TORAH AND TECHNOLOGY:

CIRCUITS, CELLS, AND THE SACRED PATH

BY

RABBI DANIEL NEVINS

IZZUN BOOKS / 2024

Torah and Technology: Circuits, Cells and the Sacred Path

IZZUN B☉☉KS

Published by Izzun Books in 2024

St. Albans, United Kingdom

izzunbooks.com

All enquiries to izzunbooks@gmail.com

Typeset in *Bona Nova*, a digitisation of Bona, a cursive typeface designed in 1971 by Andrzej Heidrich — the creator of Polish banknotes.

ISBN: 978-1-3999-7672-5

עֲנֵה דָנִיֵּאל וְאָמַר לֶהֱוֵא שְׁמֵהּ דִּי אֱלָהָא מְבָרַךְ מִן עָלְמָא וְעַד עָלְמָא
דִּי חָכְמְתָא וּגְבוּרְתָּא דִּי לֵהּ הִיא: וְהוּא מְהַשְׁנֵא עִדָּנַיָּא וְזִמְנַיָּא מְהַעְדֵּה
מַלְכִין וּמְהָקֵים מַלְכִין יָהֵב חָכְמְתָא לְחַכִּימִין וּמַנְדְּעָא לְיָדְעֵי בִינָה: הוּא
גָּלֵא עַמִּיקָתָא וּמְסַתְּרָתָא יָדַע מָה בַחֲשׁוֹכָא וּנְהוֹרָא עִמֵּהּ שְׁרֵא:

דניאל פרק ב, כ-כב

Daniel responded and said, "Let the name of God be blessed forever
and ever, for wisdom and power are God's; God changes times and
seasons, removes kings and installs kings, giving the wise their
wisdom and knowledge to those who know. God reveals deep and
hidden things, knows what is in the darkness, and light dwells with
God."

—Daniel 2:20-22

וְנָתַתִּי לָהֶם לֵב אֶחָד וְרוּחַ חֲדָשָׁה אֶתֵּן בְּקִרְבְּכֶם וַהֲסִרֹתִי לֵב הָאֶבֶן
מִבְּשָׂרָם וְנָתַתִּי לָהֶם לֵב בָּשָׂר לְמַעַן בְּחֻקֹּתַי יֵלֵכוּ וְאֶת־מִשְׁפָּטַי יִשְׁמְרוּ
וְעָשׂוּ אֹתָם וְהָיוּ־לִי לְעָם וַאֲנִי אֶהְיֶה לָהֶם לֵאלֹהִים

יחזקאל פרק יא, יט-כב

I will give them one heart and put a new spirit in them; I will remove
the heart of stone from their bodies and give them a heart of flesh,
that they may follow My laws and faithfully observe My rules. Then
they shall be My people and I will be their God.

—Ezekiel 11:19-20

CONTENTS

FOREWORD

ELLIOT N. DORFF

How can one gain moral guidance on new, hard questions? Technological advances have revolutionized major aspects of our lives, including medicine, business, communication, intellectual property, food production, and, yes, war. Some technologies that we now take for granted simply did not exist until recently. Life and death decisions today often depend on the analysis provided by machine intelligence. In some cases, the machines act on their own, sometimes for the better, and sometimes for the worse.

This raises both a moral and a methodological problem. The moral problem was described well by the philosopher Immanuel Kant in the 18th century. He pointed out that if you cannot do something, then you never have to ask whether you should; you simply cannot. If you can do something, though, you *do* need to ask whether you should because there are many things you can do that you should not. You can, for example, abuse drugs or alcohol, but you should not. You can smoke, but you should not. So, the fact that we now can use technological advances in ways that immensely amplify our ability in many areas of life does not mean that we should use those abilities wherever and however we wish. On the contrary, the increased ability that modern technology affords us makes the moral implications of using that technology more morally fraught. We urgently need advice on how to use technology morally.

That, then, raises the methodological problem: how do you gain guidance from an ancient tradition like Judaism about the use of contemporary technology that our ancestors could not possibly have known, let alone provided directions as to how we should govern its use? This problem affects some moral issues that Daniel Nevins addresses in this book. For example, when, if ever, may life support that did not exist in previous generations but that keeps a person's body functioning be removed? Under what conditions, and for what purposes, may we use genetic engineering? This methodological problem also affects ritual matters, as Rabbi Nevins describes in several chapters in this book. Modern technology, for example, affords us ways of creating a prayer quorum (minyan) online; when, if ever, should that be allowed? We can now also create lab-grown meat; is it kosher, and, if so, is it still meat, so that it may not be eaten with dairy products, or is it *pareve*, making it neutral? A much older technology is electricity, but it also eludes easy integration into the established rules of Shabbat.

One might say that because the Jewish tradition is silent about, say, artificial intelligence, another topic Rabbi Nevins addresses in this book, it has nothing to offer us about how we should use it, and we must look elsewhere for the advice we seek. That is honest – the Jewish tradition says absolutely nothing about artificial intelligence – but this approach makes Judaism irrelevant to large sections of our lives affected by technological innovations. Part of what gives Judaism meaning for Jews, though—and the same is true for people of other faiths—is the moral direction and motivation they get from their faith. Furthermore, no other religious, legal, or philosophical tradition knew about artificial intelligence either, so where should one turn for such counsel if we can get it only from explicit references in the tradition?

A second approach would be to decide that, no matter how far-fetched, we may identify an ancient precedent to govern the use of new technology. That approach would presumably make the tradition relevant to new technology and bring the authority of the tradition along with it, but it would be dishonest. That is reading into the tradition whatever one wants to see in it ("eisegesis") rather than deriving guidance from it ("exegesis").

What Rabbi Nevins wisely does in this book is first to determine whether there is anything in the tradition that, while not directly on point, nevertheless is analogous to the issues that we face with some new technology. He examines not only the mechanisms at play, but also the moral and religious implications of the new technology. That is, we need to consider the foundational convictions and values of the tradition, including its stated goals in deciding how to apply the tradition wisely to new technologies. This approach is much harder to use than simply quoting chapter and verse, as it were, from some book, but it is more realistic about the moral and ritual challenges that contemporary technology poses for us, and it is considerably more authentic in its use of the Jewish tradition.

This methodology, though, requires thorough knowledge of the tradition and a keen sense of judgment. The readers of this book will be richly rewarded by Rabbi Nevins' knowledge of both the Jewish tradition and technology, his unparalleled ability to explain both in clear terms to people who are not experts in either, and his wonderful ability to exercise judgment in a wise and compassionate way as he deals with the moral and ritual challenges posed by many forms of modern technology. One could not ask for a better guide, so read on!

Elliot N. Dorff, Rabbi, Ph.D.

Rector and Distinguished Service Professor of Philosophy

American Jewish University

INTRODUCTION

Instill in our hearts the desire to understand and discern, to listen,
learn and teach, to observe, perform, and fulfill all the teachings
of your Torah in love.

–Morning prayer before Shema

W e have been talking with machines and are no longer startled when they respond. They understand our speech, recognize our faces, our voices, our family and friends, our habits of body and mind. Powered by inscrutable processes, they complete our sentences, guide us home, and readily recommend our next purchase, news story, and show. The rapid advancement of large language models that generate texts in nearly every genre, subject, and style has blurred the boundary between natural and artificial intelligence.

Nevertheless, machines do not truly know us, at least not in the way that people know themselves or each other. Machine learning may be loosely patterned on our neural networks, and machines may be programmed to mimic expressions of affect and concern, but they lack the sensations and the sense of human minds. Artificial intelligence systems that train on vast bodies of human writing may create convincing approximations of works of art and analysis, yet these systems do not *know* anything about their subjects. Although computers can easily access the texts of Jewish tradition as strings of binary code, they have no ability to grow in wisdom and virtue, which are the essential goals of Torah study. Machines excel at processing information, which has vast benefit for those who wish to access the treasures of Torah, but their proper role is to support, not to supplant, our pursuit of holiness.

Increasingly, we refer important decisions to artificial intelligence, and instinctively accept its guidance, even on matters of spiritual significance. We keep our digital devices close at hand, sometimes wrapped around our wrists, and we may consult them more frequently than any book or person. With each technological breakthrough, we become more accustomed to life with machines.

Still, we have our limits. Roboticists speak of an "uncanny valley"— where people realize that an approximation of life is not real but artificial, and their trust suddenly dips. This uncanny valley is precious property, perhaps even holy ground. It reminds us that for all our flaws, humans possess qualities that cannot be replaced by machines. One renewed role of religion may be to remind humans to retain responsibility for their own moral lives, and to value our bodies, even when they lack or lose capacities available in machines.

Over the past two millennia, Jewish sages have sought to clarify how humans might walk with God—in kindness and integrity, towards justice and peace. Sources for their insights have included the Hebrew Bible, collections of ancient rabbinic teachings, and their own sense of logic, goodness, and truth. Our sages have worked within Jewish communities that exert a social force, keeping religious practice sustainable for the people of Israel. The cumulative product of these conversations between and within generations is a learned discourse known as halakhah.

Halakhah is often translated as "Jewish law," but the word literally means "pathway." Law is far too limited a category for the blend of interpersonal and devotional responsibilities encompassed by halakhah. Legal systems are not designed to guide their subjects toward righteousness, but merely to provide for general order and safety. True, halakhah requires some activities and forbids others, but many of these regulations relate to piety and kindness in thought and action. Moreover, *law* implies a mechanism for enforcement, but with some exceptions, Jewish religious practice today is enforced only by informal communal norms and an internal sense of obligation. As such, halakhah is less a legal system than a sacred pathway that helps us navigate the world with reverence and righteousness, and in so doing, come to know God.

While some halakhic writings are organized as comprehensive codes, halakhic instruction has largely been an interactive exercise, with students asking teachers, and communities asking rabbis, how to balance competing values and live within the boundaries of Judaism. This process began already in the days of Moses, who was frequently challenged by the people of Israel to clarify practical matters. His responses, and those of the Jewish sages who followed, were not merely a matter of legal instruction, but an effort to express Jewish values through religious practice. Most rabbinic responses to halakhic questions have been oral, but when written down, they became known as responsa (singular: responsum).

In Hebrew, this literature is called *she'elot u-teshuvot*, "questions and answers" (abbreviated as שו"ת and שו"תים). This genre developed during the Abbasid period in approximately the ninth and tenth centuries, as discussed by Robert Brody in *The Geonim of Babylonia and the Shaping of Medieval Jewish Culture*. There are contemporaneous accounts of questions sent by rabbis in, for example, North Africa, back to the academies of Babylonia (today's Iraq) where scholars of different ranks would deliberate before answering in the name of the *geon*, or greatest sage.

In classical responsa, the questioner often provides an initial analysis before identifying a novel feature of the case that requires explication. While the names of the questioner and the respondent are usually preserved, the identities of the parties may be obscured for their privacy (many questions relate to business and family law). Thus, responsa are both particular—arising from real-life scenarios—and broad, in that the respondents understood and intended that their opinions would be preserved and cited as precedents. Indeed, the responsa have been viewed as more authoritative than the codes, since they describe halakhah not only in theory, but in practice.

Responsa have often been terse. The medieval scholar known as Rashba (Rabbi Shlomo ben Aderet, Barcelona, 1235-1310) composed thousands of responsa, many consisting of just a few sentences. In contrast, the most prolific twentieth century authors of responsa, rabbis such as Shlomo Zalman Auerbach, Moshe Feinstein, and Ovadia Yosef, wrote lengthy treatises studded with hundreds of references. Some responsa hew closely to the halakhic question and the most relevant rabbinic sources, while others integrate theological, historical, scientific, and even poetic elements to inform the reader.

Responsa literature is a vast reservoir of Jewish learning that reflects our people's spiritual journey across time and space. Scholars such as Louis Jacobs, Shmuel Glick, and Haym Soloveitchik have studied the responsa as windows into Jewish history. From the Crusades to the Shoah, responsa demonstrate how Jewish leaders guided their communities under extraordinary circumstances. In recent decades, responsa have been an important genre for rabbis to address new challenges and opportunities for Jewish religious practice. While the responsa are not as familiar to most Jews as is the siddur, or prayer book, this genre of Jewish literature addresses topics that have broad application to daily life.

Jewish spirituality is expressed in many ways—through prayer and meditation, study, music, meals, social life, and acts of kindness. Halakhah touches on each of these facets of life, and collectively generates an implicit theology. The Bible and its rabbinic interpreters teach us much about God, but we can never capture the infinite expanse of divinity. Instead, our spiritual awakening emerges through daily experiences of Jewish study and practice in the embrace of a sacred community.

However, the organic experience of Jewish life has been profoundly disrupted in recent generations. First came the grand historical movements of emancipation, enlightenment, and migration. These centrifugal forces reduced communal influence and augmented individual agency. Countervailing forces of antisemitism and Zionism brought Jews back together, but the fabric of religious belonging was badly frayed. The more recent shift to technocentric culture has further isolated individuals from normative Jewish communities, and simultaneously infiltrated our very process of decision-making.

Technology has altered our sense of space, of time, and of self. Understandings of gender and sexuality have likewise raced ahead, making many recent writings sound dated within a few years of composition. Jewish migrations and minglings with people from other religious cultures have attenuated the mimetic culture of our ancestors and demanded new articulations of a meaningful, satisfying, and authentic Jewish life. Each of these developments has brought blessings, some extraordinary, yet the continuity of religious culture has been disrupted.

For Jews living in the State of Israel, the reality of Jewish sovereignty in the ancient homeland has introduced both blessings and halakhic challenges. Rabbis in Israel have responded to realities which had been largely theoretical until 1948. For example, may Israeli banks charge interest on mortgages and business loans? Should Israeli hospitals allow organ transplants? Elective abortions? How should Jewish farmers handle the Sabbatical year? After nearly two millennia without a Jewish army, what ancient halakhic guidelines should apply to the Israel Defense Forces? Given the great ingathering of Jews with varying customs from around the world, and the formation of families blending Ashkenazi, Sephardic, Ethiopian and other customs, which halakhic norms should apply, and when? While this book is set in the context of the diaspora, in most chapters I draw on the experience and expertise of Israeli scholars on the interplay of Torah and technology in the modern state.

As the pace of change accelerates, the importance of ancient wisdom increases. The vast literature of Torah contains insights that can guide us in our own path to virtue, especially when the territory we traverse seems unlike the regions crossed by our ancestors. Their resilience and resolve, their ability to reconfigure Jewish life despite dislocations and discontinuities, can fortify and guide us today.

The first section of this book includes four responsa that focus on technology itself—how it has become embedded in our moral, social, and ritual lives in ways that can both empower and undermine human agency. The second section includes three responsa on spiritual challenges highlighted by the COVID-19 pandemic, followed by a final responsum on the issue of brain death. These second-section chapters are less technocentric than are those in the first section, and yet they too contend with how technologies that are intended to improve our lives can challenge our intuitive sense of humanity.

Chapters one through three deal with the topics of artificial intelligence, genetic engineering, and lab-grown meat. Each topic is extremely dynamic, with major breakthroughs in the respective fields unfolding even as I wrote. For example, the emerging discourse surrounding organoid intelligence (the creation of miniature brains fashioned in vitro from human neurons) bears significance for chapters one and two. As such, my approach was to create models of engagement rather than final determinations of the law. These projects challenged me to probe deeper into my theory of law, considering the relative benefits of formalistic vs. values-driven interpretations, especially when contending with unprecedented technologies. My extended responsum on the use of electric and electronic devices on Shabbat (Chapter 4) considers how work itself has evolved and links the classical categories of labor to contemporary technologies.

When the COVID-19 pandemic broke out, the initial questions fielded by rabbis related to ritual. Could the mitzvah of chanting and hearing *Megilat Esther* be fulfilled by video conference? What about forming a virtual minyan? Although I did not author a written responsum at the time, I developed an approach based on a precedent from the 18th-century rabbi Haim Yosef David Azulai (Hid"a). I shared my opinion orally to allow the formation of a minyan so long as ten participants showed their faces by video, and I have now composed a chapter explaining my approach for this volume. Even as COVID-19 ebbed, other challenges to physical gatherings—from vast wildfires that blanketed regions in toxic smoke to rocket attacks that sent Israelis repeatedly into shelters—continued to raise the question of what religious services may be performed virtually.

As fascinating and important as virtual minyan was for many rabbis, COVID also raised life and death issues. The most urgent ethical questions related to medical scarcity. On what basis should personal protective equipment be distributed? Given a shortage of ventillators and the specialized staff needed to operate them, whose life should be prioritized? Likewise, as vaccines and then anti-viral drugs came to market, on what basis should they be made available, both locally and globally? My responsum on this subject addressed not only the details but also ethical theory, especially utilitarianism, which guided most secular medical responses. Does Judaism allow for a utilitarian outcome-based approach, or are we guided exclusively by rules, even in such extreme circumstances?

The third pandemic topic that I addressed related to the impact of quarantine on the time-sensitive ritual of brit milah (circumcision). Once again, I found in the writings of our ancestors halakhic precedents that are relevant for unprecedented situations in our times. I understood the broader implications of the question at a time when brit milah has been challenged by many Jews. As is often the case in responsa, I contended with conflicting imperatives—to preserve the integrity of ritual while allowing Jews to participate in communal prayer safely. These three COVID-era topics exemplify the relevance of responsa, in that they help us orient ourselves with ancient wisdom in the face of frightening change.

The final responsum included in this volume is also the earliest: "Contemporary Criteria for the Declaration of Death" (2004). New technologies have been used to shift this determination from physical observations of pulse and respiration to complex neurological studies and the analysis of blood gases. Do such determinations of "brain death" satisfy halakhic criteria? What are the implications for organ donation? What are the limits of the imperative to save a life? The original responsum is updated here, even as neurologists continue to debate confounding factors that have led some to challenge the consensus on brain death.

These responsa are my flawed efforts to understand the divine will as it continues to unfold. God is infinite, but humans live within the limits of time and space. Our yearning to live lives of holiness and goodness requires constant study, communal practice, and the willingness to admit error. Halakhic writing is not the only way—or even the primary way —that I have engaged in Torah. Weekly *drashot* (sermons), classes, and personal conversations have taken more of my time and perhaps had greater impact on the lives of my fellow Jews. Yet, halakhic literature is especially well suited for responding to shifting circumstances while retaining the core values and norms of our ancestors.

Without diminishing the importance of any of this book's chapters, the most momentous topic related to Torah and technology is missing: the ever-more-calamitous climate crisis. I will share some initial thoughts here, but plan to extend my study of this existential topic into a fuller form in the coming years, God willing.

The climate crisis is no longer a feared future but a terrifying present. As the planet warms, many once-predictable systems have veered far from standard variability. Scientists have declared our epoch to be the Anthropocene, a period in which human behavior has literally changed the weather. The results are devastating, with massive species extinction, prolonged heat waves, intensifying storms, fires, droughts, and floods already observed. Glaciers are melting, forests are aflame, seas are surpassing 100° F, and surface temperatures set new records year after year. The ground is shifting beneath our cities, while the air above is at times smoky and toxic. Much worse seems likely to come soon, with melting polar ice leading to massive sea level rises, flooded cities, and submerged islands, followed by feedback loops (such as the loss of polar reflectivity and the release of carbon from melting permafrost) to further intensify such changes.

The environmental movement, which originally focused on pollution, has in recent decades pivoted to address the causes of climate change, and urged shifting both the production and consumption of energy to clean forms, thereby ameliorating its worst effects. These efforts are important, but far from sufficient. Even if humanity were able to set aside destructive behaviors such as warfare (which itself creates vast carbon emissions) and focus on the great transition to clean energy, the chemistry of our atmosphere has already changed enough to alter the climate radically, and to imperil the survival of many species, including our own.

Geo-engineering, the attempt to adjust the climate back to a more livable range, is controversial and mostly unproven. Some methods, such as using highly reflective paints in cities, may soon make a small difference, while efforts to sequester CO_2 from the atmosphere and either store it underground or convert it to stone at a large enough scale to cool the planet seem well beyond our grasp. Seeding the skies with reflective particles could temporarily divert some of the sun's radiation, but who would fund and supervise this effort? Even more ambitious are proposals to construct a vast space parasol at a location called Lagrange Point One or L1 that would purportedly diffuse two percent of the sun's radiation and allow a 1.5 degrees Celsius cooling of Earth in just two years. But even if the engineering, financing and politics of such a plan could be settled, it would not resolve all issues with the altered chemistry of the planet, and would indeed exacerbate some of them. And, what if we overcompensated and tripped a new ice age?

In addition to the environmental movement with its focus on ameliorating the impact of human activity on earth's climate, two other broad responses have emerged, as discussed by Adam Kirsch in *The Revolt Against Humanity: Imagining a Future Without Us* (Columbia Global Reports, 2023). He calls one group of respondents the anti-humanists, in that they believe the earth will soon be rid of *homo sapiens* and much better off for our disappearance. Other forms of life will continue to evolve, but humans will not be part of the story. This school of thought denies special status to humanity—our net impact on earth has been negative, and so there is little to mourn in our demise.

An opposite perspective comes from those Kirsch calls the trans-humanists. For them, intelligence is invaluable, much more so than the biological systems that thus far allowed it to develop. While it is unfortunate that the future of human life (and the lives of many other species) on earth may be imperiled, these thinkers focus on the preservation and expansion of intelligence, whether through adapting to the changed environment, or by migrating intelligence away from biological systems and toward mechanical systems that can flourish without the limitations of human bodies.

These approaches are each antithetical to Jewish values. While the Torah does indeed include numerous stories in which people are exiled from the land because of their irresponsibility, the prospect of redemption and return is always explicit. The proper response to human failure is not the abandonment of humanity, but rather the redoubling of efforts to educate and guide people back into harmony with the Creator. And while Judaism certainly valorizes intelligence, it is not disembodied thought, but virtuous conduct that is the highest goal. True, Maimonides idealizes a non-corporeal existence of eternal contemplation of the Divine, but his great works of philosophy and law are designed to teach humans to sanctify life, not abandon it.

What halakhic questions are raised by the climate crisis? Should we reduce our carbon footprint? Of course, we should, but what is our precise obligation? Are we permitted to travel beyond walking, to eat beyond the produce of our own gardens, to consume power and products that are not carbon neutral? Halakhah works best with binaries—behaviors that are permitted or forbidden. But what would it mean to forbid all carbon-positive activities? And even if we were somehow able to pay that price, to revert to pre-modern behaviors, would that suffice to stabilize the climate, given all the changes we have made over the past two centuries? I am at the beginning of my effort to address such questions with the tools of halakhic discourse. God willing, I will be granted the time, insight, and strength to respond to them with new halakhic questions and answers in the coming years.

Responsa are a particular genre of halakhic discourse. Unlike codes of Jewish law, which set out systematic statements with minimal reference to historical context, responsa are...responsive. A question comes from a specific person, time, and place, and is addressed to a specific rabbi, who also occupies a particular context. As such, I think it appropriate to share a bit about my context—ideological, professional, and personal— so that these influences can be considered by readers as they develop their own responses to these complex topics.

Torah study and the practice of mitzvot are the threads that weave together the fabric of my Jewish identity. I am humbled by the vastness of the Torah canon, and by my own limitations of comprehension and observance. Yet the routines of daily study, prayer, kashrut, Shabbat and festivals, give purpose to my life and allow me to build religious community. While some might view these traditional commitments as a retreat from history, for me they are quite the opposite. Jewish study and practice give me frequent insights into earlier epochs and equip me to adapt to new developments in society with the confidence that the Torah is a living and dynamic force.

I should name my position within the spectrum of Jewish affiliations, even as I make the case for softening such demarcations and engaging in diverse religious discourses. I identify with the centrist stream known as Conservative or Masorti (traditional) Judaism. My ordination is from the Jewish Theological Seminary, my rabbinical association is with the Rabbinical Assembly, and I have served organizations affiliated with Conservative Judaism for my entire career, starting as a junior counselor at Camp Ramah in 1984.

That said, the English name of this denomination is confusing and unsatisfying (to me, at least). "Conservative" has nothing to do with politics, and little to do with today's cultural conservatism, but is rather a relic of late nineteenth and early twentieth century religious reforms. I prefer David Wolpe's suggestion to rebrand the denomination as *Covenantal Judaism*, since this title would more accurately reflect our commitment to join the people of Israel to God and each other through the study of Torah and the practice of mitzvot and acts of kindness.

I have been enriched by and celebrate a diversity of Jewish faith and practice. My Jewish journey began before bar mitzvah within a vibrant ḥavurah (study group) associated with my parents' Reform temple in New Jersey, and then veered dramatically to the right as I studied in Orthodox yeshivot in Monsey, New York, Paramus, New Jersey, and Jerusalem. I found much to admire in these varied settings and continue to learn from scholars across the Jewish spectrum. In my college Hillel, I eventually found a spiritual home in the traditional egalitarian minyan, yet I continued to grow in appreciation for the Jewish beliefs and practices of my friends on either side. As we sing in the prayer "Lekha Dodi," *Yamin u-s'mol tifrotzi v'et Adonai ta'aritzi,* "right and left you shall spread out, and God you will revere."

Moreover, our denominations are a recent development with uncertain shelf-life. Does it make sense to refer to pre-modern Jewish thinkers and their books through the nineteenth century lens of denominations? What type of Jew was Rambam? The Baal Shem Tov? Each, in his own way, was both traditional and radical, and neither would fit easily into today's denominational categories. I seek to follow the teachers of Jewish wisdom from across our lengthy history and ask what they have to offer us today, not to claim them for my own team.

As for contemporary scholarship, I connect to Jewish networks that are intentionally expansive—academic Jewish studies, institutes, and other independent Jewish organizations. While Jewish texts, beliefs, and practices are the foundation of my spiritual life, I often learn from science, arts, humanities, and religious studies, especially when studying the meaning of unprecedented technologies. My aspiration for this book is that it will interest any person of any faith (or none) who wonders how we might link ancient religious wisdom to the radical new technologies of our time.

A second note about the context of my work: The essays in this volume are products of my experience as a student and teacher of Torah in four professional settings: a congregation, a committee, a seminary, and a school. I spent the first thirteen years following my ordination in 1994 as a congregational rabbi at Adat Shalom Synagogue in Farmington Hills, Michigan. There, as a young pulpit rabbi, I tentatively began to practice *pesikah*—making halakhic decisions for my community. Congregants shared with me their questions and their expertise—whether in medicine, law, or communal leadership.

These conversations humbled and informed me, demanding that I dig deep and aim high, but also checking my tendency towards idealistic interpretations of halakhah. Most of this activity was oral and informal. When I became senior rabbi of Adat Shalom in 1999, I wrote my first responsum, making the case for the congregation to complete its transition to fully egalitarian worship.

That same year, I was nominated to join the Rabbinical Assembly's Committee on Jewish Law and Standards (CJLS), a body that I had previously served as student secretary from 1992-1994. Suddenly, I was expected not only to listen and record, but also to speak and to write. The CJLS has been an important forum for debating Jewish law since about 1927. By observing, supporting, and at times respectfully disagreeing with my colleagues, I gradually found my own voice in responding to contemporary questions using the insights of ancient sources. Seven of the eight responsa included in this volume were written for and approved by the CJLS. The CJLS web page includes the original authorized versions; I have edited and updated each responsum for this volume.

The first full responsum that I wrote for the Rabbinical Assembly's Committee on Jewish Law and Standards (CJLS) related to Jews who are blind. What are their ritual obligations? Might technology be used to allow them to participate in the highly significant practice of chanting Torah for their congregation? "The Participation of Jews Who are Blind in the Torah Service" was passed by the CJLS in 2003. Although it touched on technology, this was not a primary focus, and so I have not included it in this volume. However, both in the composition of this responsum and in its educational afterlife, I worked with Jews who are blind, learning from their experiences, insights, and convictions, and then returning to our sources as a better-informed student. This model of dialectical study, going back and forth between books and the people most immediately affected by an issue, is my ideal approach to halakhic inquiry.

Just as I was becoming used to the deliberations of the Committee on Jewish Law and Standards, it was drawn back into a bitterly contested conversation about gay rights (now called LGBTQI+ rights) that had begun a decade earlier when I was a student. From 2003 to 2006, the CJLS conducted a series of retreats to study, debate, and eventually vote on various approaches to the integration of openly gay and lesbian Jews into family and communal life. Ultimately, much of my effort went into seeking a halakhic key that would open what had been locked, allowing full participation in Jewish life for people who had been excluded because of their sexual orientation.

I found that key in the Talmudic statement, "So great is human dignity that it supersedes a negative law of Torah" (B. Brakhot 19b), and its halakhic application over nearly two millennia. I joined together with Elliot Dorff and Avram Reisner, two rabbis whom I view as exemplars of sensitive and scholarly halakhic engagement, to compose a joint responsum. Our core argument was that the accretion of rabbinic prohibitions that aimed to enforce celibacy for queer Jews and to prevent them from forming families was deeply humiliating and hurtful. As such, the *status quo ante* was incompatible with the well-established Jewish imperative to protect human dignity. In other words, we sought not to change the law but to harmonize two of its core values that had come into damaging conflict.

In December 2006, the matter was decided with a dramatic series of votes, including one that approved our responsum, "Homosexuality, Human Dignity and Halakhah," by a slim majority, 13-12. In fact, we needed only 6 votes for our position to be deemed a valid option, but the majority took us further, unlocking the gates of our seminaries and synagogues to queer Jews.

Several years later, the three of us consulted with newly "out" rabbinical students and ordained colleagues to develop ceremonies and documents for same-sex marriage and divorce. In 2012, the CJLS adopted our responsum, "Rituals and Documents of Marriage and Divorce for Same-Sex Couples," which has become the halakhic and ritual basis for many weddings.

Rabbis Dorff, Reisner, and I also discussed some of the pitfalls of our original paper, especially its instruction that bisexual people limit their search for life-partners to people of the opposite gender. We belatedly acknowledged that this instruction was at odds with our core quest to support the dignity of all people. An addendum to our original responsum indicating this shift in perspective was added to the official version of our 2006 responsum on the Rabbinical Assembly's CJLS web page.

Notwithstanding such flaws, I am proud of these projects and pleased with their impact. The ranks of rabbinic leadership have grown much more diverse, and our paper has influenced Jewish communities beyond the boundaries of Conservative Judaism. While these responsa do not fit within the parameters of this volume with its focus on technology and bioethics, they reflect my theory of halakhah, which integrates both formal textual analysis and the discernment of sacred values that permeate the normative realm.

Soon after our 2006 responsum was passed, I was invited to return to New York and become the Pearl Resnick Dean of the Rabbinical School at the Jewish Theological Seminary (JTS). With this move, my role shifted from that of young pulpit rabbi to that of mentor to a new generation of increasingly diverse rabbinical students. I also joined a community of scholars committed to connecting the ancient treasures of our tradition to the concerns of our day. Time and again, I was challenged by students and faculty to reconsider my interpretations and to reclaim underappreciated facets of our vast tradition.

From JTS, I had the opportunity to travel widely in the Jewish world, teaching in congregations, camps, and college campuses. Each exposure to a new collection of Torah students helped me to probe deeper into a subject and to refine my understanding of its nuances. Such experiences sharpened the essential questions, and helped me try out, revise, and finalize my findings in the form of written replies, or responsa. During this period, I began to focus my halakhic inquiry into ways that new technologies were challenging ancient Jewish norms, and I found that the writings of our ancestors could transcend the vast chasm of time and technology.

My fourteen years as dean at JTS were extremely fruitful, and I had the privilege of initiating about 300 students into the rabbinate. I also came to realize that the foundations of Jewish identity among our youngest students require attention, and so I gladly accepted the invitation to become Head of School at Golda Och Academy (GOA), a Pre-K through 12th grade day school in New Jersey. In this setting, where I work today, I see halakhah come to life with children as young as four, all the way through high school. GOA is a living laboratory of Judaism, a place where young Jews may learn to walk together as a community, and to sense the divine as they journey through life. I feel blessed in this work and optimistic that rising generations of Jews will continue to seek wise and compassionate guidance in our ever-evolving Torah.

A third contextual note, regarding teachers, family, and friends, without whom I could not function: I cannot name, nor frankly recall, every person who has helped me understand these topics or discern something worthwhile to offer. Education begins at the crib and never ends. For each of these topics I sought out experts—both in print and in person—to identify interesting questions that halakhah might be able to address. In most cases (except for the COVID chapters) I was able to take a year or two to teach the material in various settings, and each time, the questions and responses sharpened my thoughts. Whether my interlocuter was a patent judge eager to school me on intellectual property, or a high school student troubled by an inconsistency in my logic, I learned more than I taught.

I am blessed with family and friends of diverse expertise. I have leaned on them all for argument and insight. Folks from "the farm," the minyan, and family have all informed me about the intersection of technology, values, and relationships. To borrow Peter Berger's expression, they are my plausibility structure, the people who make this conversation possible—and enjoyable. I am grateful to Ellen Braitman, Judith Shulevitz, and Roderick Young for previewing the text and sharing their wise comments.

Before I was ready to submit this manuscript, I knew that I needed editing help from someone who would question every comma and help restructure passages that I could no longer see for their flaws or potential. I was blessed by the assistance of Rachel Miranda, a longtime friend and professional editor who has a brilliant eye and easy ability to improve my work.

I am thrilled to work with my friend and rabbinic colleague Adam Zagoria-Moffet of Izzun Books in St Albans, England to publish this volume. Other publishers wanted me to eliminate anything technical, and nearly all the Hebrew, but Adam was eager to share this work in all its complexity. Still, I have attempted to keep the main body accessible to most readers, while the notes contain additional treats that require knowledge of biblical and rabbinic Hebrew. I would also like to offer thanks to Mikayla Zagoria-Moffet for her time and assistance with editing and indexing the project.

Before my friends came family, and I was blessed to be brought up by wonderful parents, grandparents, and even two great-grandparents, all of whom were alive through my high school years. They demonstrated for me and my siblings, Andrea, and Teddy, how to move between worlds, how to recover from setbacks, how to live with integrity and kindness. As we each established our own families with beloved spouses, our children emerged as miraculous expressions of continuity and change.

At the end of this volume, I have appended an essay that I wrote for the journal *Conservative Judaism* in memory of my mother and teacher, Phyllis B. Nevins, פסיה בת יצחק הלוי ורחל ז"ל, shortly after her death on the second day of Sukkot in 5766 (2005). There I examined the history and meaning of the standard Ashkenazi expression of consolation, "May

God comfort you among the other mourners of Zion and Jerusalem." While that essay is not especially about either halakhah or technology, it is very much about the meaning of normative religious practice at a time of disruption and loss, and therefore seems to be a fitting close to the book.

My mother remains in my memory a beacon for all that is beautiful and good in life. She was keen, and kind, and attentive to the needs of family and friends, even if they lived across the world. Around the age of 40 she embarked on a journey of Jewish discovery that branched out in delightful directions, flowering and bearing fruit. She became passionate and proficient in Jewish art, mastering Hebrew calligraphy and producing magnificent ketubot (illuminated Jewish marriage contracts) for many fortunate couples. She joined Jewish choral groups and studied Hebrew and Yiddish music, from art songs to folk songs. Mom applied her prodigious culinary talents to mastering the art of Jewish cooking, and her challah recipe still makes a regular appearance at our Shabbat table. Wherever she lived or traveled, Mom sought out teachers of Torah. She especially delighted in supporting the Jewish development of her children and grandchildren. Her final public appearance before she died was a d'var Torah (sacred teaching) she delivered at the bat mitzvah of her eldest grandchild. We miss her in the good times and are relieved only that she did not witness many of the sorrows and outrages of recent years.

When turning our attention to the living, we say in Hebrew, she-yibadeil l'ḥaim arukhim, "may he, in contrast, be granted long life." I say this fervently of my father and teacher, Michael A. Nevins. He sets an incredibly high bar for the entire family—of kindness, creativity, and curiosity. During his long medical career, Dad distinguished himself as both a clinician and a researcher. He showed extraordinary devotion to his patients for four decades of primary care practice, and simultaneously sought new topics and disciplines for personal and professional growth. My father invited me into conversation about bioethics when I was still a teen, and we have collaborated on projects ever since. Two decades into retirement, he continues to research, write, and make new friends. Ethics, medicine, history, genealogy, art, and music—he reads, writes, and regales all who are fortunate to meet him. When I am bold enough to take on new topics such as those covered in this volume, it is his example that I emulate.

Twenty-one seems awfully young to make the most important decision in life, but I had fantastic good fortune when I began to go out with my wife, Lynn. From the beginning, we discovered the joy of walking together—in the woods, up mountains, across cities, and through the unmapped wilderness of a shared life. I am grateful to her parents, Marney and Bob, for their guidance and love. Lynn has an unwavering moral compass, a skill for observing people and finding their strengths, and an unpretentious way of improving life all around her. As a ceramic artist she turns mud into masterpieces, and as a speech therapist she helps very young people gain the gift of communication. These are Lynn's own halakhah—sacred pathways to invest life with meaning, purpose, and beauty. Her intelligence, integrity, creativity, and kindness have sweetened my life immeasurably, and allowed us to raise three spectacular children, who are already accomplished young adults. Whatever lies ahead of us, I feel fortunate to face it together.

As I consider daunting topics such as those found in this volume, I keep the voices of our children Talya, Leora and Sam in mind. Each brings their own Torah insights, and their own sense of justice and equity to the table where we noisily gather. Each has corrected my misunderstandings and opened me to new possibilities. They have brought beautiful friends to the family, and they have amazed us with their clear-eyed contributions to building a better world. I am filled with gratitude for their love, and I dedicate this book to them. May the timeless values of our sacred pathway find new expression in their lives and may the Holy One bless them on their way.

NOTE ON LANGUAGE AND SOURCES:

When transliterating Hebrew words into the English alphabet, I employ a simplified system with the letter כ (*khof*) rendered as *kh*, and the letter ח (*ḥet*) as *ḥ* with a dot underneath. For example, שלחן ערוך is cited as Shulḥan Arukh. I do not use other diacritical marks, for example to differentiate between *aleph* and *ayin*. I italicize Hebrew words unless they are in common use among my likely readers. The classical rabbinic collections known as Mishnah, Tosefta, Talmud Yerushalmi, and Talmud Bavli cover many of the same tractates, and so I identify these texts by the first letter and then tractate name. M. refers to the Mishnah, T. to Tosefta, Y. to Yerushalmi, and B. to Bavli, followed by the tractate name and location. The code of Maimonides known as Mishneh Torah is referred to as MT. Rabbi Karo's Shulḥan Arukh becomes SA, and its four divisions, derived from Rabbi Yaakov ben Asher's Tur, are rendered as OH (*Oraḥ Ḥayyim*), YD (*Yoreh De'ah*), EH (*Even HaEzer*), and HM (*Ḥoshen Mishpat*). Whenever possible, I cite from critical editions of rabbinic texts. Most citations are copied from the Bar Ilan Responsa Project, which itself draws from modern editions, though not their critical apparatus.

All texts in the body are presented in English lettering, but I have provided the Hebrew, and in the notes, only the Hebrew, as these are intended for readers with advanced skills. The webpage designed to support this volume includes bilingual study sheets encompassing the most important sources for each of the chapters and may be copied freely.

Translations of biblical and rabbinic texts in the body of this volume are my own unless otherwise noted. The frontispiece translations from my namesake prophets, Daniel and Ezekiel, are adapted from The Jewish Publication Society's Tanakh. The siddur translation at the start of this introduction is from Jonathan Sacks, *The Koren Sacks Siddur.* In several cases I have modified translations for gender neutrality, as noted.

In this volume, I identify people in both the body and the notes by their personal and family names, leaving out honorifics in the first instance. Subsequently, I refer to them by title and surname. For example, Elliot Dorff, and then Rabbi Dorff; Tamar Ross, and then Dr. Ross. I make an exception for ancient sages, following the Talmud's practice in referring, for example, to Rav Yehudah, or Rabbi Yosi, since those titles encode information about their generation and provenance, making it easier to differentiate them from sages with similar names.

The memory of past Torah scholars is a vital blessing, as their wise responses to the challenges of their times provide us with insight and encouragement as we contend with the disorienting challenges of radical new technologies. While I do not append the customary z"l (*zikhronam li-vrakhah,* may their memory be a blessing) to their names, this entire exercise is dedicated to honoring their memory.

ONLINE SUPPLEMENT:

Lesson plans, source sheets, articles, and video available at

www.rabbinevins.com/torah-and-technology/

SECTION I

HALAKHIC RESPONSES TO TRANSFORMATIVE TECHNOLOGIES

CHAPTER 1:
ARTIFICIAL INTELLIGENCE AND
AUTONOMOUS MACHINES

Among the extraordinary developments of our digital age, perhaps none is as startling as the introduction of "smart machines" that function without direct human supervision, in an open and dynamic environment, with the possibility of significant and even lethal consequences for people. An academic field of machine ethics has emerged, but there is no consensus about what type of ethical system, whether rule-based, consequentialist, or virtue, should guide the development of artificial intelligence.[1]

To date, there has been negligible engagement by halakhic authorities in this discourse, despite the high stakes for both the Jewish community and society at large.[2] In this responsum, I survey the emerging field of machine ethics, consider relevant halakhic concepts, and apply them to questions about the intersection of artificial intelligence (AI) with ethics and religion—with the caveat that the pace and scope of innovation is rapid and unpredictable. After bringing the technological and halakhic discourses into conversation, I reach three conclusions that might function as models for additional topics as they emerge from theory into practice. This chapter is based on a responsum approved by the CJLS on June 19, 2019.[3]

The field of AI has made astonishing advances, most dramatically with the introduction in 2023 of several large-language model chatbots that assimilate billions of words found on the internet and use them to predict new passages of natural language, computer code, mathematical equations and more. While the initial uses of these chatbots were entertaining, they were also quickly put to practical use (and abuse).

Chatbots are especially fascinating because the generation of language is one of the most human capacities. Indeed, this is a major focus of my responsum. However, AI theorists like Demis Hassabis of DeepMind have shown that AI is capable of even more powerful tasks, such as creating new proteins with its program, Alphafold.[4] Many of humanity's greatest challenges, such as the transition to clean energy, development of new medications, and reduction of threats borne by the climate crisis, may all benefit from the tools of artificial intelligence. Yet, as even the CEOs of the largest tech companies have stated, AI also poses existential threats to humanity.

AI is integrated into increasingly powerful military systems, some of which are designed to exercise lethal force. While most militaries claim that such systems will be kept in a semi-autonomous mode, with humans in the loop to authorize use of deadly force, the shift to fully autonomous operation could occur in a matter of seconds and be activated without oversight in the highly charged scenarios of total war.

In 2022 The White House released a "Blueprint AI Bill of Rights" featuring five broad principles designed to protect safety, security, privacy, and equity, and to make it possible to identify AI products.[5] The European Union has been engaged in similar work since 2018 and is preparing an "EU AI Act" for release in 2024. The United Nations has called for a legally binding instrument by 2026 that would prohibit all States from operating lethal autonomous weapons systems without human oversight.

While there is overlap between the concerns of government, industry, and religious communities, some of our concerns with AI are specific to halakhah. This responsum is an early attempt to name such concerns and find relevant precedents to guide the development of AI and autonomous systems in ways that differentiate them from the distinct moral and spiritual status of humans.

QUESTIONS:

With rapid advances in the development of artificial intelligence and autonomous machines have come calls for "moral machines" that integrate ethical considerations into analysis and action. It is equally plausible to develop machines that integrate halakhic norms. What halakhic principles should apply to the conduct of such machines? Specifically:

1. Are Jews liable for the halakhic consequences of actions taken by machines on their behalf, for example, Sabbath labor?

2. Should ethical principles derived from halakhah be integrated into the development of autonomous systems for transportation, medical care, warfare, and other morally charged activities, allowing autonomous systems to make life-or-death decisions?

3. Might a robot perform a mitzvah or other halakhically significant action? Is it conceivable to treat an artificial agent as a person? As a Jew?

RESPONSE:

The Rise of Artificial Intelligence and the Call for Machine Ethics

These three halakhic questions signal a portentous transition in our relationship to machines from mere tools to (potentially) ethical agents. As machines grow in their powers of analysis and action, might there be an inverse relationship to human agency and responsibility? In halakhic terms, does reliance on smart machines exonerate Jews from prohibited behaviors such as Sabbath labor? And if a Jew depends for ritual acts on machines that set their own pathways to task completion, has the person truly performed a mitzvah? What guidance, if any, does a sacred tradition like ours offer to the development of artificial intelligence? Secular ethics has begun to address related questions, but this discourse is far from achieving consensus.

Some ethicists dismiss the entire project of fashioning ethical artificial intelligence as misguided, regarding the embodied experiences of suffering, pain, pleasure, and mortality as essential contexts for moral reasoning.[6] Dramatic reports about advances in AI often obscure the fact that there has been little progress in approximating the human capacity for *understanding meaning* in machines.[7] That is, AI may be smart without ever becoming conscious. Yet, at the same time, there is little consensus about the nature of human consciousness, or why exactly it should be considered categorically different from forms of consciousness expressed by other animals or perhaps by machines.[8]

Machine learning works with data on a scale and in patterns that defy human comprehension. Deep neural networks may have up to 150 hidden layers between input and output, making them thoroughly inscrutable to humans. Inscrutability is not incompatible with intelligence, however. Indeed, humans cannot and need not fully comprehend one another's neurological processes to achieve mutual understanding and appreciate one another's intelligence.

The emerging subfield of "explainable machine learning" is working to bridge the communication gap between people and AI.[9] There has been recent activism to require that AI systems be designed with the goal of transparency and explainability.[10] Amitai Etzioni and Oren Etzioni proposed the development of an "ethics bot"[11] or "AI guardian"[12] which would supervise the functioning of other AIs to ensure that they comply not only with laws, but also with moral values.

In 2023 Anthropic, maker of the chatbot Claude, introduced a crowd-sourced attempt to develop "Collective Constitutional AI," a series of norms that the public could choose to guide the responses of chatbots. In generating responses to user prompts, should AI prioritize the free speech of individuals, or overall social equity? Should it police itself against spreading conspiracy-theories, bigotry, and calls to violence? And should such norms be based on rules such as, "do not spread falsehoods," or on utilitarian consideration for the greater good?[13] This initial attempt to elicit public input on reasonable restrictions on AI is commendable, though limited by the selection bias of those who responded to the poll, and a lack of consensus on how to balance individual rights vs. communal welfare.

Justice concerns aside, robotics researchers frequently comment on the oddness of some decisions made by AI systems, which are not attuned to the contextual cues that humans associate with common sense. The disconnect between the deliberations of humans and those of machines is a foundational problem in the development of moral machines.

An opposite problem is that the border between "natural" and "artificial" intelligence is eroding, with the integration of biological and manufactured deliberative systems well underway. Already people make momentous decisions with computer assistance, and such integration is expected to advance into more seamless and permanent forms. Algorithms that direct internet searches for information are generally hidden from the user; our decisions are unconsciously guided by the presentation of results. Machines regularly complete our sentences and even our thoughts. Humans depend upon artificial intelligence for a bewildering array of activities from navigation to financial investments to health care decisions, generally without paying critical attention to the values implicit in the guidance given by their machines. We can anticipate conflicts between humanistic or religious values and the conduct of machines; might engineers integrate moral reasoning into the design of artificial intelligence and autonomous machines?

Wendell Wallach and Colin Allen chart a continuum of ethical sensitivity and autonomy[14] required to design what they call an artificial moral agent (AMA).[15] They term the lowest level of AMA "operational morality," meaning that the machine has been designed to function within certain parameters that respect the moral principles of the programmer. From a moral reasoning perspective, this is entirely passive. The highest level would be "full moral agency," which is not possible today for an artificial agent, and may indeed not be desirable or feasible, depending on one's theory of ethics. Between these levels is a realm they call "functional morality," defined as "intelligent systems capable of assessing some of the morally significant aspects of their own actions."

Wallach and Allen situate these levels on a grid measuring low and high levels of ethical sensitivity on the x-axis, and of autonomy on the y-axis. Systems that serve in a purely advisory capacity in recommending medication dosages to physicians, for example, have low autonomy. Autopilot systems that have operated airplanes for decades possess high autonomy but low ethical sensitivity, for they do not assess the moral consequences of their actions. They possess operational morality in that their programmers have integrated moral concerns (such as not injuring or killing humans) into the design of their operating parameters (such as not banking or changing altitude at a rate intolerable to most passengers, except to avoid a collision).[16]

Autonomous vehicles have driven many millions of miles on public roads in America, though most such vehicles operate in "assist" mode, rather than functioning without any human supervision.[17] The Society of Automotive Engineers has proposed 5 levels to describe such vehicles, from no automation to full automation, with levels 4 and 5 yet on the horizon.[18] Still, that horizon is approaching rapidly, and not only for cars. Uninhabited trains, boats, and aerial vehicles already navigate the rails, waters, and skies. While many are more "automatic" than truly "autonomous," the design trend is toward autonomous machines powered by artificial intelligence.

Our greatest concern is with the development of AMAs that possess high levels of both autonomy and ethical sensitivity. Since the goal of fashioning machines endowed with high autonomy is already within reach, there is urgency in the project of developing ethical sensitivity within artificial systems before they can operate without human supervision. At the Asilomar Conference on Beneficial AI in 2017, the Future of Life Institute organized the drafting of 23 principles, signed by thousands of AI researchers and industry leaders, designed to support "beneficial intelligence"—but not "undirected intelligence."[19] Of course, even directed intelligence is not necessarily beneficial, at least not for all parties affected.

Much conversation about the moral quandaries of autonomous vehicles focuses on variations of the famous trolley problem (discussed below), raising the question of whose life a system would prioritize in an accident situation—the occupants, a pedestrian, or passengers in a different vehicle.[20] Still, this discussion presumes beneficence. What about malevolent machines?

Autonomous weapons systems (AWS) are already employed via land, sea, and air by over 90 nations. Most systems are limited to surveillance functions, but some are equipped to react to threats with lethal force (LAWS).[21] Discussions of such systems differentiate between those in which human operators are "in the loop," required to authorize each use of force; those where humans are "on the loop," consulted during the operation with the ability to cancel an attack; and those where they are "out of the loop," meaning that they are informed only after the system has acted.

Defense strategists describe four stages in military systems with the acronym OODA: **O**bserve (search for targets), then **O**rient (detect targets), then **D**ecide (make the choice to engage the target), and finally **A**ct (engage the target). If a human is required to confirm a target and any appropriate action, then the system is semiautomatic.[22] Given that computers can process some data sets far faster than humans can, the temptation is great to move people out of the decision-making loop, much as generals may set objectives and assess outcomes while leaving the real-time process of deliberation and action to soldiers in the field of conflict.[23] This would lead to a fully autonomous system, even if humans continue to set goals and review results.

The Pentagon and CIA have spent billions of dollars developing increasingly powerful autonomous systems;[24] an initiative called the Joint Artificial Intelligence Center (JAIC) was announced in June 2018, which is said to focus on safety and ethics, among other things; nevertheless, there are growing concerns from leading scientists, ethicists, and leaders of the United Nations that AI weapons may violate international treaties.[25] Of special concern are moral norms such as the principle of distinction, which requires discernment between combatants and non-combatants, and the principle of proportionality, a concept designed to limit civilian harm in proportion to anticipated military gain.[26]

One of the strongest ethical defenses of autonomous systems—whether vehicles or weapons—is the fallibility of human operators. Driver error causes 90% of the over-30,000 vehicular deaths and many more injuries annually in the United States for all the familiar reasons—drunkenness, drowsiness, distraction, and general poor judgment.[27] Soldiers suffer from these same fallibilities; fear and rage may further impair their judgment. Robotic soldiers presumably will lack these deficits, but they are likely to experience other challenges, especially in discerning intent, and in differentiating combatants from non-combatants. As noted, there has been little progress in equipping AI with understanding the meaning of a situation beyond the matching of data patterns. Will an armed robot be reliably able to discern between a child holding an ice cream cone and a soldier aiming a pistol? In its speed and efficiency, will the system fail to allow ambiguous situations to be clarified?[28]

Perhaps this is merely a technical challenge; with improvements, autonomous systems might function with greater moral consistency than humans, making their use not only permissible but, arguably, mandatory.[29] AI may not comprehend *meaning*, but it can exceed human capacities for *situational awareness* in high intensity situations. Moreover, as Ronald Arkin observes, humans do not have an impressive record for moral conduct in war, and autonomous weapons could function as a check on their baser instincts, preventing attacks that are not in compliance with international law.[30] The most highly regarded weapons programs, such as the Aegis Combat System, feature integration between human and autonomous operation, benefiting from the relative strengths of people and machines in making life and death decisions.

Israel has become a leader in developing weapons systems powered by artificial intelligence. In July 2023, Marissa Newman of Bloomberg News reported that the Israel Defense Forces had developed an AI powered targeting system designed rapidly to identify large numbers of targets if Israel were caught in a multi-front war of survival. Some news sources identified the title of this program as *ha-besorah* ("the gospel") and claimed that it allowed for the rapid generation of target lists in Gaza.[31] This system was reportedly paired with another called Fire Factory which combines target data with munitions inventory and the availability of drones and other assets to prepare battle plans.[32] These systems may have been activated in Israel's war with Hamas following its brutal attack on *Sh'mini Atzeret*, October 7, 2023. As of this writing there has not been a disinterested analysis of the accuracy of this technology, or the extent to which it has crossed legal and ethical constraints. Similar systems are presumably available to militaries of other advanced nations, especially the United States and China. It is difficult to verify claims that such systems will be kept in semi-autonomous mode with human oversight.

Additional ethical concerns related to privacy and social control are raised by AI surveillance tools, which have already expanded the dominance of the most powerful nations and corporations over their own populations and their adversaries.[33] Societies often struggle to balance individual liberty and communal security, and AI-powered systems equipped with facial recognition and video analytics may skew the balance further toward security, or perhaps more accurately, toward control by powerful governments and corporations over access to information and the freedom of action accorded to people in their domain.[34] Intelligent video surveillance systems have been developed in China as a method for regulating the social conduct of the population in general, and suppressing the Muslim Uighur population in Xinjiang Province in particular. China has found a ready export market to other nations interested in extreme forms of social control.[35]

General concerns of privacy are magnified by the expanded powers and prevalence of AI in society. Robots greatly expand surveillance powers, including in previously private spaces such as the home or even the body, given the ubiquity of smart phones and watches.[36] While there may not be a "right to privacy" in Jewish law, there certainly is a ban on "talebearing" and on injuring parties by causing them shame or other harm. AI systems often prompt people to take actions that are not in their own best interests, whether in recommending unnecessary purchases or influencing voting behaviors, as demonstrated in the 2016 United States elections. Such interventions could countervene the Torah's interdiction against placing a stumbling block before the blind.[37]

Even beneficent AI applications, such as health care assistants, may raise troubling ethical questions. When a human health care provider such as a physician or nurse makes medical interventions, there is a basic sense of relationship that anchors the interaction, creating a presumption of concern and responsibility. Systems powered by artificial intelligence may provide valuable information and analysis of risks and benefits, and their interface may mimic patterns of speech and non-verbal behaviors that approximate expressions of concern, but we generally consider such systems to be tools, not responsible caregivers. Yet already there are trends in advanced economies to rely on such systems in place of humans, whose assistance may be costlier, less readily available, and perhaps less reliable.

Indeed, the use of embodied or animated conversational agents has become common in medical settings, and meta-analysis points to improvements in outcomes when well-designed virtual agents are used.[38] Such systems are designed to educate patients and monitor behaviors, but they are not empowered to make a diagnosis or determine the course of therapy, much less assess ethical dilemmas. Looking ahead, might virtual agents be comparable to human health care proxies that make treatment decisions on behalf of a patient, or should there always be a human supervisor to finalize matters of life and death?[39]

An additional area of concern relates to fairness in machine learning.[40] Bias is not inherently problematic; indeed, the ability to discriminate between different subjects and situations is the foundation of learning. Our concern is with discrimination that leads to an unjustified bias or one that has been declared morally irrelevant.[41] Fairness in machine learning is necessary to prevent the integration of social biases by algorithms charged with assisting on momentous decisions, from medical therapies to the approval of home loans, insurance policies, and even petitions for parole.[42]

What can be done to make machines operate on a level that is at least as moral as that of beneficent humans, avoiding the pitfalls that lead people to misjudge and discriminate against one another? Given the lack of consensus about ethical principles and the pressing need to develop guidelines for the conduct of autonomous machines equipped with artificial intelligence, it is imperative that wisdom traditions such as that of Judaism contribute to the general discourse, just as it has participated in discussions of bioethics and other matters of public policy.[43]

Classical statements of rabbinic law range between extremely narrow and extraordinarily broad subject audiences. Many Talmudic norms are directed particularly at Jews who are adult, free, male, educated, physically and mentally able, and even members of the rabbinic or priestly elite. Such people were classically considered as *bar ḥiyuva*, most fully obligated, and therefore fully governed by halakhah. Yet even classical rabbinic law applies in varying degrees to people of diverse ages, genders, religions, and other categories.

Indeed, Jewish law also addresses animals, inanimate objects, and features of nature, encompassing within its scope the great chain of being.⁴⁴ Progressive halakhists have sought in recent decades to articulate a more expansive and inclusive statement of the law. Can halakhah be applied even to artificial agents? A good starting point is the rabbinic concept of "agency" (*shelihut*), specifically the appointment of agents whose status differs substantially from the principal who appointed them.

Shliḥut: What if a person's agent is not like them?

In determining the contours of legal agency, the rabbis consider differences of age, gender, religious and social status between the principal (*sholeïaḥ*) and agent (*shaliaḥ*). They also discuss the use of non-human actors (e.g., an elephant or a monkey), and inanimate objects, such as a walled courtyard, to extend the reach of a human. What is the significance of the status difference between principal and agent? In what circumstances is the principal responsible for harm or transgressions performed on their behalf by the agent? Do the terms of agency depend on the social status, cognitive state, or autonomy of the agent?

The foundational source for the laws of agency is Mishnah Kiddushin 2:1; it is developed further in both the Yerushalmi and the Bavli (41a-42b).⁴⁵

This Mishnah states that a man may betroth a woman either directly or through use of an agent, and that a woman may accept an offer of betrothal either directly or through an agent. There are several curious features to the wording of this Mishnah which occupy the sages in the Bavli and lead to important rulings, such as the prohibition of marrying off a child until she is old enough to consent to a specific marriage offer.[46] This *sugya* (sub-section) establishes that men and women (but not children) may appoint agents, and that agents may function in various legal capacities for their principal: betrothal and divorce, tithing, and also commercial transactions (such as the purchase of a paschal lamb on behalf of a group). Finally, the Talmud generalizes the rule, claiming that an agent is halakhically considered to be equivalent to the person being represented (*she-shluḥo shel adam kamoto*):[47]

> For Rabbi Yehoshua b. Karḥah states, what is the source that shows that a person's agent is [legally considered to be] like him? For it says (Exod. 12:6, regarding the paschal offering): *the entire community of the congregation of Israel will slaughter it at dusk.* Could it be that the entire community slaughtered? Wasn't it only one person who slaughtered [the lamb]? Rather, this shows that a person's agent is [legally considered to be] like him.

This legal principle had previously been cited in Tannaitic literature, including Mishnah Brakhot, Tosefta Ta'anit, and Mekhilta D'Rabbi Yishmael, et al.[48] It is assumed to apply "in all situations," except when Scripture implies restriction of a significant action to the principal.[49] This rule is widely attested in the Bavli, but several restrictions are added to its application.

In the continuation of B. Kiddushin 41b, the sages consider the implications of Numbers 18:28 for the use of an agent to separate tithes.[50] The verse emphasizes, "even you," which the rabbis understand to allow for a Jewish—but not a non-Jewish—agent in the act of tithing:

> Then [it could have stated,] *you.* Why was it needed to state, *even you?* It was needed according to the statement of Rabbi Yannai, for Rabbi Yannai said: *Even you*—just as you are parties to the covenant [i.e., Jewish], so must your agents be parties to the covenant.

To be clear, Rabbi Yannai's restriction is contextual—to the religious obligation imposed on Israelite farmers to tithe for the Temple. Because non-Jewish farmers had no such obligation, they could not serve as agents for this task.[51] This might imply that in other situations, non-Jews *could* serve as agents, and indeed there are a few such cases from the realm of financial law.[52] Still, the general principle is that a Jew may not appoint a non-Jew as an agent, because gentiles are not obligated to observe the mitzvot of Jews.[53]

Sometimes this ruling is restated as, "for gentiles have no agency," but this phrasing is imprecise, as noted by Moshe Schochet (1878-1947) in his Mishneh Torah commentary: obviously gentiles do serve as agents *for each other*, and in this way, their status is not to be compared to people who are physically or intellectually incapable of such service.[54] Moreover, a responsum of Moshe Sofer (1762-1839) claims that when gentile law parallels Jewish law, then the action of a gentile agent may be accepted.[55]

There is also a distinction between pure agency, which is set up as a voluntary act, and employment, in which the servant's hand is an extension of the hand of the employer (*yad eved ke-yad rabo*). A gentile may, for example, transport an object for a Jew, even one of ritual or legal significance, such as a *gett* (writ of divorce).[56] The codifiers are most exclusive of gentile proxies in ritual contexts, such as the sale of *ḥametz* on Passover, and most inclusive when it comes to business practices that are shared between Jews and gentiles, or when gentile workers are hired for the task. As Shneur Zalman Fradkin of Lublin (1830-1902) explains, gentiles may conduct business for Jews, but may not complete mitzvot on their behalf.[57]

Another helpful distinction is illustrated at B. Eruvin 31b, in a discussion about using an agent to deliver a food item that will be placed in a location to extend one's *eruv* (Shabbat boundary):

> For it is taught in a *beraita*: If they gave it [i.e., an item to establish an extension of the *eruv*] to an elephant, and it carried it, [or] to a monkey and it carried it—this is not a [valid] *eruv*. But if one said to another [person] to receive it from [the animal], then it is a [valid] *eruv*. But what if it [the animal] does not deliver it? Rav Ḥisda says, this case [is valid] when the [principal] stands and watches [the entire sequence]. And what if [the human receiving agent] refuses to accept it from [the animal]? Rav Yeḥiel says, it is established that an agent [can be expected to] complete his appointed task.

Generally, the agents must themselves be like the principal—Jewishly obligated and, in the case above, accepting of the rabbinic rule about *eruvim*. For example, a Samaritan who rejects the rabbinic law of *eruvim* may not serve as an agent for this purpose. This accords with what we learned in the previous paragraph. But if there is a second *receiving* agent who is equally obligated, then the first *messenger* agent need not be committed to the religious content of the task. Indeed, the item could even be placed on an elephant or a monkey to convey, so long as the principal can observe the transfer, and the receiving agent is in place.

This ruling establishes a precedent for intermediate steps that are not considered to be true agency but are mechanical. In later halakhic literature, this comes to be called *ma'asei kof,* the "act of a monkey," and serves to justify, for example, using a postal or courier service to send a bill of divorce to a location where a second agent will receive it.[58] The carrier is not a true agent in the sense of legally representing the sender. In other words, both at the outset and at the conclusion of the legal act, there must be a properly qualified actor (whether principal or agent) who can bear full responsibility, but in the middle, it is permissible to use animate or mechanical means of conveyance.

From the first example of tithing and the subsequent ones regarding *eruvim* and *gittin,* it appears that there is a higher standard of agency for ritual actions than for monetary transactions, but even ritual acts may use a non-obligated agent for an intermediate step such as transportation. *We may infer that if a ritually obligated individual both initiates and completes an action, then a non-obligated agent, and even a non-human agent, might be permitted to carry out an intermediate segment of the task.*

A second important restriction on agency is the rule, "there is no agency for transgression" (*ein shaliaḥ le-d'var aveirah*). For example, if A says to B, "Go get me an ox from the barn of C," and B goes and steals C's ox, B is responsible for their own action and cannot claim to have simply followed A's orders. As the Talmud puts it, "If the master speaks, and a student speaks, to whom do we listen?"[59] God is the master, and the agent remains responsible to obey divine law, regardless of the instructions of the principal. Agency breaks down at the border of transgression. When a principal appoints an agent for a legal act, then the "agent is like the principal." But if it turns out that the action is illegal, then the agent is liable for their own misdeed (at least if the agent shares the same halakhic obligations as the principal). However, the principal remains morally culpable for leading their neighbor into transgression.[60]

This rule sounds reasonable but could lead to absurd or even mischievous results, as the sages realized (not even anticipating AWS). Should a child or a slave be held liable for obeying a parent or a master? Could a courtyard be held to the same liability? After all, rabbinic law allows a person to claim ownerless property based on it landing in their domain—within 4 cubits of their body in a secluded space, or in their courtyard—even without the person establishing physical contact.[61] But what if the "claimed" object is not truly ownerless? Can a person be held responsible for the acquisition committed by his courtyard? Might an inanimate object be considered an agent?

At B. Bava Metzia 10b, the sages entertain the possibility that a courtyard could be considered an agent of a person, for example, in acquiring ownerless property for them or receiving a bill of divorce. As Rashi explains, [then] "her courtyard could be like her agent."[62] Yet, this position is rejected. Why? Amoraim Ravina and Rav Sama limit the transfer of liability from principal to agent in cases where the agent has little or no autonomy, with each offering a different explanation for the limitation [emphasis added in both quotes]:

> Ravina says, when we said that "there is no agency for a transgression," that was *only when the agent was personally obligated* [for that transgression]. But as for a courtyard, which is not itself obligated, the principal is liable. If so, when a man tells his wife or slave, "go steal for me," since they are not obligated to pay [the "double" penalty], shall we say that the principal is liable? You could say, wives and slaves are [after all] responsible [not to steal] but are not obligated [to pay the fine for theft, since they do not control their own assets]. For it is taught in a Mishnah, if the woman is divorced or the slave is freed, then they become liable to pay [their own fines].

Rav Sama says, when we said that "there is no agency for a transgression," that was *only in the case* when [the agent] acted if he wished to, and [the agent] did not act if he didn't wish to. But as for a courtyard, where items are placed without its consent, the principal is liable.

Before proceeding, we must pause to acknowledge the offensiveness of the common comparison of women to slaves in a patriarchal society, and of the ancient permission for slavery altogether. We further acknowledge the painful reality that, though most nations no longer sanction slavery, and though they may have enacted formal gender equality in many realms of law, no society is fully egalitarian, and various forms of slavery remain prevalent throughout the world, including in democratic countries.[63] For the Talmud, a stratified social structure is assumed, and the presenting question pertains to the implications of such hierarchies for the legal institution of agency, not to the (in)justice of such structures.

Instead, the editor ponders the practical distinction between the positions of Ravina and Rav Sama, proposes some cases where they might yield different results, but concludes that in the end, their positions are compatible. The rule that "there is no agency for a transgression" applies only when the agent possesses the ability to resist the mission, and to pay consequences for transgression. In the end, the courtyard is not really an agent. *Obligation is an essential qualification for agency; an inanimate object cannot become an agent.*

A related discussion is found in Midrash Mekhilta[64] regarding a person "who sends their livestock to graze in another's land" (Exod. 22:4). The verb for "send" is read by the rabbis to imply that the owner used an agent to perpetrate this misdeed. The Midrash says:

He sends his livestock. From here they said, if he handed his sheep to his son, to his agent, to his servant/slave, then he [i.e., the owner] is exempt, but [if he handed his sheep] to a person who is deaf-mute, mentally ill, or a minor, then he [i.e., the owner] is liable.

The Midrash here distinguishes between an agent who has the capacity for independent judgment, and therefore is responsible for their own actions, and an agent who does not have such ability, and is therefore not held responsible.[65] The sages have established a distinction between agents who are independent moral actors and those who are not.

This rabbinic discourse around agency and crime has implications for our discussion of machine ethics. When we say that machines are functioning autonomously, we currently mean this in a very limited sense. Machines are given a task and the capacity to complete the task within certain parameters, usually by following algorithms built on a series of predetermined "if...then" rules they have been programmed to follow. They are not capable of establishing independent goals or refusing to act on orders that fall within their operational parameters. Nor are they accorded legal personhood, no matter how personal people may get in conversations with virtual assistants.[66] Just as it would be absurd to punish a courtyard for "stealing" a goat, so would it be absurd to whip an autonomous vehicle in punishment for "murdering" a pedestrian.

Legal standing and free will are essential components of moral stature and liability.[67] At this stage, artificial intelligence functions like a tool, and so, moral liability must remain with the principal. Or perhaps the machine is more like an animal, in which case its owner is responsible to a greater or lesser extent, depending on its typical performance. In any event, the machine is not obligated, as Ravina puts it, nor does it have free will, as Rav Sama emphasizes. *Without these capacities, liability remains with the principal who appointed the agent—the person, not the machine.*

Even so, questions remain. Who is the principal? Those who designed the system? Its manufacturer? The vendor, or the end-user? Liability for an action conducted by an autonomous system should reside with the person most responsible for this specific action. If a user instructs an autonomous vehicle to convey them to a location, and the vehicle causes damage or injury on the way, the vehicle is not a free agent and does not have legal or moral standing (unlike a human driver).[68] A person should be responsible, but who? With consumer products in general, there is overlapping responsibility between the manufacturer, who must build a reliable product, and the user, who must maintain the product and use it according to directions. What is different here is that AI-directed machines are designed to operate in unpredictable circumstances. Still, humans design, manufacture, license, sell, purchase, and use these machines—surely there must be a doctrine of joint or several liability to account for damage and assign fault to one or more responsible humans.

What about future iterations of artificial intelligence? Recalling the schema of Wallach and Allen, what if future machines progress from operational to functional morality? Some researchers (and many science fiction writers) anticipate artificial *general* intelligence, which would not merely complete delimited tasks, but could pursue more abstract goals (e.g., fighting crime) using contextual reasoning. Just as human neural networks have been used as a model for developing artificial neural networks, so might moral values be used as a model for training machines to differentiate and prioritize goals.

Imagine, for example, an AI assistant that has observed that a user is an alcoholic, and thus declines to transport them to a liquor store unless there is consultation with another family member, physician, or legal official. Such pairings of AI with autonomous machines might eventually qualify as "full moral agency." At that point might machines be deemed persons, responsible for their own conduct, expected to comply not only with laws, but also with moral values? We will return to this question below.

Currently, autonomous machines do not possess well-developed capabilities for moral reasoning. We have suggested that the people who make use of their services be held responsible for their actions, but is this position reasonable, when that person does not understand or minutely control the implementation of commands that activate such machines? When autonomous vehicles cause damage, should full liability be assigned to their occupants? These occupants may not understand, much less direct, the algorithms guiding their vehicle. They will not truly be drivers, but rather passengers. Is it reasonable to hold them liable? For this question, we turn to the rules of damages (*nezikin*).

Limited Liability for Indirect Actions

Beginning with the Torah (Exodus 21:25-36 and 22:4-5), Jewish law holds owners responsible for damage caused by their property, whether animate (such as a donkey or an ox) or inanimate (such as a pit or a fire). There are many variables that can mitigate or amplify liability, such as whether the damage was intentional or accidental, direct or indirect, predictable or surprising, whether due caution had been exercised, or whether freak circumstances conspired to cause harm. These subjects are discussed extensively in the first six chapters of Bavli Bava Kama.

It is well established in Jewish law that people are partially responsible for damage caused by an animal or tool that is under their domain.[69] It is also established that people bear full responsibility for damage caused by actions they have initiated, such as shooting an arrow, even once the object has departed from their control. This category of damage is known as *be-koho* ("by his force"). But there is a third category of damage caused by a sequence of events initiated by a person that proceeded in unpredictable ways. For example, a person throws a stone, which ricochets and hits another stone, which loosens and falls, damaging property in the process. This is called *b'koah koḥo* ("by force of his force") and is more controversial, with differing opinions about liability.[70]

A major distinction is made by the sages between animate and inanimate property.[71] This distinction plays out in many areas of halakhah, such as whether animate property (say, a tethered donkey) might be used as a wall for a Sukkah, a post for an *eruv* (a Sabbath boundary), or as parchment for a *gett*. In the laws of damages, a further distinction is made between behavior expected of animals (which increases liability for the owners) and unexpected behavior (which limits owner liability).[72] How shall we regard the conduct of autonomous machines—like inanimate property that might move and cause damage (as with a fire), or like an animal that moves of its own volition, and may surprise its owner with unexpected behavior? Should autonomous machines powered by artificial intelligence be regarded as "alive," at least to the extent of animals? And if so, should this comparison narrow or expand the scope of owner liability?

In *Teḥumin*, an Israeli journal of halakhah and society, Yosef Sprung and Yisrael Meir Malka discuss liability for the actions of autonomous vehicles in light of the laws of damage.[73] Avraham Yeshaya Karelitz (1878-1957), known as the Ḥazon Ish, had declared operators liable for the actions of machines such as cars or motorized plows they had set in motion, even if they had removed their hands from the controls, since they had clearly caused such machines to operate.[74] Yet Sprung and Malka note that autonomous vehicles are different—they act independently and in ways that the user cannot always anticipate.

A precedent within established halakhah is the case of work animals that are sometimes kept under direct control, and other times allowed to follow their own course. Animals yoked to a plow are an example of the former; unfettered animals carrying a pack across a field at the urging of a person are a type of the latter. At B. Shabbat 153b, we learn that a man who plows on Shabbat with his animal is fully liable for the labor; but if he places a load on an animal to carry from one domain to another, he is not. Why? Both are forbidden labors!

The answer is technical in part—the sages imagine the person placing his package on a moving donkey and removing it when the animal stops. Being fully liable for the labor of transporting requires the same person to lift the object, carry it, and then deposit it. But if person A places an object on person B, who transports it, and then A retrieves it, they are both free from full liability—yet are still forbidden to act so, by decree of the rabbis. Rav Pappa then says that any action that is biblically forbidden when done by one (active) person, and only rabbinically banned by means of another (passive) person, is completely permitted when done by means of an animal.[75] This is because the animal is not itself liable for the mitzvot.

A second and more interesting distinction is found in Ramban's comments to B. Shabbat 153b.[76] He distinguishes between situations where the animal is controlled and those where it is relatively independent:

> This [liability] is stated because when a person plows with his animal, he places a yoke on it, and he controls it by force of his hands, and it remains under his control. Any labor is done for the person, and it depends on him, and the animal is no more than a tool in the hands of an artisan. This is not comparable to the donkey driver, because the animal walks of its own accord, even if it is somewhat mindful of the donkey driver.

Rabbis Sprung and Malka suggest that this distinction may apply as well to an autonomous vehicle. Even though it is given a task by a human "driver," the fact is that the driver does not control the machine directly. It will stop and start, turn, avoid obstacles, re-route, and otherwise operate independently, as it works to complete its mission. This would imply that a person is not responsible for work done on their behalf by an autonomous machine, so long as it is acting independently.

A similar inference is drawn from discussion of a person who encourages an animal to graze in a neighbor's field—only if they push the animal to cause damage is the person fully liable. Otherwise, the animal is understood to have acted independently (see Rema to SA HM 394:3). So, too, with a person who sets a dog or a snake to bite a foe—this is forbidden, but the damage is not considered to be directly caused by the person, since the animal directs its own action.

As Sprung and Malka summarize these cases, a person is fully responsible for malicious damage caused by an animal, but only if the person is directly controlling the animal's action. If the animal acts independently, then the damage is not considered to be caused by the person, though the owner may be held indirectly responsible for common damages under the less severe categories of *shein va-regel*, "tooth and hoof." This area of established law (see Mishnah Bava Kama, ch. 2) would imply that damage or ritual violations caused by autonomous machines would not be the full responsibility of the owner, though the owner might nevertheless bear partial responsibility, as with any damage done by one's animals or other possessions.[77]

Rabbis Sprung and Malka also discuss the concept of *ba-koaḥ sheni*, "second force," a term which comes from a discussion of murder in B. Sanhedrin 77b/Ḥullin 16a. If A unleashes a force (such as a stream of water) in a way that directly kills B (say A had bound B and placed B in the path of the water), then A is liable for murder—it is as if his arrows accomplished his goal. But if A's action was more indirect—for example, causing a flood that *might* overtake B—one could argue that the lethal force of the floodwaters was independent of the actor, and thus the death was not caused entirely by A. In that case, A would not be liable for murder (though perhaps for manslaughter). Similarly, if a person requested that an autonomous vehicle convey them to their office, and the vehicle did damage on the way, the damage could be said to have been caused by a second force, leaving the person exempt from personal liability—especially in a case when there is no reason to expect an accident.

Jewish laws on liability differentiate between damage caused by a person and damage caused by their property. The archetype of the latter category is fire. If A starts a fire and it spreads to damage B's property, then A is liable for the damage. But as we have seen, the introduction of intermediate factors that separate between the action of a person and the ultimate results can lessen or eliminate liability. Likewise, when a person's property causes damage, we consider outside influences. For example, if a person sets a controlled fire in their yard in a manner that is normally safe, and then an unusually strong gust of wind spreads it quickly and it destroys neighboring property, that person is not fully liable. Whenever damage is caused by a combination of factors, some of which were absent at the time of the person's initial act, liability is limited.

Jewish law includes the category of compulsion (oness); one may be held liable for damages that they set in motion even if they did not intend the destruction. The Mishnah from Bava Kama cited above states that "a person is always forewarned" and may not claim ignorance and freedom from liability for the consequences of their actions. Yet this description of liability assumes control over the action. If there was very low risk of damage, and if the process happened outside the person's control, then they should not be held liable for the damage caused by their vehicle.

The authors next discuss the category of "permitted harm." For example, if person A chooses to go running in the park, and they collide with person B, who is also running in the park—both runners had permission to run in public, and both were aware of the risk of such collisions. Unless they acted with wanton disregard for the safety of others, there is a normative expectation permitting such conduct (and even more if they were racing home for Shabbat). As autonomous vehicles become prevalent, Rabbis Sprung and Malka conclude, people journeying on roadways will expect these machines to function according to their design, and users should not be held responsible for freak accidents or failures that they could not have anticipated.

A complicated and controversial topic in the laws of damages is liability for indirect action.[78] There are two similar categories known as *grama* and *garmei*. In the laws of damages, a person implicated by *grama* is exempt from liability, but is liable for *garmei* (following the opinion of Rabbi Meir in the Talmud). Everything about this topic is complicated, from the definition of terms and the nature of liability for *garmei*, to whether it is true liability, or merely a penalty to prevent people from damaging the property of others with impunity. Generally, for an act of negligence to result in liability for damages as *garmei*, the damage must be direct, immediate, and certain. None of these conditions is expected to apply to autonomous vehicles, and thus, not even a penalty is justified for damage caused by one's autonomous machinery.

Sprung and Malka's presentation regarding damages is excellent, and yet the project that they have set for themselves is limited. They have not considered the larger implications of autonomous technologies. How shall we regard the decisions of the autonomous machine—is it like an extension of the owner, or like an independent actor? Should distinctions applied to animals as either harmless or dangerous be applied to AI-driven machines?

What if the machine does not cause physical damage, but violates other rules of the Torah? For example, if a person pre-orders an autonomous vehicle to take them on a Shabbat journey—have they violated Shabbat? Sprung and Malka do not address this question, but their conclusion that passengers are not responsible for the damage done by autonomous vehicles suggests that they are likewise not responsible for forbidden labor done by the vehicle on their behalf. This is implicit in their citation of the Ḥazon Ish regarding the operation of a plow on Shabbat. Certainly, it would be less problematic to allow a machine to conduct labor autonomously than to drive the plow oneself, but is it permitted?

A further limitation of this presentation is that it does not address the integration of Jewish principles into the design of the autonomous vehicles and of the algorithms that guide them. One expects that such vehicles will be safe, safer even than those driven by people, yet accidents will continue to occur. If a vehicle must choose between hitting a pedestrian in the roadway or diverting and striking an inanimate object, thereby risking the lives of its occupants, what will it do? Whose life should a machine prioritize when mortal danger is inevitable?

Canteens, Trolleys, and Cars: Prioritizing Between Lives

Perhaps the most universal ethical principle is the one stated unequivocally in the Decalogue as *lo tirzaḥ,* "do not murder." Yet the Torah itself states that the punishment for murder is execution, so intentional killing is sometimes sanctioned.[79] Then there is killing in self-defense, and negligent homicide, both of which are treated more leniently by the Torah, as well as justified warfare. Even if a person intentionally murders an innocent victim, rabbinic law requires elaborate (and largely unfeasible) evidentiary standards of intention and action before permitting execution. How might a machine determine whether a killing is justified or even necessary?

In 1942, the science fiction writer, Isaac Asimov, wrote his Three Laws of Robotics, with Law One a prohibition on harming humans— but nothing about such rules has ever been simple. What is the difference between murder and manslaughter? What is the definition of intention? Who is authorized to assess risk? Is there a meaningful ethical distinction between action and inaction, even if both are conscious decisions that may cost a life? And what should be done when loss of life is inevitable, and only one person or party can be spared?

This final question played out gruesomely in England during the summer of 1944. The German army developed V-1 missiles and began launching great numbers of them at London, causing enormous damage and ultimately, 6,000 deaths. Most of the missiles fell to the south of the city, where the damage they caused was far less than if they had hit their intended target. British Intelligence engaged in a campaign of misinformation to convince the Germans that their missiles were mostly striking Central London. In so doing, they exposed people to the south of the city to greater danger, and indeed, some 57,000 homes were damaged in Croydon alone. And yet, it was claimed that because of this deception, the casualty total was reduced, sparing as many as 10,000 lives. After the war, British philosopher and ethicist Philippa Foot explored the dilemma through publication of a verbal puzzle that has come to be known in philosophical discourse as the Trolley Problem.[80]

The puzzle begins with a trolley rolling out of control towards five victims who are tied to the tracks. A bystander can throw a switch and divert the trolley onto a spur, to which only one person is tied. Inaction will result in five deaths, whereas action can reduce the toll to one. What is the moral response? This puzzle, with many permutations, has been used to clarify different systems of moral reasoning. The most famous variable is that, instead of pushing a switch, the bystander may push a large person onto the tracks to stop the trolley and save the five.[81] Surveys reliably show that most people would throw the switch but would not push the person, even though the death toll would be the same.

From a utilitarian perspective, one looks to the result and reasons backwards. If forced to choose between 1 victim and 5 (in the trolley problem), or between 6,000 and 16,000 victims (in the WWII case), the moral choice is to minimize loss. The mechanism should not matter since the goal is always the best outcome for the largest number of people. Yet this approach involves intentionally causing the death of specific people. Is that defensible?

In a rule-based (deontological) ethical system, the focus is on the person deciding how to act. The rule "do not murder" would preclude a witness either from throwing the switch or pushing the man, since by doing so, they would have chosen to kill the person on that track. Yet this ruling will cost four additional lives and is in tension with another rule, not to watch passively while another person is killed.

Most deontological systems have developed ways to reconcile rules, such as the doctrine of double effect associated with the thirteenth century Christian theologian, Thomas Aquinas.[82] In this case, the bystander who throws the switch, diverting the trolley to the spur, does not *intend* to kill the lone person tied to the tracks over there, but only to save the lives of the five trapped on the current route. True, the bystander may *foresee* the death of the solitary victim before throwing the switch but would be delighted if that person were somehow to escape injury. The same cannot be said about pushing a large person onto the tracks, since their death is not merely a *consequence* of the act of saving but is the very *means*. Still, from the perspective of the poor person tied to the tracks in the first scenario, the intention of the bystander is of little significance. Is this fine moral distinction why so many people differentiate between the two?

The divergent responses to the two scenarios (in numerous surveys, 90% would throw the switch, but only 10% would push the man), despite their equal outcomes, may reveal less about moral reasoning than about neurology. Recently, the field of "neuroethics" has examined the respective roles of the brain's limbic system (associated with emotional responses and drives) and the prefrontal cortex (associated with abstract reasoning) and shown that the former is more powerfully activated by the prospect of pushing a person onto the tracks. Assessment of intent is often an after-the-fact rationalization designed to justify instinctive decisions, rather than an objective measurement.[83] Many other variables illustrate the interplay of these systems, indicating that people frequently act first for emotional reasons, with ethical theories such as utilitarianism and deontology serving as after-the-fact rationalizations.[84]

There are other approaches to decide the most ethical course that focus more on the moral development of the actor. Perhaps best known is an approach traced to Aristotle known as virtue ethics (restated in modern terms by Philippa Foot). Here, the focus is not on abstract decisions but on conflicting dispositions *within the person* empowered to act. What would be the most honest or brave or responsible action? Again, such considerations would make little difference to the doomed person tied to the tracks. Yet the Torah also frames its rules in terms of righteousness and integrity. What might rabbinic sources contribute to this discourse?

One of the most famous moral dilemmas included in the Bavli (at Bava Metzia 62, and paralleled in Midrash Sifra, Behar 5:6:3) frames the question in the context of a road trip gone bad:

> Two people were walking on the path, and one held in his hand a canteen of water. If they both drank from it, they would both die [of thirst], but if one of them drank from it, they may reach the settled area. Ben Petora explained— better that they both drink and die, that one not (passively) observe the death of the other. But then Rabbi Akiva came and taught that the verse, *Let him live by your side* (Lev. 25:36) means that your life precedes the life of your fellow.

The Talmud might have summoned a consequentialist argument, saying that a toll of two dead is worse than one, but that perspective is not mentioned. Jewish law does not permit the killing of one person to spare the life of a second, except in self-defense, so consequentialism seems to be unacceptable.[85] Ben Petora comes closest to the virtue ethics position. What kind of person would take the water and leave his friend to die? This argument has the unfortunate consequence of a maximal death toll. Rabbi Akiva's *drash* unearths a "rule" in the Torah that justifies and even requires what might otherwise look like a selfish act or a coldly consequentialist calculus—but has the benefit of reducing the body count.

Later commentators seek to harmonize the two perspectives. Rabbi Samuel Eliezer ben R. Judah HaLevi Edels (b. Cracow 1555) argues that Rabbi Akiva's rule applies only if the canteen *belongs* to one person, but if it belongs to both, then Rabbi Akiva would surely agree with Ben Petorah and instruct the person in possession to share and die.[86] I am not convinced. Rabbi Akiva might then argue that *the one in possession has presumption of ownership*, as he does in numerous other cases.[87] In this example, a rule allows conduct that would otherwise be condemned as selfish.

Should Rabbi Akiva's rule be made the basis of the algorithms that guide autonomous vehicles? In an accident situation where the vehicle must either strike a pedestrian or divert into a hazard that would endanger the occupant, Rabbi Akiva's rule would doom the pedestrian if needed to save the passenger (assuming the vehicle is loyal to its occupant).

However, at Bavli Pesaḥim 25b, the rabbis argue against permitting the killing of a bystander even for the sake of self-preservation.[88]

How do we know that murder is forbidden, [even if necessary to save one's own life]? It is logical, as seen in the case of one who came before Rava, saying, "the lord of my town told me to kill so-and-so or if not, I will kill you." [Rava] said to him, "Let him murder you, but you must not murder. Why do you think that your blood is redder than his? Perhaps that fellow's blood is redder than yours!"

This story, which is founded on rabbinic reasoning, becomes exalted into a cardinal rule known by the expression, *ein doḥin nefesh mipnei nefesh,* "one may not kill one person to save another." Rava thus follows a relevant rule; his position also seems closer to the virtue-ethics perspective of Ben Petora: better to die than to become a murderer. In the accident scenario described above, this logic might yield the opposite outcome. The autonomous vehicle would need to divert from striking the pedestrian, even if that caused mortal injury to its passenger (and totaled the vehicle).

It is possible that Rava does not truly disagree with Rabbi Akiva, since Rava's case would require the active murder of one's neighbor, whereas Rabbi Akiva simply advises the canteen holder to walk away. This reconciliation was offered by Ephraim Oshry in his *Responsa Mima'amakim* from the Kovno ghetto during the Shoah.[89] Rabbi Oshry argues that we may act to preserve our own lives, even if this might passively endanger another person, but we may not actively kill another person since "why do you think your blood is redder than theirs?" Ben Petora might argue that simply by keeping the water to himself, the first person is actively killing or at least shortening the life of the second, but Akiva and perhaps Rava would counter that in this desperate circumstance, a person may act to preserve their own life.

Rabbi Oshry notes that Rabbi Moshe Isserles concludes that if a person is about to suffer damage, he may protect himself, even if this causes another person to be harmed.[90] This logic allowed Rabbi Oshry to justify the distribution by Jewish officials of work permits to half of the working population of the Kovno ghetto, even though it made the deaths of the other half more likely.

Do we prefer that autonomous machines identify with and prioritize the lives of their owners (or users), as Rabbi Akiva's rule would indicate, or that they act altruistically, as Ben Petora and perhaps Rava would argue? Rabbi Akiva's principle has been well established, and thus we might conclude that autonomous vehicles should prioritize the lives of their occupants, though of course they should be designed to spare the lives of bystanders as well, whenever possible.

Algorithms can be designed to reflect whatever ethical approach programmers prefer, but many would object to the entire premise of this exercise. After all, both Rabbi Akiva and Rava were addressing human actors, not machines, which have no "skin in the game." On the other hand, encoding into AI whatever rules and principles we settle on would probably make compliance more likely in difficult situations.[91] Paradoxically, AI can either be used to ensure greater compliance with Jewish ethical teachings or, since artificial agents are not party to the Torah's covenant, to avoid them altogether.

Indirect Actions and the Evasion of Moral Liability

We have now come upon the limitations of formalist models of religious law.[92] It may be possible to pair autonomous machines with the halakhic doctrine of indirect causation to evade legal liability for damage done, for crimes committed, and for social and ritual obligations evaded. What then of our general obligation, "you shall do that which is right and good in the eyes of the Lord your God" (Deut. 12:28)?[93] Once we have delegated duties to smart machines, are we absolved of responsibility?

Consider the progression within recent decades, from writing orders in pen and ink, to entering data by means of a keyboard, to the use of natural speech to instruct digital assistants to act on one's behalf. In my responsum on electricity and Shabbat, I argued that using digital devices such as keyboards or cameras should be considered a derivative form of writing and therefore be forbidden on Shabbat. Might the same be said about speech that is captured by digital assistants that are always listening, and suggesting actions based on what they hear? Arguably, the use of speech recognition introduces one or more degrees of separation between the person and the action. After all, the AI-driven machine must make use of a large database of sounds to interpret the speaker's words, with many opportunities for error. This would seem to downgrade the process from active writing to an indirect interaction that could be permitted as *grama*.

We already differentiate between direct and indirect speech when it comes to non-Jewish employees performing tasks for a Jew on Shabbat. For example, if a Jew were to announce, "I am cold," or "I would like a cup of coffee," and a gentile employee or friend were to respond by adjusting the thermostat or brewing a cup of coffee, this action would be acceptable for many Shabbat observers. Would the same not be true for a speech-activated smart thermostat or coffee machine? Certainly, such indirect action would not be the equivalent of a physically forbidden action taken directly by a Jew; yet such speech acts are increasingly common and powerful in our technological environment. Permitting them outright may signal the erosion of distinction between Shabbat and weekdays. For example, a Shabbat observer might use voice commands to summon an autonomous vehicle to drive them across town, to order the delivery of food or other merchandise, to cook, clean, or engage in commerce, all without directly "acting" in a forbidden fashion.

The principle of *shvut* reminds Jews to guard the restful experience of Shabbat and Yom Tov, and not to lean too heavily on techniques that avoid technical violation while substantially undermining the restful spirit of the day. Ramban describes just such a concern in his commentary to Leviticus 23:24.[94] *Only if there is a positive religious obligation at stake, such as caring for people's comfort and dignity, should speech acts that cause a machine to complete labor be permitted on Shabbat.*

Near the end of his life, Aharon Lichtenstein (1933-2015) delivered a series of lectures based on Ramban's "Treatise on the Law of Indirect Damage," which, as discussed above, is a complex topic of great interest to the medieval sages.[95] He voices concern that technology might be used to evade responsibility for harm and calls on rabbis to address the matter:

Within the developing technological reality, there is a constantly increasing ability to inflict significant damages, physical or even virtual, without becoming liable based on the criteria of Ramban or the R"I [Rabbi Yosef ibn Migash]. The damage can be more abstract, and the process more indirect, than the minimum required to cause liability in the laws of *garmei*—and yet, the results can be extremely severe. A skilled and brilliant thief could commit a perfect crime, using an indirect mechanism for the intrusion without getting caught up, according to those who hold this view, with liability for direct or indirect damage. Will the gap in time between an act and its consequence, and the autonomy of an advanced system, be allowed to separate a person from [responsibility for] their actions? Will this approach—which has been used by *poskim* to ease liability for the laws of Shabbat—also be used to dismiss liability for damage? And even if we can set aside this example, differentiating between Shabbat and damages, since regarding labor we focus on the process, whereas with damages we look at the results—will this problem not recur in many other cases? The need is apparent, the [rabbinic] authority exists, and the eyes [of the public] are raised. If the leading authorities can address this matter and repair this substantial societal problem, they will succeed and raise high the banner of Torah.

Rabbi Lichtenstein named a major problem, even if only as a valedictory message at the close of an extensive discourse. He is hardly alone or even early in worrying that technology has created plausible moral deniability, with vast social damage to follow, but his call for rabbinic activism is noteworthy. Perhaps, as he suggests, we ought to be lenient on matters of ritual, which are between people and God, but more stringent with actions that can damage other people, whether immediately, or even over the course of generations.

Philosopher Hans Jonas argues in *The Imperative of Responsibility* that classical ethical discourse is inadequate to the powers of the technological age.[96] Previous ethics focused on interhuman relations and were geared "to the proximate range of action," given the presumption that humans could not cause damage to future generations or to the earth itself and had no sense of cumulative impact. He observes that no ethics outside of religion have adopted the needed perspective, which includes nonhumans within the realm of human responsibility. For Jonas, the greatly expanded powers of advanced technology require a commensurate expansion of moral responsibility.

Jonas focuses primarily on environmental ethics; this is a concern of ours as well. Here, however, our task is to delineate responsibility not for actions done by humans with machines, but for actions done by machines on behalf of humans. Shall our ethics expand yet again to encompass artificial intelligence? Can machines themselves be taught to act ethically? From the perspective of halakhah, is it legitimate to join Allen and Wallach in imagining an artificial moral agent? Might we ever say that a machine has attained personhood? If so, could the machine also acquire a religious identity, become subject to divine command, and be considered Jewish? Outlandish as this may sound, the concept is not unanticipated. In the early modern era, several prominent sages pondered a similar question: *may a golem count in a minyan?*

Androids as Religious Agents

As noted above, while the rabbis focused much of their norm-building attention on individuals like them, they also expanded their gaze to other types of people, as well as to animals, objects, and topography. Rabbinic law, like all law, is anthropocentric, with human life most carefully protected and regulated. Yet, this is not a full account of biblical and rabbinic thought, which is concerned with animal suffering, imposes responsibilities on humans for animal welfare, anthropomorphizes certain animals as "crafty" (the snake in Eden), and others as loyal and innocent (Balaam's donkey), or wise and industrious (the ant in Proverbs 6). In one famous Talmudic passage (B. Eruvin 100b), animals are proposed as a possible source for natural law.[97] The rabbis even apply the same court procedures required for the execution of criminals to certain animals.[98] The Land of Israel is viewed in Leviticus as a living organism that cannot tolerate moral turpitude.[99] Indeed, it is possible to extend Judaism's "image of God" concept beyond humanity to the earth's ecosystem.[100]

Still, these are natural phenomena. What about creatures created by people? There is a long history in Jewish thought extending to the early rabbinic period, discussing the possibility and implications of using mystical methods to create an android or "golem." Gershom Scholem, Byron Sherwin, Moshe Idel, and others have produced extensive studies of the history of the golem.[101] The golem enters halakhic discourse in the 17th century with obvious implications for our subject. I will provide a brief review of the essential sources, citing Idel's book as the latest statement on the subject.

Early rabbinic texts, such as Midrash Bereshit Rabbah and the mystical book Sefer Yetzirah, may imply some measure of human partnership in the creation of the world, and specifically, in the creation of humanity. Idel finds support for this claim in early rabbinic traditions related to Abraham. Midrash Bereshit Rabbah plays on the unusual word b'hivaram ("in their creation") in Gen. 2:4 and rearranges the letters to render b'Avraham ("through Abraham")—that is, God created the world through the merit of Abraham.[102] Sefer Yetzirah, which may include material from as early as the second century, begins with discussion of the methods of combining numbers and letters by which the universe is formed. Toward the end, it includes a passage describing the special role of Abraham:

Because Abraham our ancestor, blessed be his memory, contemplated and looked, saw and investigated, understood and engraved, extracted and combined and formed, and succeeded [in the creation of people, as it says, "and the souls that they made in Ḥaran"]; the Master of the Universe was revealed to him and He made him sit in His bosom and He kissed him upon his head and called him My beloved and set him as His son." [103]

Idel believes that Sefer Yetzirah hints here at Abraham's ability to create a person (which is made quite explicit in the bracketed text). In any event, the 13th century commentator, R' Eleazar of Worms, based on traditions from his master Rabbi Yehudah he-Ḥasid, understood Sefer Yetzirah in this way. The ability to create a person was considered within reach for the righteous, though only God could endow a person with intelligence and speech.

This idea that humans are distinguished by *intelligence and speech* is found in the comments of Rashi to Genesis 2:7: "All animals are called *nefesh ḥaya* [vital life], but humans have additional vitality, since they also possess intelligence and speech."[104] This claim of human distinction relating to speech, based perhaps on the Aramaic translation of Onkeles, *l'ruaḥ m'mal'la* (a speaking spirit), was also integrated into liturgical poetry, most famously in the Yom Kippur poem, *Ha-aderet v'ha-emunah*.[105]

The belief that righteous sages might create a person, but could not endow them with speech, is based on the most important text regarding the creation of an android, Bavli Sanhedrin 65b:

Rava said, if they wished, the righteous could create a world, for it says, "But your iniquities have been a barrier [between you and your God]" (Isaiah 59:2). Rava created a man and sent him [to appear] before Rabbi Ze'era. He [Rabbi Ze'era] spoke to him, but he [the man] did not reply to him. [Rabbi Ze'era] said to him: You came from the fellowship [of magicians], return to your dust! [106]

This strange story claims that certain rabbis were able to use "The Book of Creation" to create life forms. Rashi explains Rava's method for creating the man: "He created a man by means of Sefer Yetzirah, for they learned the combination of letters of the [divine] name."

It is hard to know quite how Rabbi Ze'era regarded Rava's artificial man. Idel translates ḥevraya as "the pietists," though it literally means "the fellowship" or "the magicians."[107] It appears that this man was able to understand and follow Rava's directions yet was unable to speak in response to Rabbi Ze'era, or perhaps at all. This story established the template for all later descriptions of a golem as a man-made creature of limited intelligence. In Ashkenazi circles, we begin to hear stories of rabbis who created a golem with Rabbi Shmuel He-Ḥasid, father of Rabbi Yehudah, in the 13th century, and then Rabbi Eliyahu of Ḥelm in the late 16th century.[108]

For our purposes, the significance of this topic is its entrance into halakhic discourse among the descendants of Rabbi Eliyahu of Ḥelm. His grandson (or perhaps great-grandson), Rabbi Tzvi Ashkenazi,[109] reports the family tradition that his grandfather created a "man" and asks whether he might have been counted in a minyan.[110] After all, the Talmud states (B. Sanhedrin 19b), "whoever raises an orphan in his home is deemed by the Torah to have given birth to him."[111] This might imply that the golem could be considered Jewish. But based on the Bavli's story of Rabbi Ze'era dissolving the golem, Rabbi Ashkenazi concludes that such a person could not have been useful in a sacred service such as making a minyan. Moreover, he offers a *drashah* on Gen. 9:6, *ha-adam ba-adam*, that only a person who came from *within* a person, i.e., was born from a woman, is considered human and protected by the prohibition against murder.[112] [113]

Rabbi Ashkenazi's son was an even more influential halakhic authority, Rabbi Jacob Emden.[114] In his collection of responsa, he returns to his father's question, focusing on the relationship of speech to legal standing.[115] He concludes that the golem is not like a human who is incapable of speech, but rather, is to be compared to a beast in human form. At the end, Emden adds a fascinating detail, apparently from family traditions, that Rabbi Eliyahu of Ḥelm grew concerned that his golem might "destroy the world," and thus detached the divine name from his forehead, returning him to dust, but not before the golem scratched Rabbi Eliyahu badly.[116] This postscript seems to be the source for some of the stories told later about the Maharal and his golem in Prague.

While it might be tempting to dismiss mystical texts in a discussion of contemporary halakhah, we ought to resist this temptation. First, while fantastical, these discussions of the status of a manufactured man (and in some cases, a woman) come from the core of rabbinic discourse and involve some of the greatest halakhic authorities of our tradition.[117] Early modern masters such as Yosef Karo and Eliyahu, the Gaon of Vilna, are counted among the giants of both mystical and legal scholarship. Second, as the modern commentators Jacob Katz and Moshe Ḥallamish have demonstrated, kabbalah has exercised a substantial influence on halakhah, especially following the publication of the Zohar.[118] Third, as our late colleague Byron Sherwin argues, the mystical and halakhic discussions of the golem are an important model for understanding the religious significance of technology.[119]

What, then, might we learn from this discourse with reference to artificial intelligence? The idea that humans can create entities that mimic the physical and cognitive features of humanity has not exceeded the imagination of our halakhic predecessors. Resemblance, however, did not secure equal status. A golem was not born, it lacked speech and creative capacity, and therefore, while it could be useful, it could not sanctify God.

In our time, AI is quickly developing convincing capacities for intelligence. In some ways, machine learning already exceeds human learning, including in what we would like to see as creative ability. Yuval Noah Harari notes that judges of chess tournaments tend to be suspicious of human—but not computer-generated—moves that appear completely original.[120] Yet machines lack the most distinctive human tendencies, which may be more emotional than intellectual. They may compute, they may even generate speech. But they cannot feel responsible, fear failure, or experience love.

The nature of consciousness in humans and other animals is hardly well understood. Giulio Tononi has developed an "integrated information theory" which argues that consciousness emerges as a product of informational complexity.[121] In *Consciousness and the Social Brain*, Michael Graziano notes the limitations of this and other hypotheses and offers an "attention schema theory," by which consciousness is a "schema" (simplified rendition) of information attended to by the brain. He says, "Attention is not data encoded in the brain; it is a data-handling method. It is an act."[122]

Toward the end of Graziano's book is a chapter called "Some Spiritual Matters," including a section on "Computer Consciousness" (216-220). Having described the peculiar features of the human brain's attention schema that yield the distinct sense of being conscious, he offers a pathway to developing a similar ability in machines. When asked about such a computer's awareness of feelings, Graziano said it would "provide a human-like answer because the information set on which it bases that answer would be similar to the information set on which we humans base our answer."

Graziano suggested in 2015 that with proper resources and effort, such a conscious machine could be designed within a decade. Some would say that the uncanny approximations of human personality expressed in early 2023 by ChatGPT, Bing, and other chatbots fulfilled this prediction. Journalist Kevin Reese published an alarming account in February 2023 of his interaction with a beta version of Microsoft Bing's chatbot, codenamed Sydney, which he says tried to convince him to leave his wife.[123]

Yet, it is far from evident that such approximations of consciousness are tantamount to human character. It is not only that our brains are social, with a theory of mind to predict what another person thinks, but that we feel *responsible* for each other's well-being. This interpersonal bond is the essence of ethics. A machine may be developed that can mimic the reports of awareness made by humans, but it will still not achieve the status of humanity unless it can present the essential aspects of personhood. What are they?

The definition of personhood and its parameters is a vexing philosophical and legal problem.[124] Scholars working in the field of critical animal studies have "conceived of animals as persons, agents, and subjects." This is at variance with the established characterization of animals as things and property. In her study of Bavli Sukkah 22b-23b, Beth Berkowitz shows how the sages problematize their initial characterization of animals as objects and establish a category, *davar she-yeish bo ruaḥ ḥayyim* (a living entity), that acknowledges that animals are "bad things," even if they are not exactly persons.[125]

Dr. Berkowitz suggests that the ancient rabbis were navigating between Roman law, which clearly and consistently classifies animals as property, and Zoroastrian law, which divides animals between beneficent and noxious classes, accepting them as subjects that can be innocent or guilty, much as the sages did in applying court procedures to animals accused of crime. In the Babylonian Talmud, she argues, the rabbis confront the limitations of animal "thingness" and open the possibility of animal subjectivity.

Personhood is at the heart of our discussion of whether AI-directed machines can, likewise, escape their status as "things" and achieve something closer to subjectivity. Analytic intelligence is only one aspect of personhood. It is difficult and even dangerous to define personhood precisely, since one can always find categories of people who lack an "essential" ability. It is reductive to state that a person is someone born to a person, but that is the sense of the above *drashah* by Rabbi Tzvi Ashkenazi.

Another approach is to consider personhood as a social construct—a person is an actor who relates to themselves and to other actors with responsibility and reciprocity. This understanding does not, however, apply to all or only to humans. Some humans are either temporarily or permanently incapable of such relationships, yet they nevertheless remain part of the class of people who do have such abilities. This is not the case with machines, which currently have no sense of self, no experience of obligation, of concern, of guilt, or of moral grandeur. These terms are admittedly imprecise, but it is just such spiritual qualities that define personhood in Jewish life as found in our liturgy, our commandments, and our theology.

Abraham Joshua Heschel considered the distinctive qualities of humanity in his 1964 address to the American Medical Association, "The Patient as Person." In his poetic style, he writes:

> What constitutes being human, personhood? The ability to be concerned for other human beings ... The truth of being human is gratitude, the secret of existence is appreciation, its significance is revealed in reciprocity. Mankind will not die for lack of information; it may perish from lack of appreciation. Being human presupposes the paradox of freedom, the capacity to create events, to transcend the self ...

The ultimate significance of human being as well as the ultimate meaning of being human may be wishful thinking, a ridiculous conceit in the midst of a world apparently devoid of ultimate meaning, a supreme absurdity. It is part of the cure to trust in Him who cures. Supreme meaning is therefore inconceivable without meaning derived from supreme being. Humanity without divinity is a torso. This is even reflected in the process of healing. Without a sense of significant being, a sense of wonder and mystery, a sense of reverence for the sanctity of being alive, the doctor's efforts and prescriptions may prove futile.[126]

If Heschel were alive today, he would likely add the biotech engineer to the doctor. Intelligence can be manufactured, but not the soul, and without a soul, artificial life is always virtual, never quite real. Our halakhists denied that a golem could join a minyan. It is evident that for an action to count as fulfillment of a mitzvah, a command, one requires still distinctive human capacities such as compassion, gratitude, wonder, and reverence.

FROM THEORY TO PRACTICE:

Foreseeable Implications for Real Life

We have considered four halakhic discourses that seem relevant to our consideration of AI and autonomous machines: the rules of agency and the role of non-human agents; the rules of damage caused by animals and property under indirect control of a person; the prioritization of lives when loss is inevitable; and the (im)possibility of including a human-made android or golem in the minyan. Now we turn to practical questions, realizing that this technology is new and that we can hardly anticipate all the capabilities that will be developed and the religious dilemmas they will engender.

Smart Appliances and the Laws of Shabbat

It is already common for "smart appliances" to employ facial recognition to identify users, and for machine learning to anticipate their needs. Such interactions may quickly move from the digital to the physical realm. For example, a kitchen appliance might learn to prepare hot beverages or to cook certain foods customized for each member of the household. Or an autonomous car service might be ordered to transport members of the family to certain locations each day, including on Shabbat, based on their appointment calendar or by monitoring their digital messages and location history. Let us assume that the machine's completed actions would not require a human user to engage in any direct financial transactions or physical data entry on Shabbat. Is such labor permitted, given that it is automated, or is it forbidden, given that it requires human participation?

Currently, there are many appliances such as elevators and timers that have been modified to operate for human benefit on Shabbat, but these devices follow a fixed schedule without human input at the time of the action. True, Shabbat elevators check to make sure the doorway is clear, and the car is not overloaded before moving, but there is no need for human action other than standing in place while the machine completes its task. In contrast, smart appliances and vehicles guided by artificial intelligence will engage the user, recognize them, perhaps request voice confirmation of instructions, and modify their actions in response to or in anticipation of human need. Should actions that would be forbidden for a Jew be permitted to a robot acting on their behalf?

God commands the People of Israel to observe the Sabbath, not only for themselves, but also for their animals and non-Jewish staff. However, automatic work processes set up prior to Shabbat, such as a water mill to grind kernels of grain into flour, or an irrigation trench to water a field, may continue through Shabbat, since Jews are not responsible for work done by tools as long as the process is not managed on Shabbat, and there is no concern that others will think a Jew is doing the labor.[127]

Although non-Jews are not themselves commanded to rest on Shabbat, Jews are restrained from requesting that they perform forbidden tasks on their behalf. The restraint on "speaking to a gentile" is complex, with various explanations, stringencies, and leniencies.[128] In general, a Jew may not ask for nor profit from labor done by a gentile on Shabbat. Such requests introduce weekday concerns into Shabbat and turn the gentile into an agent for the Jew.[129] The status of this prohibition is rabbinic, or *shvut*. If the task was *not* formally prohibited as transformative labor but only from the command to rest, then a Jew may ask a gentile to do such tasks for the sake of the ill or infirm, or to assist with a mitzvah (for example, by setting up materials for havdalah). This is because there is no "*shvut* on a *shvut*," meaning that the expanded ban on asking gentiles to work (*shvut* #1) does not extend to the expanded ban on imperfect or impermanent forms of the prohibited labors (*shvut* #2) if the purpose is to allow performance of a mitzvah, to help the ill or infirm, to protect dignity, etc. It would seem reasonable to be at least as lenient with an autonomous machine, and probably more so, if there is a halakhically significant motivation.

Earlier in this chapter, we learned that an agent generally bears responsibility for prohibited actions, but not if they lack the freedom to refuse the assigned task or the ability to pay fines for misconduct. A smart appliance or autonomous vehicle does not have the freedom to refuse a task or the ability to pay for misconduct. As such, it might be considered a tool in the hands of the user, and it would be forbidden to ask or even allow the machine to perform labor on one's behalf. Yet we also found that intermediate factors between the will of the user and the actions of their animals or the interactions of their property and environment could reduce liability for consequent actions.

Arguably, the very premise of artificial intelligence is that it is autonomous—it considers variables such as traffic reports, and determines the best route, and in this sense, it is acting independently of the user. The user's request for forbidden labor could be designated as indirect, but since there is immediate correlation between the command and the action, we would deem it to be *garmei*, and for the user to still bear partial responsibility for the action.

As I argue in my responsum regarding electricity and Shabbat (Chapter 4), there is a contest of values between preserving the distinctive experience of Shabbat and Yom Tov on one side, vs. protecting life, preserving human dignity and the environment, and completing positive mitzvot on the other side. Regarding biblically forbidden labors, only the mandate to save life can override the prohibition. Thus, a person would be forbidden from typing instructions during Shabbat for a machine to do labor on their behalf.

However, passively permitting a system to initiate actions on one's behalf during Shabbat without instruction, or even speaking instructions to a machine that will independently design a course of action, is to be considered akin to a partially indirect action and is therefore of a lower-level concern, the rabbinic concept of *shvut*. The person does not supply or even anticipate all the information required for the activity; autonomous machines gather data required to realize goals, and thus they are not mere tools in the hand of a person. Still, the experience of asking a machine to complete tasks for a person is close enough to the experience of asking a non-Jew to do the same that it should be governed by the same rabbinic concern for *shvut*. Competing Jewish values such as human dignity may outweigh rabbinic bans. Nevertheless, everything possible should be done to honor both values and to minimize conflict between them.

Therefore, it would seem to be permissible to arrange for an autonomous vehicle to transport a person under special circumstances (illness, frailty, disability, danger) within the local limits of travel on Shabbat. Interactions with AI-powered autonomous machines on Shabbat itself should be considered as generally banned by force of rabbinic law, but amenable to override due to urgent competing halakhic values. That said, we are also bound to a positive commandment to preserve the restful nature of the day by avoiding weekday actions and concerns, and we should avoid such technological solutions unless necessary for the experience of Shabbat itself. Moreover, we must not use this leniency to order services during Shabbat for *after* Shabbat or the holiday, since this would be considered preparing for the work week, which is itself forbidden under the category of *shvut*.

There is an established pattern among halakhic scholars of seeking leniencies in the realm of Shabbat law that are not applied in other situations.[130] We would therefore find that during Shabbat or Yom Tov, asking for or acquiescing to biblically prohibited labors to be done on one's behalf by a machine is banned, but under the least severe prohibition, is *shvut*.

Training Autonomous Cars for Accident Situations

Engineers working on autonomous vehicles presume that they will be far less likely to endanger the lives of passengers or pedestrians than are vehicles driven by humans. There have been several well-publicized fatal accidents caused by autonomous vehicles, but none in which the car was forced to choose between two potential victims. Human drivers are not generally trained in the prioritization of lives either, except not to swerve to avoid small animals in the road, and so perhaps it is unnecessary to worry about the moral reasoning of vehicles.

Moreover, most of the ethical systems that are candidates to guide the development of artificial moral agents are problematic for one or another reason. Consequentialism might lead an autonomous vehicle in an accident scenario to consider the relative market value of nearby cars (or even the net worth of their occupants), swerving to hit the least expensive (or least wealthy) among them. Such considerations might be rational but would be judged as morally unacceptable for human drivers.

Deontology might lead an autonomous vehicle to continue into a potential multi-fatality collision if veering aside would introduce the risk of a single fatality (for example, avoiding a head-on collision only by killing a pedestrian beside the road), since a moral agent should never intentionally kill an innocent person. Yet such conduct would maximize the lethality of this incident.

Somehow, human drivers are expected to do the right thing even during the confusing and chaotic experience of a crash, even without ethical guidance, and somehow, we anticipate designing autonomous machines that can also "do the right thing." How? One relative strength of machine intelligence is situational awareness, the ability to process information from many sources at once—which might overload a human actor—and to act according to the established decision tree. What might that be?

Recalling our earlier discussion of the teaching of Rabbi Akiva, we would conclude that a vehicle should prioritize the life of its own passenger(s) in an accident scenario where it is a choice between their life and that of another person, since "your life comes first." But remembering Rava, we would want the autonomous vehicle to give every priority to sparing life, and never intentionally to kill a person, even if that allows an accident to take the life of its passenger(s). Rabbi Oshry's citation of Rema balances these values, allowing for self-rescue even if that puts other lives at risk. A halakhic algorithm might be structured as follows:

i.   If there is risk of a collision, then the vehicle should first avoid danger to all people in the area, by swerving, slowing, or accelerating as necessary.

ii.   If a collision is unavoidable, then the priority should be to avoid fatality or severe bodily harm to humans. The vehicle should swerve to avoid striking a pedestrian or passenger vehicle, even at risk of property damage.

iii.   If the risk of fatality is unavoidable, then each vehicle should prioritize its own occupants. To avoid striking a pedestrian on the roadway, the vehicle should not swerve off the road into danger unless there is little risk of fatality to the passengers. Rather, the vehicle should take all available measures to reduce danger to the pedestrian, such as slowing down or switching lanes, while still protecting the lives of the passengers.

While such an algorithm might approximate the moral reasoning of a person and could even exceed their analytic abilities in an accident situation, the machine itself is not to be considered a moral agent. Moral agency reflects the embodied experience and moral accountability of humans—their sense of self, of mortality, of responsibility, and of guilt. A moral actor must be able to do a minor wrong to accomplish a major right. *Humans should be consulted in any life-or-death scenario unless the delay required for such consultation will imperil human life.*

Regarding autonomous weapons systems, military strategists have noted that requiring a human to be in the loop on all lethal actions will disadvantage that side. Once autonomous weapons systems have become part of a nation's arsenal, humans are not likely to retain constant control over the systems. This argues against the use of AWS that target humans (rather than inanimate targets such as mines, missiles, sensors, etc.) altogether, and indeed, this should be our primary position. Certainly, the laws of war should be updated to ban fully autonomous systems from attacking humans without specific human permission. Otherwise, there will be an accountability gap, and commanders might unleash such weapons without the constraint of being held personally responsible for the results.

Given that semiautonomous weapons are already integrated into the armed forces of dozens of nations, some have argued that the next best approach may be to integrate tight ethical controls into command systems. Michael Saxon and Christopher Korpela make this case:

> So, does the need for responsibility in Just War Theory require that humans remain "in the loop" for decisions involving potentially lethal force? This might be illuminated by imagining a human-in-the-loop LAWS system that satisfies all of the requirements of IHL [International Humanitarian Law]. First, it is discriminate, in that it is capable of differentiating between combatants and non-combatants. Second, it adheres to the rule of non-combatant immunity. Third, it is proportionate, using morally appropriate levels of force. These must all be subject to the checks provided by the human mind in control. Aside from legitimate questions about the *ease* with which a system might allow the nation to go to war unnecessarily, this sort of machine seems ideal.[131]

While such a sensitive machine may seem ideal in secular terms, and might even satisfy Wallach and Allen's standard for an AMA, can the same be said for the requirements of halakhah? True, the Talmud (B. Brakhot 62b) has David lecture Saul, "The Torah says, if one comes to kill you, rise up quickly to kill him."[132] A human pursuer is considered forewarned, allowing a human defender to strike the attacker dead without warning. Yet the halakhic codes teach that the minimally lethal use of force is necessary (as exemplified in the Bible by David, who spares Saul's life), and that a defender who kills an attacker when non-lethal options are available is liable for the death.[133]

We must not offer authority to a non-human actor to differentiate among human targets and decide whom to kill. Paul Scharre concludes his book, *An Army of None*, with a call for "a conscious choice to pull back from weapons that are too dangerous, too inhumane" (362). He warns that autonomous systems are hackable, and that they may be turned against their owners by adversaries, or even by simple error. In *Foreign Affairs*, he argues that "the United States should work with other countries, even hostile ones, to ensure AI safety" (144). International activism to limit the autonomy of lethal weapons has begun, and halakhists must join humanists in mandating human judgment in matters of life and death. Autonomous defense systems that attack objects such as missiles or malware are one thing; those that select human targets and attack them without human consent are quite another. Maintaining human control over such systems may require structures such as 24:7 human operators to authorize lethal attacks; humans must always retain control of preemptive uses of force. Jewish law is exceptionally cautious about the evidentiary standards required to justify killing a human. *Autonomous weapons systems must not use lethal force against humans without human direction.*

Robotic Assistance in Jewish Ritual Performance

Robotic attendants might be able to assist Jews in various physical tasks required to complete mitzvot. For example, they might retrieve ritual objects such as a siddur, tallit, tefillin, lulav, and etrog, and bring them to an immobile person at the time of prayer. We learned above that ritual actions such as separating tithes or establishing a Sabbath boundary must be *initiated and completed* by a Jew, not by a non-Jew (e.g., a Samaritan) nor by an animal (e.g., an elephant or a monkey). However, we saw that a Jew might rely on one of these "agents" for an *intermediate* step such as carrying an object from one location to another. Based on this analogy, a robot or other type of smart appliance might be used to position or prepare an object for ritual use, but the ritual itself must be performed by a person for whom it is a sacred obligation. The same would be true for social commandments such as performing acts of *ḥesed* ("kindness")— visiting the ill, comforting the bereaved, supporting the poor. A machine might assist, but a human must initiate and complete this action.

We have traced the history of the golem not only as an occult figure, but also as a possible player in the ritual life of a community. Jacob Emden asked whether such an android might be counted in the minyan required for certain ritual acts. He concluded that because the golem discussed in our sources lacked human capabilities of speech and apparently reasoning, and because it was not formed within a human, it could not be considered human, nor could it be included in ritual life.

Digital assistants today are already capable of voice recognition and of generating contextually appropriate responses. The field of affective computing addresses the emotional content of communication with the goal of helping people form bonds with machines. Studies have demonstrated that people of all ages are eager to engage such speaking machines as if they were persons. And yet, the distinction between human and artificial intelligence remains significant. Artificial agents may *approximate* the decision-making process of humans, but they do not have the capacity to *appreciate* the significance of an action, to accept or reject responsibility, to experience human emotions of fear, pain, pleasure, or love, or to act in service of an abstract value, the divine. This distinction between machines and humans is essential and demands our active defense.

PISKEI DIN

1. *Are Jews liable for the halakhic consequences of actions taken by machines on their behalf, for example, Sabbath labor?* Perhaps, but only at the lowest level of *shvut* (lower-level concerns). During Shabbat or Yom Tov, a Jew should not request that a smart machine initiate or complete forbidden labor unless there is a mitigating factor such as illness or frailty, threat to human dignity, or the specific need to facilitate a commanded act on that day. Arranging for such activities prior to the onset of Shabbat or Yom Tov, even absent such mitigating factors, would be permitted if it is understood that these services were pre-arranged, and if they did not undermine the general experience of Shabbat.

2. *Should ethical principles derived from halakhah be integrated into the development of autonomous systems for transportation, medical care, warfare, and other morally charged activities, allowing autonomous systems to make life-or-death decisions?* Autonomous systems may have capacities to process and communicate information that exceed those of humans, and they may help humans avoid common failures as moral and religious actors. That said, only humans have the right and the responsibility to make life-or-death decisions. Humans must supervise AI systems and authorize lethal actions, whether in transportation, medicine, or in warfare.

3. *Might a robot perform a mitzvah or other halakhically significant action? Is it conceivable to treat an artificial agent as a person? As a Jew?* Artificial agents may be used to facilitate the

performance of mitzvot, for example in conveying ritual objects to a person. They may follow commands, but they do not become humans, much less *b'nei brit*.

These distinctions are not to diminish the value of artificial intelligence, which can be vast, but to recall the very purpose of the mitzvot that have been revealed to and developed by the people of Israel—to bless God Who, despite our frailty and fallibility, has sanctified our lives through the commandments.

CHAPTER 2:
JEWISH PARAMETERS FOR
GENETIC ENGINEERING

P erhaps the greatest disruption wrought by modern science is our ability not only to understand how organic forms evolve, but also to intervene and modify the genetic code. Our ancestors understood breeding and permitted it in some cases, but they also expressed great concerns about the mingling of life forms to create new species.

As I was writing my 2015 responsum, news of the gene-editing system known as CRISPR became public, challenging religious communities to decide whether the easy ability to modify the genome was a blessing or a curse. CRISPR inventor and future Nobel laureate, Jennifer Doudna, invited me to a multidisciplinary conference in 2017 at her lab in Berkeley. There scientists, ethicists, lawyers, and religious thinkers debated the uses and abuses of this new technology. My responsum had sought a middle path which would allow responsible interventions that promised significant health benefits while cautioning against using gene editing to refashion life simply for pleasure.

In the subsequent years, CRISPR has become a standard tool in biotechnology, allowing remarkable new therapies—from an Israeli lab that modified peanut proteins to help desensitize people with peanut allergies, to the advancement of xenotransplantation to allow for the safe transplant of hearts and other organs from pigs to people. These early uses of CRISPR are not dystopian, but they do pose ethical challenges, and many more quandaries will come from our enhanced power to reprogram the code of life. Such quandaries are ethical, legal, and even theological, as I anticipated in this responsum.

QUESTION:

What halakhic values and norms should be applied to the genetic modification of organisms, whether plant or animal, particularly when using recombinant DNA? May Jewish consumers receive medical, nutritional, and commercial benefit from genetically modified products? Must modifications to the human genome be limited in scope?

RESPONSE:

What are humans, that You have been mindful of them, mortals, that You have taken note of them, that You have made them little less than divine, and adorned them with glory and majesty? You made them master over Your handiwork, laying the world at their feet, sheep, and oxen, all of them, and wild beasts too; the birds of the heavens, the fish of the sea, whatever travels the paths of the seas. O Lord, our Lord, how majestic is Your name throughout the earth!

Psalm 8: 5-10[1]

That you have made them little less than divine—This refers to Jacob, for it says (in Genesis 30:39), *and since the goats mated by the rods* .... Rabbi Hoshaya explains, "He would draw an image, and just as he drew, so the seed formed in the water of their wombs, and so did they give birth. This teaches that [Jacob] lacked only the ability to give them a soul."

Midrash Bereshit Rabbati, *VaYetze*

Humans have influenced the evolution of plants and animals since our prehistory, often without intention or awareness. For example, the evolution of fearsome wolves into friendly dogs may have originated from the advantage conferred on those canines with smaller jaws to access food from human encampments.[2] People are frequently unaware of the impact of their activities on the adaptation of other species. There is evidence of recent evolution of fish to favor thinner bodies, the better to evade the nets of fishermen; and of elk to favor smaller racks of antlers, which are less valued by human hunters.[3] By catching and killing specimens with specific traits, humans may paradoxically exert evolutionary pressure that causes the diminution of those very desirable qualities.

Of course, farmers, herders, and—since the work of mid-19th century monk-biologist Gregor Mendel was rediscovered—scientists, have also successfully bred plants and animals to favor certain qualities and avoid others. The domestication of eight plant species and four animal species in the Neolithic era was essential for the expansion of civilization in the Fertile Crescent and other regions.[4]

Charles Darwin opened his great work, *On the Origin of Species* with a discussion of the impact of human selection (in contrast to natural selection) in a first chapter titled, "Variation under Domestication." Yet, for all his remarkable prescience, Darwin did not have knowledge of genetic theory, and he could not foresee the direct modifications recently made possible by genetic engineering. He wrote, "Man ... can neither originate varieties, nor prevent their occurrence; he can preserve and accumulate such as do occur."[5]

Darwin considered his work to be compatible with religious faith, yet it was and remains challenging to a traditional worldview that asserts not only the special creation of each species of plant and animal, but also the stability of these species across time. These two foundations of early monotheistic faith are grounded in the first two portions of the Torah, *Bereshit* and *Noah*, and are implicit in the writings of great sages such as Ramban, when he writes in his commentary to Leviticus 19:19:

> One who grafts together two species alters and undermines
> the work of creation. It is as if he thinks that the Holy
> Blessed One did not complete the needs of His world, and
> he desires to assist in His creation of the world by adding
> more creatures to it.

Ramban developed a doctrine of species preservation which has religious significance to this day. The divine origin of life on earth remains an important if mysterious belief for many religious people, but faith in the immutable permanence of species does not. Indeed, the Torah itself mentions Jacob's breeding technique for producing hardy dark sheep and speckled goats (Gen. 30:37-39).[6] Isaiah's messianic prediction of an end to carnivorous diets assumes dramatic changes in nature.[7] On a practical level, the sages of Israel were familiar with techniques for grafting plants and interbreeding animals to form hybrids, which though forbidden to Jews under the rubric of *kilayim* (artificial hybridization), were nevertheless common in antiquity.

Belief in an unchanging natural world was already problematic in antiquity, and has become untenable in the past two centuries.[8] While there remain religious practitioners of various faiths who insist that all species currently in the world were created literally according to the timeline laid out in Genesis 1 (even though it is contradicted in Genesis 2), Jews from across the spectrum have long since integrated the concept of natural history into their religious world view.[9] As we consider the halakhic implications of reengineering plant and animal life, it will not be the preservation of a mythic stasis of all creation that guides our inquiry. Rather, Jewish norms that mandate a ban on *kilayim*, the protection of human life (*pikuaḥ nefesh*), and the prevention of animal suffering (*tza'ar ba'alei ḥayyim*), will form the fertile ground for our study of genetic engineering.

Darwin devoted an entire chapter of *On the Origin of Species* to hybridism; in recent decades, biologists have increasingly regarded natural hybridization as an important factor in speciation.[10] Intentional hybridization by farmers and agricultural scientists is an essential practice for the cultivation of fruits such as apples and grapes. Since the 1950s, researchers have used hybridization and backcrossing to create lines of wheat and other grains that have improved disease resistance, thereby feeding the rapidly growing populations of developing countries.[11] In a sense, they were merely continuing the process of improving crop yields that began in the Neolithic era. Still, until recently it was not possible for humans to directly manipulate the genome. New methods are yielding radically new results and eliciting urgent new questions.

Modern Advances in Genetic Engineering

Genetic engineering, which involves the direct modification of DNA, was first demonstrated in 1973 by Herbert Boyer, Paul Berg, and Stanley Cohen (who coaxed bacteria to develop foreign proteins), and the field has grown rapidly since then—from manipulating the DNA of yeast and bacteria to that of plants, fish, birds, and mammals. By the 1980s, researchers were capable of inserting DNA from one species into the fertilized egg of a different species, producing new specimens with hybrid characteristics, referred to as transgenic.

Zebra fish have received the DNA of coral and sea anemones to make them glow; salmon have been artificially endowed with the DNA of deep sea eels (ocean pout) to make them grow year-round; and goats have had snippets of human DNA inserted into their fertilized ova to cause them to produce enzymes such as antithrombin and lysozyme for human benefit.[12] The resulting recombinant DNA includes sequences from both original organisms, even though they are of different species that could not naturally reproduce together. The use of transgenic mice has become commonplace in contemporary laboratories, with companies such as The Jackson Laboratory's JAX Mice making hundreds of variants—their targeted genes "knocked out," activated, or added— easily available to researchers.[13]

Methods for blending the DNA of different species have become ever more sophisticated, from the initial insertion of foreign DNA into a fertilized egg using a micro-syringe, to more recent efforts that employ a "gene gun," agrobacteria, or modified viruses to transfer DNA from one organism to another. The discovery of a naturally occurring RNA system for splicing targeted sections of viral genomes, now widely known as CRISPR, and the adaptation of this system for humans to edit DNA, has vastly expanded the ability of scientists and even amateurs to change the code of life cheaply and with relative accuracy. This is fascinating, but is it good to blend the DNA of different species?

Hybrids have been created in laboratories between species (e.g., lions and tigers) and even between genera (e.g., sheep and goats).[14] An international industry known as "pharming" has arisen to develop genetically modified (GM) organisms to grow medications and other substances such as biofuels that are useful to humans.

Genetic engineering is a field of great promise in combating hunger and disease.[15] GM crops, first introduced in 1994 with the FlavrSavr Tomato, had by 2013 been planted on 420 million acres, including half the world's soybeans and a third of its corn.[16] Many scientists believe that it will be impossible to feed the world's rapidly growing human population without genetically modified crops.[17] Not only may such crops reduce the need for herbicides, but some seeds, such as Golden Rice, are engineered to include Vitamin A, and thus can help combat vitamin deficiencies that cause blindness in a half million children each year. J.R. Simplot's USDA-approved modified potato has been designed to produce less acrylamide, a possible carcinogen, when fried.[18]

Some crops would be wiped out by fungi or infestations without their genetic modification. However, concerns about the safety of some of these products persist; for example, GM corn may be grown using neonicotinoids, a class of neurotoxic insecticides that activists claim have played a role in the collapse of honeybee populations, and may even disrupt nerve cell activity in mammals.[19] Scientific reviews have not, however, confirmed these claims.[20] GM cotton crops often integrate the insecticide Bt in every cell, which may be causing the selection for resistance in "superbugs," leading farmers to increase the use of pesticides. Attacks and defenses of GMOs on health grounds are contentious and complex, defying simple conclusions. Regulations to alert consumers to the use of GM products (such as those already in place in Europe), and continued study of their ramifications for animal and human health, are certainly warranted.[21]

Aside from the development of new foods, genetic engineering has become increasingly significant in medical research and therapy. Long-term safety trials have already been completed for certain GM medications, some of which are indispensable to contemporary pharmaceuticals. In 1978, the first synthetic human insulin was bioengineered using E. coli, and in 1982, Eli Lilly and Company marketed the first commercial bioengineered insulin under the brand name Humulin. In 2007, the company SemBioSys announced plans to bioengineer insulin by introducing the human gene for insulin production into safflower plants, thereby reducing the costs of creating this vital medication. The company went bankrupt in 2012,[22] but most insulin produced today is made from biosynthetic processes using bacteria and yeast to grow this ever-important medical product.[23]

In December 2023, the United States Federal Drug Adminstration and the European Medicines Agency both approved Cevgeny, the first CRISPR/Cas9 based therapy to cure sickle cell disease. Cevgeny modifies a patient's blood stem cells to allow them to increase production of fetal hemoglobin, which prevents the sickling of red blood cells and improves oxygen delivery.[24] This therapy does not involve blending human DNA with that of other species, and so it avoids the primary halakhic concerns that we will discuss below. Other therapeutic uses of CRISPR/Cas9, however, do indeed blend human DNA with that of another species, specifically, the pig.

Cancer researchers have capitalized on the human immune system's intolerance for certain foreign DNA to stimulate auto-antibodies to inhibit the growth of cancer cells. For example, NewLink Genetics developed a product called HyperAcute that, according to its web site, is "...composed of human, tumor-specific cancer cell lines. These cells have been modified to express alpha-gal, a carbohydrate to which humans have preexisting immunity. These alpha-gal-modified cancer cells stimulate a rapid and powerful immune response that trains the body's natural defenses to seek out and destroy similar cancer cells in the patient. The objective of HyperAcute™ immunotherapies is to elicit an antitumor response by 'educating' the immune system to attack a patient's own cancer cells."[25] Another anti-cancer gene therapy involves modifying DNA from a pig and introducing it to a tumor site within a human to induce an autoimmune response from the host to attack the tumor.[26]

One of the most spectacular recent uses of CRISPR/Cas9 has been to raise specially modified pigs as a source for human organ transplants. The field of xenotransplantation (transferring an organ from one species to another) involves many technical and ethical challenges. On the technical side, recipients often reject foreign organs, especially from different species. CRISPR has been used to remove some of the sequences of the pig's DNA and to add other sequences of human DNA. The organs of such genetically modified pigs are more likely to be accepted by human recipients, without requiring lifelong administration of anti-rejection medications. Is it permitted to mingle human and porcine DNA for the sake of saving human lives? Is it ethical to change the nature of other species, often causing suffering to many generations of test animals, for the ultimate benefit of humans?[27]

A less ethically fraught field is immunoprophylaxis by gene transfer (IGT), a form of genetic engineering that seeks to reengineer human DNA for permanent resistance to a broad spectrum of viruses.[28] A detailed analysis of the science involved in these projects is well beyond our scope, but the significance of genetic engineering is manifest, as is the need to consider the ethical and religious implications of this rapidly growing field.

Our focus in this responsum is primarily on the field of transgenics, which impinges on established halakhic concerns. I note, however, that genetic engineering has begun to focus on "cisgenic" products that artificially blend materials from different members of the same species, and thereby evade government regulation,[29] Such intra-species blends sidestep our halakhic concerns related to the Jewish prohibition on blending species (kilayim). I will not focus on the fascinating field of synthetic biology, which involves engineering organisms from synthetic sources (even creating DNA from nucleotides other than the four found in nature). These forms of genetic engineering raise issues of human safety and animal welfare, and perhaps other halakhic issues as well, but they do not trigger the same religious concerns with the blending of species that are found in transgenic organisms, and they will need to be considered separately.[30]

While the methods employed by contemporary biotech researchers are stunning to consider, in many ways they are employing mechanisms already evident in nature. Horizontal gene transfer (HGT) has been studied since the 1950s. Recent research indicates that HGT occurs naturally, not only among bacteria and viruses, but in the development of animals, including primates. Alastair Crisp and Chiara Boschetti and their collaborators demonstrated that as many as 145 human genes (from among 20,000 in the human genome) have been picked up from other species.[31]

Blending the DNA of different organisms can produce scientific, medical, and financial benefits to academic researchers and for-profit businesses, which increasingly work in concert.[32] Humans are profiting (in both senses) from many of these new products, and genetic engineering is already being used to combat cancer and other diseases. Yet, as the "code of life" gets reprogrammed, and the genomes of different organisms are artificially combined, difficulties arise regarding intellectual property, ethical limits of experimentation, and the long-term consequences of these scientific interventions.

Independent organizations such as the Union of Concerned Scientists have warned of potentially harmful side effects of GM crops, such as the evolution of "super-weeds" that incorporate the herbicide resistance intended for GM rice or corn.[33] In the United States, the National Institutes of Health established a National Human Genome Research Institute in 1990 with a program called ELSI (Ethical, Legal, and Social Implications), "to foster basic and applied research on the ethical, legal and social implications of genetic and genomic research for individuals, families and communities."[34] What is missing is a systematic and sustained discourse among religious people regarding genetic engineering.

OVERVIEW OF HALAKHIC CONCERNS

Even as scientists and businesses around the world rapidly transform the genetic structures of plants and animals, religious thinkers have been relatively slow to engage in these profound matters, whether in support, in criticism, or simply from curiosity about the implications for established theological and moral principles. However, we are not in the starting position. In recent decades, several of our scholars from the Committee on Jewish Law and Standards (CJLS), together with rabbis from other circles, have initiated inquiry into the halakhic ramifications of genetic engineering.

In 1980, Seymour Siegel, who was then chair of the CJLS, published an article titled, "Science and Ethics: A Creative Partnership."[35] He called for a "creative partnership between the scientific community and those who express the values of our society," and expressed confidence that even revolutionary advances in DNA research could be compatible with monotheistic ethics, since nature itself is not deemed divine, and, "illness, disability and disease are, in a sense, challenges which God puts to man."

The CJLS subsequently approved two responsa that considered the kashrut implications of genetically modified organisms. In 1994, Kassel Abelson (also the CJLS chair at the time of his writing) determined that microbial enzymes that had been isolated from an animal source, or genetically engineered, should be considered kosher.[36] Avram Reisner followed this in 1997 with an extensive study of kashrut and other halakhic issues raised by genetic engineering, concluding that "the kashrut laws of prohibited admixtures do not apply to the microscopic manipulation of genetic materials." Although there have been significant biotechnology developments in subsequent years, and his focus was primarily on matters of kashrut, Rabbi Reisner also discussed broader questions that will be integral to our investigation.[37]

Besides questions of kashrut, what are the other relevant halakhic concerns? The following list is not exhaustive or conclusive; I shall return to the most salient halakhic concerns below. First, Judaism prohibits the infliction of needless animal suffering.[38] A formidable amount of animal suffering is engendered by these experiments, and many sterile and severely deformed animals are being created for uncertain human benefit. Second, the introduction of genetically modified species could undermine the survival of extant species,[39] although minor modifications could also allow current species to survive in changing environmental conditions. As we have seen, scholars such as Ramban hold humans responsible for species preservation.

While early fears about the creation of transgenic diseases that could cause human pandemics have not been realized (despite disproved theories that the COVID-19 virus was engineered in a lab in Wuhan, China[40]), there remains the possibility that new transgenic viruses or antibiotic-resistant bacteria could be created through these processes, with dire consequences. The Torah commands Israel, "be very watchful of yourselves," (Deut. 4:15) and this verse has been interpreted to convey special responsibility for preserving one's life from danger.[41]

The genetic modification of organisms raises thorny issues of identity. When the human genome is blended with the DNA of other species, what are the religious implications? The concept of humanity's creation in the divine image is a cornerstone of Jewish belief; a doctrine of human exceptionalism is inherent in the ban on murder and the special responsibility to protect human life (though the ancient sages mentioned other species that resembled humans in one way or another).[42]

Over the entire enterprise hangs the specter of eugenics, the quest to fashion an ever more perfect human species and to eliminate undesirable specimens, which was used to justify enormous evil in the past century. While the new "consumer eugenics" is voluntary and does not involve killing people, there is a growing ability to screen fertilized eggs prior to implantation for various qualities, and to "enhance" human abilities, both physical and intellectual. These issues were studied in Mark Popovsky's 2008 responsum on preimplantation genetic diagnosis.[43] David Golinkin also addressed several of these concerns in a brief responsum, concluding that, "Jewish law supports gene therapy that seeks to eliminate serious or fatal genetic diseases," but arguing that gene therapies employed for enhancement or eugenic purposes should be banned on ethical and theological grounds.[44] Finally, in *Jews and Genes: The Genetic Future in Contemporary Jewish Thought*, editors Elliot Dorff and Laurie Zoloth include 22 chapters by leading scholars, with an entire section dedicated to genetic engineering. I will refer to several of these essays below.

Genetic engineering raises questions about what is meant by terms such as "illness" and "health," and what forms of intervention may be

justified as medically necessary.[45] Positive halakhic values are also at
play in this discourse, since genetic engineering holds the promise of
improving human nutrition and general health, and we are obligated to
feed the hungry,[46] heal the ill,[47] and preserve human health.[48] Before I
can turn to such broad mandates, I begin with the most direct halakhic
concern, which is the Torah's prohibition on kilayim, the breeding of
different species of plants and animals together.

Kilayim: The Ban on Interspecies Breeding / Biblical Texts

Chapter 19 of Leviticus begins with the statement that all of Israel
should become holy, "for I the Lord your God am Holy."[49] Following
the chapter's climactic verse 18, "love your neighbor as yourself," the
foundation of Jewish interpersonal ethics, the Torah turns in verse 19
to an apparently different concern, the mingling of species:[50]

> You shall heed my statutes: you shall not let your cattle
> mate with a different kind; you shall not sow your field
> with two kinds of seed; and clothing made of two kinds of
> yarn you shall not put on yourself.[51]

These laws banning the interbreeding of different species of animals
and plants, and even of wearing mingled garments, are perplexing, as
is their dramatic location in Leviticus 19 under the headline, "you shall
keep my statutes."

The laws of kilayim are restated in Chapter 22 of Deuteronomy, v.
9-11:

> You shall not sow your vineyard with a second kind of
> seed [else the fullness from the seed you have sown, and

the yield of the vineyard, may not be used]. You shall not plow with an ox and ass together. You shall not wear cloth combining wool and linen.

Each of the three regulations found in Leviticus is modified by Deuteronomy. The prohibition of mixing seeds is extended (or perhaps limited) to the vineyard, and the produce of such forbidden mingling is itself forbidden; the unfamiliar term *shatnez* is explained as (or perhaps limited to) a blend of wool and linen; and, most surprisingly, the ban on *breeding* different species is transformed into a ban on *hitching* an ox and an ass to a single plow.

Ramban harmonizes Deuteronomy's ban on hitching the ox and ass together with Leviticus's prohibition against crossbreeding by saying that farmers tend to house their plow team together in a single barn, which could lead to interspecies intercourse.[52]

Modern Bible scholars, however, are not inclined to harmonize the texts. Jacob Milgrom explains the disparity between the two presentations as a conflict between the interests and contexts of the holiness source (H) and the Deuteronomist (D).[53] Perhaps, he speculates, in the interim between the composition of H and D, the use of mules had been introduced to the region, causing the modification of the law to allow for the use of these hybrids.[54] It is also possible (if farfetched), as Michael Fishbane has surmised, that Deuteronomy's reference to "plowing" is a biblical-era euphemism for sexual intercourse, as found in the book of Judges, where Samson charges, "If you had not plowed with my heifer [that is, his wife], you would not have found out my riddle" (Judges 14:18).[55] If that is the case, then both traditional and modern scholars may find no practical difference between Leviticus and Deuteronomy, both of which prohibit interspecies breeding.[56]

Curiously, the rabbis treated the first clause in Deuteronomy (regarding the vineyard) as additive (extending the ban from field crops to vines), while the third clause was read as restrictive (limiting *shatnez* specifically to linen and wool blends).

Rabbinic Understandings of Kilayim: Grafting Plants

Leviticus instructs the Israelite not to "sow mixed seeds" in the field but leaves uncertain what precisely is the problem. Rabbinic interpreters have argued that when different species of plants draw moisture from the same soil, they may interfere with each other, and perhaps also cross-pollinate. This, of course, could happen even if different crops were planted in distinct rows or separate plots. In the Mishnah, the sages dutifully prohibit blending crops in the field, but then focus on a more direct form of "mingling" known in rabbinic literature as *ha-markiv*, the grafting of one plant's stem onto the rootstock of another plant.

Grafting is prevalent in contemporary gardening and agriculture, and it also occurs naturally when the branches of two trees grow together. Gardening author Ken Druse explains the process:

> The branches squeeze tighter as they grow, until the cambium layers of both are exposed at the contact point. If the branches remain in place, the cells will knit together and may merge into a single limb. The horticultural process starts with a section of stem, called a scion, that is surgically attached to a growing plant, called the understock or the rootstalk.[57]

Druse adds that grafting confers many advantages, from speeding the process of producing salable fruits to imparting disease resistance or winter hardiness from the understock to the scion. Nearly every apple eaten today comes from a grafted tree and, as he explains, it is even possible to graft a different variety of apples onto each branch of a single tree. Likewise, nearly all grapes produced for winemaking are the result of cuttings, grafting, or layering.[58]

Ancient grafting techniques were presumably distinct from some of today's methods, but the basic principles were the same. Tractate Kilayim discusses (and prohibits) grafting in chapter one, Mishnah 7 and 8 (Soncino translation):

> It is not permitted to graft from one tree to another, or from one herb to another, or from a tree to an herb, or from an herb to a tree. R. Judah permits it from an herb to a tree.

> It is not permitted to plant herbs in the trunk of a sycamore. It is not permitted to graft rue on white cassia, since that is [grafting] an herb onto a tree. It is forbidden to plant a young fig-shoot in a cistus shrub for the purpose of providing shade for the latter, or to insert a vine-shoot into a melon in order that the latter might contribute its moisture to the former, since that is [grafting] a tree onto an herb. It is prohibited to place gourd seed into the juice of a mallow for the purpose of preserving the former, since that constitutes [grafting] an herb onto a [heterogeneous] herb.

There is no Babylonian Talmud to Tractate Kilayim (though as we will see, this subject is discussed in B. Kiddushin 39a). The Yerushalmi discusses grafting as follows:[59]

> How do we know that one may not graft a barren tree onto a fruit tree, nor a fruit tree onto a fruit tree of a

different species? Because it [the Torah] states: Guard My statutes. R' Yonah [quotes] R' 'Lazar in the name of Kahana: It is in accord with R. 'Lazar's saying—"the statutes—are those that I have established in My world." Henceforth it is forbidden [to blend species] since Adam the First. R' Yosi in the name of Rabbi Hila [says], all agree that [the prohibition derives from the word] "statutes" that I have established in My world. Henceforth it is forbidden to graft a black fig [tree] onto a white fig [tree].[60]

The Yerushalmi here is quite prohibitive, banning not only the mingling of different fruit species but even the grafting of varieties of the same fruit, for example, dark and light figs. The parallel text in Midrash Sifra, Kedoshim 2:17, does not include Rabbi Hila's extension of the ban to grafting varieties of the same fruit, but offers an unqualified ban on grafting in general:

> What is the source for prohibiting the grafting of a barren tree upon a fruit-bearing tree, or a fruit-bearing tree upon a barren tree or a fruit-bearing tree upon a fruit-bearing tree? This is taught by the verse, "guard My statutes."

The sages are apparently not concerned with the grafting of a non-fruit-bearing tree upon another non-fruit-bearing tree, and indeed, Rambam limits the ban of horticultural blending to edible fruits and vegetables, explicitly permitting such mixed sowing for medicinal purposes:

> The prohibition on mixed seeds is limited to species fit for human consumption, but bitter grasses and such from roots which are not fit except for [consuming as] medicine,

and similar [plants] are not included in the ban on mixed seeds.[61]

Rambam's limitation of the ban to medicinal edibles draws the objection of his commentators, starting with Yosef Karo in *Kesef Mishneh*. He is surprised by Rambam's claim considering the Mishnah and the Yerushalmi's broader statements that would ban any mingling of crops, even for animal fodder, and in turn limits Rambam's permission to blended bitter grasses that have no nutritional value for either people or domesticated animals.[62] Nevertheless, Rabbi Karo reiterates Rambam's ruling nearly word for word in the Shulḥan Arukh.[63]

While halakhic sources ban the sowing of seeds in the field and the grafting of trees, it is only *the process, not the product*, that is banned. Rambam states this clearly in Halakhah 7:

> Although a person who sows mixed seeds, and one who grafts mixed species of trees, is to be lashed, nevertheless their [fruits] are permitted for consumption, even for the very person who transgressed and sowed them, for the only prohibition is in their sowing. And it is permitted to plant a shoot [i.e., a cutting] from the grafted tree and to sow from the seed of a plant that was cross-sown.

Rabbi Karo accedes to this ruling in Beit Yosef YD 295:7, citing the Rosh and the Yerushalmi itself to permit use of the produce of grafting, both for consumption and for replanting.[64] Grafting trees is considered biblically banned, but enjoying their produce is permitted. The one exception, based on the verse in Deuteronomy and formulated as a unique prohibition by the rabbis, is a ban on enjoying the fruit of grafted vines, even outside Israel (*kilei ha-kerem*), apparently due to the additional phrase about "fullness of the seed" with reference to grapes.[65]

It is not evident why the rabbinic sages were so lenient in permitting benefit from the produce of forbidden hybrids. After all, the sages forbade benefit from *ḥametz* owned by a Jew on Passover (M. Pesaḥim 2:2), libation wine acquired from an idolater (M. Avodah Zarah 5:10), meat mixed with milk (M. Ḥullin 8:4) and many other products of ritually forbidden activities.[66] It is possible that the Torah's phrasing of these prohibitions, which focus on the act rather than the result, is the reason, but perhaps the sages were simply being realistic. They had no certain method for identifying the provenance of produce in the market. If they were to declare all vegetables and grains that were grown in mingled plots to be forbidden, and likewise were to ban all grafted fruits, they would essentially be cutting themselves off from the food supply of their region. The sages might have suspected the local population of neglecting their tithes, yet such doubts could always be addressed by re-tithing purchased produce. But if the fruits of *kilayim* were forbidden, there could be no remedy for them. Mishnah *Shekalim* 1:2 attests to the prevalence of transgressors of the rules of *kilayim*, and perhaps this explains why the sages chose to forbid the act of mingling, and to use their influence to disrupt such practices, but not to go so far as to ban the produce.

Rambam and the later codifiers go into extraordinary detail on gardening techniques for keeping different species apart, even when attempting to grow a diverse crop in a small plot. In chapter 3 of MT Kilayim, he discusses plants that look similar but are of different species, which must be kept distinct, and others that look different but are in fact related and may be mingled. He explains that the unique qualities of the plot (today known by the French term *terroir*) and cultivation techniques can produce different forms from the same species. Though they look distinct, they may be sown together.[67] Some plants are best identified by their fruit, others by their leaves, and yet others by their flowers. These details indicate our sages' intimate knowledge of botany, yet the details are not essential for our inquiry. Their overarching concern was *to prevent the blending of different species,* whether of plants or of animals.

Despite Shmuel's statement in B. Kiddushin 39a (see below) forbidding all forms of *kilayim* in both the land of Israel and abroad, halakhic codes limited the prohibition of mixing seeds in the field and vineyard to the Land of Israel, reading the biblical words "your field" and "your vineyard" restrictively. They may also have been influenced by the closing words of the Mishnah in Tractate Orlah (3:9), "New grain is biblically forbidden in every place, and *orlah*-fruits are forbidden [outside Israel] in a tradition [going back to Moses], and *kilayim* are forbidden [outside Israel] according to the sages."

In his Mishnah commentary there, Rambam explains that because grapes produced from vines that have been grafted onto a rootstock of a different species are forbidden even for sale in Israel, the sages were strict in adding a ban on the grafting of grapes abroad.[68] Nevertheless, the grafting of different species of trees, and the interspecies breeding of animals, neither of which is restricted by the Torah to "your field" or "your vineyard," are prohibited biblically both in Israel and abroad, according to all of the codes. Thus, while Shmuel's claim for the universal application of *kilayim* within and without the land was not accepted, the established halakhah maintains a broad prohibition, whether rabbinic or biblical in force, of most forms of *kilayim,* except for mixing seeds in the field, which is permitted abroad.[69]

Crossbreeding Animals

Chapter 8 of Mishnah Kilayim focuses on the mingling of animals, and itself mingles the respective concerns of Leviticus and Deuteronomy, namely breeding different species together, and yoking different species together as beasts of burden. The Yerushalmi (Y. Kilayim Ch. 8, Halakhah 2) asks whether it should be forbidden to house males and females of different species near one another, lest they mate, but concludes that the verse forbids only actively causing them to mate. Rambam (9:1) provides an explicit image that is restated by the later codes:

> He is not lashed unless he inserts [the male's organ] with his hand like a kohl applicator into its tube, but if he mounted them onto one another or encouraged them with his voice then he is [only] lashed for rebelliousness [against the sages, but not for violating the biblical decree].

As with the fruit of mixed plants (other than grapevines), the progeny of mixed animal breeds are permitted for subsequent benefit and, in the case of "pure" species, sacrifice and consumption. When it comes to the offspring of mixed-species parents, the one prohibition is not to crossbreed them for a second generation. What then is one to do with such mixed breeds? Rambam rules (at 9:6, reflecting M. Kilayim 8:5) that the identity of the mother is determinative. Thus, a mule that has a donkey for its mother and a horse for its father may be bred with a donkey, but not with a horse. If one is uncertain of the pedigree of the animal, then checking its ears, tail, and voice will suffice to determine if it is suitable for breeding with another animal (that shares these characteristics). These rulings are restated by Rabbi Yaakov b. Asher in Tur, YD 297 and by Rabbi Karo in the Shulḥan Arukh.[70]

While the rabbis were intent upon reinforcing the Torah's prohibitions on cross-species breeding, as with vegetables, they were rather lenient in permitting the use of the mixed progeny. Perhaps they were convinced that such animals are generally sterile (as Ramban comments at Lev. 19:19) or believed that the total number of species has remained constant since the time of creation. Again, they may also have been realistic about how much control they could hope to exert on animal husbandry, and the great difficulties that would ensue if only "pure breed" sheep, goats, and cows were permitted to their community. Nevertheless, the rabbis understood their role to be the prevention of activities banned by the Torah to the best of their abilities. Before I extrapolate from these pre-modern prohibitions to the remarkable innovations of biotechnology it is necessary to explore the theological underpinnings of the halakhic ban on *kilayim*.

The Significance of Species: Theological and Scientific Perspectives

What was the Torah's objection to the crossbreeding of plants and animals and to the blending of wool and linen cloths? The text does not state its rationale, but the headline of "Heed my statutes," and the situation of this text within the great holiness code of Leviticus 19, has led generations of interpreters to discern a cosmic concern in these regulations. The first-generation Babylonian Amora, Shmuel,[71] is cited at B. Kiddushin 39a:

> As Shmuel taught, "guard my statutes" means, the statutes that I have enacted for you already [i.e., before Sinai]: do not crossbreed your cattle, and do not [mingle species] in your field. Just as [it is forbidden] to crossbreed your cattle, so [it is forbidden] to graft species in your field. And just as [the prohibition regarding] your cattle applies whether in the Land of Israel or abroad, so too does [the prohibition] regarding your field apply whether in the Land of Israel or abroad.[72]

That is, the Creator has determined the development of plant and animal species, and thereafter, humans may not modify them, whether by crossbreeding or by grafting, whether in Israel or abroad. The idea that "My statutes" alludes to a cosmic order is reinforced by a verse from Job, "Do you know the statutes of heaven? Can you establish their dominion on earth?" (38:33). In Midrash Bereshit Rabba, Rabbi Simon claims, "There is no single grass which lacks a heavenly patron that goads it and says, 'grow!' This is the meaning of the verse, 'Do you know the statutes of heaven? Can you establish their dominion on earth?'"[73]

Even a simple reading of the Torah reveals the conviction that observing divine statutes leads to blessing, whereas violation of the divine order leads to devastation. Leviticus 26:3-4 states:

> If you walk in my statutes, and keep my commandments, and do them, then I will give you rain in due season, and the land shall yield her produce, and the trees of the field shall yield their fruit.

Midrash Vayikra Rabba understands this verse, considering other verses from Jeremiah and Proverbs, to mean that there is a "natural order" to creation—God creates the celestial bodies, the sea, the sand, and the depths, all with a specific design.[74] The combination of respecting natural law and observing the mitzvot will ensure blessing for the world and for Israel.

This theme is greatly developed in the Jewish mystical tradition, which views human conduct as playing a direct role in supporting or interrupting the flow of blessing from heaven into the world. The Zohar (Kedoshim, III: 86b) builds upon Rabbi Simon's statement in *Bereshit Rabba*, concluding:

> Thus, it is written, *ḥukkotai*, My statutes you shall keep. [Your cattle you shall not mate *kilayim* with a different kind; your field you shall not sow *kilayim* with two kinds; two kinds of threads—*shatnez*—shall not come upon you]

(Lev. 19:19)—because every single one is appointed over a specific object in the world by that ḥok. Consequently, it is forbidden to switch species, to insert one species into another, because one thereby uproots each power from its place and negates the celestial family, falsifying the royal solemnity.[75]

The Zohar here warns of the dire consequences of creating new species; they disrupt the harmony of heaven and earth.

Writing in the same era, as we have seen, Ramban argues at Leviticus 19:19 that for humans to breed new species would be to imply deficiency in the divine creation and thus in the Creator.[76] Rabbeinu Baḥya restates this concern (31:2). Moreover, hybrid progeny such as mules are, Ramban observes, generally incapable of reproducing themselves, and ultimately undermine the preservation of species ordained by God.[77] Rabbinic texts from the classical and medieval period thus support the idea that the mitzvah of kilayim is a shield for the cosmic order. The identification of this mitzvah as a statute, a ḥok, is not meant to strip it of apparent reason, but rather to invest it with ultimate significance.

While Ramban's perspective is in harmony with midrashic and mystical texts, there are, as always, different currents within the stream of Torah. Midrash Bereshit Rabba encapsulates the tension between viewing the natural world bequeathed by God to be perfect, while simultaneously assigning humanity the responsibility to improve life.[78] In Parashah 12:1, the midrashic voice mocks the idea of "improving" on the human form by adding a third eye or leg, and then concludes, "As it were, God takes pride in His world, saying, look at this creature that I have created, and this shape that I have formed."[79] But in Parashah 11:6, a midrash defending the need for circumcision to "repair" the male body argues, "Everything that was created in the six days of creation requires further labor—just as mustard needs sweetening, and lupine needs sweetening, and wheat needs to be ground, so too does man need to be repaired." Do the sages conceive of the world as perfect, and the responsibility of humanity to preserve it as is, or is God's creation just the beginning, with the role of humanity to extend and improve life? Despite the piety of the former position, it is the second view that has become normative.

Rabbi Judah Loew, the Maharal of Prague (c.1520-1609), comments in *Be'er HaGolah* on a *beraita* found in B. Pesaḥim 54a.[80] There, Rabbi Yosi claims that God conceived of two additional creations just before the first Shabbat but did not complete them. Rather, at the end of Shabbat, God gave Adam the idea to make them. The first task was to create fire from stones, and the second was the method for crossbreeding two species (i.e., a horse and a donkey) to create a mule.[81] The Maharal views these two actions as symbolic of the human role in completing God's creation (using the same term that Ramban employed to ban the practice, *hashlamat ha-olam*, "completing the world"). While the creation of fire is an obvious benefit to extend human sight in the dark and is indeed deserving of blessing as part of the weekly havdalah ritual, the creation of a mule is forbidden by the Torah. Yet the Maharal develops a nuanced idea that posits God's separate agendas for humanity and for Israel. Humanity has an *obligation* to create new species such as the mule, because it is possible, even though Israel is forbidden to do so:

As for those who are surprised by [God's instruction to Adam for] grafting of two species, certainly according to the Torah given by the Holy One to Israel this practice is forbidden as *kilayim* (Lev. 19:19). But Adam the First was to do this act, because this [new species] deserved to be in the world, so that the world would be completed. And even though the Torah that the blessed God gave forbids this [mixing] as *kilayim*, this is only according to the way of Torah. There are many species that were created in the world, and the Torah forbade [Jews] from eating them, and yet they were made in the world to complete the world. And the prohibition of kilayim is not a matter of sexual perversion, for the Torah also prohibited plowing with them together. This indicates that the prohibition against kilayim is only about joining two separate species together, according to the way of Torah. And we have already explained that the way of Torah is one thing, and the completion of the world is another.

The Maharal finds evidence here of a dual agenda for the world. Israel is prohibited from mixing seeds to form new hybrids; yet, the Creator wants the world to be "completed" with creatures beyond the initial creation, and thus empowers humanity to play a role in the extension of life. It is perhaps not surprising that the Maharal is credited with the most dramatic Jewish legend of the extension of life, the creation of his "golem" in Prague. The Maharal establishes a counterweight to Ramban's theology of restraint: God wants humans to complete the world, which was bara la'asot, "created for making" (after Gen. 2:3). This perspective accords with Psalm 8, cited at the beginning of this responsum, which proclaims that God has made humanity "little less than divine," with stewardship over all life, and concludes that human mastery expands the glory of God's name across the earth.

There is something rather modern about the Maharal's concept, and indeed he has been cited by Rabbis Byron Sherwin, J. David Bleich, and Avram Reisner in arguing for a broad mandate to permit genetic engineering.[82] Yet, it remains true that the Torah bans interspecies breeding, and the halakhic codes extend the ban to Jews hiring a non-Jewish breeder to mingle species of animals.

As we explore the theological implications of Jewish texts regarding mingling species, a certain level of cognitive dissonance is unavoidable.

All pre-modern sources, and even some contemporary rabbinic sources, accept the creation narrative in Genesis, in which each species of plant and animal was created "in the beginning" (as Darwin describes this view, "separately created"[83]), and they have remained constant as part of the divine plan. Even the Maharal's idea of a human role in expanding the animal kingdom seems to have been a "plus one" concept to develop the divine-human partnership. None of these sages anticipated the modern concept of evolution, in which all life forms mutate in reproduction, with species evolving throughout their generations in response to the competitive environment within which they live. The sages were not aware of the mass extinctions that are part of earth's natural history (and of humanity's recent unnatural history).[84] Even in the story of Noah's flood, they claimed a perfect survival rate. Why, then, bother with the views of our ancestors on matters of biology?

Some contemporary apologists find hints of anticipation among our ancient sages of the discoveries of modern science, but such attempts are neither credible nor necessary. We read our ancient sources for their moral and theological ideas, and we construct normative practices in continuity with their teachings, combined with contemporary insights, for the sake of constructing a richer and more nuanced religious life. Whether or not Ramban or the Maharal would have accepted Darwin's theory of evolution, their ideas regarding the religious significance of humanity's stewardship of the world remain cogent. Ramban teaches us to conserve species as a way of honoring the Creator; the Maharal adds a religious value to human creativity in completing God's world.

As mentioned earlier, one perspective that has largely been shared by religious and scientific thinkers since antiquity is the belief that hybrids are generally sterile, and that the mixing of breeds is problematic in part because it creates a "dead end" in life. This opinion has been remarkably durable, counterevidence notwithstanding. As noted above, in *The Origin of Species*, Charles Darwin dedicates an entire chapter (9) to hybridism, observing that hybrid plants and animals do not seem to suffer universal sterility, and in fact, hybrids may in some instances outperform their parent species. Moreover, Darwin does not see evidence of a sharp distinction between the categories of *species* and *variety*. These observations of his were largely ignored in the early twentieth century, when speciation tended to be viewed as an essential and permanent form of differentiation (a view that coincided in some cases with racialist abhorrence of human "miscegenation").

In recent decades, however, biologists have come to view naturally occurring hybridism as a common and often beneficial response to environmental challenges, allowing species to adapt to changed circumstances within a generation—far faster than is typically the case with random mutation and natural selection.[85] Reticulate evolution is another phenomenon in which lineages diverge and then recombine, involving "the processes of natural hybridization, horizontal transfer and viral recombination . . . and is now well established as having affected the origin and adaptation of organisms from all of the domains of life."[86]

Moreover, one of the newest fields of biological inquiry, epigenetics, shows that DNA alone is not determinative of gene expression. The environment within which an organism develops and its experience in life play enormous roles in its physical development down to the molecular level, mostly through a process known as DNA methylation.[87] Under the banner of "evodevo" (evolution and development), researchers are continuing to examine the complex relationship between inherited genes and their expression.[88] Species are not identical to their genomes; indeed the entire concept of "species" as an ontological category has been undermined by both biological and philosophical inquiry.[89]

Skepticism about the inherent traits of species is expressed already in the 12th century by Maimonides. He writes in his *Guide for the Perplexed* that "no species exists outside of the mind, but that the species and the other universals are, as you know, mental notions and that every existent outside the mind is an individual or a group of individuals."[90]

That is, discussion of "species" is a heuristic device, a means to describe individual organisms which share common traits, not an ontological claim about their essence. He does not deny here that which he affirms so consistently in his legal writings: distinctions between species must be maintained among plants and animals for kashrut, lulav, kilayim, korbanot, and many other mitzvot.

All our sages ultimately affirm the Torah's ban of kilayim, the mixing of different species of plants and of animals. What, in their mind, is so wrong with such hybrid beasts? Little is said by the ancient sources to explain this abhorrence, but modern Bible scholars read something deeply symbolic at stake in this passage of the Torah banning the mixing of species. Jacob Milgrom notes that the cherubim were described as hybrids, with human faces and birds' wings (Exod. 25:20, 37:9), and that they guarded access to sacred zones such as the Garden of Eden (Gen. 3:24) and the Holy of Holies, where they were embroidered into the curtains (Exod. 26:1, 31), and stood guard over the Holy Ark (Exod. 25:18-22). Ezekiel describes hybrid beings with the four faces of a human, a lion, an ox, and an eagle, bearing the divine chariot (Ezek. 1:10). He also depicts the cherubim as accompanying God in the Temple and on journeys (Ezek. 9:3; 10:1-20; 11:22).[91] These hybrid creatures were heavenly beings that guarded the divine throne from encroachment.[92]

Milgrom argues (p.1661) that the regulation of shatnez—clothing that mingles linen and wool—is symbolic of the distinction between the sacred and the profane: "Israel is commanded to be holy, but is warned that it is not allowed the privilege of breeding different animals, sowing mixed seed, or wearing fabrics of mixed seeds [sic.]—for these are reserved for the sacred sphere and, in the case of clothing, to the priests." He notes that the lower cover of the tabernacle, the curtain of the holy of holies, and the costume of the high priest all included shatnez, as did the belt of the regular priest.[93] The rabbis read the juxtaposition of the ban on shatnez in Deut. 22:11, and the command to attach tassels to one's garment in the very next verse, to imply that *tzitzit* are the exception that proves the rule.[94] It is even possible that the *tzitzit*, or tassels, that the regular Israelite was commanded to wear in Numbers 15:37-41, were also designed to be an intentionally blended garment, *shatnez*, with three white cords of linen, and one woolen cord dyed blue.[95] If so, then these blended garments would remind all of Israel of the boundary between heaven, where life forms are blended, and earth, where distinctions must be maintained.

Regarding *tzitzit*, the Israelite is told "so that you do not follow your heart and eyes in your lustful urge," recalling all the commandments. The maintenance of boundaries between species is central to the doctrine of holiness, and this may explain the placement of these regulations in chapter 19 of Leviticus (and the interpolation of this mitzvah in Numbers 15 between the narratives of the twelve spies and of Korah's rebellion, when social order was suddenly in disarray).

Moreover, the Bible apparently considers the blurring of species to be perilous to human life. Chapter 6 of Genesis relates with disapproval the mating of "divine beings" with the "daughters of men," which leads directly to God's decision to blot out life from the earth. Alan Cooper argues that the identification of Noah as, literally, "a man who was innocent, perfect in his generations" (Gen. 6:9), refers not to his moral strength relative to his contemporaries, but rather to his genealogy; Noah was purely human, not from one of the human/divine hybrids just described, and thus his line alone was worthy of salvation.[96] Rabbinic interpreters likewise believed that the great crimes that precipitated the flood included interspecies intercourse. Only those species that had maintained "their families" were deemed worthy of salvation.[97]

These texts are important for understanding the theological concerns of our ancestors regarding the mixing of species. Many of them are quite speculative, but they do yield values that are relevant to our consideration of modern biotechnology. They demonstrate awareness of the possibility and benefits of hybridized life forms but express anxiety about blurring the established boundaries of life. If this was true for ancient methods of breeding, how much more so in the contemporary laboratory. Nevertheless, we must not assume that new technologies match old prohibitions. Rather, we must carefully consider the legal and moral ramifications of each new technology before determining the proper halakhic ruling.

A VALUES-INFORMED HALAKHIC ANALYSIS

When it comes to novel questions of halakhah that are not addressed in our ancient sources, we may choose between two broad approaches: legal formalism, and values-informed or purposive (or nonformalist) legal interpretation.[98] Tamar Ross describes the relative advantages of each approach:

> If, for the formalist, the room for judicial discretion lies in the areas *not covered* by law and its formal prescriptions, for the nonformalist it lies in the application of those general principles *within* the law in a manner that realizes their purposes to perfection.[99]

While formalism has an austere reputation, and indeed leaves little room for the evolution of established law, in novel areas it may lead to lenient results. If a contemporary practice is not precisely forbidden by a halakhic precedent, then it may be permitted even if this seems to be excessively lenient.[100]

A non-formalist or values-informed interpretation of halakhah considers both precedent and the stated *telos* or purpose of the law, incorporating moral as well as legal statements of the tradition in producing a just decision. Sometimes the nonformalist approach may lead to leniencies, as halakhists consider the broader goals of an area of law, narrowing unhelpful precedents to make room for deeper and more prevalent strands, while in other cases, the result may be stricter than a purely formal analysis of precedent would indicate.[101] In either case, the halakhah is respected as a multifaceted literature that offers nuanced moral and spiritual instruction in addition to practical guidance in the cultivation of religious virtue.

An important basis for halakhic formalism is found in *Tiferet Yisrael*, the Mishnah commentary of Yisrael b"r Gedalya Lipshuetz (Germany, 1782-1860), to M. Yadaim 4:3. This chapter records the dramatic decisions made on the fateful day when the Sanhedrin deposed Rabban Gamliel and installed Rabbi Elazar b. Azariah in his place as chief justice. Mishnah 3 presents an extended debate between Rabbi Tarfon and Rabbi Elazar b. Azariah about tithing practices, during which Rabbi Yishmael charges the latter with bearing the burden of proof, since his position is more stringent. On this point, *Tiferet Yisrael* comments:

> For regarding any matter where there is no known reason to forbid it, then it is permitted without [necessitating] a reason, for the Torah did not mention the entire range of permitted actions, only those things that are prohibited.

Rabbi Yishmael's assertion that stringent positions in halakhah bear the burden of proof is a much-neglected principle in contemporary practice. Indeed, some contemporary halakhists, such as bioethicist Avraham Steinberg, cite *Tiferet Yisrael's* reading to establish that, absent any precise prohibition, new scientific and technological advances should be cautiously adopted.[102] Discussing the permissibility of cloning, he argues (based on dominion theology from Genesis 1:28) that humanity is ordered to subdue the earth, and concludes that modifications of creation are permitted, with three conditions:

a) There is no *inherent halakhic prohibition* in the acts involved in the technological advancement.

b) The effort towards improvement of Creation does not *result in an irremediable prohibition.*

c) The *benefit/harm ratio* for humans is positive.[103]

From this formalistic perspective, one could argue that while the Torah vigorously prohibits the blending of *seeds in the field*, which the sages extended to *grafting plants* together, and to the interspecies *mating* of animals, only these precise activities ought to be considered forbidden. Because neither the Torah nor the ancient sages were familiar with DNA, they could not prohibit what they did not know. Therefore, while it is strictly forbidden to breed, for example, a horse and a donkey by causing them to mate, it would not be forbidden to combine the DNA of a horse and a donkey *in vitro* to create a mule. According to Steinberg, one still must engage in a rational cost/benefit analysis before adopting a new technology, but even a radical innovation such as human cloning need not be forbidden if there is no specific prohibitive precedent.

J. David Bleich likewise adopts a formalist approach in his survey article on genetic engineering.[104] Citing the Ḥazon Ish to M. Kilayim 2:6, he states (p.71) that "artificial insemination designed to produce an interspecies is not forbidden," and continues, "it is quite obvious that genetic manipulation, since it does not entail a sexual act involving partners who are members of different species, cannot be regarded as forbidden." Rabbi Bleich considers several halakhic concerns, such as whether the fruit of an etrog tree that was pollinated by a lemon tree would be acceptable for use on Sukkot (yes), and whether fruits grown on a young sapling that was grafted onto a mature rootstock would nevertheless be prohibited as *orlah* (no). He is aware of the theological concerns expressed by Ramban but sets them aside based on a broader mandate for humans to conquer the world and complete the work of the Creator, as explained by the Maharal text studied above. Since modern methods of genetic engineering are distinct from the activities banned by the Torah and Jewish sages as *kilayim*, there is no need to ban the creation of new hybrid species.

In a sense, the distinction between *in vitro* fertilization in a lab and the sexual breeding methods employed on the farm is like the distinction made in kashrut between naturally occurring animal products and chemically altered substances such as rennet and gelatin. The latter have been identified as *davar ḥadash*, a "new entity," with some *poskim* finding that their transformation into an inedible state neutralizes their kashrut status.[105] With this comparison in mind, we might argue that the blending of genetic materials in a laboratory is not halakhically comparable to sexual mating, even if the cellular mechanics and the result of *in vitro* fertilization are identical to *in vivo* process found in nature.

An even more audacious approach for setting aside concerns about genetic engineering is to declare microscopic phenomena to be of no halakhic relevance. Yeḥiel Michel Epstein (1829-1908), author of Arukh HaShulḥan, does just this when considering the kashrut implications of microscopic organisms that are prevalent in rainwater and in the air. He concludes, "In truth, the Torah did not forbid anything that the [naked] eye cannot perceive, for the Torah was not given to angels ...."[106] This is an important principle in modern kashrut, subduing some of the excessive restrictions that modern technology makes possible, but it is uncertain whether Rabbi Epstein would have approached genetic engineering in the same way.

Does it make sense to use such broad declarations about the insignificance of microscopic structures to declare the Torah's regulations of breeding to be utterly inapplicable to fertilization techniques in the lab? After all, lab workers are highly proficient at working on the microscopic level using ever more sensitive tools. Perhaps it would not exactly be incest for the harvested semen and eggs of a brother and a sister to be mixed in a petri dish, but surely the Torah's concern with incest is not only in the sexual act but also in the creation of a child whose parents are siblings. While it would be a mistake to view DNA as a pristine "code of life" that functions independently of the environment, it would also be implausibly naïve to ignore the significance of genetic inheritance and its implications for a normative religious system such as halakhah.

Shlomo Zalman Auerbach rejects the "naked eye" argument regarding genetic engineering since lab workers regularly manipulate microscopic materials.[107]

> Regarding his question regarding genetic engineering, where they insert cellular materials from one organism to another, and in so doing transform the structure of the second, whether this action can be exempted from the prohibition of kilayim since these cellular materials are not visible to the [naked] eye: [In my opinion,] since the workers are manipulating these materials, and transferring them from one species to another, this should certainly be considered as "visible to the eyes," and it is not comparable to [the permission to eat] microscopic worms, which are not seen.[108]

He then differentiates between the prohibition of the physical mating of two species of animals and that of kilayim, which he limits to the blending of their genetic materials. In his opinion, in vitro fertilization avoids the first prohibition, but leaves the second one intact. This novel distinction allows him to honor both the formal precedent (interspecies sexual intercourse is forbidden) and the targeted value (the genetic integrity of species should not be compromised). However, Rabbi Auerbach does not address the question of whether the prohibition of kilayim should be invoked when only a snippet of

DNA is involved, rather than the blending of the entire genomes of two different species to form a dual-species chimera. I will return to this important distinction below.

In contrast to legal formalism, a values-informed legal analysis considers the purposes of the laws, whether or not they are made explicit.[109] Regarding our very subject, kilayim, Rashi on Leviticus 19:19 states, "These laws are a royal decree, and there is no reason for them."[110] This formalistic-sounding comment elicits a vociferous response from Ramban, which I have cited in part above: "While the common people might not understand the divine will, every word of God has a purpose which must be discerned."

Ramban understands the rationale for the mitzvah of kilayim to be respect for the divine creation. He writes, "And one who breeds together two species alters and undermines the work of [God's] creation." To apply the law without seeking to understand its values is literally to devalue the Torah, and to strip it of its purpose. Halakhic observance then becomes a matter of obsequious conformity. While obedience is a necessary aspect of Jewish devotion, it alone does not suffice. The declaration of, "we shall heed and hear!" (Exod. 24:7) gives priority to compliance but follows it immediately with comprehension. In our case, to assess the permissibility of genetic engineering on strictly formalistic grounds—whether the modern lab procedure is the physical equivalent of the ancient methods of farming—is to ignore the theological concerns expressed across the centuries of Jewish interpretation of the Torah's ban on kilayim.

Even the halakhic texts I have cited give reason to consider with caution new methods for blending DNA. The sages required that fields with blended crops be weeded into homogenous plots, even if the farmer had not intentionally sown them together (they might have grown together, or seeds from a prior season might have sprouted). And while the strongest prohibition on breeding different species of animals together might have been reserved for "hands-on" mating,

Jewish farmers were warned not to verbally encourage their animals to mate between species and were forbidden to bring their animals to a non-Jewish breeder for such purpose.[111]

Does the ban on crossbreeding apply to non-Jews as well as to Jews? In B. Sanhedrin 56b, Rabbi Eliezer states that the ban on crossbreeding animals and grafting plants (but not the wearing of *shatnez* or sowing seeds together) applies to gentiles.[112] It is unclear on what basis Rabbi Eliezer extends this rule beyond Israelites. As Meiri points out, the ban on crossbreeding does not derive from the seven Noachide laws, which are discussed on the same page.[113] On *Sanhedrin* 60a, the Bavli answers this question with the statement of Shmuel from *Kiddushin* 39a: The ban on *kilayim* is part of the natural order that God established from creation and entrusted to all descendants of Noah.[114] Ovadia Yosef traces this line of reasoning through the generations in his collection of responsa, *Yabia Omer*.[115] The establishment of *kilayim* as a meta-principle that applies to all people from the time of creation reinforces the idea that the ban on interspecies breeding ought to be understood as a theological value for all God-fearing people, not a narrow legal regulation imposed on Jews alone.

Returning to halakhic formalism, Rabbis Steinberg and Bleich see no inherent difficulty in genetic engineering. A values-informed interpretation reads precedent somewhat differently, understanding the ban on *kilayim* as Ramban did, as a foundation for limiting human interventions in the natural world, preserving extant species, and preventing the creation of new hybrids. Rabbi Reisner generally follows the line of the formalists in permitting genetic modifications of species, yet he too is troubled by the possibility of "gross modifications." He writes (p.109):

> The burden of this paper is lenient and would permit even such a genetically engineered plant. Still, when we are

able to change not a single trait, but much of the genome of a creature, to create, as it were, a creature of our own devising, then we must ask, is that the point at which we must stop?

It appears to us that the sages conceived a broad prohibition of blending different species, which they understood to be a measure of respect for creation. While they were unfamiliar with DNA and could not know how the genes of two parents were blended in their children, they understood well enough that the Torah intended to keep species distinct, at least when it came to fruits, vegetables, and animals, and that this mandate was the collective responsibility of all people.

Medieval sages were also concerned with the imposition of animal suffering because of *kilayim*. Yaakov ben Moses Moelin (Maharil, 1360-1427) writes in Responsum #124 that it is forbidden to force a bird to nest on eggs from a different species of bird because of the ban on causing animal suffering.[116] Observant Jews are responsible for minimizing such suffering, even in the service of medical research; western governments are belatedly developing stricter standards for the humane treatment of laboratory animals.[117]

Although the sages were vigilant in preserving and indeed expanding the ban on interspecies mating, they were nevertheless quite lenient in concluding that the *produce* of hybrid fruits (other than vines, given Deuteronomy's phrasing) is permitted for cultivation and consumption. Moreover, Rambam offers a significant exception in permitting cross-cultivation of "bitter grasses" for medicinal purposes, and this exception is restated in the Tur and Shulḥan Arukh as established law.

Judaism's ban on *kilayim* is understood to apply to all people, places, and circumstances. It would seem, therefore, that the default position of halakhah is to forbid the blending of genomes of different species, for much the same reason. Our ancestors were aware of possible benefits of such crossbreeding, but they nevertheless forbade Jews from engaging in such practices or in asking non-Jews to do so.

However, the sages were also clear in permitting the produce of such forbidden efforts. It was permitted to ride a mule, for example, to eat the fruit of a grafted tree, and to replant cuttings from such a hybrid. Thus, contemporary Jews may certainly benefit from the hybridized products on the market, whether they are apples or mules, or even from transgenic animals such as the GloFish.

Moreover, Rambam makes a significant exception for medicinal purposes, and his narrowing of the prohibition against crossbreeding or grafting plants to apply only to food is significant. Even if the ban on *kilayim* did apply to medicinal herbs, the great principle of *pikuah nefesh*, rescuing human life, would override such concerns. This point is made dramatically in B. Yoma 82b (Soncino translation):

> Our Rabbis taught: If a woman with child smelt the flesh of holy flesh, or of pork, we put for her a reed into the juice and place it upon her mouth. If thereupon she feels that her craving has been satisfied, it is well. If not, one feeds her with the juice itself. If thereupon her craving is satisfied it is well; if not one feeds her with the fat meat itself, for there is nothing that can stand before [the duty of] saving life, except for idolatry, incest, and bloodshed [which are prohibited in all situations].

While this text describes an intense craving for forbidden food, the same leniency would apply to medicines derived from forbidden sources. If, for example, it were possible to use porcine DNA in a therapy that induced a human autoimmune response to attack a life-threatening tumor, halakhah would certainly favor such an intervention. Likewise, researchers are making progress in xenotransplantation (cross-species transplantation) by, for example, genetically modifying pigs so that their organs may be transplanted into humans without triggering an organ rejection response.[118] This, too, would be halakhically justifiable under the rubric of *pikuaḥ nefesh*, as an action that might save human life.

Even absent such a life-or-death scenario, the use of genetically modified organisms (GMOs) to enrich the nutritional value of rice, for example, which is a subsistence crop for billions of humans, would seem to be indicated, so long as any concerns over health side-effects and ethical issues can be satisfactorily resolved by responsible agencies. There are certainly valid concerns about the health and economic consequences of introducing GMOs, and in large swaths of the world such as Europe, Africa, and South Asia, a broad consensus against the genetic modification of food crops has taken root. Yet, many experts argue that the fears upon which this consensus is based are tragically mistaken, and that GM crops will be a necessary component of any successful strategy to feed the rapidly growing human population, which could rise to ten billion by century's end.

. While the blending of two species to form a new hybrid is forbidden under the rubric of *kilayim*, it is not evident that this prohibition should apply to the transfer of sequences of DNA from one organism to another. As we have seen, the human genome already has 147 "foreign" genes, and we are aware that humans share the preponderance of their genetic material with members of other species.[119] Plants and animals into which DNA sequences from the human genome have been inserted so that they may produce insulin, lysozyme, and other useful products, remain modified plants and animals. They may be transgenic, but they have not become human/plant hybrids.

As such, we would limit the application of kilayim to the full blending of genomes to form a dual species chimera, as in sexual reproduction, whether in the barn or in the lab.[120]

Halakhic formalists exclude such genetic modifications from

the ban of *kilayim* since the mixing is not sexual, but even a values-informed analysis recognizes that this mitzvah is intended to prevent the creation of new hybrid species, not the minor modification of organisms to produce proteins or develop other qualities that might produce tangible benefits for humans and other species.

Ethical Concerns Regarding Genetic Engineering

Before we offer a broad-based exception to permit genetic modifications (but not chimera) whenever there is a plausible human benefit, whether for health or hunger, we must pause to consider some of the relevant ethical and theological values that suffuse Jewish teaching.

From the opening chapters of the Torah, we learn that there is something distinctive about human identity, something that reflects God. It is this sensibility that underlies the prohibition against murder (Gen. 9:6), and it is this same belief that animates the Torah's great mandate to protect human life by nearly all possible means. Saving human life trumps all other Jewish values, except the prohibitions against murder, idolatry, and sexual acts categorized as *ervah*. Our contemporary challenge is that some lifesaving therapies may paradoxically undermine the sanctity of life, specifically through the popularization of what has come to be called "consumer eugenics."

While most people are familiar with the horrors of Nazi ideology and the mass murder of Jews and others whom they considered a threat to the genetic stock of their so-called Aryan race, it is less well-known that eugenics was a popular interest of scientists and leading legal and political figures in the United States and other countries by the late nineteenth century.[121] Indeed, practical eugenics was a common practice in America in the first half of the twentieth century, leading to the institutionalization and forced sterilization of citizens with epilepsy or those deemed to be "feeble-minded."[122]

The current project of sequencing and modifying the human genome may be motivated by therapeutic concerns, but there is danger that our market-driven society will also allow for new eugenics promising the enhancement of human offspring.[123] It is or will soon become possible to design humans with DNA that not only limits susceptibility to cancers and other diseases,[124] but also adjusts physical qualities such as height, eye and hair color, and skin tone. The temptation to "borrow" from the genomes of other species to integrate some of their physical attributes might soon become overwhelming.

Enhancements might not be limited to appearances, either, but might make possible the improvement of musculature, vision, hearing, and even memory. For example, current research focused on multiple sclerosis, a disease that impairs neurological function, seeks to create therapies that would promote functional remyelination, allowing MS patients to establish new neuronal connections; such a therapy if successful, might also benefit healthy people who seek improved intellectual performance.[125] Likewise, genetic research into cell senescence is focusing on ways to prevent cells from "turning off," thus extending both cell life and human life. These proposed enhancements are not "eugenic" in nature but are intended to cure disease and enhance health for all people.

While efforts to date have focused on somatic gene therapies that affect only the present generation, it is also possible to intervene with germ lines that will alter future generations. The motivation to repair a mutation such as the one that causes sickle cell anemia, and to prevent its transmission to future generations, is considerable. Likewise, some people have a genetic mutation that apparently confers natural immunity to HIV. Should this mutation be introduced to the population at large?

It is difficult to anticipate what side effects might follow from such permanent alterations of the human genome. Moreover, human diversity is an important biological, social, and theological asset.

Germline genetic therapy is thus banned in many countries (including Israel), and is regulated in others (including the United States) since the impact on future generations is unknown.[126] However, researchers in China have already used CRISPR/Cas9 technology to "edit" the DNA of human embryos.[127] Although the experiment was on nonviable embryos, and failed in its goals, it is alarming to consider that the editing of humans in ways that could affect future generations has already begun. Indeed, a group of prominent researchers led by Nobel laureate David Baltimore called for an open discourse on genetic engineering, while "strongly discouraging, even in those countries with lax jurisdictions where it might be permitted, any attempts of germline genomic modification for clinical application in humans, while societal, environmental and ethical implications of such activity are discussed among scientific and governmental organizations."[128]

Philosopher Michael Sandel mounts a broad argument against genetic enhancement therapy in his 2007 book called *The Case Against Perfection: Ethics in the Age of Genetic Engineering*. Yet, the author concedes that genetic engineering might be considered comparable to other, noncontroversial interventions made by people to improve their bodies and minds, or those of their children or clients. Not only medical interventions but also education and athletic training are all efforts to augment human performance. We do not leave much in our lives to chance, at least not when we can improve outcomes. Genetic engineering may be considered just another method used for such ordinary purposes.

Still, Sandel is concerned with what he calls hyperagency, "a Promethean aspiration to remake nature, including human nature, to serve our purposes and satisfy our desires. The problem is not the drift to mechanism but the drive to mastery. And what the drive to mastery misses and may even destroy is an appreciation of the gifted character of human powers and achievements" (26-27).

Sandel, who is Jewish, does not refrain from appealing to a religious sense of "giftedness," but he also identifies in genetic engineering threats to three secular foundations of morality: humility, broad responsibility, and social solidarity (85). Of course, these secular values are also very much Jewish values. Belief in God, specifically in God as our creator and teacher in the path of holiness, is the religious foundation for humility, causing us to accept responsibility for the lives and well-being of others, and giving us a sense of communal solidarity, both within the covenanted community of Israel and with all of God's creation.

Sandel (94) anticipates criticism that his approach is "too religious" and offers the work of John Locke, Immanuel Kant, and Jürgen Habermas to buttress the secular philosophical basis for the giftedness of life. Yet he does not consider the possibility of a religion-based critique that would defend genetic engineering as a form of *imitatio dei*, imitating God by acting to protect and strengthen life (as seen above in texts from Rambam, Tur, and Maharal).

Judaism has been willing to permit nearly anything to protect human life, although there are some limits (again, one may not murder, commit idolatry, or perpetrate a sexual crime to protect life). We would be wise to recall Ramban's teaching that the ban on *kilayim* is an indication of respect for the Creator, and a necessary restraint upon God's most audacious creatures. Yet Sandel's preference for chance over choice (92) does not resonate deeply with Jewish sources. The story of King Asa, who turned to physicians rather than to God to heal his leg (2 Chron. 16:12),[129] is accepted in Jewish sources as reasonable if not virtuous conduct.[130] Both halakhic formalism and values-informed analysis provide ample precedent for the modification of human bodies to improve function and extend lifespan.

The Torah itself anticipates that affluence can cause humans to forget the giftedness of life, leading them to say, "My own power and the might of my own hand have won this wealth for me."[131] Likewise, the Torah is concerned with the human tendency to abandon personal responsibility and to break with communal solidarity, but these are ancient human proclivities, and are not uniquely triggered by genetic engineering. Human perfection may be an unrealistic goal, but the improvement of our physical and spiritual abilities is, as Rambam writes in *Hilkhot De'ot*, chapter 3, the essential human endeavor.

Physician and ethicist Jeffrey Burack provides a close examination of Jewish perspectives on enhancement, emphasizing the importance of humility (*anavah*) in Jewish thought.[132] He challenges Sandel's argument that genetic enhancement poses a unique threat to these foundational values. After all, we already make many radical adaptations to the human body through corrective surgeries, organ transplants, and mechanical implants, not to mention cosmetic surgeries. While distinctions can be made between interventions that are demanded (and deserve insurance coverage), and those that are merely to be tolerated, we do not perceive these remarkable interventions as a form of "hyperagency" that threatens our sense of the giftedness of life. Rather, Burack argues that our emphasis should always be on humility. Are our motivations consistent with our duties to be stewards of the human body for God?

Burack raises an important concern that I have already mentioned: are we confident that we understand the consequences of genetic engineering for both current and future generations? Many researchers have sought to limit gene therapy on humans to somatic cells, avoiding modifications to the germline that could be inherited by future generations. Yet, there is some evidence of "leakage" of viral vectors used to deliver gene therapy that are later detectable in semen, making it possible that even these genetic interventions are heritable.[133] For Burack, these questions point to a Jewish paradox—we are responsible for repairing the world, but are warned to maintain appropriate humility about its unknowable ends. Likewise, our halakhic examination leads to conflicting imperatives—both to preserve life and to improve it, to use our gifts of mind and spirit, and to remain humble about the limits of our comprehension.

Philosopher Alan Mittleman concludes his 2015 book, *Human Nature and Jewish Thought*, with a reminder about the importance of limiting the human drive to mastery:

> We have the creativity and freedom to remake the world, and now, increasingly, to remake ourselves. Our own survival might well depend on cultivating anew a sense of limits. Adam and Eve were expelled from the Garden of Eden for transgressing a limit. Limits there will always be, many imposed by human nature. Our dignity inheres in knowing when and how to master them, and when and how to accept them with respect.[134]

Aaron Mackler offers the biblical concept of creation in the divine image as the core principle for considering the ethics of genetic engineering.[135] It implies "a general commitment of respect for persons and urges that "care must be taken not to treat a person as an object" (281). Rabbi Mackler cautions at the beginning of his article that it is both too early and too late to make final determinations on this subject. Genetic engineering has already accomplished dramatic changes in the genomes of plants and animals, but we still know quite little about what developments the near and not-so-near future will bring us.

We are both early and late in the development of genetic engineering. Knowing that the determination of halakhah to govern genetic engineering will remain an unfinished task, I nevertheless have sought to add to the Jewish discourse. I have examined the key texts and values that are currently at stake. It is now time to offer my conclusions.

HALAKHIC CONCLUSIONS

In this responsum I have discovered many causes for concern with genetic engineering, whether from a theological sense of humility toward the Creator; an imperative to observe the mitzvah of *kilayim*; or worries about the safety of GMOs. Each of these concerns has practical applications. Nevertheless, I have not established a general prohibition on the genetic modification of DNA in plants, animals, or indeed, in humans. Most modern methods of genetic engineering are not directly comparable to the actions forbidden as *kilayim* by the Bible and rabbinic literature, since recombinant DNA generally includes just snippets of foreign genomes that function as widgets in their recipient.

Even if the creation of transgenic organisms were to be considered halakhically equivalent, based on a values-informed analysis, to the forms of *kilayim* forbidden by our tradition, the fruits of such efforts would remain permitted after the fact. And even before the fact, the motivation to save human lives and enhance health with therapies that use genetic engineering to combat cancer, feed the rapidly expanding human population, or produce medications, would suffice to permit that which might otherwise be forbidden. Still, we remain responsible for the prevention of animal suffering, and for the possible health dangers to humans and animals posed by GMOs.

Because biotechnology is a revolutionary field, with real benefits and real risks that cannot always be anticipated, halakhic considerations indicate the importance of vigilant attention to the emerging technology and its applications.

PISKEI DIN

REGARDING THE GENETIC MODIFICATION OF PLANTS
AND ANIMALS

1) The Torah's ban on *kilayim*, the physical blending of different species of plants or animals, does not extend to the modification of gene sequences via the introduction of foreign DNA to convey a specific capability in the new organism. Jews may benefit from the fruits of hybridized plants and animals, but they should not intentionally create entirely new species.

2) The health implications of genetically modified foods must be examined on an individual basis, without making broad assumptions that all GMOs are either salubrious or dangerous. The Torah's command (Deut. 4:15) that we guard our health requires vigilant attention to the safety of our food supply.

3) When considering the genetic modifications of organisms, Jews must, as informed and engaged citizens, seek to minimize animal suffering and to protect extant species.

PISKEI DIN

REGARDING THE GENETIC MODIFICATION OF HUMANS

4) The creation of dual species human/animal chimera is forbidden.

5) Modifications of the human genome intended to combat illness are permitted, for they may promote human health and protect human dignity.

6) Genetic modifications intended to enhance the aesthetics of otherwise healthy humans are forbiddcn, for they violate Jewish teachings about the sanctity of human life. Modifications to the human genome must be limited to changes needed to restore health. Because the line between therapy and enhancement is often ill-defined, consultation with a scholar versed in these halakhic, ethical, and biological considerations is required before such therapy is commenced.

CHAPTER 3:
THE KASHRUT OF
CULTURED MEAT

In the summer of 2013, Mark J. Post, a medical researcher at Maastricht University in the Netherlands, made headlines by presenting the world's first hamburger made of "cultured meat," a product developed in a lab from a sample of skeletal stem cells taken from a live cow.[1] Dubbed the "$325,000 Burger," this product was clearly not close to reaching market, yet as a proof of principle, it dramatized the potential of cultured or cultivated meat, which had been discussed for many decades.[2]

By 2016, companies such as Memphis Meats had announced their intention to bring "clean meat" to market within five years, and an Israeli start-up called SuperMeat claimed to be close to producing kosher cultured chicken.[3] In May 2017, Technion University in Haifa hosted a conference called "Future Meating," dedicated to clearing the path for the commercialization of cultured meat. The Good Foods Institute reported in 2022 that European governments had invested half a billion Euros in sustainable meat production, including the development of lab-grown meat.[4] In 2023, the United States Department of Agriculture for the first time approved the sale of laboratory grown meat from chicken cells, by which point over 100 companies worldwide were focused on producing cultivated meat.[5]

In January 2024, Aleph Farms announced that Israel's Chief Ashkenazi Rabbi, David Lau, had agreed to certify their steaks as kosher. In an earlier responsum, discussed below, Rabbi Lau suggested that because this company's method takes starter cells not from a cow, but from a fertilized egg that had not yet implanted, it could theoretically be considered both kosher and *pareve*. In contrast, Rabbi Menachem Genack of the OU ruled that such meat was inherently non-kosher since the source cells were ultimately derived from the body of a live cow.

In this responsum, passed by the CJLS in 2017, I had examined rabbinic sources most relevant to this innovative technology, which lead to the following questions. Does the removal of cells from a live animal violate the Torah's ban on vivisection? What about cells from a non-kosher species—would their DNA suffice to render subsequent generations of the cell line non-kosher? Would a meat product that is biologically identical to conventional meat be considered *besari* ("meaty" from a kashrut perspective)? The challenge here was to identify relevant principles and norms from traditional texts and test if they could prove useful for contemporary quandaries.

The rapid expansion of plant-based meat-like products may have reduced the market for animal-cell sourced lab meat, but the questions raised by this technique remain pertinent for this and other technological topics. This responsum was approved by CJLS on November 14, 2017, and has been updated to reflect further developments in the scientific and halakhic literature.[6]

QUESTION:

May cultured meat—also known as *in vitro*, clean, cultivated, or lab-grown meat—be considered kosher?

RESPONSE:

Before we examine the halakhic concerns raised by cultured meat, what are the general arguments advanced on its behalf? Proponents of cultured meat make numerous claims:

> *Ethics.* Conventional methods for producing meat cause animal suffering at each stage of the process. Cultured meat would not involve a nervous system, and thus there would be no animal suffering.
>
> *Health.* Pastured meat often contains antibiotics and growth hormones, as well as contaminants such as Salmonella and E. Coli that can be harmful to humans and animals which consume them in large quantities. Cultured meat would be produced in sterile conditions with no need for such additives and a lower risk of contamination. It might also be possible to include healthful components such as fat tissue rich in omega-3 fatty acids.
>
> *Environment.* Animals raised for meat pollute the environment through their waste products, including the emission of carbon dioxide and particularly methane, a potent greenhouse gas. Cultured meat would be cleaner to produce because there would be no excrement or emission of methane (a by-product of rumination and fermentation involved in raising cattle for pastured meat).

Ecology. The vast tracts of land and quantities of freshwater currently dedicated to livestock production could instead be dedicated to cultivating diverse fruits and vegetables, enriching human nutrition; fields could also be fallowed and returned to nature. Wildlife could benefit from the reduction of herds and flocks raised for meat (since many wild animals are killed during hay harvesting).[7]

Energy efficiency. Cultured meat's proponents claim that, in ideal conditions, it should require far less energy to produce than does the system of raising animals (especially cattle) for slaughter and then butchering them for sale. These claims have been challenged in the scientific literature; it is too early to know how the efficiency debate will be settled.[8]

Halakhah addresses these general concerns under classical rubrics such as minimizing animal suffering (*tza'ar ba'alei ḥayyim*), promoting human health (*ve-nishmartem me'od li-nafshoteikhem*), and protecting the environment (*bal tashḥit*).[9] While these categories have been greatly expanded in contemporary Jewish discourse, perhaps beyond the point of connection to their classical contexts, the declared goals of developing cultured meat appear to be consonant with traditional Jewish norms and values.

Rather, our halakhic concerns will focus on production methods, specifically questions such as the species of animal used as a source of cells to culture meat, the prohibition of removing a limb or even flesh from a living animal, the kashrut of ingredients used in the growth medium and as additives for flavor, texture, and shelf-life, and the ritual valence of the final product—whether it should be considered "meat" in halakhic terms, or rather neutral (*pareve*).[10]

On the meta-level, these questions all point to a broader one of identity transmission. To what extent do subsequent generations of a cell line inherit the qualities of their genetic ancestors? We are accustomed to viewing biological organisms as related to their ancestors and yet also as distinct entities shaped by their environment. This is even more true on the cellular level. The field of epigenetics has demonstrated that environmental factors play an enormous role in gene expression;[11] viruses may alter an organism's DNA over the course of one generation. The cellular modifications at play with cultured meat are immense, with transformations between stem and differentiated states changing the structure of the units. Indeed, cells altered in a lab environment may not be recognizable to the original animal's immune system.[12] We must remain cognizant of this reality when considering whether subsequent generations of cells should be assigned the halakhic attributes of the first cells taken from a live specimen. Let us begin our halakhic inquiry with the source—must the original cells used to produce cultured meat come from a kosher animal?

"That which comes from the pure is pure"

The first step in creating cultured meat is to collect a sample of stem cells from a living animal; these cells are manipulated in a nutrient-rich lab setting called a bioreactor to induce proliferation. They are then coaxed into differentiating to form muscle fibers and are subjected to tension to develop into tissue that can be layered into meat.[13] Living cells may also be harvested immediately after kosher slaughter, which would have halakhic implications but is not the anticipated practice. An Israeli company has announced plans to source stem cells from amniotic fluid in a pregnant cow; the collection of such cells would arguably avoid many halakhic concerns, as Chief Rabbi David Lau has argued.[14] I will discuss this method and Rabbi Lau's analysis below. In the future, it may also be possible with synthetic biology to recreate the muscle and fat cells that comprise meat entirely from non-biological sources (which, like plant-based meats, would obviate most of our concerns), but for now, cultured meat is being designed to derive from a live animal source.

Because the resultant "edible biomass," or synthetic meat will never have been part of an animal, the established signs of kosher species (split hooves and rumination for mammals; fins and scales for fish; traditional identification of birds) will not be observed. However, the harvested cells may be compared to eggs and milk collected from a fully formed specimen and inherit the species status of their source. True, the harvested cells are microscopic and are not edible in the normal sense. Still, the comparison to eggs is apt given that yolks are essentially large cells produced by a live animal that may be fertilized for the sake of reproduction, eaten, or put to some other use. The stem cells mined from a live animal likewise have the capacity to be used in any of these ways, albeit with significant technological assistance.

Eggs produced by a kosher bird or fish are considered kosher, whereas eggs produced by a non-kosher bird or fish are not kosher. This rule is derived by the rabbis from the "extra" word *bat* (daughter) in the list of non-kosher birds in Leviticus 11:16 and Deuteronomy 14:15: "and the ostrich [daughter]." While the sages in Bavli Ḥullin 64b discuss if *bat* is not merely part of the name of the ostrich, from the apparently extraneous word, they derive a ban on ostrich eggs:[15]

> Ḥezekiah says: what is the source that teaches that the egg of an impure bird is biblically forbidden? For it says: "and the daughter of the ostrich." Does the ostrich have a daughter [i.e., a chick born hatched]? Rather, what is this? An impure egg.

Likewise, milk from a kosher mammal is permitted for kosher consumption, whereas milk from a non-kosher mammal is forbidden (the exception being human breast milk).[16] This rule comes to be known in halakhah as, "that which is derived from an impure/forbidden source is also impure."

Mishnah Bekhorot 1:2 opens with the status of offspring that do not resemble the species of their mother (presumably because of cross-species hybridization). If such an animal is considered "pure" (like a cow) and it is a firstborn, then it would have to be turned over to the Temple, whereas if it is deemed impure (like a donkey) and is a firstborn, then it would have to be "redeemed," meaning, bought back from the priests.

The Mishnah next considers whether the subsequent offspring of a "pure" animal may be considered kosher to be eaten, even if it does not resemble its "pure" parent:

> What about for the purposes of eating? If a pure animal gives birth to one resembling an impure species, [the offspring] is permitted for eating. If an impure animal gives birth to one resembling a pure species, [the offspring] is forbidden for eating. That which emerges from the impure is impure, and that which emerges from the pure is pure.

Based on this mishnah, its discussion in B. Bekhorot 6a-7b, and the sources we have seen regarding eggs, Rambam prohibits any food that derives from an impure animal:[17]

> Any food that emerges from one of the forbidden species that one is to be whipped for eating—this food is biblically forbidden to eat. For example: milk from impure domesticated and wild beasts, and eggs from impure birds

and fish. For it says, "and the daughter of the ostrich"—this
refers to its eggs. And this rule applies to any [animal] that
is forbidden like the ostrich, and for all things like eggs.

The sages at B. Bekhorot 7a debate the kashrut of animal by-
products such as donkey urine which, repulsive as it may sound, was
apparently used in some ancient food preparations.[18] Rosh considers
donkey urine to be biblically banned, whereas Rambam permits it (as
implied in the halakhah above that forbids only "any food" from an
impure species). Rabbi Yosef Karo in Beit Yosef (YD 81) and Shulḥan
Arukh (YD 81.1) sides with Rosh to prohibit even this non-food product
under the rubric of, "that which emerges from an impure animal is
impure."[19]

Based on the principle that derivatives of non-kosher animals—milk,
eggs, edible skins, and even urine—are not kosher, we conclude that
regarding cultured meat, too, the kashrut status of the animal *species*
is significant. It is true that taking a biopsy of cells is quite different
from the natural process of collecting eggs or milking cows, but it is not
more invasive than is the taking of meat, skin, or bones. *Simply put, cells
from a non-kosher species may not be used to produce kosher food.*

Rabbi J. David Bleich gives a less simple explanation, citing Rabbi
Chaim Soloveitchik in differentiating between two forms of *yotzei*,
substances that *separate* from the original animal.[20] The first he applies
to the flesh of the original animal and of its descendants, which is
forbidden in Lev. 11:8 and Deut. 14:8 under the expression, "do not eat
from their flesh." The second form of *yotzei* refers to derivative products
such as milk and eggs. Rambam, in *Forbidden Foods* 3:6, says that eating
the flesh of forbidden animals calls for the penalty of being lashed,
while eating forbidden milk and eggs incurs a less severe whipping
for rebelling against rabbinic authority, even though the act is itself
biblically banned.[21] Rabbi Bleich claims that the cells harvested to

culture meat would be the latter form of *yotzei*, separation, like milk and eggs. However, this is not an obvious conclusion since the cells' source is "flesh," and so too is their intended end. To paraphrase Rabbi Shimon b. Lakish in B. Pesaḥim 84a, *batar basof azlinan*, we should consider the final intended result.[22] Rabbi Soloveitchik said of eggs and milk that "they are not a kind of meat," but it would be difficult to say this of a tissue sample taken from a cow that is cultured to make a hamburger. Like us, Rabbi Bleich generally understands that cells taken from a kosher species may be compared to other substances produced by living animals such as milk and eggs, and are permitted. Curiously, he does not address a major consideration of ours and other halakhic researchers, the way that the cells are removed from the living specimen.

A Limb Taken from a Living Animal

The prohibition on eating a limb taken from a living animal (hereafter, "the limb ban") is derived by the sages from three or four verses in the Torah. Bavli *Sanhedrin* at 57a and 59a-b cites Genesis 9:4, where God tells Noah and his children: "You must not, however, eat flesh with its lifeblood in it."

Bavli Ḥullin 102b presents a debate between Rabbi Yoḥanan and Reish Lakish.[23] Both agree that the limb ban is based on Deuteronomy 12:23, where Moses warns Israel, "But make sure that you do not consume the blood; for the blood is the life, and you must not consume the life with the flesh." These two sages derive similar laws from Exodus 22:30, where God commands Israel, "You shall be holy people to Me: you must not eat flesh torn by beasts in the field; you shall cast it to the dogs."

Rabbi Yoḥanan argues that the Deuteronomy text also establishes a ban on "flesh from a living animal," while the Exodus text refers to the ban on *tereifah*, eating from a carcass killed by other animals in the field. Rabbi Shimon b. Lakish derives both the second and third rules from the Exodus text. In either case, the limb ban is located by these sages in Deuteronomy 12:23, and both agree that there is an additional "flesh ban" against eating meat taken from a living creature, even if it does not meet the rabbinic definition of a limb. The "flesh ban" is also derived from Exod. 22:30, based on the Onkeles Aramaic translation, "You shall not eat flesh *torn* from an animal." Such meat is forbidden as *tereifah*, "torn," if the animal is mortally wounded in the process but has not yet died.

The Exodus verse, which speaks of "meat from the field," reinforces the idea that these bans apply only to land animals, not to fish (or permitted grasshoppers). Fish do not require ritual slaughter, and their blood is not forbidden. As such, they are not protected from being eaten alive, though to do so would be considered cruel conduct and forbidden under the rubric of *tza'ar ba'alei ḥayim*, causing excessive suffering to animals, and as a repugnant behavior banned under the category of *bal tishkotzu*, "you shall not draw abomination upon yourselves" (Lev. 11:42).[24,25]

Finally, a *beraita* cited in B. Nazir 53b[26] bases the limb ban on Numbers 19:16, a text regarding ritual purification following corpse contamination: "And in the open, anyone who touches a person who was slain by sword, or who died naturally, or [touches] human bone, or a grave, shall be unclean for seven days."

The limb ban is understood by the rabbis to be one of the seven universal commandments given to all descendants of Noah, that is, to all humans, which was then repeated and included within the Sinaitic revelation to Israel. In B. Sanhedrin 59b, we read:

> Rav Yehudah says, citing Rav: Adam the First was not permitted to eat meat, for it says, "To you and to the beasts of the earth are [the fruits of the field] given to eat" (Gen. 1:29-30)—but the beasts of the earth are not given to you.

When the children of Noah came, [God] permitted [meat] to them as it says, "As with the green grasses, I give you all these" (Gen. 9:3). Is it possible that [the ban on] limbs from living creatures would not apply [to the Noahites]? Thus, it says, "You must not, however, eat flesh with its lifeblood in it" (Gen. 9:4).

The proof-text for the limb ban as applied to gentiles comes from Genesis, not from one of the post-Sinaitic verses. It is extended to Israel based on the verse in Deuteronomy and on rabbinic logic. Midrash Sifre Devarim to Re'eh (Piska 76) states:

And thou shall not eat the life with the flesh (12:23): This refers to a limb cut from a living animal. But is it not obvious that if flesh seethed in milk, which was permitted to all descendants of Noah, was (later) forbidden to Israel, the limbs of a living animal, which was forbidden to all descendants of Noah, should certainly be forbidden also to Israel? (Not necessarily so,) as evidenced by the case of the (captive) *woman of goodly form* (Deut. 21:11), who was forbidden to all descendants of Noah but was (later) permitted to Israel, and by other similar cases. You should therefore not be surprised if the limb of a living animal, too, were (later) permitted to Israel although previously prohibited to all descendants of Noah. Hence, *thou shalt not eat the life with the flesh*, referring to the limb of a living animal. R. Ḥanina ben Gamliel, however says: This refers to the blood of a living animal.[27]

The rabbis first seek to extend the limb ban to Jews based on the premise that Jewish law is always stricter on Jews than on gentiles. Contending with contrary evidence, they switch tactics to establish an independent biblical source of the limb ban that is indisputably addressed to Israel.[28]

Indeed, in several senses, the limb ban is considered by the rabbis to be more severe for gentiles than for Jews. Gentiles are prohibited to tear a limb from any land animal, whereas for Jews, the prohibition applies only to "pure" species that they are permitted to eat.[29] For example, if a limb were torn from a pig, it would be forbidden to a gentile under the limb ban, but for the Jew, only under the pork ban.[30] Moreover, according to Rambam, the system of minimum measurements established by the rabbis as a threshold for liability on eating forbidden foods applies only to Jews.[31] Thus, the limb ban takes effect for Jews only when a *kezayit* of forbidden flesh is consumed, whereas for gentiles, even a tiny amount is prohibited. Still, this is a theoretical distinction since the meat remains forbidden for everyone.

Classical rabbinic sources discuss whether one act of cutting a limb from a live animal could simultaneously violate as many as three prohibitions. In B. Ḥullin 103a, a case is imagined in which the flesh sample is a) taken from a live animal, which b) was mortally wounded in the process, and c) the flesh was itself forbidden fat. Is the transgressor in triple jeopardy? The medieval commentators debate the consequences (see novella of Rabbi Shlomo ben Adrat here for a summary). In our case, however, the cell collection does not constitute a limb, the source animal is not permanently injured, and the targeted cells are skeletal stem cells, not forbidden fats.

Moreover, the halakhic principle of "one act is not punishable for more than one prohibition" would tend to rule out an accretion of bans (there are exceptions, as when the acts are simultaneous).[32] For example, if a non-kosher species (such as a pig) were slaughtered in a non-kosher fashion, then a Jew who ate the meat would be punishable only for eating the forbidden species, not also for eating meat lacking *sheḥitah* (kosher slaughter). In our case, if the species is kosher, and the cells are not from inherently forbidden fat or blood, then the active prohibition would be against eating flesh from a live animal.

With many halakhic food prohibitions—such as on mixing meat and milk, and ḥametz during Pesaḥ—the ban covers not only eating the food, but also benefiting from owning it. However, the limb ban is limited at B. Pesaḥim 22b to eating, because of the comparison to blood. Deut. 12:23 emphasizes, "but make sure that you *do not eat* the blood," which is understood by the rabbis to imply permission of benefit.[33] In addition, the verse in Exodus speaks of throwing such food to the dogs (possibly one's own pets), which may indicate that flesh from a living animal may be used so long as a person does not eat it.[34]

What constitutes the limb that one is forbidden to detach from a living animal? The sages discuss two types of "limb." One is a body part that includes flesh, bone, and sinew, such as a hand or leg. Another type of "limb" is an organ that is entirely "flesh," such as the tongue, spleen, kidney etc. The limb ban seems to apply only when the entire limb is removed. Some say that to elicit punishment, the entire limb would have to be eaten, but the halakhah sets a minimum for Jews at consumption of a *kezayit* of any part before liability is established.

As we have seen, there is a related ban on eating "flesh from a living animal." Rashi on Ḥullin 102a states that this concept bans consumption of a limb, even if it lacks a *kezayit* of flesh, and of a *kezayit* of flesh, even if it does not constitute a limb.[35] Rambam rules this way in chapter 5 of his *Laws of Forbidden Foods* and is followed by later codifiers. Here is the summary given by Yaakov b. Asher in the Tur (YD 62):

"You must not consume the life with the flesh" (Deut. 12:23). This warns not to eat a limb from a living animal. It applies to cattle, beasts, and birds, but only to pure species. If a limb is removed from a living animal, whether it has flesh, sinews, and bones, or whether it is only flesh, such as the tongue, spleen, kidneys, and testicles, it is prohibited to eat it whether there is a *kezayit* or not.[36] And likewise, flesh removed from a living animal is prohibited, even if it is not considered to be a limb from a living creature; it is prohibited because of the verse, "you must not eat flesh torn by beasts in the field" (Exod. 22:30).

There is a surprising line of rabbinic thought that if not for explicit biblical permission to drink milk and eat eggs, these products of live animals would be forbidden under the rubric of the limb ban. They, and only they, are biological products permitted for consumption even when collected from live animals.[37] As such, eating cells removed from a live animal would clearly violate the limb ban, though if the quantity remained below the threshold of a *kezayit*, the ban might be reduced to a rabbinic level.

Zvi Ryzman completely dismisses the prohibition against eating "flesh from a living animal" because, he notes, the targeted cells are stem cells, not muscle tissue. He points to the famous statement in B. Yevamot 69b that, during the first forty days of gestation, a human fetus is considered as *maya b'alma*, "simply water,"[38] a classification that is cited in several modern responsa to permit early-term abortions even in non-life-threatening circumstances.[39] Rabbi Ryzman then argues that the stem cells taken by biopsy to culture meat from a cow or other animal permitted for kosher consumption are comparable to the cells found in an early term human fetus. On this basis, he claims that stem cells are not considered "alive" but rather, "just water," and thus not "flesh" that could trigger either the limb ban or the flesh ban. He concludes,

Therefore, it appears that a cell taken from a pure animal is not considered to be "a limb from a living animal" or "flesh from a living animal," for it is actually "just water," and is not a limb or flesh.[40]

While a human fetus before 40 days may be largely unformed and is, indeed, not considered by halakhah to be an independent life until birth, the cow from which stem cells are harvested is very much alive in the world. Moreover, when technicians take a biopsy from an animal, they remove many types of cells at once, not only stem cells, and only later isolate them. The stem cells taken are mature, not embryonic.[41] Indeed, it is not evident that cultured meat may be developed only from stem cells. Other types of cells, including fibroblasts, may be used as the foundation for the growth of the trillions of cells required to produce an edible form of meat.

In response to his critics in the journal *Teḥumin*, Rabbi Ryzman reiterates his position in volume 36, extrapolating from a text focused on human development *in utero* to the context of flesh removed from a mature cow for the sake of forming meat, but this is not convincing.[42] It does not appear that calling biopsied cells "simply water" will suffice to permit their consumption.

Rather, another approach seems preferable. It is forbidden to eat even a minute amount of flesh taken from a living animal, but with cultured meat, *there is no intention to consume the source cells themselves.* The act of "eating" is said to involve "pleasure in the throat," but these cells will never be placed in a human throat and would be undetectable if they were.[43] They certainly do not meet the halakhically significant threshold of *notein ta'am*, giving flavor.

Like most cells, these will eventually degrade and die. Far more significantly, the final product is extremely unlikely to contain remnants of the original stem cells. It is only much later—after their descendant cells will have transformed from stem into muscle and fat cells, multiplied by the trillions within a growth medium, and been structured under tension to form strips of muscle tissue and then layered into meat—that an edible product will emerge. By one estimate, from ten source cells it could be possible in ideal conditions over two months to culture 50,000 tons of meat.[44] Muthuraman Pandurangan and Doo Hwan Kim have claimed that a billion pounds of *in vitro* meat could be produced from one animal.[45] Even if such estimates are wildly optimistic, in any given portion of the end-product, it is exceedingly unlikely that there will be consumption of the actual source cells taken from an animal.

Although it is theoretically possible that one or more of the original cells might survive into the final product and be unwittingly eaten by someone, liability for the limb ban for Jews is triggered only with the consumption of a *kezayit*. A kosher consumer could be confident that the cultured meat they consume will contain no cells that ever lived in an animal (at the level of one in many hundreds of trillions). Mishnah Makhshirin establishes that when an unmarked piece of meat is most likely to be kosher, then it may be assumed to be kosher.[46] In our case, any portion of cultured meat is extremely unlikely to contain one of the original source cells.

Moreover, we have the oft-cited argument of Yeḥiel Mikhel Epstein, author of Arukh HaShulḥan, regarding the kashrut implications of microscopic organisms that are prevalent in rainwater and in the air. He concludes, "In truth, the Torah did not forbid anything that the [naked] eye cannot perceive, for the Torah was not given to angels ...."[47] If a stem cell taken from the original animal makes it to the final consumer product, blended in with trillions of new cells, it will be impossible to identify, impossible to taste, and of no halakhic consequence to the consumer, for whom it would be as undetectable as any microscopic organisms found in food.[48]

However, we ought not rely on Rabbi Epstein's argument altogether to dismiss the significance of the original biopsied cells. His exclusion was focused on the unavoidable ingestion of microscopic organisms when drinking water and breathing air, not on the expert manipulation of cells by scientists in the lab (a distinction first made by Rabbi Auerbach).[49] Those cells, harvested from a living animal, *derive their species identity* from that animal, whether they are fertilized and bred into a full specimen, or cultured to develop a mere component, such as muscle tissue. There will be no kosher pork chop.

J. David Bleich struggles to reconcile the general dismissal from halakhic consideration of subvisual phenomena with the fact that current biotechnology allows technicians working on the microscopic level to create macroscopic results (like a hamburger).[50] He cites Rabbi Auerbach's responsum to expand the realm of responsibility to include subvisual actions intended to produce visual results.

Rabbi Bleich further suggests that Rabbi Auerbach's observation may be related to the halakhic concept known as *aḥashveih* ("ascribed value"). This is the concept that some actions may not initially be regulated by Jewish law unless they come to be associated with a specific forbidden result.[51] This resembles discussions within Shabbat laws regarding intention—the same act might be either permitted or forbidden, depending on the clarification of intention. In this way, Rabbi Bleich arrives at a defense of the halakhic significance of microscopic interventions that are intended to yield macroscopic results. While not all his reasoning resonates with us (he gives credence to the notion that pre-modern rabbis had microscopic vision), the general conclusion is similar (we will return to this concept below).

Rabbi Ryzman includes the microscopic effects exclusion in his list of factors that may cumulatively make cultured meat permissible. Rabbi Yaakov Ariel has published an extensive and stringent critique of Rabbi Ryzman's original article in *Teḥumin* (vol. 36), waiving permission based on the dismissal of microscopic phenomena. He writes, "But because these small cells that were taken from flesh that is visible to the eye, reproduce and assume large proportions that are visible to the eye, their legal status is like regular flesh. And because their source is from forbidden meat, so too is the product that inherits their status, like the forbidden source."[52]

Rabbi Ariel argues that the passage of a product through a

microscopic stage does not inherently annul the significance of the visible source and edible end-product. Rabbi Auerbach first made this declaration, and I argued for it in my 2015 paper on genetic engineering (see previous chapter). A broad-spectrum declaration that nothing microscopic has halakhic significance is counter-intuitive and counterproductive in an era when scientists regularly work on this level. While a formalistic halakhic approach might set aside the significance of these stem cells, a value-informed approach such as mine will take them, their source, and their destiny seriously. If the microscopic realm were to be declared beyond the jurisdiction of halakhah, then many of humanity's most consequential decisions would be denied the insights of our ancient and profound tradition. Our approach, therefore, is not to dismiss the significance of all microscopic manipulations, but rather to establish which forms of identity are retained by subsequent cell-line generations, and which forms of identity are erased.

The Question of Identity Across Generations

Although we have found precedent for maintaining the *species identity* of cells derived from permitted and forbidden animals, just as is done with milk from mammals, and eggs from birds and fish, it is reasonable to ask how much individual history those source cells convey with them. Species identity across generations is compelling for several reasons. First, this is the default position of both biology and halakhah, summed up nicely in the Mishnah at Bekhorot 1:2: "that which comes from a pure species is pure and that which comes from an impure species is impure." Second, we might compare the DNA preserved in these cells to the halakhic concept of *davar ha-ma'amid*, a "sustaining substance."[53] In rabbinic sources, this is a minute additive that nevertheless has a pronounced, durable, and readily discernible impact, such as rennet on cheese or gelatin on gelatinous foods.[54] The DNA from the original cells is, of course, not an additive, but given that it is only one ingredient in the recipe for making cultured meat, and that it persists in the subsequent generations, conveying to them the particular qualities of the species from which they were collected, the comparison is apt. From these cells, an entire new specimen could be created bearing the hallmarks of its parent species.[55] Even though DNA itself is not visible to the naked eye, its effect certainly is, and thus it has the status of *be'ayin*, something that may plainly be detected.

If species identity can be preserved across the generations, what about other attributes of the source cells? If the original cells were cut from a live animal, do the successor cells inherit the status of "torn flesh," even though they were never part of a living specimen? This is a fundamental question. Those who would apply the limb ban to descendant cells—a trillion or more cells cultured from an original animal cell—are claiming that the descendants are identical to the source, not only in genotype but in phenotype. This is false on both scientific and halakhic grounds.

Biologically, the successor cells are transformed by their own "experience"—the material environment in which they are nurtured, differentiated, and multiplied. They have transformed cell type, grown in a distinct environment, and become far removed in generation and experience from the animal in which the first cells grew. They do not bear a "flesh memory" of the original cells,[56] and as Dr. Post has observed, the descendant cells might not be recognized by the original animal's immune system were they to be returned by autologous transplant. The DNA might be the same, but everything else is different. They are like eggs collected from a chicken—the same DNA, but different substance and halakhic status.

It is possible that a gene editing technology such as CRISPR will be employed to modify the DNA of the harvested cells. This could be done to increase yield by modification of the myostatin gene (whose mutation leads to a condition called "double muscling"),[57] or perhaps to augment the nutritional content of the meat. The halakhic concept of *davar ḥadash*, a "novel entity," is usually applied to a substance that has passed through an inedible state, but in this case, the product would be modified at the genetic level, so that the descendant cells might arguably be deemed a new substance.[58] However, single-gene modifications do not suffice to change the species identity of the organism. Further, Mark Post says that concerns about GMOs argue against the use of gene editing of the cells.[59]

Halakhic concerns are not necessarily satisfied by scientific findings of fact. It is helpful, when possible, to connect contemporary phenomena to established categories that have settled law, even if the fit is not perfect.[60] Yaakov Ariel finds a fascinating precedent in the realm of tithed grain. Mishnah Terumot (Ch.9) considers the status of crops grown from tithed seeds that had been dedicated for the exclusive use of priestly families, or from seeds that were supposed to have been left for the poor. By the third crop-generation, the plants lose the status of the first generation, at least for annual plants. Regarding perennials, which may produce several seasons of fruit from one seed, the later generations inherit the ritual status of the source. Rabbi Ariel points to Mishnah 9:6 to prove that later generations of seeds may inherit the ritual status of their source. This is hardly the only explanation—our Sages could simply have made an enactment to discourage sinners from "burying the evidence" of their illicit retention of grain. Still, Rabbi Ariel concludes that cultured meat grows exclusively from the power of the original cells, and therefore, that the product is the equivalent of the source. If the original cells were forbidden as "torn meat" or limb meat, then the subsequent generations would be precisely the same.

To strengthen his point, Rabbi Ariel argues that while seeds of grain depend on other factors—such as the soil and its nutrients—to grow, and thus lose their identity by the third generation, the cells of cultured meat depend *entirely* on the source cells, and thus later generations are undiminished in their inheritance. But this is patently false—without receiving nutrients in the lab, the cultured meat will never reproduce. Ze'ev Weitman critiques Rabbi Ariel, arguing that stem cells in their growth medium are precisely like seeds planted in the ground:

> However, it appears that the matters are indeed comparable, for just as the earth provides a plant with the nutrients needed for it to grow and develop, exactly so with cultured meat—there the growth and development are made possible due to the materials that nourish the cell and serve it as a growth platform. And if a plant which grows and develops from a seed is considered a new entity (lit. *new face*) it appears that so too meat which grows and develops from a cell may be considered like a new entity.

Rabbi Weitman is correct in drawing a more direct comparison between the cells of cultured meat and plants grown from seeds of tithed or untithed produce. The source cells alone cannot reproduce to create the descendant product. We may apply to them the halakhic principle *zeh va-zeh goreim*, "both factors are necessary" for the new cells to grow, and thus, even if one element is forbidden, this ban is not conveyed to the end-product.[61]

We would go further and say that the stem cells are comparable to a plant whose seed desists—the original cells will die, and only with intensive interventions from lab technicians will new cells grow and develop in the desired fashion. Therefore, the model from replanted tithes fails to establish the transmission of ritual status between generations of cells.

To conclude this section, the easiest argument for inherited identity relates to *species status*. Germline cells from a species convey the same qualities to their genetic heirs, even with the mutations that attend all reproduction. DNA is like a sustaining substance, and the species identity is reproduced at the cellular level. Culturally, too, we recognize later generations of plants and animals as belonging to the same species, even with the minor variations that are readily observed. However, it is less coherent to claim that later generations of cells should inherit the *ritual status* of "torn meat" from their source cells, which themselves have long since perished. The later generations of cells were never connected to a living animal, even as later generations of plants and animals were not part of their ancestors. In other words, *cells that are cultured over time to produce beef remain identified with the same species of cow, but not with the experience of the specific cow or cows from which they ultimately derived, just as ears of barley lose the ritual tithing status of earlier generations, while remaining barley.*

As we have seen (B. Pesaḥim 22b), while there is a comprehensive prohibition on *eating* the limb or flesh or blood taken from a living animal, there is no prohibition on *benefiting* from it. These microscopic cells may be cultured in a lab setting to produce muscle cells and other components that will eventually resemble meat. The harvesting process will not render the original animal as "mortally wounded" and so, as Rema taught, there is no true limb ban, but only a stringency. And even if the original flesh should be forbidden as a stringency, the amount taken is less than the *kezayit* that is forbidden to Jews. And even if we nevertheless forbid the cells, since non-Jews receive a stricter standard, this will apply only to the original cells, not to the trillions of descendants. These later cells are the product of many inputs—DNA from the source, and nutrients from the growth medium. All aspects are essential; this triggers the principle of *zeh va-zeh goreim* and renders the final product permissible.

Therefore, the derivative cells do not inherit the prohibited status of flesh torn from a living being. However, given that all the derivative cells come from the same species as the source, and that they could, in fact, be used to reproduce an entire animal, they retain the species-status of the original specimen, just as milk and eggs do. Cultured meat from a cow, but not from a pig, may be made kosher. However, what about the other ingredients that might be part of this product?

Non-Kosher Additives

How does one develop an edible biomass (i.e., meat) of trillions of cells from just a few original stem cells? Technicians embed these cells within a sponge-like matrix that is perfused with a culture medium that provides nutrients and growth factors. The most common recipe[62] for such a medium contains an additive of fetal bovine serum, which is generally non-kosher.[63] Gels used in Petri dishes are often made from porcine sources. Plant-based replacement additives are possible and desirable to the general consumer for various reasons: they have the potential to be cheaper, are safer from infectious agents, and are preferable for vegetarians. Should livestock be drastically reduced because of meat being mostly cultured, there would no longer be an adequate source of serum.[64] However, plant-based media may introduce allergenic factors. This problem will require attention from commercial producers but is not a kashrut concern.

Dr. Mark Post has made progress in developing a vegetarian growth medium; without this development, there would be little benefit to cultured meat, since many cows would need to be slaughtered to provide the serum. Dr. Amit Gefen of Technion University has proposed using apples for the armature needed as a foundation for cultured meat. He told *Ha'aretz*, "Experience accumulated abroad shows that it is possible to grow cells from a mammalian source on apples because of the structure of their porosity. The pores are a sort of niche that provides the mammalian cells with a protected habitat in which the biological processes necessary for one day becoming a tasty piece of steak can occur."[65] Even with a plant-based armature, there will still need to be a medium to supply nutrients for cell growth.

It would be in the interest of the kosher (and vegetarian) consumer for cultured meat to be developed in an exclusively plant-based medium that is certified kosher. Rabbi Bleich (56-58), like Rabbi Ryzman, raises the halakhic principle discussed above of *zeh va-zeh goreim* (both this and that are causative). If two factors are required to produce cultured meat, one permitted and a second forbidden (because of the limb ban), then there are grounds for leniency to permit the product. Thus, even if the source cells were forbidden on some level, their inability to grow without the kosher medium would yield a permitted product. If both the source cells and the growth medium were deemed non-kosher, then so would be the end-product.

For cultured meat to mimic the pastured product and seem *besari*, it may be necessary to add ingredients to enhance taste, aroma, appearance, and bite, just as is done with soy and wheat-based meat products. These additives will also need to be kosher-certified. To win over the public to this new form of meat, it may well be in the interests of producers for kosher supervisors to help certify that aside from the original cells mined from a live animal, the product is entirely vegetarian.

Would the use of fetal bovine serum in the currently common growth medium render the product inherently non-kosher? The finished product would be removed from the medium, or the reverse. Yet, just as food that is cooked in a forbidden substance is forbidden, so, too, is food that is soaked in a forbidden substance, according to the principle, "soaking [food] is like cooking it." True, the growth medium would not necessarily imbue the product, once removed, with its taste, either good or bad, which makes moot the traditional concern of whether a non-kosher admixture is tasty or repulsive. In the final form, any residual amount of medium left in the meat would certainly be less than 1:60 of the product volume and, because there was no intention to retain it, could be considered retroactively nullified.[66]

Perhaps the very process of metabolizing the growth medium can be considered a form of nullification. Haifa chief rabbi Sha'ar Yashuv

Cohen discusses the use of a wheat-based medium to grow mushrooms—could the mushrooms be considered kosher for Passover?[67] He notes that in general, forbidden foods convey their prohibition to subsequent substances, unless there is a *ḥidush*, a novel permission implied by the Torah itself.[68] This is not the case here, but if the medium had been formulated before Passover, then the substance was not initially forbidden, and its products would not inherit a forbidden status. However, if the wheat-based product were indeed rendered *ḥametz*, would the mushrooms that were nourished by it also be forbidden? Or could we say that the biochemical process of breaking down the growth medium effectively creates a new substance?

Rabbi Cohen compares this question to the status of an animal endowed with a gland that produces a fragrance (musk) that may be burned as incense, or even added to flavor food. The medieval sages concluded that this substance may be eaten, since the "blood" of the animal has been transformed by the animal itself into a permitted fragrance.[69] Rabbi Cohen concludes:

> Accordingly, the *ḥametz* that has been consumed by the mushroom and then secreted is certainly already a different substance. This is apparently no less so than the case of blood consumed by the body of an animal that is transformed into a fragrance, and thus it is possible to permit it.

Rabbi Cohen concludes his article by sharing that a corn-based alternative medium has been identified, ultimately allowing his finding to go unimplemented. Having consulted with the great authorities of his time, however, he asserts that even the wheat-based medium would have been permitted. This argument could similarly be employed to nullify the halakhic significance of a forbidden growth medium such as fetal bovine serum, which is "consumed" by the muscle tissue. As with his case, however, we would do better with a medium whose kashrut status is beyond doubt.

These arguments might lessen the severity of prohibition against a meat product cultured with animal-derived growth media such as fetal bovine serum. Still, such blood-based additives introduce new halakhic and health problems. For these reasons, it should be mandatory that growth media and all other additives to cultured meat be animal-free for the product to be certified kosher.

Should Cultured Meat Be Considered "Besari" from a Kashrut Perspective?

We have already learned that meat removed from a living animal, even a pure animal, is considered *treife* (unkosher) and is forbidden to be eaten.[70] If, however, the flesh taken from the animal is not itself eaten, but is rather used as a source to create new generations of cells, are those subsequent cells—which have never themselves been part of a living animal—considered meat? We have argued that they should not be considered "limb meat," but are they meat altogether? Cultured meat will lack the features of an animal and not be subject to slaughter and inspection. It would be plausible to compare it to eggs laid by a live bird. They derive from an animal and, in certain conditions, would have the capacity to grow into an animal, but instead, they have been kept in a cellular state, and might be considered *pareve*, or neutral, like eggs or a vegetable. On the other hand, the end-product is intended to look, feel, and taste like meat, and it will be biologically identical to meat. How could it be deemed *pareve*?

We may look for precedent to the discussions regarding rennet and gelatin, which were debated extensively by halakhists in the twentieth century.[71] These are substances derived from an animal source which are not themselves considered to be "meat" and have been found by some halakhic authorities, after extensive processing, to have become a "novel entity," and therefore neutral. In the case of rennet extracted from the lining of a calf's stomach, there is precedent to consider the dried-out product to be "like wood."[72] Moreover, the rennet may be nullified in a volume of ingredients 60 times greater than itself.[73] Regarding gelatin, the addition of toxic chemicals like hydrochloric acid have arguably removed the substance from the status of food and turned it into a new substance.[74]

Aharon Kotler considered whether, in certain contexts, gelatin should be considered *besari* based on the principle of *aḥashveih*, ascribed status, and should not be cooked with dairy.[75] In his conclusion, however, he states that if gelatin were prepared from kosher slaughtered animals in kosher vessels, the end result would be *pareve*: "and even to use a mixing process which blends the gelatin with milk appears to me as permitted."

Still, both gelatin and rennet pass through an inedible and even a toxic stage, whereas the cells gathered from a live animal will, despite all manipulations, remain some sort of muscle cell. It is less plausible to dismiss the *besari* status of a biological structure that never departs significantly from its original state.

There is also the precedent of chymosin, a microbial enzyme originally harvested from ruminant animals, but since 1990, cultured through recombinant genetic engineering. It is employed to produce kosher cheeses; chymosin itself is considered kosher and *pareve*.[76]

Nevertheless, cultured meat is different—it is "flesh from the flesh." If the biological structure of the product and the experience of eating it is deemed identical to that of eating pastured meat, then the principle of ascribed status as meat ought to be applied.

The discussion in Bavli Ḥullin (75b, and then SA YD 13:2, 64:2 and its commentaries) of *ben pakua*, a live calf fetus collected from the carcass of a slaughtered cow, is instructive on this point; if the animal is fully formed but has never touched the ground, it may be eaten based on the mother's ritual slaughter, and its normally forbidden blood and fat could be considered permitted.[77] This establishes that the sages could conceive of a biological meat that is not, in halakhic terms, considered to be *besari* because it has never lived an independent existence as an animal.[78] Still, the moment such an animal "touches ground," it is deemed *besari*. It seems that the sages are struggling to acknowledge the unique qualities of this unusual case while nevertheless reestablishing the connection to conventional forms of eating in which meat is considered *besari*. This resonates with our case.

An additional unusual "precedent" comes from the realm of rabbinic legend rather than halakhic sources, though the boundaries between the two are not always discernible. Most articles in the Jewish press on the halakhic possibilities of cultured meat mention two Talmudic legends involving miraculous meat.[79] In B. Sanhedrin 59b, a story is told of the sage Rabbi Shimon b. Ḥalafta who, while walking on his way, was attacked by lions. He prayed for assistance, and two beasts fell from the sky. One was eaten by the lions, but Rabbi Shimon survived and was able to collect the second animal and bring it to the Beit Midrash, where he raised the question of its kashrut. The answer was: *nothing impure comes from heaven.*[80]

In another rabbinic legend at B. Sanhedrin 67a, Rabbi Ḥanina and Rabbi Oshaya were studying the mystical *Book of Creation* (Sefer Yetzirah) and magically managed to create a calf.[81,82] The Talmud itself does not seem interested in the halakhic implications of this miracle meat. Does the animal require kosher slaughter? Is its flesh even considered meat? The implication is that this meat is kosher, but is it *besari*?

Rabbi Ryzman cites the Torah commentary of Isaiah Horowitz (*Shelah*) to Genesis 37:2,[83] as well as that of Meir Leibush Weiser (*Malbim*) to Gen. 18:7 considering the story of Rabbi Ḥanina and Rabbi Oshaya (Rabbi Bleich also focuses on this text). Malbim states that meat created from the *Book of Creation* is not like meat cut from an animal, and it may be eaten with milk. This is his explanation of how

Abraham was allowed to offer meat and milk to his angelic visitors in Gen. 18—it was not natural meat, but "miracle meat." After all, the text refers mysteriously to the "calf that [Abraham] had made."[84] Rabbi Ryzman suggests that biotech's cultured meat might be comparable to the magical meat made by the Talmudic rabbis and even to Father Abraham using secrets from the *Book of Creation and* would therefore be classified as *pareve*. This is an entertaining suggestion, but it is difficult to rely on for a halakhic opinion addressing technological developments of our day that are remarkable and even astonishing— but are ultimately based on scientific methodologies. At the very least, these stories demonstrate a rabbinic openness to accepting the kashrut of unnatural methods of meat production and the possibility of *pareve* meat. Still, it is implausible to cite these stories as precedents for applied law.

Based on what we have seen above, the source of cells used to create cultured meat must be kosher, just as the animal source of eggs and milk must be kosher for the derivative products to be acceptable for kosher consumption. The original cells harvested from a kosher animal may themselves be considered *treife* meat, and forbidden to eat, even though liability for a Jew is limited to a case in which a *kezayit* of vivisectioned flesh is consumed. Moreover, we have learned that it is permitted to benefit from such cells, and we have argued that later generations of cells which were never part of the original animal should not be banned as part of its body. Likewise, because the original cells were not part of a slaughtered animal carcass, they never became "meat." In cell generations after the initial harvest, and weeks, months or years later in the lab, muscle and fat cells will be formed into a tissue culture resembling meat, but these cells will never have seen the inside of an animal and might in principle be considered *pareve*.

However, we anticipate that it would be confusing for kosher consumers to differentiate between conventional pastured meat, which is *besari* and may not be mixed with dairy products, and cultured meat, which if deemed *pareve*, could be mixed with any food. The concern of misleading impressions, *marit ayin*, could be triggered by a kosher cheeseburger. A similar concern might have convinced the ancient sages to ban placing poultry and dairy products on the same table, lest Jews become casual and end up violating the rabbinic ban on eating them together (or the biblical ban on beef with milk).[85]

Moshe Isserles discusses the use of almond milk to cook beef and poultry, raising the concern of *marit ayin*, misleading appearances, with the former, given the biblical ban on beef and milk (SA YD 87:3, Rema). He recommends placing some almonds by the dish to signal that the milk is plant-based. Commentators such as Pri Megadim (#6) argue that *marit ayin* applies even for a rabbinic ban such as on mixing poultry and milk, and recommend that almonds likewise be placed beside such a dish at large banquets in order to avoid confusion.

Still, kosher consumers have long since passed the stage of assuming that anything that looks like meat or milk is what it appears to be. We regularly eat soy or wheat-gluten based "meat" at dairy meals, and *pareve* "milk" from soy, almonds, cashews, coconuts, and other plants at meat meals. Old customs such as placing almonds on the table are no longer in practice. The task of keeping kosher now depends on kosher seals and supervisors to ascertain that there are no forbidden ingredients or mixtures of food.

A middle position is to argue that cultured beef is not "as *besari*" as traditional pastured beef, since the cells of the final product were formed outside of an animal, and there is no need for or possibility of slaughter, deveining, soaking, and salting to remove non-existent blood. And yet, because the product is, in the end, muscle and fat tissue that is designed to be indistinguishable from traditional meat, it might be considered "meat according to the rabbis," somewhat like chicken. If so, then it, too, would be forbidden to eat with dairy products, but the prohibition would be of a lower level. Likewise, on the nine initial days of Av, days when Jews are instructed not to eat beef, the ban might not apply to cultured meat.

David Lau, the Chief Ashkenazi Rabbi of Israel, discusses one company's distinct method of collecting stem cells for the purpose of producing kosher cultured meat. Fertilized cow eggs that have not yet been implanted on the uterine wall are flushed out of the womb and isolated. The plan is to use these cells to produce muscle and fat cells and to culture them in a plant-based or synthetic growth medium to culture beef. Rabbi Lau argues that this method avoids some of the concerns that I have discussed above since the cells were never attached to a live animal.[86]

Rabbi Lau believes that the resultant product is comparable to a vegetable that grows from the ground and is therefore both kosher and *pareve*. He does not explicitly address the additional question of the species of the source animal. His arguments could in theory apply equally to stem cells gathered from a pig, treating them too as comparable to a plant. Nevertheless, he concedes that *marit ayin* may apply to the preparation of cultured beef with milk and would presumably say the same about pork created from the stem cells found in a fertilized pig embryo.

We likewise conclude that cultured meat ought to be regarded as essentially kosher and *pareve*, while still avoiding mixing it with cow milk for the following reasons: 1) to maintain our practice of ruling stringently on matters of possible biblical prohibition; 2) to preserve the classical kosher separation of meat and milk; and 3) to avoid confusion between both forms of meat, so long as they are on the market. Caution would dictate that cultured meat, which is intended to be identical in both substance and style to pastured meat, should be treated as "*pareve*, meat equipment," in kashrut terms, at least until a transition has been completed in the kosher market away from conventional pastured meat.

While a purely vegetarian or even vegan diet has many benefits, and may even comprise the morally ideal diet, most humans still seek to fill at least part of their protein requirement with meat. Meat is a significant part of many cultures and cuisines, including the Judaic one, which recommends meat consumption on Shabbat and festival meals In the Talmud, Rabbi Yehudah b. Beteirah claims that while the Temple stood, there was no joyous meal without meat, though without the Temple, "joy" can still be had with wine.[87] Rambam rules that on festivals, even absent the Temple, there remains a need to eat meat to rejoice properly.[88] This should be understood as a culinary recommendation, not an absolute mandate to eat meat. Still, cultured meat, if developed as promised, has the potential to be a clean, compassionate, and healthful source of protein which could augment the values of Jewish eating within a sustainable framework.

SUMMARY

The original cells removed from a live animal as a biological source for cultured meat are themselves forbidden for consumption under the rubric of "flesh from a live animal." Normally, forbidden foods do not yield permitted foods. However, the severity of this ban is reduced for several reasons: 1) the amount of cells biopsied is below the threshold of a *kezayit* for which a Jew is liable; 2) the original cells will not persist into the final product except at a rate of "one in a trillion," and in uncertain circumstances, halakhah considers the most likely scenario; 3) the descendant cells are grown outside of the body and depend on more than one factor to multiply, rendering them permitted; 4) the new cells will have been manipulated from stem to muscle or fat cells, and may also be edited to achieve desirable mutations such that they are no longer identical to the source cells—they are arguably a new substance with new features. This final contention may be the weakest, since *davar ḥadash* remains a controversial topic in halakhah, and after all, the cells remain identifiable with their source, and have not passed through an inedible or dead state. Still, with these four reasons, we conclude that the prohibition of eating flesh taken from a live animal does not apply to the final product of cultured meat.

As for the growth medium, even if blood products that are metabolized by the tissue might be considered transformed into a neutral new substance, vegetable-based growth media are preferable for reasons of both kashrut and avoiding the need for animal slaughter. A kosher growth medium will allow for a kosher end-product.

Species identity will be retained under the principle, "what comes from the pure is pure," and because the still-active DNA may be considered a "sustaining substance." Cow cells may produce permitted cultured beef, but pig cells will produce still-forbidden cultured pork.

While it may be argued that cultured meat should be ruled *pareve*, this is a matter of doubt, given that the skeletal muscle stem cells remain edible throughout the process, unlike gelatin or rennet, which are rendered inedible. Moreover, judging cultured meat to be *pareve* would cause confusion and undermine an important aspect of kashrut practice. The concept of "ascribed value" indicates that we ought to compare cultured meat to traditional pastured meat (much as poultry was likened to beef) unless efforts to replicate the consistency and taste of meat fail. Finally, in matters of possible biblical prohibition, we rule stringently.[89] Nevertheless, cultured meat that is sustainable and morally beyond reproach may soon be available for kosher consumption.

PISKEI DIN

1) Should cultured meat become a viable consumer product, it will be important to ascertain that it derives from a kosher species of animal and that the growth medium and any additives be plant-based or synthetic and certified kosher. Indeed, the entire process will require kosher supervision.

2) Cultured meat derived from cells taken from a kosher species of animal will not be prohibited as a limb or flesh taken from a living animal, because the original cells will not be eaten, and they alone would not suffice to create the final product.

3) While cultured meat might be deemed *pareve* like eggs, because the product is designed to mimic the biological structure and eating experience of pastured meat, it would be confusing for one meat to be *besari* and another apparently identical meat to be *pareve*. If a transition is completed away from the marketing of conventional pastured meat in favor of cultured meat, then this *marit ayin* concern may be removed, just as concerns related to using almond milk with meat dishes have been eliminated.

4) If cultured meat fulfills the promises of being less cruel to animals, less destructive to the environment, and more healthful to consume, then it will be not only acceptable, but even preferable to eating conventional pastured meat.

CHAPTER 4:
THE USE OF ELECTRICAL AND ELECTRONIC DEVICES ON SHABBAT

W hen I first embarked on the path of traditional Jewish observance, I was puzzled by the mismatch between classical norms and contemporary realities. The ancient sages spoke of a world in which the production of food, shelter, and clothing occupied many hours of each week, but in our modern world, "work" refers most often to earning income through various services, many of them mediated by digital devices by the early 2000s. This shift became even more pronounced during the COVID pandemic, which accelerated the disassociation of work from established times and places. While it is often possible to extrapolate from ancient actions to contemporary technology, the translation involves the loss of values that animated the Shabbat and made it a distinctive day.

This concern cuts both ways, with surprising stringencies and leniencies made possible and even probable by the changes in both the material and social realms. To my mind, what was needed was a sustained examination of the laws of Shabbat, the values that underlay them, and finally, a determination of their application to contemporary reality. I built on the 1950s work of Conservative rabbi Arthur Neulander, and on the prolific writings of Israeli Orthodox rabbi Shlomo Zalman Auerbach.¹ Their analyses were invaluable for my consideration of the realm of electrical appliances, but today's concerns also involve electronics and the management of data. I adopted a systematic approach so that this paper could be the foundation of a curriculum on the laws of Shabbat.

My responsum was passed by the CJLS on May 31, 2012.[2] Eight years later, in the throes of the COVID-19 pandemic, the CJLS approved an emergency accommodation to allow the use of video conferencing to give Jews access to public worship on Shabbat and Yom Tov when it was unsafe to gather in person. Because the creation of temporary screen views and minor modifications such as clicking on the mute/unmute button is a rabbinic level concern, and the motivation was based on public health in a pandemic, and because these settings could be activated before Shabbat, I voted in favor of this accommodation. I recognized the dangers of isolation, and the blessings that this permission had for homebound people across the world. However, the concerns that I noted in this responsum over the recording of data, and the erosion of our special Shabbat atmosphere, remain in place. Outside such crises, it is important to affirm the value of Shabbat as a day to separate ourselves from technology and its many distractions, and to reengage face to face with people and with the divine.

In 2023, the CJLS passed two new responsa that addressed the use of electric vehicles (EVs) on Shabbat and Yom Tov. I had tried to avoid this subject back in 2012 but given the rapid growth of the EV sector of transportation, I have added a new section to my original responsum at the end of this chapter.

QUESTION:

May electrical appliances and electronic devices be used on Shabbat? If not, then why not? If so, then with what restrictions? What other halakhic values should be considered regarding the use of electricity on Shabbat? May some restrictions on the use of electricity be waived in favor of the needs of disabled or frail individuals?

RESPONSE:

> In the tempestuous ocean of time and toil there are islands of stillness where one may enter a harbor and reclaim their dignity. The island is the seventh day, the Sabbath, a day of detachment from things, instruments, and practical affairs, as well as of attachment to the spirit.
>
> Abraham Joshua Heschel, *The Sabbath*[3]

The flick of a switch. This action, so effortless and casual, is nonetheless a powerful marker of modernity. The switch completes or breaks a circuit, unleashing or suspending the flow of electrons that power every conceivable type of machine.[4] With electricity, we control our physical environment, altering the shape and structure of objects and yielding light and dark, heat and cool, sound and silence, and innumerable other environmental adaptations. Electrical motors move people and objects in every direction, enabling those with disabilities to function more fully, and all to avoid unwanted exertion.[5] Motion sensors are increasingly embedded in appliances such as public sinks, toilets, lights, and doors, and security cameras have proliferated, making it challenging to function in modern buildings[6] without an electronic transaction.[7]

We use electricity to control not only our physical reality, but also the digital information integral to contemporary life. The prevalence of batteries and wireless networks has untethered the digital device, giving us instant access to people and information to help us navigate our lives no matter where we are. Adults and older children seldom venture forth without some sort of electronic assistant. Electronic networks are tapped for transactions that once required physical acts such as entering a store and handling currency. In addition to commercial transactions, smart phones are increasingly employed to manage physical tasks, such as unlocking and heating cars and homes; the technology of near field communications has allowed phones and fobs to function as electronic keys and wallets.[8] Digital devices are replacing their analog predecessors, though print has remained popular for books.[9] Social networking programs are playing an increasing role in the establishment and maintenance of personal identity.

The pervasive use of electricity and electronics defines modern living,[10] and the integration of electronics into all aspects of life has been accelerating. Wearable technology has become commonplace and biometric data is automatically monitored and shared by many users. Speech recognition has improved to the point that buttons and key clicks are no longer necessary to control our machines, or for them to prompt us to modify our own behavior. The line between people and machines grows thinner and harder to delineate.

Using electronics makes us powerful, yet there is a cost to being permanently networked. Our digital servants tend to become tyrants, and it is nearly impossible to escape their reach. Instant access leads to the loss of privacy and the erosion of social intimacy.[11] Work that used to end when we left the office now follows us out the door, down the street, and into our homes. Even on vacation, it is common to see people with laptops and smart phones, busily keeping up with their demanding tasks. Simple pleasures such as sitting with family and friends over an undisturbed meal, reading in a quiet room, and taking a leisurely stroll, have become rare in our culture. We need a break, and Shabbat is here to help us, even as it helped earlier generations rest from the physically intensive tasks that typified their work.

As we will see, Shabbat fosters a different state of consciousness through its detailed regulation of human behavior. Each action is analyzed through two lenses: Is it *melakhah* ("transformative labor"), the type of work prohibited by halakhah? And does it undermine *shvut*, the positive obligation to rest on Shabbat? In this book, I examine these questions to reach conclusions grounded in tradition and reflecting the realities of contemporary technology and culture.

Why is this necessary? Why can't everyone simply rest when and how they like? Of course, they may; Jewish practice today is voluntary, at least for most Jews. This chapter, like many contemporary presentations of halakhah, is an effort to explain the meaning and the benefits of normative observance in addition to clarifying the technical legal aspects of the matter. What differentiates Shabbat from an ordinary vacation is that it is a communal and sacred enterprise. When Shabbat is observed as a day of intentional rest, it allows community to emerge. When Shabbat is sanctified, then our resting becomes something more than relaxation; it becomes an act of devotion, highlighting those values and relationships that have ultimate significance. Many Jews suffer from a lack of Shabbat and a consequent loss of purposeful community. Studying and reclaiming these sacred traditions is an essential step to rebuilding a meaningful and hardy Jewish life.

Once a week, many Shabbat-observant people already power down their devices and choose to abstain from their use for the duration.[12] To be more precise, they avoid *directly operating* electrical devices on Shabbat, but nearly all continue to benefit from the lights, refrigerators, thermostats, clocks, and countless other devices that carry on their assigned tasks. Shabbat law applies not only to Jews but to an extent also to non-Jewish employees.[13] It applies even to work animals owned by Jews, but not to appliances—so long as they are left to function on their own.[14] Sometimes these devices are programmed before Shabbat with timers to heat, elevate, illumine, and darken at appointed times, thereby giving many of the benefits of electrical use even while avoiding the direct performance of forbidden labor on Shabbat.[15]

For many Shabbat observers, the manual flick of an electrical switch is tantamount to *ḥillul Shabbat*, the desecration of Shabbat—such a profound transgression that it was considered a capital offense (Exod. 31:14), although Judaism has not practiced the death penalty for two millennia.[16] The identification as a *shomer Shabbat*—a Sabbath observer—is in many circles associated with rendering electrical switches inaccessible or inoperative before sundown on Friday, and in the setting of timers to adjust lights and other appliances as necessary until nightfall on Saturday.

Maintaining a comprehensive ban on the direct operation of electrical and electronic devices on Shabbat is a policy with many advantages. It is relatively simple to explain and to enforce—even a toddler can be trained to avoid operating electronics on Shabbat. Forbidding even arguably permissible actions may be considered a *s'yag la-Torah*, a "fence around the Torah," preventing people from inadvertent performance of truly forbidden activities. And the result of a comprehensive "electric-free Sabbath" is to create a day that is dramatically different from the rest of the week. Moreover, the motivations for not using electricity on Shabbat go well beyond the formal requirements of the law. Some young adults have published a "Sabbath Manifesto" promoting a weekly 24-hour respite from technology,[17] though not necessarily within the bounds of the Jewish Sabbath, and many people cherish vacations from their digital devices.[18] Finally, reducing the use of electricity once a week can help train people to consume less power overall, and thus mitigate the harmful impact of our consumption habits on the environment.

Nevertheless, other Shabbat-observant Jews make distinctions between electrical appliances whose operation they find to be permitted and those which they deem prohibited. Such people claim that it is possible to avoid forbidden activities and to achieve the necessary state of tranquility on Shabbat, even while making limited use of electricity.[19] For example, dozens of Orthodox rabbis endorsed a special light switch designed to avoid forbidden labor, promoted under the slogan, "Control Electricity on Shabbos!"[20] The Zomet institute in Israel has justified specially designed public telephones[21] and computer keyboards[22] to allow Shabbat observers to gain access to data without violating the laws of Shabbat.

Some may shun the use of electricity unless it is indicated by another Jewish value, such as assisting people who are ill, frail, or disabled; performing necessary military services; avoiding great exertion and waste on Shabbat; or preventing animal suffering.[23] Since many Shabbat observers leave unused appliances such as lights, air conditioners, and elevators running all day, the refusal to adjust appliances according to need is not necessarily a green solution.

This subject is complicated, requiring sustained study of the issues and vigilance in practice. Not every action that is permitted should be recommended. The extensive use of timers and specially adapted appliances can easily undermine the distinctive atmosphere of Shabbat. Yet in some cases, the trade-off in Jewish values may be justified. This subject is complex but being *shomer Shabbat* has always required study of the laws of Shabbat, and simplicity itself is not a halakhic goal. Just as there are detailed regulations about how, for example, one may re-heat food on Shabbat without transgressing the ban on cooking or use house keys without violating the ban on carrying, so, too, is it possible to develop careful policies about what electrical appliances may be used without violating the laws of Shabbat.

Whether one adopts a comprehensive ban or a partial permission, it is worthwhile to study the halakhic issues involved in operating electronics on Shabbat. The purpose of this responsum is to examine the salient issues and give guidance to people who wish to observe the traditional Sabbath rules while also guarding Jewish values such as protecting the dignity of people who are frail or have physical disabilities, the preservation of the environment, and the joy of Shabbat. Instead of presenting a narrow discussion of one particular action, we have chosen to begin with a broad review of Shabbat laws. This survey will allow our specific findings to be judged within their broader context and will also provide our community with a better sense of this important area of Jewish law. Because the use of electricity has come to permeate nearly every aspect of contemporary life, and because prior halakhic studies of the use of electricity have generated considerable ambiguity on core concepts, it is not possible to issue a simple and terse ruling. This project has become extensive, yet it, too, will require expansion and revision as the technology continues to develop.

Our discussion begins in Section I with a technical analysis of *melakhah*, the form of creative work prohibited on Shabbat. Some actions are considered *assur de-oraita*, forbidden by the rabbis' understanding of the biblical prohibition, and call for severe punishment in the classical literature. Other actions are considered *patur aval assur*, exempt from full liability, but still banned by the rabbis' own authority. Finally, some actions are considered *mutar l'khathilah*, permissible from the outset.[24] We will discuss various actions involving electricity and seek to clarify to what extent the categories of *melakhah* are involved.

Yet our subject is not limited to determining whether operating a given electrical appliance is physically comparable to the work traditionally prohibited on Shabbat. Another category known as *shvut*, or "rest," is designed to protect the special atmosphere of Shabbat and to safeguard the observant from unwitting transgression. But what is *shvut*, and how should it be defined in contemporary life? This is the focus of Section II, involving the exploration of rabbinic values specific to Shabbat and Yom Tov, such as *tirhah yetirah*, avoiding excessive exertion; *uvdah de-hol*, distinguishing Shabbat from workdays; and *muktzeh*, keeping a protective distance from the performance of forbidden labor.

The observance of Shabbat does not occur in a vacuum devoid of other halakhic values. Section III explores the interaction between such values, some of which reinforce a ban on using electricity, while others would rather mandate its use in certain situations. In it, I consider a representative sample of electronic devices which may be helpful to frail and disabled individuals who are mindful of the laws of Shabbat. Finally, in Section IV, I summarize my conclusions, indicating which actions involve *melakhah*, and are thus forbidden unless needed to safeguard health; which actions involve considerations of *shvut*, and are thus forbidden unless overridden by competing Jewish values; and which are to be considered permitted. An appendix applies these findings to a representative sample of electrical and electronic appliances and applications. We begin now with a technical discussion of the definition of *melakhah* before considering its relevance for the use of electricity.

I

MELAKHAH:

THE PROHIBITION AGAINST TRANSFORMATIVE LABOR

Defining Melakhah: Biblical Sources

The primary halakhic vocabulary used to regulate Shabbat is that of *melakhah*, transformative labor. The Torah emphatically prohibits all *melakhah* on pain of death (Exodus 31:14) but is vague about the definition of such activity. What is this *melakhah*? In the Torah, God commands Israel not to burn fire in all of its habitations (Exod. 35:3), to stone to death a man who gathers firewood (Num. 15:32-35), and not to plow or harvest in the field (Exod. 34:21).[25] Jeremiah adds a ban on carrying from one domain to another (Jer.17:21-22),[26] and Nehemiah admonishes the men of Judah for treading on winepresses and loading wares on Shabbat (Neh. 13:15-18).[27] Jeffrey Tigay observes that a ban on cooking is implicit in the Exodus manna narrative.[28] Baruch Schwartz reviews the treatment of Shabbat in the Torah's four documentary traditions, arguing that each source is distinctive and consistent in its presentation of the purpose of the seventh day.[29]

Nevertheless, it is unclear from the biblical texts how many discrete actions are cumulatively included in the melakhah prohibition, and how these activities are to be differentiated from other, permitted behaviors. Ancient Jewish writings such as the Book of Jubilees and the Dead Sea sect's Damascus Document include distinctive lists of prohibited Sabbath labors,[30] but these are not in accord with the (generally more lenient) standards later adopted by the rabbis,[31] nor do they clarify the theoretical framework of the ban on melakhah.

While the Torah repeatedly bans melakhah in the strongest of terms, it does not provide an abstract description of the nature of melakhah which could fill the void left by its sparse list of banned activities. Still, we may extrapolate some of the meaning of the term from other contexts in which melakhah is mentioned. The term melakhah is employed in reference to God's creation of the cosmos (Gen. 2:2-3) and to Israel's construction of the tabernacle (Exod. ch. 36). These associations imply that there is something creative about melakhah—it is the language of creation both for God and for people.[32] In desisting from creative labor on Shabbat, even the labor of tabernacle construction, the Israelite identifies with both the active and the resting states of God. The type of creativity discussed here is one in which material reality is transformed, rather than the artistic creativity of song, speech, and other expressions of emotion and ideas. In fact, the cessation of physical creativity functions as a catalyst for spiritual creativity on Shabbat, as it says, shavat va'yinafash, God "ceased from work and was refreshed" (Exod. 31:17).[33] Rabbi Shimon ben Lakish taught that the cessation of physical labor and all of its frustrations leads to the gift of *neshama yeteirah*, an "additional soul" on Shabbat.[34] The seventh day has long functioned as an incubator for the most spiritually creative and productive insights of the week.

The importance of Shabbat is indicated by the fact that it is the only ritual practice included within the Decalogue. In the Exodus version, the command to desist from *melakhah* is explained as a reminder of how God desisted from *melakhah* on the seventh day (Exod. 20:7-10).[35] Yet in the second rendition, Shabbat is said to be a reminder of Israel's liberation from slavery (Deut. 5:14). Curiously, the Torah does not spell out precisely how observing Shabbat is reminiscent of the exodus from Egypt. Perhaps it is because slaves are not permitted to rest, and so Shabbat reminds Israelites that they were once enslaved and were rescued by the Lord. The point of resting is thus to inspire gratitude to God for our freedom. This explanation is supported by Rabbi Avraham ibn Ezra in his comments to Deuteronomy 5:14, "Some say that [it is because] the slave may not rest. Behold, the Lord took you out of slavery and commanded you to rest so that you would remember that you were a slave."

Yet, this explanation is rejected by Ramban, for whom Shabbat functions purely as a reminder of God's creation; the Exodus from Egypt is yet another demonstration of God's renewal of creation, *ḥiddush ha-olam*. Sabbath rest therefore reminds us of God's creative power, not of our improved circumstances.

Bernard Goldstein and Alan Cooper suggest that Deuteronomy's version of the Decalogue originally included *ḥag ha-matzot*—the Passover holiday—as the fourth commandment, since Shabbat was not significant to the Northern tradition; later priestly editing in Judea substituted Shabbat but incongruously left the motive-clause regarding the exodus in place.[36] In any event, the two associations of Shabbat with the creation and the exodus were combined by the sages in the *kiddush* prayer for Friday night. The command not to work thus reminds Israel of the Lord's great gifts of life and liberty.[37]

A different (and perhaps primary) motivation for the Sabbath laws is implicit in the narrative regarding the manna in Exodus 16:22-30, where the Israelites are instructed to collect a double portion on the sixth day so that they might rest from gathering food on the seventh day. This narrative precedes the prohibition against Sabbath labor, which is first mentioned in Exodus 20:7. The statement in 16:30 that "the people rested on the seventh day" is a unique claim in the Torah.[38] The purpose of Shabbat here seems to be an amplification of the lesson of manna—to foster a sense of trust in God's reliability as a provider for the people's physical sustenance. Shabbat is called a sign between God and Israel (Exod. 31:13, 17), apparently because the Lord and His people share the experience of working during the week and resting on Shabbat. According to Moshe Greenberg, it is this shared experience of resting from manna production and collection that Israel is commanded to "remember" in the Decalogue (Exod. 20:7).

Stephen Geller argues that Exodus chapter 16 contains two distinct traditions about the manna and Shabbat, one covenantal, and the second cultic or priestly.[39] The covenantal tradition views both the manna and the Sabbath as examples of God testing Israel's obedience. Despite the warnings about not hoarding manna from day to day, and not going out to collect it on the Sabbath, some Israelites persist in this behavior, drawing rebuke from Moses and God. The point of Shabbat rest in this perspective is for the Israelites to accept divine sovereignty. The second and more extensive perspective is priestly in nature. The daily gift of manna is a reenactment of the creation narrative in Genesis 1, and the double portion of manna on the sixth day recalls the emphatic pronouncement that the creation was "very good." The command to rest from collecting manna on Shabbat is an Israelite imitation of God's desistence from the work of creation on the seventh day—the divine act of separation between ordinary and sacred times. Geller writes, "Observant humanity makes each Sabbath a shared act of creation with God." This priestly perspective also connects the Sabbath to a later mechanism of divine-human partnership, the tabernacle.

The command not to perform *melakhah* on Shabbat is repeated just before the section detailing the command to build the tabernacle (Exod. 35:1-3). The rabbis understand this juxtaposition to indicate the primacy of Shabbat over the tabernacle project,[40] and to limit the scope of *melakhah* forbidden on Shabbat to those acts involved in building the tabernacle. In Bavli Ḥagigah 10b, the rabbis explain that *melakhah* is categorically limited to intentional labor, *melekhet maḥshevet*, actions intended for the same purpose as their equivalent activities in the tabernacle.[41]

Modern Bible scholars have observed that the institution of Shabbat rose in prominence following the destruction of the first temple in 586 BCE and came to symbolize the entire covenant at that time.[42] Whereas the festivals required a physical center for full ritual observance, the Sabbath could be observed anywhere, including in exile. Moreover, as Michael Fishbane has written, post-exilic ideology "saw in the desecration of the Sabbath the principal reason for Judea's destruction, and, correspondingly, believed its reconsecration to be vital."[43]

Defining Melakhah: Rabbinic Sources

The association of Shabbat with the great biblical narratives of the creation, exodus, tabernacle, exile, and restoration lends extraordinary significance to *melakhah* but does not define it with legal precision. What is *melakhah*? The biblical materials alone do not suffice to explain how, exactly, one might observe the day of rest. Into the void steps Mishnah Shabbat (7:2), proclaiming a list of "forty less one"[44] primary categories of *avot melakhot* (forbidden labor):

Principal occupations are forty less one: to sow, to plough, to mow, to gather into sheaves, to thrash, to winnow, to sift [grain], to grind, to sieve, to knead, to bake, to shear wool, to wash wool, to card, to dye, to spin, to warp, to shoot two threads, to weave two threads, to cut and tie two threads, to tie, to untie, to sew two stitches, to tear thread with intent to sew two stitches, to catch a stag [game], to slaughter it, to skin, to salt [cure] a hide, to singe a hide, to tan, to cut up a skin, to write two letters, to erase with intent to write two letters, to build, to demolish, to extinguish fire, to kindle fire, to hammer, to carry [or convey] from one *reshuth* [domain] into another. Thus, these principal occupations are forty less one.[45]

This list may be broken into five functions. Labors 1-11: the production of bread; labors 12-24: the production of clothing; labors 25-33: hunting and preparing hides as parchment for writing; labors 34-38: the construction of tools and shelter; and labor 39: the transportation of goods. We may summarize the list by stating that the rabbinic understanding of *melakhah* regards *the transformation of material reality to serve the needs of civilized people for food, clothing, writing, shelter, and tools.*[46]

Labors that leave no durable impact on the material environment are not considered to be forbidden as *melakhah*. As Mishnah Shabbat 12:1 declares, "this is the rule: anyone who performs work, and his work is stable (or endures) on the Sabbath[47] is culpable." This general principle is stated in a Mishnah which functions as a header to the second half of the tractate and its discussion of the first 38 labors.

The immediate focus of this Mishnah is on the cluster of building activities, but the principle of "durable impact" relates to other clusters as well. For example, tying a knot is the 21st archetype of labor, but the rabbis limited this ban to "permanent" knots intended to last for at least 24 hours. A professional knot used to secure a camel's bridle, which is forbidden, is in this way distinguished from tying a shoelace, which is allowed. Durability is the focus of the sections dealing with writing[48] and is implicit in the later ruling about cooking that from a halakhic perspective, a substance may be cooked only once.[49] Rabbi Vidal di Tolosa states in Maggid Mishnah, his commentary to Rambam's Mishneh Torah, that, "all Sabbath labors require a durable result."[50]

The one *melakhah* that appears to be an exception to this rule is the final one, "and one who carries from domain to domain" since the change in location does not necessarily alter the object itself. Indeed, this category is viewed as a *non sequitur* in the list of the *melakhot*, as Avraham Goldberg discusses in his commentary to Mishnah Shabbat, and this may account for the Bavli and Yerushalmi's attempts to base it separately on verses in the Torah[51] and the overwhelming attention to carrying in Mishnah Shabbat (which occupies the first half of the tractate). It may be that the transportation of tools is considered essential to the building process described in the prior set of categories, or that once an item is completed, it is then carried for use. Only when the object has been used is the labor of construction deemed complete. In any event, transporting goods from domain to domain is ultimately a transformation of material reality and conforms to our general understanding of *melakhah*.

It is not evident how the early rabbis of the Talmud (Tannaim, 70-200 CE) transitioned from the Torah's rather vague prohibition against *melakhah* to the detailed list in Mishnah Shabbat 7:2. In Bavli Shabbat 49b, the later rabbis (Amoraim, 200-450 CE) discuss this subject among themselves as an apparently unsettled question: "That Mishnah which lists forty minus one *melakhot*—what is its basis?" Rabbi Ḥanina bar Ḥama asserts that the Mishnah's list is in accord with the tabernacle labors; other theories indicate that the Torah supplied the quantity but not the identity of the labors. One claims that 39 is the number of references to the word *melakhah* (in three forms) in the entire Torah; at B. Shabbat 49b, the rabbis struggle to identify which instances should be included on the list. Elsewhere in the Bavli[52] and in the Yerushalmi,[53] the rabbis derive the number 39 from plays on the *gematria* (numerical value) of the words *eleh ha-devarim* in Exodus 35:1.[54]

These theories may address the quantity of categories, but not their specific identities. Are the 39 categories an accurate and exhaustive list of the tasks of tabernacle construction? Where does the Torah mention or at least imply activities such as those described by the rabbis? After all, the most extensive description of the tabernacle construction comes in Exodus chapters 36-39, where the dominant verb is simply, *vaya'as*, "he made." The physical actions involved in this making are left largely to the imagination. From a logical perspective, how could desert nomads have performed extensive agricultural tasks such as plowing, sowing, and harvesting, especially during the few months between the exodus and the building of the tabernacle?[55] Given the Torah's description of the tabernacle labors, why are so many of the rabbis' *avot melakhot* focused on food and cloth production, and so few on carpentry and metalwork? For example, why did the Mishnah identify *ofeh*, baking, as the banned archetype, whereas the Amoraim considered it to be a mere subcategory of *bishul*, seething, an activity said to have been performed to boil the dyes for the tabernacle coverings?

Notwithstanding such basic questions, the view that the banned Sabbath labors were derived from the tabernacle labors came to dominate rabbinic thought. The Yerushalmi states, "All the principal categories of labor were learned from the tabernacle."[56] Bavli Shabbat 49b states that any labor not performed in the tabernacle cannot be considered to be one of the archetypes.[57] Indeed, the Torah itself links Shabbat to the tabernacle with the expression, "Guard My Sabbaths and revere My sanctuary; I am the Lord" (Lev. 19:30 and 26:2).

We may think of the Sabbath as a mirror image of the tabernacle: the tabernacle is built through 39 discrete actions; the Sabbath is "built" through 39 discrete inactions. While the Sabbath appears to be less substantial than the tabernacle, it is the Sabbath that has endured as a permanent structure of Jewish life, whereas the tabernacle has receded into mythic memory.

The rabbis wax eloquent in their praise of Shabbat, saying that guarding Shabbat is the equivalent of keeping all mitzvot in the Torah, and that if Israel would only guard the Sabbath properly, the messiah would promptly arrive.[58] Later mystical authors go further, seeing proper Sabbath observance as instrumental in maintaining cosmic harmony.[59] This extraordinary praise of Shabbat should give pause to our desire to expand the use of tools, whether mechanical or electronic, on a day whose most valuable feature may be its enforced break from *melakhah*, physical creativity—labor that transforms.

PRIMARY AND DERIVATIVE LABORS:

Although the *melakhot* were initially limited to a list of 39, many other activities were banned by association. One of the many complicated questions in the laws of Shabbat is the relationship between the primary categories (*avot*) and their derivatives (*toledot*). In the Talmud Yerushalmi, we read that Rabbi Yoḥanan and Rabbi Shimon ben Lakish studied the topic of the primary and derivative labors for three-and-a-half-years and produced a list of 39 *toledot* for each of the 39 *avot!*[60] Joel Roth and Yitzḥak Gilat have each produced detailed studies of this subject.[61]

Shabbat is not the only halakhic topic in which the terms *avot* and *toledot* appear—they are found also in the definition of damages (*nezikin*)[62] and of the sources of ritual impurity (*tuma'ah*).[63] In the latter usage, derivative sources of ritual impurity have diminished severity, but regarding both damages and Shabbat labor, derivative acts have legal consequences equal to those of the primary categories.[64]

Derivative Shabbat prohibitions are said to resemble the primary categories in their physical function, purpose, or result.[65] One example of a *toledah* is watering plants; this is forbidden as a derivative of the primary category of *zore'ah* (sowing seeds). Both activities have the purpose of making a plant grow in the soil, but the mechanisms are physically distinct. Thus, watering is not banned as a form of sowing, but rather, is a derivative labor sharing the same goal of causing plants to grow. *Avot* and *toledot* are further differentiated by the fact that the primary categories generally appear on the list of Mishnah Shabbat 7:2, whereas derivatives include forms of labor absent from the list but comparable to its categories.[66] Primary categories are also said to have been "important" to the work of building the tabernacle, which was not the case for the derivatives.[67] In the classical setting, the major purpose of differentiating primary and derivative Sabbath labors was to determine how many sacrifices of purification (*korban ḥattat*) were necessary to restore an unwitting transgressor to good standing before God.

For our purpose, it is immaterial whether a *melakhah* said to be involved in the use of electricity is from a primary or derivative category; all are equally forbidden. Nor are we immediately concerned with the quantity of sacrifices required in the ancient Temple. However, we will see that the *av/toledah* relationship is essential when considering whether a *melakhah* such as cooking or writing, when performed in a completely distinct process (such as using a microwave oven or committing written words to digital memory), should be forbidden as a derivative form of the primary prohibition. If the *pe'ulah* (physical mechanism) is different from that of the primary prohibition, but the *takhlit* (purpose and result) are identical, then an activity is considered forbidden as a *toledah* or derivative of the primary category. If the mechanism, purpose, and result are different, then the activity under consideration would not be forbidden as *melakhah*, though it might still be inconsistent with the command to rest on Shabbat.

INTENTIONAL LABOR

In Mishnah Ḥagigah 1:8, the rabbis declare that "the laws of Shabbat ... are like mountains suspended by a hair, for they have few verses, but many laws."[68] Given the large number of references to Shabbat across the Hebrew Bible, the significance of this claim is unclear. In the Bavli (Ḥagigah 10b), the rabbis clarify the Mishnah's puzzling statement by saying that while there are, in fact, many verses about Shabbat in the Bible, the matter of intentional labor is not explained in the text, but must be inferred.[69] Indeed, the question of intention is essential to the rabbis' determination of whether any given action is considered to have violated an established prohibition.

The great significance granted to intention indicates that the Sabbath rules as developed by the rabbis are concerned not merely with external reality, but also with the internal experience of the Sabbath observer. Indeed, Mishnah Shabbat 7:2 is set within a larger chapter named for its first Mishnah, whose subject is the psychological context of Sabbath transgressions. Stephen Wald writes in his commentary to Bavli Shabbat that the "root idea" of the chapter is "that one is not liable for the number of transgressions performed but rather for the number of errors which caused the transgressions. This root idea moves the focus of our attention from the concrete and objective plane to the more abstract and subjective plane of discourse."[70] Understanding both the physical and psychological impact of each activity involving electricity on Shabbat will likewise be essential to our project.

There are four categories of intention significant to *hilkhot Shabbat* (the laws of Shabbat):

A) UNINTENDED AND UNANTICIPATED MELAKHAH: DAVAR SHE-AINO MITKAVEIN.

If a person performs a permitted act on Shabbat knowing

that it is *possible* but not inevitable that a *melakhah* might result from their activity, such action is permitted despite the unintended consequence. The classic examples are dragging a chair on a dirt floor, which could cause a rut, but is not considered to be "plowing," and walking across a lawn, which could uproot some grass, but is not considered "harvesting."

B) UNAVOIDABLE MELAKHAH: PESIK REISHEI VE-LO YAMUT.

If a person performs an action on Shabbat for a permitted purpose but knows that it is inevitable that a beneficial *melakhah* will result from the activity, such action is deemed by the rabbis to be forbidden by biblical law as an unavoidable and beneficial consequence.[71] This category's name comes from its classic example—a man wants to give a child a chicken head to play with (!) on Shabbat (as "playing" is a permitted activity); he cuts off the head, not intending to kill the chicken per se, but, "if you cut off its head, will it not die?"[72]

C) UNAVOIDABLE AND UNDESIRABLE MELAKHAH: PESIK REISHEI VE-LA NIHA LEI.

If a person intends to perform a permitted act on Shabbat knowing that it is *inevitable* that a *melakhah* will result from the activity, except that he will receive no benefit from this result (and may suffer a loss), many authorities permit the action, though some Ashkenazi *poskim* rule stringently.[73]

D) INTENTIONAL ACT, BUT FOR A DIFFERENT PURPOSE: MELAKHAH SHE-AINAH TRZRIKHAH LE-GUFAH.

Finally, if a person intentionally performs a *melakhah* on Shabbat, but for a permitted purpose unrelated to its forbidden result, this is the subject of debate. In the Talmud, Rabbi Shimon considers such an act to be permitted, whereas Rabbi Yehudah forbids it. Later authorities mostly side with Rabbi Shimon's leniency, ruling that such an action is not banned by the Torah, but they nevertheless ban it by force of rabbinic decree.[74] The classic citation is Bavli Shabbat 73b, though there are other references to the debate throughout the tractate and other volumes. This case refers to a man who digs a hole on Shabbat, which is normally forbidden as either the *melakhah* of *ḥofeir* ("digging") or *boneh* ("building") depending on whether the hole is inside or outside of the home. In this case, however, this man's interest is not in producing a hole, but rather in gathering some dirt. Rabbi Shimon permits the act, whereas Rabbi Yehudah forbids it—almost. In the end, even Rabbi Yehudah permits it, because in this case, the act of digging is considered destructive (*kilkul*), since it leaves an unhelpful and even hazardous hole in the field or floor. While the majority view is that such *melakhah* does not violate the biblical ban, the rabbis prohibit it of their own authority.

The question of intention is significant when considering the *melakhot* possibly involved in using electricity. For example, some electrical switches may create an arc of flame when flipped. It is forbidden to light a fire (*mavir*) but in this case, the creation of sparks is not *inevitable* and is not the actor's *intention* and is generally not even *observed*.[75] Causing such sparks would therefore be considered only a *possible* consequence of the act, and certainly not one which benefits the actor. Thus, we would deem their creation to be permitted as *davar she-aino mitkavein*, "unintended and unanticipated."[76]

To summarize this introductory discussion, to establish that a given action is *biblically prohibited* as *melakhah*, one must show that the act is physically comparable or has comparable intentions and results to one of the primary categories (*avot*) or its derivations (*toledot*). Absent such results and intentions, the act may still be forbidden by authority of the rabbis but will not be considered biblically prohibited. Rabbinic prohibitions are generally binding, but they bear lesser penalties and may be superseded by competing halakhic values, as we will see in Section III. We now consider various categories of *melakhah* and their applicability to the operation of electrical appliances and electronic devices.

Categories of Melakhah Most Relevant to the Use of Electricity[77]

From the outset of this discussion, we should note that there are many established forms of *melakhah* that are performed through the operation of various electrical appliances. From sowing seed to transporting produce, all thirty-nine categories of labor might be performed with electrical assistance, and all would be banned under the same rubric as if done without electricity. Here, the prohibition is in the activity itself, whereas the use of electricity to facilitate the labor is of secondary importance. One may not claim that they did not intend, for example, to trim shrubs, but merely pushed the button that operated the motor of the power trimmer.[78] If one's action is intended to result in a *melakhah*, then one is liable for that *melakhah* on Shabbat or Yom Tov, whether the tool was manual or powered. We cannot list every type of appliance, but the following brief list should alert the Sabbath observer to the types of labors to consider with some household appliances used to perform them:

Kotzeir (pruning) – electric trimmer or lawn mower

Toḥein (grinding) – electric coffee grinder or pepper mill

Lash ve-ofeh (kneading and baking) – electric bread maker

Gozeiz (shearing) – electric shaver

Tofeir (sewing) – sewing machine

Koteiv (writing) – using an electric typewriter or printer to apply ink to paper

Any labor that is forbidden manually is also forbidden with electrical assistance, since the physical mechanism of labor is either similar or identical, and the intention and product of the manual and power-assisted actions are identical. Moreover, the Sages do not maintain unsustainable distinctions (*lo plug rabbanan*).[79]

Most electrical appliances and electronic devices, however, do not involve the direct performance of established *melakhot* with the same physical mechanism as their manual predecessors. Is the use of electricity inherently problematic, as implied by the blanket prohibition on the use of electricity by many Shabbat observers? If so, then why? The following *avot melakhot* have been frequently mentioned as *general* objections to the operation of electrical circuits:

Molid, "Making New"

When a live circuit is closed, electrical current is caused to flow into an appliance, generally with desired results (sometimes, of course, the results are negative). One 19th century rabbi, Yitzhak Schmelkis,[80] argued that this action could be compared to a case discussed in the Talmud (B. Beitzah 23a) in which a cup of perfume was spilled onto a piece of ceramic or a garment to infuse it with fragrance.[81] This action was rabbinically forbidden because the absorbing agent was permanently transformed by the infusion. So too, argued Rabbi Schmelkis, should the operation of all electrical appliances be rabbinically banned on Shabbat as a form of *molid*, because the appliance absorbs the current and is transformed by the change.

If this comparison were accepted, then the closing of any electrical circuit would be rabbinically banned, regardless of the function of the device itself. However, prominent 20th century halakhic authorities such as Shlomo Zalman Auerbach[82] and Eliezer Waldenberg[83] rebutted this argument. *Molid reiha* is not used in halakhah as a source from which to extrapolate other prohibitions. Even within the case of transferring fragrance, the rabbis banned only perfuming clothes, presumably because this was a permanent (or at least durable) transformation. In contrast, electrical appliances are constantly being turned on and off; introducing current does not make them "new" or render a durable transformation.[84] Perhaps the *initial use* of an appliance which had never been previously tested could sustain this argument,[85] but *molid* makes little sense when applied to the ordinary use of electrical appliances.

Boneh, "Building"

A more influential argument for the prohibition of operating all electrical appliances was advanced by the Tel Aviv-based rabbi Avrohom Isaiah Karelitz, generally known for his book of responsa, *Hazon Ish*.[86] He argues that closing an electrical circuit may be compared to the primary category of labor called building, noting that in the Talmud, the ban on Sabbath "building" is applied even to the assembly of pre-existing parts (like sections of a pole that were attached for use in whitewashing walls).[87] So too, according to Rabbi Karelitz, should the introduction of electrical current into an appliance be banned as a form of construction. The category of building is linked to its opposite: *soteir* ("breaking"). It is forbidden to break something down, though this ban is generally limited to cases where the intention is to prepare the site or materials for new construction, rather than just breaking something for the sake of disposal (*kilkul*). Turning off an appliance would, according to the Ḥazon Ish's reasoning, be forbidden as "breaking" it down to prepare it to be "built" again.

While Rabbi Karelitz's position banning the operation of electrical appliances based on *boneh* has received more support than has the ban based on *molid*, it too has been refuted, most vigorously by Rabbi Auerbach. He argues that opening and closing a circuit is comparable to opening and closing a door or window and is unlike building a wall. When we close a door, we don't consider that we have built a wall, nor do we say that we have destroyed a building when we open the door. Thus, closing a circuit is not properly considered to be building, nor is opening a circuit considered to be breaking down. Doors and windows are designed to be opened and closed constantly, and so, too, are electrical circuits.

On a technical level, appliances that operate with alternating current are constantly cycling on and off. If so, then turning off an AC appliance can be viewed as merely preventing it from cycling on or off again—even more reason to refute this line of prohibition. Battery-powered electronic devices that have no moving switches and are not connected to a power grid are even more resistant to this argument. Rabbi Auerbach's critique of the Ḥazon Ish's reasoning has been accepted by many authorities.[88] Rabbi Auerbach's arguments are convincing for electrical appliances and even more so for electronic devices that have no moving parts.

Makeh B'fatish, "Completing Labor"

Rabbi Karelitz mentions another category of *melakhah* in connection to closing an electrical circuit. *Makeh b'fatish*, literally, "the final hammer blow," refers to completing a type of building. This is a broader category than *boneh*, which generally is limited to actions involving hard construction materials used to create an object, whereas *makeh b'fatish* can also refer to building with pliable materials like cloth. In Mishnah Shabbat 12:1, this category is included in the general principle mentioned above, "this is the rule: anyone who performs work, and his work is stable (or endures) on the Sabbath, is culpable." The Gemara adds in the name of Rabba and Rabbi Zeira that any action which completes labor (*gemar melakhah*) is also deemed *makeh b'fatish*.[89]

Rashi explains the source activity as the final step in chiseling a square of stone out of a cliff and states that any other construction technique that requires a final blow is considered a derivative of *makeh b'fatish*.[90] The Tosafist Rabbi Yitzhak questions whether stone-carving was a tabernacle labor, and explains that the expression refers to the final hammer blow for creating a utensil.[91] Rambam applies this category to the final stage of creating utensils of glass, ceramic, and metal.[92] The Talmud Yerushalmi cited above (which claims that Rabbi Yoḥanan and Rabbi Shimon ben Lakish identified 39 derivatives corresponding to each primary category of labor) also states that whatever they couldn't identify, they called a derivative of *makeh b'fatish*.[93]

This category thus has broad application, but can it be applied to the normal operation of electrical appliances? The same objections summoned above may be applied here: electrical circuits are designed to open and close constantly. Turning on an appliance is no more the "completion" of its construction than is twisting a doorknob or shutting a window. *Makeh b'fatish* refers to the permanent completion of a labor, as in the case of a hammer splitting rock or driving a nail into a wood plank. Perhaps soldering electrical wire to a circuit board could qualify as this type of labor, but it is implausible that it applies to daily operations. As mentioned above, AC appliances are constantly cycling between states; solid state electronics have no moving parts. This category, then, is not convincing as a catch-all prohibition against using electrical appliances on Shabbat (but see further discussion below).

Mitakein Mana, "Preparing a Utensil"

This term falls under the prior one, but it is often listed separately. Eliezer Waldenberg argues that closing an electrical circuit to allow for the operation of an electrical appliance is forbidden as "preparing a utensil," citing the precedent of winding a watch, which had been forbidden by several early modern authorities.[94] As with the previous two arguments, this one comes down to whether one considers an electrical appliance, in Rabbi Waldenberg's words, to be "dead" without electricity and "alive" with it, and whether its operation should be considered a type of construction.

Our opinion remains that electrical appliances are prepared at the time of their assembly. Adding current allows them to function, just as causing water to run through a tap or toilet allows those appliances to function, but we do not consider these normal operations to be acts of creation that cause durable change. Rather, they are mechanical manipulations akin to dozens of other activities done by Sabbath observers such as opening doors, cabinets, and windows. Increasingly, modern appliances and electronics do not truly turn on and off, but merely switch from "standby" to "active" mode. Activating an electrical appliance is not to be viewed as a form of construction.

That said, this category of *mitakein mana* does plausibly fit into the category of actions that involve assembling an appliance—connecting it to the electric power grid, or inserting a battery without which it would be useless.⁹⁵ Just as considerations of *molid* would indicate that new appliances should not be used for the first time on Shabbat, so, too, would concerns of *mitakein mana* indicate that repairs to electrical and electronic appliances and their attachment to a power source would be forbidden on Shabbat, as would recharging batteries.⁹⁶

Bishul, "Cooking"

Rabbi Karelitz writes that the phenomenon of electrical wires growing warm because of resistance might be beneficial to the conduction of electricity. If so, then the heating of the wires could be considered forbidden as a type of cooking. This theory is flawed on many levels. The generation of heat through resistance is the result of inefficiency in electrical wiring that is undesired and unhelpful to the transmission. Indeed, the hotter the wires, the less efficient they are at transmitting current.⁹⁷ Moreover, the wire does not generally get hot to the point of halakhic significance known as *yad soledet bo* ("the hand retracts from it"),⁹⁸ and thus the warming of wires is not considered *bishul*. Even if the wire did get sufficiently hot and there was some benefit to the heating, people are not generally aware of the warmth of electrical wires, and this action would therefore be permitted as an unintentional act. Finally, there is a general principle of *ein bishul achar bishul* ("there is no cooking after cooking," in other words, a substance is not cooked twice).⁹⁹

Nevertheless, there is one type of heating electrical wires that could meet the conditions of *bishul*—the intentional use of a resistor to generate heat, as in the case of an electric range or oven, a space heater, electric kettle, or hair dryer. The ancient rabbis considered "cooking" to be forbidden whether the cooked substance was a food or not (the source activity in the tabernacle was the boiling of dyes), and whether or not the cooked item came into direct contact with the fire. If food is cooked in a substance such as water that had been heated and then removed from the fire (e.g., an egg in a pot that had boiled and then been turned off), this is forbidden as a derivative form of cooking (*toledat ha-or* or *toledat ha-eish*).[100]

Still, in all these cases, *bishul* requires actual fire. What about "cooking" with electricity? Many contemporary families do all their cooking with electric ovens, microwaves, and toasters and do not even own a gas oven or range top. Indeed, gas-fired appliances have fallen out of favor lately, since they have been found to introduce dangerous compounds into the home, and of course, they produce greenhouse gases such as CO_2. The ancient rabbis, too, knew of ways to cook without a fire—for example, in sand that had been heated by the sun or in the hot springs of Tiberias[101]—is this type of cooking forbidden as *bishul*? The source text for this discussion is Bavli Shabbat 39a, and there is a full discussion in the medieval commentaries and codes. Rambam rules leniently, but the Shulḥan Arukh considers such cooking to be forbidden.[102]

Rabbi Moshe Feinstein reviews these sources, arguing that activities similar to those performed in the tabernacle are rightly considered to be forbidden as derivative prohibitions.[103] He interprets the lenient rulings of Rashi, Ra"N and other authorities who permit cooking with the sun to have referred to a different and less effective cooking method, and argues that a microwave oven is designed to cook food just as effectively as fire does, and therefore is biblically forbidden as a *toledah* of *bishul*. Rabbi Feinstein's arguments are convincing.[104] Electric ovens are far closer in function and result to gas ovens than to the indirect and inefficient forms of cooking mentioned in the Talmud, such as using thermal springs or solar-heated sand and rooftops to cook eggs. Both the intention and the result of cooking are identical, whether the source of the heat is gas or electricity. For this reason, we consider the use of electrical heating elements to cook food, or to heat air or water, to be *toledat bishul*, a derivative form of cooking, and biblically forbidden on Shabbat.[105] Any device that directly heats food or water to a scalding temperature may not be operated on Shabbat.[106] On Yom Tov, when cooking with fire is permitted for food preparation, the normal use of electrical heating elements should also be permitted.[107]

What about the incandescent light bulb? This device also runs an electrical current across a metal resistor so that it generates light and heat. The filament, and indeed the entire fixture, certainly gets so hot as to cause the hand to retract. As we will see below, Ravad[108] (in contrast to Rambam) argues that heating metal to the glowing point for the purpose of softening or annealing it is banned under the category of *bishul*. Nevertheless, we would argue that operating a light bulb is not a form of cooking, for the simple reason that the generation of heat does not produce any durable change in the metal and provides no benefit whatsoever. The metal returns to its former state after cooling and is not "cooked." There is no benefit to the metal filament's heat as described in the Talmud and codes—not to warm water, nor to sweeten mustard, nor to soften the metal itself for shaping or annealing. Indeed, the heat is extremely inefficient, wasting up to 90% of the energy used by the appliance.

Moreover, when a person flips a light switch today, they often do not know whether the fixture is incandescent, fluorescent, or LED. The latter two forms of lighting are gaining in market share, and do not involve heating metal to the glowing point (fluorescents excite mercury vapor, which emits ultraviolet light, which in turn causes phosphor to glow in the visible spectrum; LEDs allow electrons to recombine with electron holes and release photons of different colors).[109] Even if a person is aware that by turning on an incandescent light fixture they are heating metal, there is no intention of accessing and reshaping the metal, nor indeed any possibility of doing so, much less of dousing the glowing filament in water to anneal it. For all these reasons, it is not appropriate to ban the use of incandescent light bulbs under the rubric of "cooking."[110]

Mavir, "Burning" and M'khabeh, "Extinguishing"[111]

Surprisingly, the most severe and prolific argument against the use of some forms of electrical appliances, among many Orthodox *poskim* at least, is also the one most at odds with physical reality. This is the argument that turning on lights is forbidden as "burning," and that turning them off is forbidden as "extinguishing." Burning wood or any other combustible material on Shabbat is, of course, explicitly forbidden by the Torah (Exod. 35:3). It is perhaps no coincidence that the creation of light was the first act ascribed to God in Genesis, and that creating fire is the Torah's most clearly prohibited labor.[112] Lighting fire is used as a type of bracketing ritual to indicate the start and conclusion of Shabbat. Both in Hebrew and in English, it is conventional to speak of "kindling" electric lights.

Nevertheless, electric lights are not on fire, no matter how often we use words associated with fire to describe them—and the rabbis prohibited burning, not causing light to shine.[113] Indeed, we insist on the use of actual fire for mitzvot such as lighting candles for Shabbat, Yom Tov, Hannukah, and havdalah.[114] The incandescent light bulb generates light when its metal filament is heated to the glowing point by its resistance to an electrical current. There is no combustion, no flame, and no production of charcoal, and yet many rabbis still consider the operation of an electric light bulb to be forbidden on Shabbat as if it were truly "burning."[115]

This argument is made with greatest force and thoroughness by Shlomo Zalman Auerbach in his collection of responsa, *Minḥat Shlomo*. His focus on the incandescent light bulb is perhaps a consequence of the fact that for over a century (and his entire lifetime) it was the most popular and useful electrical appliance. This humble device was the "killer app"—the appliance that motivated cities and nations to construct vast power grids for the distribution of electricity, so that homes and businesses could be illuminated in a way that was dramatically easier, cleaner, safer, and cheaper than using fire.

Coincidentally, this appliance functions in a way that is not completely unknown to classical *halakhic* sources: by heating a piece of metal. The Talmud discusses the status of a hot metal ember, *gahelet shel matekhet*, in several locations. Mishnah Shabbat 3:5 describes a metal pot containing water that has been removed from the stove on Shabbat: "If one removed a boiler, he must not put cold water into it to make it hot, but some may be put in it or into a cup to make it lukewarm."[116]

This Mishnah is difficult to understand, but it is discussed rather extensively in the Bavli (Shabbat 41a-42a) and in later commentaries.[117] According to the Bavli, the Mishnah describes the case of a metal utensil that has absorbed heat from a fire and then been removed while still hot. Putting a small amount of liquid into the pot might boil the liquid, which would be forbidden as cooking, but putting a large quantity of liquid that will merely be warmed is permitted. If the pot had been emptied of liquid, then dousing it with water could have the effect of *tzeiruf*, annealing[118] the metal, a rabbinic prohibition.

This discussion leads to a statement (42a) in the name of Shmuel that differentiates the metal ember from a burning piece of wood, "One may extinguish a metal ember in the public thoroughfare [on Shabbat] lest it cause people injury, but not a wood ember." Rashi makes explicit the Talmud's distinction between hot metal and burning wood in two successive comments:

A *metal ember* [*may be doused*]. One may toss outside [hot] metal waste, for the biblical category of "extinguishing" does not apply to [hot metal], though the rabbinic [form of the prohibition] does ban it, but where there is a public hazard, they did not enforce *shvut* [i.e., a rabbinic ban].

But *not so with* [*a burning ember of*] *wood.* For this [dousing a burning wood ember] is a biblical prohibition [of "extinguishing"] punishable by stoning.

It seems likely that the metal being discussed here is not "glowing" but is nevertheless scaldingly hot. Hot metal is particularly dangerous, since it is impossible to discern its temperature simply by looking at it, which is not the case with burning wood. Since the metal is not "burning," causing it to cool down by dousing it with water is not the *melakhah* of "extinguishing," but is merely a rabbinic prohibition lest the metal is doused to anneal it. But since the presence of this hot piece of metal is a danger in the public domain, it may be doused. Rashi teaches us that the sages did not enforce their rule of *shvut* in consideration of public safety.

In his great code of law, the *Mishneh Torah*, Rambam discusses the heating of metal in several locations. In the *Laws of Shabbat* 9:6 he refers to heating metal until it glows to soften and then shape it as *cooking*, but in Halakhah 12:1 he states the following: "A person who heats metal to anneal it in water—this is a derivative form of burning and is forbidden." Rabbi Auerbach seizes on this line, despite its explicit qualification, to prove that Rambam generally considers heating metal to be considered "burning." Even though Rambam earlier calls heating metal a form of cooking,[119] and Ravad protests Rambam's designation here of burning,[120] and even though Rambam himself includes the condition "to anneal it in water," Rabbi Auerbach insists that Rambam would (if available for comment on modern technology) ban the heating of a metal filament in an incandescent light bulb under the category of burning.

Rabbi Auerbach reads the words *kedei l'tzarfo ba-mayim* not according to their simple meaning, "to anneal it in water," but rather, "to the temperature sufficient for it to be annealed in water." This reading assumes that Rambam considers heating metal until it is hot enough to shape to be considered "cooking," but heating it a little further so that it is hot enough to then be annealed in water to be "burning." How a person is supposed to measure this distinction is nowhere evident.[121] As Rabbi Abraham ben David of Posquieres (Ravad, 1120-1198) points out in his Mishneh Torah commentary, annealing metal is not biblically forbidden on Shabbat, but only by rabbinic authority. Yet Rabbi Auerbach uses this text as the foundation for claiming that turning on an incandescent light bulb should be considered biblically banned as burning.

Why does Rabbi Auerbach insist on this unlikely argument, despite his awareness that the metal is not "burning"?[122] Having systematically refuted all the other arguments for prohibition, he seems to feel that this is the only way to establish a biblical ban on using electricity on Shabbat. As he says in section 2 of his responsum, "if we do not claim that hot metal is considered fire, then even cooking with electrical heating elements would not be cooking," and there would be no biblical prohibition.[123]

Shlomo Goren[124] published two essays in the Israeli journal, *Sinai*, in 1949, arguing that the use of electricity cannot be compared to the biblical prohibitions against burning and extinguishing on Shabbat.[125] After examining our text from Tractate Shabbat, Rabbi Goren proceeds to compare it to Yerushalmi Yoma 3:5,[126] and then to Bavli Pesaḥim 75a.[127] The most compelling explanation of these texts is that the rabbis did not consider heating metal to be a form of burning, nor did they consider cooling metal to be extinguishing, for the simple reason that metal does not undergo combustion to create heat, but rather absorbs energy from another source, and returns to its prior state after releasing the energy as radiant heat. Rabbi Goren cites the words of Magen Avraham (OH 334:35), "but regarding metal there is no [prohibition of extinguishing] for it is not burning." Rabbi Goren insists on an accurate physical description of fire—a substance that combusts material and creates flame—and concludes that the heat generated by a metal resistor to an electrical current is neither fire nor even a derivative form of fire (*toledat eish*).

Rabbi Goren proceeds with a straightforward interpretation of Rambam: only when one heats metal, and then suddenly cools it with the intention to anneal it, can the process be associated with "burning" and "extinguishing." It was, according to Goren, the comparison of annealing to extinguishing—both of which involve suddenly cooling a substance to preserve its altered state—that led Rambam to categorize heating metal in this situation alone to be a derivative form of burning. But since both stages (heating and cooling) are necessary for the *melakhah* of annealing to be completed, and since neither action is intended nor accomplished with the operation of an electrical lamp, the category of burning is inapplicable to electrical lights. In the conclusion to his first essay, Rabbi Goren categorically rejects the application of both "burning" and "cooking" as reasons to ban the use of electrical lights on Shabbat.

In his second essay, Rabbi Goren expands on his former reasoning, citing *geonim* (early medieval sages) and later medieval sources to buttress his argument that heating metal and cooling it without the purpose or effect of annealing are not biblically forbidden on Shabbat. He boldly writes that the use of a telephone on Shabbat may be completely permitted (he was obviously referring to land lines, not to cellular phones which had not been invented yet, and which pose other halakhic issues as discussed below; in any event, he maintained a rabbinic ban on using phones on Shabbat). However, he argues that there is still a rabbinic prohibition on turning off an electric light based on the Talmud's description of dousing a metal ember as *shvut*, and of turning on a light based on the rabbinic prohibition against starting a new fire (*molid ohr*).[128] These arguments of his are not well developed. The Talmud's *shvut* category refers to dousing a hot piece of metal with water, which could cause annealing. It makes sense to prohibit this rabbinically, but that is not at all the case with turning off a light switch. "Starting a new fire" refers to making physical sparks for the sake of igniting combustible materials, which is not relevant here. Since Rabbi

Goren has amply proven that a metal filament is not on fire, this claim to a rabbinic prohibition is unclear. It seems to us that Rabbi Goren has made a convincing case against the biblical prohibition of using incandescent lights on Shabbat and has not established a rabbinical prohibition in its place.

Nevertheless, the "stringent ones" (as Rabbi Goren calls them, perhaps alluding to Rabbi Auerbach), who argue that turning on incandescent lights is prohibited as burning, have won broad acceptance in the Orthodox community. Indeed, disabling light switches prior to Shabbat is a standard marker of Shabbat observance in the Orthodox community and is also common among observant Conservative Jews, as is the idea that the operation of electrical light fixtures is biblically prohibited.

From our perspective, the claim that heating a metal filament is to be banned on Shabbat as "burning" is not convincing for incandescent light bulbs and is not even relevant for other types of light fixtures or for any other electrical or electronic appliances. Already in 1950, Rabbi Arthur Neulander wrote for the CJLS a simple but clear refutation of the use of burning as a reason to ban electrical lights, and his argument remains cogent today.

A NEW LIGHT IN ZION?

The fact that incandescent light bulbs are being replaced by compact fluorescent bulbs, light emitting diodes (LEDs), and other cool-running appliances that do not heat metal to the glowing point, only augments this perspective. These newer lighting fixtures do not involve the concerns mentioned by twentieth century sages; they do not result in any material change to the substance; and they are designed to run relatively cool and to last for thousands of hours of use. As such, the concerns discussed above about the *melakhot* of cooking, building, completing, and burning all appear to be irrelevant to the operation of such fixtures.

Avram Reisner has countered this perspective, arguing that the creation of light is one purpose of the *melakhah* of burning.[129] He supports this position with the Torah commentary of Ramban, to Exodus 35:3, in which Ramban mentions a variety of uses of fire, arguably including for the sake of light.[130] Ramban's point here is that, in contrast to Yom Tov, when it is permitted to burn fire for the sake of cooking, on Shabbat the prohibition on burning is absolute, regardless of the desired result, whether it be for food preparation or for physical pleasure in the heat and light of the fire. Rabbi Reisner believes that this implies that any action that yields the results of fire, including the creation of light, is included within the *melakhah* of burning, regardless of the mechanism. This understanding would result in a biblical-level ban on the use of all light fixtures on Shabbat.

Rabbi Reisner's argument accords with our explanation of derivative labors, *toledot*, which accomplish a forbidden purpose via a mechanism distinct from that of the primary labor and are considered biblically forbidden. Nevertheless, we respectfully disagree with his analysis. The prohibition against burning known as *mavir*, which is the thirty-eighth *melakhah*, was associated with heating a kettle to make dyes in the tabernacle, or to create charcoal for use in smelting metal.[131] As Rabbi Goren demonstrated, this prohibition against burning is dependent upon the physical action, because combustion causes a lasting change in a substance. The luminescence caused by electrical appliances does not involve combustion, so even for Ramban it is not included in the category of burning. Creating a fire on Shabbat is forbidden, whether for the purpose of cooking, heating a room, or enjoying the light. But electrical lighting is distinct in both the original tabernacle-related purpose and the mechanism from the *melakhah* of burning and should therefore not be included in this category of prohibition.

The creation of light itself is not mentioned as a *melakhah* in classical or contemporary sources. Indeed, "light" does not exist independently of the eye, which perceives certain wavelengths of radiant energy as light of various colors.[132] Light is emitted and manipulated via an extraordinary range of physical and chemical interactions, including bioluminescence, none of which are considered in the halakhic literature.[133] The conversion of potential energy to kinetic energy (as in lowering an object, or in allowing the flow of electrons from a cell to an LED) is not itself forbidden as *melakhah*. The creation of light does not meet the standard of *melakhah* established in the Mishnah—the creation of a durable change in material reality—unless the light is a by-product of combustion. It is evident from the rabbinic sources that the basis for banning burning was the combustion of the fuel, and the durable transformation of materials consumed by its heat.

Rabbi Dr. Dror Fixler of Yeshivat Sha'alvim and of Bar Ilan University's engineering faculty[134] examines the question of whether creating light (with an LED bulb) is itself prohibited on Shabbat, and concludes that there is no such prohibition.[135] As he notes, Moroccan and Egyptian rabbis generally permitted the use of electricity on Yom Tov until the middle of the twentieth century, but eventually came to ban it due to concerns about the erosion of the special atmosphere of Yom Tov and the possibility that such leniency would be extended to Shabbat, where they felt there was a prohibition against "burning" that might be violated in operating incandescent lightbulbs (following the position of the "stringent ones," as Rabbi Goren called them above). Rabbi Fixler accepts this stringent ruling for incandescent light bulbs because of their heating of metal to the glowing point but finds that the creation of light with an LED bulb is not forbidden as either *melakhah* or *shvut*.[136] Nevertheless, he concludes that because LEDs are used with consumer electronics, they should be banned as leading to activity inappropriate for Shabbat and Yom Tov.

We shall return to the subject of protecting the tranquility of Shabbat below in Section 2. For now, we may conclude that creating light with an electrical fixture is not properly considered to be *toledat mavir*, a derivative form of the *melakhah* of burning, since the process, the purpose, and the result of using an electrical lighting fixture are all dissimilar to the process, purpose, and result of burning wood, gas, or any other fuel.

Furthermore, we have argued that *melakhah* is limited to actions that result in a durable change in physical reality. Causing light to shine with a lighting fixture does not meet this standard.[137] As Rabbi Goren demonstrated, burning is paired with extinguishing, just as building and breaking down are paired (similarly to the categories of tying and untying, writing and erasing). An item that cannot be "extinguished" in the sense of preserving it in an altered state such as turning wood to charcoal or annealing metal, also cannot be "burned." For this reason, we insist that the category of *mavir* does not apply to the normal operation of light bulbs or other electrical appliances. It obviously does apply, however, to any appliance that uses an electric starter to generate sparks for the ignition of gas or other fuels.

GENERATING ELECTRICITY

Before we conclude our discussion of burning, we must address the *generation* of electricity. Electricity is generated by numerous processes—nuclear fission, hydroelectric turbines, windmills, photovoltaic (solar) cells, geothermal, biomass, etc., but unfortunately, burning coal and natural gas remain common sources of electricity in the United States and many other countries. A person who uses electricity on Shabbat could be considered as indirectly causing such combustion to occur.

However, this is not a halakhic concern, for several reasons. The power grid is constructed to generate a steady supply of electricity in response to general demand; when one appliance is turned on, it is probable that another is turned off, resulting in no net increase in demand. Indeed, there is equipment to ensure that power production and consumption are kept equal. Turning on household appliances has no direct effect upon the power plant unless it is a mass phenomenon (such as the use of air conditioning units in hot weather) and even then, no individual action by a consumer would directly affect the burning of coal or natural gas at a power plant.

Moreover, power is generated for the general population, most of which is not Jewish, and thus one is using a resource that is not produced by an action forbidden on Shabbat specifically on behalf of a Jew. This is less the case in Israel, where many utility workers and most of the population are Jewish, but even there, the generation of electricity is generally an automated and steady process that does not require human interventions in response to typical consumer activity. If we were to worry about generation issues, then we would also ban the use of tap water on Shabbat, since water pressure is maintained by electric pumps that are triggered by water use. Thus, the generation of electricity is not of immediate concern to the Sabbath observer; this is even more the case when using battery-powered devices.

To summarize our discussion, we have concluded that opening or closing an electrical circuit should not be prohibited as a form of building, that the warming of wires is not cooking, and that the generation of light in electrical appliances, including incandescent light bulbs that heat metal until it glows, should not be prohibited as either cooking or burning. Thus, there is no comprehensive ban covering all uses of electricity as *melakhah*. On the other hand, we have found that the use of electricity to generate heat for the sake of cooking food or heating air and water is forbidden as a derivative form of cooking, even without the use of fire. We have also noted that new appliances should not be used for the first time on Shabbat, and that devices ought not be assembled on Shabbat (e.g., replacing a bulb, a battery, or plugging a new appliance into a socket). Our discussion of *melakhah* so far would result in a ban on operating electrical appliances designed to generate heat for the purpose of cooking food or heating air or water on Shabbat, but it would not ban the operation of circuits in general for other electrical appliances. In Section II, we will discuss other halakhic considerations that would limit the use of electrical appliances out of concern for *shvut*, the imperative to rest.

Even for those who consider opening or closing circuits to involve one or more *melakhot*, solutions have been found to allow the use of such devices, whether with a timer or with a buffer mechanism (called a *grama* device) that uses a capacitor to render the action indirect.[138] This can be understood as moving a switch into a position in which it is likely to be activated soon, rather than activating it directly.[139] The circuit is left open prior to Shabbat, and the operator controls the intensity of electrical current indirectly. Adjusting the accelerator of a scooter yields a delayed response and is therefore considered indirect. But if the general electricity ban based on *melakhah* is unconvincing, as we have argued, then such measures are unnecessary.

Koteiv, "Writing"

A category of *melakhah* that is of relevance to the use of electronic devices is the prohibition against "erasing two letters" and "writing two letters" on Shabbat. Many digital devices automatically generate electronic logs of their activities and are regularly used to record and display information. While video displays (whether CRT, LCD, or LED[140]) are volatile, constantly being erased and refreshed, and are therefore dissimilar to the permanent form of writing banned as *melakhah*, the storage of digital information to flash memory or disk is non-volatile and is comparable to forbidden forms of writing.[141]

It is interesting that Mishnah Shabbat 7:2 establishes a "two-letter" standard for writing. According to Mishnah 12:3, this standard recalls the practice of marking the bottom of the planks for the tabernacle with a two-letter code. This limitation is apparently linked to the fact that Hebrew has no single-letter words (though individual letters are used to indicate numbers). Likewise, in the various binary codes that have been developed in recent decades, such as ASCII, Unicode etc., letters, numbers and other symbols are each formed by distinctive series of zeroes and ones. True, writing generally involves a graphic representation that is visible, but digital data is stored for future display and is thus similar in function to classical forms of writing.

With electronic appliances, we "write" all manner of data files (text, sound, images, etc.) through a process of translation in which analog inputs (e.g., typing on a keyboard or speaking into a microphone) are digitized and then stored in vast strings of binary code. The prohibition in Mishnah Shabbat 12:3 includes any language or symbolic system within the realm of writing: "whether with two symbols[142] or in any language he is liable," and this policy is reasonable for our situation as well. The normal method of writing today involves digital devices that we use to store and display information, just as we do with printed media.

However, a contrary perspective about the broad prohibition against writing emerges from Talmud Yerushalmi. In reference to Mishnah 12:3, it states: "Who taught *simiyonot*? Rabbi Yossi. What is 'every language'? Even *aleph/alpha*."[143]

On this basis, the 12th century rabbi Eliezer ben R. Yoel Halevi (Ra'avyah) takes a distinctive stand, limiting the biblical prohibition against "writing" to either Hebrew or Greek:

> Even though *Rabbeinu* [Shlomo, viz. Rashi] explains in *Perek ha-boneh* that one who writes two letters in any language is liable, in the script-appearance of every people, it is a mistake, for we read in the Yerushalmi, "what is 'every language'? *aleph/ alpha, beitha/beta*," namely, in [Hebrew or in] Greek. But as

for [writing in] other languages he is not liable, as I have previously written. [144]

Based on Ra'avyah's bold and unusual claim—that the Mishnah's prohibition against "writing" on Shabbat is limited to writing in either Hebrew or Greek[145]—writing in binary code would arguably not qualify as the biblically banned form of writing on Shabbat. This leniency, while fascinating, is unconvincing. Rashi and other commentaries to the Mishnah, such as Rambam and Bartenura, understand the Mishnah to prohibit writing in any script. It is not clear why the *melakhah* would be limited to Hebrew and Greek—especially if we consider the *melakhot* to originate with the tabernacle project. In any event, Ra'avyah's position is idiosyncratic, and today we consider the prohibition against writing to include the creation of a physical record of any letter or symbolic system.

Aside from the subject of what letters are written, the rabbis also consider the type of ink and surface used, as well as the writing method. In chapter 12 of Mishnah Shabbat, the rabbis limit liability for writing on Shabbat based on these considerations. A person is not liable for "writing" unless they use their dominant hand to write two or more letters in one session with a durable ink[146] on a durable surface. Mishnah Shabbat 12:5 states, "If anyone wrote with liquids, or with fruit juice, or in road-dust, or in writer's-sand, or with anything that does not last, they are exempt."[147] Tosefta Shabbat 11:8 summarizes: "They are exempt [from liability for writing on Shabbat] until they write with a durable substance on a durable surface."[148] Rambam restates this law thoroughly in the *Laws of Shabbat* 11:15[149] and Yisrael Meir HaKohen Kagan (Ḥafetz Ḥaim, 1839-1933) provides an extended comment on the subject in Mishnah B'rurah to OH 340, #22.

Some rabbis have argued that recording to electronic media may be differentiated from pen and ink writing based on another distinction offered by the Mishnah: kel'aḥar yad—"like [writing] with the back of the hand." For example, the Mishnah states that if a person writes with their non-dominant hand or uses their foot or even their neck to scratch two letters, that person is not liable for the melakhah of writing. The theory seems to relate to the idea of "intentional labor." If one's intention was really to perform labor, then they would have done it in the most efficient and effective way possible. Writing with the back of the hand, foot, or neck may allow the creation of a legible mark, but it is not the intentional labor prohibited by the Mishnah. Therefore, a person who writes imprecisely is not biblically liable for the labor of "writing."[150]

Obviously, writing with a keyboard—whether physical or virtual—or any other input device is not the "normal" way of writing known to our ancestors. Yet this principle refers to an *awkward and imprecise* form of labor. No one today would consider typing on a keyboard or touch screen to be more awkward or imprecise than writing with pen and paper. On the contrary, using digital recording devices is extremely precise and efficient. Which is likely to be more accurate and legible for a later reader, a typed transcript, or scrawled notes? Which will be more realistic, a digital photograph of a bird, or a pen and ink drawing? The various forms of recording data to digital memory are the modern equivalent of writing with quill and parchment and are often a more durable and effective medium for recording information.

During the 1980s, the CJLS discussed the question of recording video to magnetic tape on Shabbat. In his 1989 responsum, Arnold Goodman cited earlier discussions from the 1950s regarding audio recordings and argued that tape recording is not forbidden since it is indirect, and not the way that "they did the labor."[151] Other CJLS authors and committee members disagreed, arguing that recording on magnetic tape performs the same function of preserving a record as do traditional methods with ink and paper, and therefore it is forbidden on Shabbat as a form of writing.[152] Gordon Tucker argued that the operation of video or audio equipment by a Jew on Shabbat or Yom Tov is forbidden under the rubric of "writing." However, he (later joined by Elliot Dorff) allowed for such operation by a non-Jew or by an automatic recording device.[153] Mayer Rabinowitz rejected Rabbi Goodman's arguments and rejected the hiring of a gentile to record worship services.[154] Committee members added additional aesthetic and spiritual concerns in opposition to the practice of recording Shabbat services.

We agree with the arguments made by Rabbis Tucker, Dorff, and Rabinowitz in the 1980s that recording audio and video on magnetic tape is to be considered forbidden on Shabbat under the category of "writing," unless the process was set up before Shabbat to operate automatically. The same is true for the use of contemporary digital storage media such as hard drives and flash memory. This is also true for cloud computing, since in the end, the data will be stored in some non-volatile device. In this discussion, Rabbi Rabinowitz made the same comparison used by Rabbi Feinstein regarding microwave ovens: the purpose of cooking is to transform food from a raw to an edible state; the purpose of writing is to store information for later recall. What matters is not the process but the purpose and the result. However, we would clarify that the process does matter somewhat. Writing saved into digital memory can be considered *toledat koteiv*, a derivative form of writing rather than the original form. As such, it remains biblically prohibited on Shabbat. Other concerns about writing and erasing divine names on digital displays and memory media (as discussed below) are not involved.

Digital writing performs the same function as conventional writing, though the process is different. As seen above in the discussion of cooking, an activity that shares the same purpose and result as a primary form of *melakhah* but accomplishes it via a different process is viewed as a *toledah*, a derivative form of the labor. This differentiation is significant since the category of writing has other halakhic ramifications. If we were to consider "writing" saved to digital memory or to a video display to be the exact equivalent of the original form of "writing," then we would never be allowed to "erase" a screen view or digital file that contains one of the divine names. The CJLS has approved Avram Reisner's arguments against considering such erasures to be forbidden.[155]

For our purposes, then, the issue is whether "writing" with electronic devices is the functional equivalent of writing with pen and ink; if so, then it is forbidden as a *toledah*, a derivative form of the activity called "writing," just as watering plants is forbidden as a derivative form of "planting," and using a microwave oven is forbidden as a derivative form of "cooking."

Although "writing" is associated with letters and numbers, this creative labor equally applies to recording imagery, sound, and other types of data. Joel Roth has written, "If the function of writing is appropriately defined as the production of a lasting imprint upon some substance, it seems virtually incontrovertible that the function of photography would have to be considered forbidden under the category of writing."[156] As with Rabbi Feinstein regarding cooking, we find Rabbi Roth's conclusions about photography to be convincing.

What about the use of electronic paper in e-readers?[157] If our concerns about writing to digital memory could be addressed by disabling network functions,[158] it remains the case that each fresh page view effectively creates a new durable image. Within the electronic paper are microcapsules that are arranged by electrical charge to display pigment and form an image. This image endures even without any refreshing of the display. E-ink is a stable form of writing and would therefore appear to be biblically forbidden as *toledat koteiv*.

Nevertheless, most current e-readers are set automatically to erase the written image after a brief period of inactivity, either by darkening the screen or by displaying a stock image in place of the written text. If so, then the creation of a screen-view does not meet the halakhic standard of liability seen above in Tosefta *Shabbat* 11:8 of "writing something with a durable substance on a durable surface." The status of creating a screen-view that will auto-erase after a few minutes would be that of *patur aval assur*, "forbidden but exempt"—meaning it is exempt from full liability for the biblical *melakhah*, but still forbidden by rabbinic decree, much as writing in sand on Shabbat is rabbinically banned.

The use of e-readers on Shabbat raises additional halakhic problems. Beyond displaying text, they also provide users with the ability to record notes and to download additional content. Both activities are forbidden under the biblical category of *toledat koteiv*, a derivative form of writing. Purchasing content would also violate the *shvut* ban on commerce discussed below in Section II. Many e-readers are really tablet computers with full functionality and can quickly lead the user away from passive reading and into active writing and the creation of new content. True, one could say the same of reading a paper book—the passive activity of reading can lead to using a pencil or highlighter to mark the book, and therefore to violation of Shabbat. Yet this distinction is more sustainable, since marking up a paper book is frequently impermissible—if the book is borrowed from another person or a library, for example—and writing in the book requires a separate tool. In contrast, computers use the same input devices (touchscreen, keyboard, trackpad, mouse, etc.) for reading and writing, and the markings the produce are easily removed and considered inconsequential, thus making the distinction unsustainable. For all these reasons, it seems that the use of e-readers as currently configured is not permitted on Shabbat.[159] We will discuss accommodations for disabled users below in Section III.

The intentional recording of data—whether of text, images, or sound—is forbidden on Shabbat as a derivative form of writing. While this form of recording may not employ the same mechanism as the writing used in the tabernacle (whatever that was), it has the same purpose and result—to preserve information for later display. We cannot claim that such writing is akin to the category called *kel'ahar yad* ("with the back of the hand"), because this form of writing is efficient and effective to an extent equal to or greater than that of conventional writing. Rather, this form of writing should be considered a derivative form of the activity that is biblically prohibited on Shabbat and Yom Tov.

Thus, we would prohibit the Sabbath operation of a digital phone, camera, voice recorder, or computer used for writing text or recording audio or video files. These activities are all derivative forms of "writing" and are therefore biblically forbidden on Shabbat and Yom Tov.

What about the use of cellular phones? These devices automatically record activity such as the time, number, duration, and even location of each call, both within themselves and on the service provider's register for billing purposes. While such recording may not be the primary intention of a person who initiates or accepts a call, this recording of data is unavoidable and beneficial, and is thus banned as *pesik reisha*, an unintended but unavoidable consequence. Moreover, the categories of phone and computer have now converged, and even the simplest cellular phones are used to send and receive text messages, take photos, and complete financial transactions. Absent extraordinary circumstances necessary for preserving life, the use of such phones would appear to be forbidden as the *melakhah* of *toledat koteiv* on Shabbat and Yom Tov. We will discuss the use of phones further below under the rubric of *shvut*.

Another ubiquitous form of electronic device is the magnetic stripe card, "a type of card capable of storing data by modifying the magnetism of tiny iron-based magnetic particles on a band of magnetic material on the card."[160] Such cards come in a variety of formats, with black, brown, and silver tapes typically containing three bands for the storage of data. Some magnetic stripe cards, such as those used for automatic teller machines, credit and debit cards, driver's licenses, telephone cards etc., contain basic information about the user, but account balance and other detailed information is stored on a remote database that must be accessed to process transactions. Other forms of stripe cards, such as hotel key cards and bus and subway fare cards, may store data and account balances on the card itself and can be used without immediate reference to a networked database.

The type of card used to transfer data across the network (ATM, credit card, etc.), involves the recording of transaction data and would therefore be forbidden as *pesik reisheh*, an action that inevitably results in a derivative form of writing. Bus and subway cards that store account balances are also problematic, in that each swipe of the card results in a notation on the magnetic strip. This, too, involves a derivative form of writing as well as a commercial transaction.[161] We shall refer to both categories of card as "Type I." However, hotel key cards and fobs used for building access arguably avoid both issues. So long as they are programmed prior to Shabbat, their use on Shabbat would not seem to involve either writing or commerce. When swiped or brought close to the reader, they merely show the proper entry code to unlock the door (as established above, the LED indicator light is of no halakhic significance).[162] We shall refer to this form of stripe card and contact-less fob as "Type II." Because there is no intention, and often no result of recording entry data from their use, they may be considered permitted. Keys are generally used to secure an area and safeguard a person and their property. We again cite Rashi in saying that safety concerns supersede those of *shvut* in this case, and therefore justify permission to use such a magnetic key card or fob.[163]

Is it permissible to request that a gentile swipe one's Type I magnetic card for a commercial transaction (thus creating a durable record)? Asking a non-Jew to perform *melakhah* on one's behalf is considered rabbinically prohibited. Such a request may also be viewed as a desecration of God's name in that it publicly demonstrates one's desire to circumvent the laws of Shabbat. Asking non-Jews to perform an act of *shvut* for the sake of a mitzvah or to relieve a non-life-threatening health challenge is, however, permitted under the rubric of *shvut d'shvut*, a tertiary concern for Sabbath rest.[164]

Therefore, we consider the use of Type I magnetic stripe cards such as a credit or debit card to be forbidden as a derivative form of writing and often also as a commercial transaction. The use of Type II cards and fobs of the sort used in hotels and dormitories as room keys is a practical exception: so long as these cards are not carried outside of a single domain and are not used for commercial purposes, they may be used without performing *melakhah* and without compromising the experience of Shabbat as a day of rest.

A Non-Formalistic Definition of Melakhah

Until now, we have considered classical definitions of *melakhah* and their relevance to contemporary electrical and electronic appliances. However, it is worth considering a modern approach that adopts a non-formalistic definition. Joel Roth, in agreement with Isaac Klein, cites modern theological writings from scholars as diverse as Samson Raphael Hirsch, Mordecai Kaplan, and Abraham Joshua Heschel to argue that the classical ban on *melakhah* is meant to prevent people from exercising "mastery" over their environment.[165]

In addition to the standard methods of identifying *melakhot* by comparison to established forms, Rabbi Roth writes that any activity that demonstrates mastery is forbidden on Shabbat as a *melakhah*, even if the intention is *not* like that of an established category of *melakhah*. In other words, the issue in evaluating the permissibility of any given action is *not only* whether it resembles a forbidden category in mechanism, in intention, or in result, *but also* whether it demonstrates "mastery over nature." Rabbi Roth considers operating electric lights on Shabbat to be biblically banned as *melakhah* since they demonstrate mastery over nature.

Following the example of Rabban Yoḥanan and Rabbi Shimon ben Lakish as cited in the Yerushalmi, he classifies such actions under the general category of *makeh b'fatish*.[166] Turning on an electric light may not resemble any category of *melakhah*—as we have seen, the rabbis prohibited cooking and burning, not making light—but it would still be forbidden according to Rabbi Roth, because this action demonstrates mastery over nature.

This approach initially appears persuasive, but it is problematic on several levels. The Yerushalmi text bears the hallmarks of *aggadah*, claiming that these rabbis had identified 1,521 forbidden forms of labor, but giving no examples. What does it mean that they "found" labors? Were they relying on oral traditions or making up their own system? When they assigned miscellaneous actions to *makeh b'fatish*, did they have any rubric? This Yerushalmi text gives us no useful information, which is perhaps why it is not cited in the halakhic codes.

Rabbi Roth suggests a system—actions that exhibit mastery over nature may be called *makeh b'fatish*. As we have seen from the Mishnah, however, *makeh b'fatish* is linked to *boneh* ("building") and is generally associated with the construction of objects of stone, metal, or glass. Moreover, if we accept this argument, then why stop with electricity? Modern plumbing is an equally impressive and complex system—should we ban taps and toilets because they exhibit mastery over nature? How about door handles and locks? This theory of "mastery" to explain the purpose of banning *melakhah* has no source in biblical or classical rabbinical literature, as Rabbi Roth concedes, and it seems unwieldy in practice (especially since faucets and toilets are often controlled by electronic sensors).

In fact, resting on Shabbat is itself an assertion of mastery. Israel is told to imitate both the activity and the rest of God—and to feel secure enough in their efforts that they can stop working each week and enjoy their accomplishments. Observing Shabbat is a form of *imitatio Dei*—God rested from labor on the seventh day, and so should Israel. God stopped providing manna on the seventh day, and Israel stopped collecting it. As noted above, Shabbat is a "sign between Me and the Children of Israel"—that is, it is a shared experience that binds Creator and creature. Thus, Shabbat is hardly an experience of submission; it is a day when the children of Israel don garments of glory, eat fine foods without effort, and imagine themselves already to reside in a tranquil world of perfection.

It appears to me that with their 39 categories of *melakhah* the rabbis were concerned with the avoidance of *making permanent, or at least durable, changes to one's physical environment.* Labor is an indication of inadequacy, of lack, and Israel is commanded on Shabbat to rest and appreciate the resources that they already possess. As we have seen, the understanding of *melakhah* as an action that renders durable and constructive change is stated explicitly in Mishnah Shabbat 12:1 regarding the labors of *boneh* (building) and *makeh b'fatish* (completing), and it is also stated regarding labors such as *kosheir* (tying) and *koteiv* (writing). Using available resources and leaving the minimum impact on our environment during the holy hours of Shabbat is a way of focusing the mind on the divine creation and on the twin gifts of life and liberty that are mentioned in the Torah and in our liturgy.

The Mishnah's list focuses specifically on labors needed to produce food, clothing, writing, and shelter. Until recently, such activities absorbed the greater part of the day for most people. Resting from such exertions on Shabbat is a weekly form of thanksgiving. Nevertheless, Rabbi Roth is certainly correct to focus on the *intention* of any given activity as relevant to whether it should be permitted or forbidden. While we may not agree with this line of reasoning regarding *melakhah*, it will be useful when considering the secondary level of Shabbat restrictions called *shvut.*

||

SHVUT: THE OBLIGATION TO REST

> Six days you shall do your labor, and on the seventh day
> you shall rest; so that your ox and donkey will rest, and
> your servant's child and the stranger will relax. (Exod.
> 23:12)

This verse differs from those examined at the beginning of Section I regarding *melakhah*.[167] Instead of prohibiting the Israelite from working on Shabbat, it gives a positive commandment to rest.[168] The Torah is interested not only in creating an internal state of tranquility, but also in fostering a public atmosphere of rest that includes not only the free Israelite but also his or her livestock and servants. The command to rest is repeated in Exodus 34:21, and there are numerous references to "guarding" Shabbat and to making it and other festivals into a *shabbaton*, or day of rest.[169]

Medieval lists of the 613 mitzvot mention *resting* as one of the 248 positive commandments,[170] though the status of the *shvut* restrictions is considered rabbinical. The term *shvut* (rest) is used somewhat loosely in halakhic discourse. In a masterful address delivered to the Rabbinical Assembly in 1945, Rabbi Boaz Cohen traces the development of *shvut* from the Tannaitic period through the works of the *amoraim, geonim,* and medieval codifiers.[171]

One of the earliest texts regarding *shvut* comes from the description of how to observe Passover in Exodus 12:6. Midrash Mekhilta D' Rabbi Yishmael states: [172]

Therefore, shall ye observe this day. Why is this said? Has it not already been said: "no manner of work shall be done on them" (v.16)? From this, I would know only about work that can be regarded as labor [*melakhah*]. What about activities that can be regarded just as detracting from the restfulness of the day [*shvut*]? Scripture therefore says: "Therefore, shall you observe this day," thus prohibiting even such work as only detracts from the restfulness of the day.[173]

It is noteworthy that this Midrash does not frame *shvut* as a rabbinic fence around the Torah's prohibitions, a decree lest any specific *melakhah* be performed. Rather, it describes *shvut* as its own biblical imperative—to rest on Shabbat, beyond the bare minimum of avoiding *melakhah*.

Two additional early Midrashic sources examine *shvut* and enumerate its various categories. Midrash Sifra lists eighteen forms,[174] whereas Mekhilta D'Rabbi Shimon bar Yoḥai lists only ten.[175] The most authoritative source, Mishnah Beitza 5:2, provides fourteen examples of *shvut*, divided into three categories:

Any act for which one is liable on the Sabbath, whether because it is a rabbinical abstention from work acts, or by virtue of an optional act, or regarding a religious duty, on the Sabbath, they are culpable for it on a festival. And these are the ones under the category of rabbinical abstention from work acts: they must not ascend a tree, nor may they ride upon a beast, nor swim on the water, nor clap hands, nor slap the thighs, nor dance. And these come under the category of optional acts: they must not sit in judgment, nor may they betroth, nor may they perform the ceremony of ḥalitzah; nor contract a levirite marriage. And these come under the category of pious duties: they must not dedicate, or make any valuation vow, or devote anything, or separate priest's dues or tithes. All these they have proscribed on a festival, even more so on the Sabbath. There is no differentiation between a festival and the Sabbath except for the preparation of necessary food. (trans. Philip Blackman)

This Mishnah has been parsed by many scholars who are puzzled by its three apparently distinct categories of *shvut*, *reshut*, and *mitzvah*. The consensus seems to be that the Mishnah's three categories are all forms of *shvut*. The latter two are distinct categories within *shvut* in that they are generally performed as part of a religious or judicial rite.

It is conventional to explain each of the Mishnah's forbidden acts as a safeguard to prevent a person from violating the more serious category of *melakhah*. One mustn't climb a tree lest they break off a limb, nor swim lest they displace water or later squeeze out wet garments. We do not perform acts of court or make dedications to the Temple on Shabbat lest we be tempted to write a record of the activities. These explanations may be understood as rabbinic decrees to prevent the performance of any specific *melakhah* (*gezeirah shema*—decree just in case) or as a buffer between the states of permission and prohibition (*s'yag* - fence, *harḥakah* -distancing). Yet if one reads the Mishnah without this preconception, it prohibits these activities without reference to *melakhah*. It is possible to understand *shvut* in this Mishnah, as in the early Midrashim, as an independent category of activities that are simply viewed as inappropriate for a day dedicated to rest.

Although this view of *shvut* as an independent tradition regarding Shabbat laws is evident in the earliest rabbinic sources, the category of *shvut* came to describe activities surrounding *melakhah*, such as labors done imperfectly (with the back of the hand, or impermanently, as seen above) or without full intention. In these cases, *shvut* prohibitions are considered of rabbinic provenance, despite the clear biblical origin for the core concept.

Of the many scholars to study this paradox, the most influential is Ramban. Leviticus 23, one of the fullest descriptions of the festival calendar, includes in verse 24 the positive commandment to rest in reference to the day of shofar blasts, which is known to us as Rosh HaShanah: "Speak to Israel, saying, in the seventh month the first day will be a Shabbaton, for recalling trumpet blasts, a holy occasion." From this verse, the Bavli derives the idea that "resting" is a positive commandment from the Torah (Shabbat 24b-25a). In his Torah commentary to Lev. 23:24, Ramban comments on this verse, considering the Midrash Mekhilta cited above:

It seems to me that this Midrash is saying that we have been commanded from the Torah to have rest on the festival, even from activities that are not *melakhah*: a person should not labor all day measuring grains, weighing fruits and merchandise, filling casks of wine, emptying vessels, and transporting stones from house to house and place to place. And should the city be walled and locked by night, they could be loading the donkeys, and delivering wine, grapes, figs, and all goods on the festival so that the market would be full of all forms of buying and selling, with the shops open and the merchants attending and the vendors with all their wares displayed with their coins before them, and the workers would be rising early to hire themselves out for these and similar tasks as if it were a weekday—and all this is permitted on the festivals and even on Shabbat itself, for there is no *melakhah* in all of this! For this reason, the Torah said "Shabbaton"—that it be a day of rest and relaxation, not a day of effort. And this is a good and accurate explanation.

Yitzhak Gilat traces the evolution of Ramban's thoughts from this passage in his Torah commentary to his notes on Rambam's *Sefer HaMitzvot*, to his sermon for Rosh HaShanah.[176] Ramban was apparently troubled that such a clearly stated and important biblical commandment could be treated as a mere rabbinic decree, and he kept returning to this topic and refining his position. According to Gilat, Ramban's final verdict is that *shvut* is differentiated from *melakhah* not in kind but in degree. Both are biblical laws, but *melakhah* is forbidden in even the most minor action, whereas *shvut* restrictions are forbidden biblically only when accomplished with great effort. A minor transgression of *shvut* is considered just a rabbinical ban. The positive commandment is to create an atmosphere of rest; minor deviations from this psychological goal are tolerable, but at the point that a person changes the atmosphere of Shabbat to that of *ḥol* (weekday), then they have failed to fulfill the biblical command to rest. In contemporary terms, speaking briefly and socially with a business associate at a Shabbat kiddush is different from sitting down afterwards to discuss marketing strategies. In the latter scenario, the commandment of *shvut* would be violated, even if the associates were careful not to write down their ideas.[177]

Some rabbis piously extended the concept of *shvut* to include even aesthetic and introspective concerns. Not only did they prohibit conducting business on Shabbat, but even *thinking* about business. Not only did the sages prohibit playing instruments on Shabbat,[178] but also making loud noises (or even excessive conversation).[179] Rabbi Abbahu states in Talmud Yerushalmi that we are to imitate the divine silence on Shabbat: "Rest to the Lord—like the Lord! Just as the Holy One rested from speaking so too should you rest from speaking."[180] Even the method of walking on Shabbat was meant to be different from the hurried scurrying of the workweek.[181] Some of these practices were embellished in legends such as the famous story of the man who noticed a gap in his fence on Shabbat, thought first to fix it, and then vowed not to repair it since the forbidden thought had come to him, and was rewarded for his piety.[182]

Nevertheless, the Talmud declares that thoughts of labor are permitted, and these directives to think and move differently on Shabbat are considered aspirational rather than normative.[183]

A complex category of Shabbat and Yom Tov law deals with handling objects and has come to be known as *muktzeh*, literally "set aside." Mishnah Shabbat 17:4 preserves debates among Rabbi Akiva's students about what types of objects may be handled and for what purpose. Rambam explains that the ban on handling items that have no Sabbath-appropriate use is designed to protect the distinctly tranquil nature of the day, but Ravad maintains that the purpose of *muktzeh* is to prevent inadvertent transgression (MT Shabbat 24:12-13). This is a replay of the classic definition of *shvut*, which brings up the same question—is it primarily a safeguard to prevent *melakhah*, or does it have its own psychological value? Rambam points us in the more expansive direction whereby *shvut* is broader than a mere protective measure; it is a guide to making Shabbat and Yom Tov distinctive and holy.

Shulḥan Arukh (OH 308:1) summarizes the rules of *muktzeh* this way:

> All utensils may be handled on Shabbat, except for *muktzeh*, out of concern for financial loss. For example: a knife used for ritual slaughter or circumcision, and a barber's shears, and a knife used by scribes to sharpen their quills [may be moved for safekeeping]. Since they are cautious not to use [any of] these utensils for another [permitted] purpose, it is forbidden to carry them on Shabbat, even if only to clear the space they are occupying, or to use their mass [e.g., as a paperweight].

Objects that have a permitted use on Shabbat may be handled

to protect them, or to clear the space they occupy. Only items used exclusively for a forbidden purpose, such as matches, may not be touched on Shabbat. This rule thus plays a dual function: it helps to preserve the special atmosphere of Shabbat, and it safeguards against inadvertent transgression.

To summarize our introduction to *shvut*: actions banned by the rabbis as *shvut* may be divided into three categories:

A DECREE TO PREVENT VIOLATION OF A MELAKHAH:

This is perhaps the most common form of *shvut* and is presumably behind the Tannaitic examples. Thus, one should not climb a tree lest they break a branch, nor make legal rulings lest they write down the verdict. In these cases, the act banned as *shvut* is not inherently problematic, but is to be avoided as a fence around the Torah.

ACTIONS DISTINCT FROM THE BIBLICAL PROHIBITION

Liability for performing *melakhah* on Shabbat is limited by the restrictions of action and intention described above. As we saw, writing is defined as forming two letters using durable ink on a durable surface with one's dominant hand. Absent these conditions, the action cannot be considered the biblical *melakhah* of writing, yet the rabbis still prohibited writing in a different fashion. This rabbinic level of prohibition is known as a *shvut*. So, too, the biblical prohibition on carrying was limited to instances where the object was lifted, carried four cubits in a public domain,[184] and then put down, all by the same person. This category of *shvut* also includes asking a gentile to perform a *melakhah* on Shabbat. Such instruction is considered banned by the rabbis, even though the biblical prohibition covers only work done by a Jew. This second form of *shvut* may be understood in two ways—it is either another type of fence around the Torah to prevent a Jew from getting used to a behavior and inadvertently violating the prohibited form, or as a means of enforcing the spirit as well as the letter of the law.[185]

PROTECTING THE RESTFUL NATURE OF THE DAY:

The third and perhaps most interesting category of *shvut* describes activities that are truly distinct from the *melakhot* but are considered incompatible with Sabbath rest. From a very early time, commerce was considered improper on Shabbat, and not only because it might lead to writing, but because Shabbat was designed to be a day of delight. This important concept is based on a prophetic text, Isaiah 58:13-14:

> If you refrain from trampling the Sabbath, from pursuing your affairs on My holy day; if you call the Sabbath "delight," the Lord's holy day "honored"; and if you honor it and go not your ways, nor look to your affairs nor strike bargains—then you can seek the favor of the Lord. I will set you astride the heights of the earth, and let you enjoy the heritage of your father Jacob—for the mouth of the Lord has spoken. (trans. NJPS)

Isaiah's words were understood to exclude business dealings from Shabbat.[186] So, too, was excessive exertion (*tirḥah y'teirah*) considered to be forbidden under the category of *shvut*. For example, one should not carry heavy furniture up and down stairs within the home, even though this is not banned as *melakhah* either by the Torah or by the rabbis. Making loud noises or even talking excessively (*ivaludei kala*) was considered by some to be inappropriate on Shabbat.[187] A vague but important application of this category was called *uvdin d'ḥol*, [avoiding] weekday behaviors.[188] Actions that are commonly associated with working—even though they do not involve *melakhah*—should be avoided. Eventually, even *thinking* about weekday activities like business and politics[189] came to be included in the prohibition called *shvut*, though this level of observance was considered the practice of saintly individuals and was not banned by halakhah.

Returning to our topic of electricity, the obligation of *shvut*, rest on Shabbat, has multiple applications. If the use of a particular electrical appliance or electronic device does not involve *melakhah*, one still must ask whether it could expose one to the risk of performing *melakhah*. For example, some e-readers may be used in a "read-only" manner, in which images are displayed in a transient fashion that would not be deemed "writing." Nevertheless, the normal operation of these devices is to follow links to download new content, whether free or for a fee, thus leading to both *melakhah* (*toledat koteiv*) and violation of *shvut*. Moreover, they track usage and store information such as the current page view, so that when the reader returns, it will be easy to resume reading. Each of these objections could arguably be addressed, and in this way allow for the reading of content on Shabbat that would otherwise be inaccessible. At this point, it appears to us that the border between permitted and prohibited activity with e-readers remains impossible to articulate, leaving the operation of such devices in the middle category of *patur aval assur*, exempt from liability but still forbidden absent a competing value, as described below.[190]

Moreover, the use of many electronic devices undermines the distinctive tranquil nature of Shabbat or Yom Tov. For example, turning on a radio or television may not involve any form of *melakhah*, and yet it introduces audio and video that are broadcast from another locale, bringing with them music, news, and advertisements that may distract the listener from his or her immediate surroundings and from the special atmosphere of Shabbat. Using the phone can also shatter the distinctive culture of Shabbat as a day focused on one's immediate surroundings and the people with whom one is "making" Shabbat. Shabbat is a day dedicated to localism, as the Torah says, "one should not leave their place on the seventh day" (Exod.16:29).[191]

Contemporary families spend much of their time "together" focused on their individual electronic devices. Faces lit by glowing screens large and small, ears attached to headphones, they busily interact with friends and strangers across the world—while making minimal contact with the people around them. Shabbat can and should be different. Aside from the issues of *melakhah* that have occupied most of our attention to this point, there is the positive value of creating a tranquil environment of spiritual community on this holy day. It is understood that one person's tranquility is another person's boredom, but Shabbat can be a day to reclaim interactive entertainments occurring in real time, without the mediation of technology. Focusing on the people around us rather than on communication with those far away creates a powerful sense of community that is not virtual. Refraining from calling, texting, video-chatting, and participating in the ever-expanding menu of social media for 25 hours, preserves the simple art of face-to-face communication, and differentiates Shabbat from other days. *Shvut*, the positive command to rest on Shabbat, is undermined with the use of electronic communication.

We must acknowledge, however, that for some people who are physically isolated, it is not possible to "make Shabbat" with others. For them, telecommunications may be the only avenue for connecting with friends and family, and even for participating in Torah study or communal prayer.[192] Calling an elderly parent may be an expression of *kibbud horim*, honoring parents, just as reaching out to an ill person may be the best chance for *bikkur ḥolim*, visiting the sick—both important mitzvot. The principle of acting *l'tzorekh mitzvah*, for the sake of a mitzvah, will be discussed below, and may ameliorate concerns regarding *shvut*, but it does not suffice to permit the *melakhah* of writing on Shabbat. From our perspective, this means that a phone call to check on a person's wellbeing is preferable to a text message or email, which come closest to the banned category of writing, even if the phone call also generates a record on the device and server, since these residual effects are unintended.

If Shabbat and Yom Tov are to succeed in focusing the mind on Torah and on appreciation for the natural environment created by God, then we have a positive reason to avoid digital distractions and make Shabbat a day unlike any other. Of course, the same may be said about reading newspapers and business journals. Ideally, we should spend Shabbat reading and discsussing Torah and other subjects which increase our sense of appreciation for the world and that do not engage us in business. However, most of the Shabbat-observant community does read secular literature on Shabbat, and this has become normative. Nevertheless, the principle of *shvut* indicates that we should make special effort on Shabbat to study Torah, and to avoid subjects such as business and finance that are antithetical to the spiritual focus of the seventh day.[193]

Under normal circumstances, we therefore should not use a phone, computer, or any other electronic device that distracts attention from our immediate surroundings. Yet what about the use of digital devices necessary to protect human dignity, such as hearing aids, or the use of a motorized chair, cart, or lift to help a disabled or frail individual get about the home or congregation? Such questions pit the value of *shvut* against competing Jewish values, such as human dignity, and thus, they call for nuanced prioritization. This is the focus of our next section.

III

PRIORITIZATION OF HALAKHIC VALUES

Since the period of the Maccabees, there has been consideration for the balance between observing Shabbat and *pikuaḥ nefesh*, protecting human life.[194] The rabbis declared that *pikuaḥ nefesh* is so important that it overrides the prohibition against doing *melakhah* on Shabbat. They debated the precise *drashah* or literary clue to this important principle,[195] but determined that whenever a person's health is at serious risk,[196] considerations of *melakhah* and, all the more so, *shvut*, are waived.[197] The rabbis were emphatic on this point, instructing a rescuer not to hesitate to violate Shabbat, and even making allowances for the rescuer to violate Shabbat once again to return home after their heroic act, lest the halakhically observant public hesitate to take lifesaving action.[198] As Rav Yehudah says in the name of Shmuel, "the Torah says, 'you shall live by them' [the mitzvot]—not die by them."[199] This principle naturally applies whether or not the action involves the use of electricity.

The rabbinic prohibitions that are classed together under the rubric of *shvut* are treated leniently in the face of the "demands of a mitzvah," though the permission to request such actions from non-Jews is often limited to tasks associated with the performance of brit milah.[200] The rabbis have a general principle of *mitzvah ha-ba'ah b'aveirah*, that one may not violate one mitzvah to fulfill another one, especially when the violation is active, and the failure to fulfill the second mitzvah is passive (for example, one may not steal to give charity or to fulfill the mitzvah of possessing a lulav).[201] As such, it does not generally suffice to claim a positive purpose to justify the performance of *melakhah*.

Additional halakhic norms bear upon our discussion of electricity on Shabbat, but none has the same legal force as *pikuaḥ nefesh*, the preservation of life. Only serious risks to health can justify the performance of *melakhah* on Shabbat. Still, other halakhic norms are relevant when determining whether a given action that is arguably banned as *shvut* should be permitted in certain circumstances. The most important such value is the dignity of people, or *k'vod ha-briyot.*[202] Jewish law requires us to prevent the humiliation of others, and to act to protect that precious quality, known as dignity, that derives from the divine reflection evident in every human life. While considerations of dignity do not supersede *biblical* prohibitions, they do negate later additions made by the rabbis to Jewish law. If we were to determine that a given activity was prohibited by rabbinic law, but was necessary to preserve human dignity, then accommodation would be mandated.

Within the Orthodox community consideration for human dignity has led to lenient rulings regarding the use of a hearing aid on Shabbat,[203] and the permissibility of using an electrical wheelchair or scooter that is equipped with a *grama* switch (see discussion above). Conservative rabbis have likewise permitted the use of assistive devices to allow people with various physical disabilities to participate more fully in communal life. For this reason, we would permit the use of devices that could be considered rabbinically prohibited, such as an infrared radio transmitter to allow people who are hard of hearing to participate in prayer and Torah study. This same concern justifies the use of microphones and other technologies to amplify voice,[204] and the use of electric-powered wheelchairs, carts, lifts, and elevators on Shabbat, since these do not involve *melakhah*. Indeed, the same consideration for avoiding excessive strain on Shabbat that serves as a form of *shvut*, limiting us from activities such as moving furniture, may also justify the use of electricity, for example, the use of an elevator[205] rather than climbing stairs.

Returning to the subject of e-readers, as we have seen above, the use of these devices on Shabbat is problematic on many levels. Downloading new content and making notations are biblically prohibited activities under the category of *toledat koteiv*, derivative forms of writing. Purchasing new content is additionally forbidden by the rabbis under the rubric of *shvut*. Using e-readers to display new screen views that are transient in that they automatically shut off after a few minutes of inactivity would not be biblically prohibited but would be banned rabbinically as *toldat koteiv d'rabbanan*. However, *if such an e-reader had its network functions disabled and were used to display text in a temporary fashion (thus reducing the prohibited act of writing to the rabbinic level) for the sake of a visually disabled person who had no other way to read, we would suspend the rabbinic-level prohibitions in deference to the demands of human dignity.*

The prophet Isaiah praises a person who calls Shabbat a "delight" and the sages developed the concept of *oneg Shabbat* (Sabbath delight) to involve eating delicious foods and avoiding fasting on Shabbat.[206] In Midrash Yalkut Shimoni, the concept of *oneg Shabbat* is extended to "even a small thing."[207] While this value (which was traditionally applied to allow keeping foods warm, and to prohibit anxiety-inducing activities such as sea-travel close to Shabbat)[208] has arguably been overextended and used to justify violation of Shabbat norms for the sake of individual pleasure, there is some precedent for treating issues of *shvut* leniently to augment the celebration of Shabbat.

Another halakhic value relevant to our discussion is *bal tashhit* ("do not destroy"), the command not to waste physical resources.[209] Desisting from using electrical devices altogether is certainly one way to reduce one's carbon footprint and is therefore consistent with Jewish values for every day, and not only on Shabbat. Likewise, the practice of walking to synagogue and to meals is a "green solution" that is particularly appropriate for a day dedicated to recalling God's creation.[210] On the other hand, we are not expected to sit in the dark on Shabbat as did the Karaites and make the day one of gloom. Rather, we should make reasonable use of our resources on Shabbat, carefully avoiding *melakhah* and creating a positive atmosphere of rest, *shvut*.

If we are commanded to recall the majesty of God's creation on Shabbat, then surely, we should not observe it in a way that wastes the resources God has so graciously provided. Many observant Jews leave lights, air conditioners, and other appliances running for all of Shabbat, even when unneeded. This practice is understandable if one considers the operation of all electrical switches to be biblically forbidden, because the principle of not wasting resources does not supersede the prohibition of *melakhah*. Thus, if we were to consider turning off an appliance to involve a *melakhah*, then we would not permit it just to save energy.

Indeed, Mishnah Shabbat 2:5 rules out saving resources as an excuse for performing the *melakhah* of *kibui*, extinguishing, while permitting such action when motivated by concerns for physical health and safety:[211]

> One who extinguishes a lamp out of fear of idolaters, thieves, or evil spirits, or to help an ill person sleep, is exempt. If [he extinguished the lamp] from concern for the lamp, or the oil or the wick, he is liable. Rabbi Yossi exempts him from all of these except for the wick since it makes charcoal.

This text indicates that it is permitted to perform the *melakhah* of "extinguishing" for the sake of safety and health, but not to preserve material resources. Of course, the Mishnah's concern is not the reduction of carbon emissions, but the preservation of a person's property. Rambam notes in his commentary that the stringencies of the second half of the Mishnah reflect the view of Rabbi Yehudah, that labor done for a purpose other than its forbidden result (i.e., creating charcoal) is still forbidden. He also notes that putting out the lamp prepares it to be used to burn fuel again in the future, so this action cannot truly be called an unintentional form of labor.[212]

We have determined that turning off electrical appliances does not involve *melakhah*, whether intentional or unintentional; turning an appliance off does not make it easier to turn it on, as is the case with relighting wicks, and this Mishnah therefore does not apply. The principle of conserving natural resources indicates that we should indeed turn off unneeded appliances on Shabbat.

This principle may also be applied to the use of e-readers, since purchasing or borrowing books in electronic form avoids many wasteful activities, such as producing paper, printing, transporting, and storing the finished product. Some reading materials may be accessible only in digital form. For these reasons, there is a positive motivation to use e-readers on Shabbat that could arguably justify the relaxation of certain *shvut* concerns. Nevertheless, as discussed above, the current generation of e-readers and tablets include many applications that record data in a way we understand to be biblically forbidden as writing. Indeed, these devices are becoming more fully featured and networked with each generation. A Shabbat-observant Jew who wishes to use an e-reader would need to disable all features for address all concerns of data downloading, recording, and display, lest they violate fundamental principles of Shabbat law.

A related halakhic value often considered in reference to Shabbat and holidays is known as *hefsed merubeh*, preventing substantial financial hardship.[213] One example in the codes regards a wedding that was delayed on a Friday afternoon until after dark. While the Mishnah at Beitza 5:2 states that we do not perform weddings on Shabbat (because of *shvut*, lest one sign the marriage contract), in this case, delaying the wedding until after Shabbat would waste all the food that had been prepared and would embarrass the family; Moshe Isserles rules that the wedding is permitted, but this leniency is limited to emergency situations, not for planned events.[214] This consideration does not suffice to permit *melakhah*; still, if inaction will result in great financial loss, and a simple response can prevent the loss, one need not worry about *shvut.* Thus, one can and should put leftover foods back in a refrigerator for use after Shabbat, without worrying that this is to be considered "preparation" on Shabbat for afterwards.[215]

The rabbis declared that certain *shvut* prohibitions did not apply within the ancient Temple (*ain shvut ba-mikdash*), but this permission did not extend to other worship spaces.[216] In cases of need, especially to perform a mitzvah, they permitted asking a non-Jew to perform an act of *shvut*.[217] Thus, within a modern congregation, Jews should not perform acts banned as *shvut*, but may request such support from non-Jewish staff.[218] Janitorial staff might be instructed to keep the building clean, lit, and organized for congregational use (e.g., unstacking and arranging chairs for a service), and catering staff might set tables and otherwise arrange a dining space on Shabbat, but even non-Jewish staff should not be instructed on Shabbat to perform *melakhah* such as cooking, transporting supplies to the synagogue, performing construction, etc.

Rabbinic Sabbath prohibitions are generally treated leniently for the sake of a mitzvah at dusk.[219] The Talmud and codes also permit certain violations of *shvut* for a sacred obligation, such as accommodating unanticipated guests for a Shabbat meal. For example, if one did not have sufficient space cleared away to seat all of the guests, they may move produce out of a storage area to make room, so long as this does not require excessive effort.[220] So, too, is it permissible to accommodate the non-*melakhah* needs of a person who is ill but not in danger (*holeh she-ain bo sakanah*), and to ask a non-Jewish attendant to perform such tasks, and even *melakhot*, on such a person's behalf.[221] People who would not otherwise use electricity on Shabbat would be justified asking a non-Jewish attendant to help in this way, to assist a frail or ill person and make them more comfortable. There is a long tradition of permitting an action that is not ordinarily associated with Shabbat, but is not specifically prohibited, through a variation (*shinui*) that highlights the action and consciously differentiates it from weekday behavior.[222]

To summarize this discussion, Shabbat is meant to be a day of delight that augments one's appreciation of the twin blessings of life and liberty, and that allows a person to become attuned to the spiritual partnership with God. In general, the rules of *melakhah* and *shvut* function well in fostering this sensibility, but other Jewish values, such as the preservation of human life, health, and dignity, as well as our resources, may at times supersede considerations of *shvut* and even rabbinic forms of *melakhah*. When electrical appliances and electronic devices are needed to further these values, they allow one to fulfill the positive mandate to remember and sanctify Shabbat, and they may therefore be used in the manner delineated below.

As mentioned above, there is a broad permission for the performance of *melakhot* on Shabbat to save life and prevent significant threats to human health. Yet many of the assistive devices used by people who are ill, frail, or disabled are not necessarily of a lifesaving nature, though they may be necessary for such people to become physically comfortable, and to overcome isolation. There is a continuum of physical and social comfort that is directly related to health. People who experience physical or psychological distress often also experience a decline in health, and it is not always apparent at what point such declines become serious enough to invoke the *pikuah nefesh* exception to the ban on *melakhah*.

The benefit of the doubt in matters of health should always be towards leniency, and the judge of medical necessity must be the patient or their medical surrogate.

We realize that every such accommodation has the potential to involve other problematic actions. For example, if it is permissible to use a wheelchair lift on Shabbat, is it also permissible to repair such a wheelchair lift on Shabbat? To call the company that services lifts? May one pay the workman and sign an invoice? Such activities are all banned on Shabbat, unless there is danger to an individual (for example, someone stranded on the lift or trapped in an unsafe area). There is an understandable tendency, therefore, to prohibit even related activities out of concern for their unintended consequences. We should not allow such slippery-slope arguments to incapacitate decision-making, but it is appropriate to try to anticipate such issues.[223] There is already precedent for allowing Jewish ambulance drivers and other rescue workers to drive—not only towards the hospital while bearing a patient who is urgently ill, but also to drive home again aftwerward, lest they become hesitant to violate Shabbat to save a life again. Still, we must exercise caution to minimize Shabbat violations to those directly necessary for protecting health.

In June 2023, the CJLS approved two responsa, one by Mordecai Schwartz and Chaim Weiner, the other by David Fine and Barry Leff, that dealt with the use of electric vehicles (EVs) on Shabbat. The first responsum argued that all vehicular travel is forbidden on Shabbat, but only under the rabbinic rubric of *shvut*. Rabbis Schwartz and Weiner did not differentiate between gasoline and electric vehicles, deciding that the use of an internal combustion engine should not be defined as "burning" (*mavir*) because one does not directly ignite the fuel. Their overall intention was to make the case for walking on Shabbat, which I share, but by collapsing any distinctions between types of motors, they removed an incentive to switch to the less problematic (both ritually and environmentally) class of EVs. Moreover, they declined to offer general permission to classes of individuals, such as the frail and disabled, to use an EV to reach synagogue. For these reasons, I voted against their responsum.

Rabbis Fine and Leff came closer to my understanding, differentiating electric motors from internal combustion engines, and they argued that EVs are preferable forms of transportation on Shabbat for those with legitimate need. I agreed with this argument and appreciated their attention to limiting such travel to the neighborhood and avoiding carrying items to and from the car. While I voted for this responsum, I remain concerned that there remain many potential stumbling blocks when using EV's on Shabbat (such as the need to pay for tolls, parking, and recharging batteries) and that their permission may be too broad. An opportunity to reinforce the value of localism on Shabbat may have been lost. Micah Peltz and I explained our concerns in a statement available at the CJLS webpage.

My position is that all Jews ought to prioritize walking on Shabbat and Yom Tov, and not use any form of transportation on those holy days if possible. For those with special needs, it is permissible to use electric vehicles, if necessary to allow participation in communal prayer and meals, so long as they avoid intercity travel, expenditures (tolls, parking, charging, maintenance), and carrying goods. But in an emergency, everything is permitted to preserve life.

When considering the permissibility of using any device on Shabbat, we first consider potential violations of the ban on melakhah, and then whether the proposed action is compatible with the general obligation to rest. While the use of electricity is not inherently forbidden, we have seen that many issues of both melakhah and shvut can arise from the ordinary use of common devices. Most electronics generate durable records even if that is not the user's primary intention. Therefore, they should not be used on Shabbat.

Simple appliances such as fans, lights, and elevators can be used without performing melakhah or violating the tranquil spirit of Shabbat. Indeed, they may enhance the traditional observance of Shabbat by avoiding exertion and discomfort. Electronic appliances are often problematic and should be avoided unless mandated by one of the contravening halakhic values described above.

Finally, we return to the matter of intention. There is a difference between intentionally recording data by, for example, operating a digital camera, and unintentionally being recorded by, for example, walking past a security camera. The former action is forbidden as the performance of melakhah, but the latter is permitted as an unintentional consequence of a permitted action. We hold this distinction to be true even when there is awareness of the possible recording of data, as in the case of using a hotel key card that notes the time of use, or walking across a lobby equipped with cameras, so long as that data is not accessible to the user. Such permissibility is reinforced by the fact that the equipment is automated, and the field of view is recorded regardless of the presence of a given individual. In such cases, we consider the recording of data to be an unintended consequence that is permitted.

Over the course of these three sections, we have examined the core concepts of *melakhah* (labor) and *shvut* (rest) and considered how the contemporary uses of electricity interact with Jewish teachings about marking the seventh day as a separate and sacred time. From the biblical materials, we have learned that Shabbat is a day dedicated to appreciating the gifts of life and liberty. From the rabbis, we learned to avoid actions that make a durable change to our surroundings, and to preserve a tranquil atmosphere on Shabbat that amplifies the sense of divine presence.

While we have found support for some uses of electricity in certain situations, we have also discovered numerous ways in which the operation of electrical appliances is incompatible with the observance of Shabbat. This is a countercultural finding, because the constant use of electronics is extremely seductive to our generation. In the face of this great desire to "stay connected," we often forget the cost of losing the precious hours of quiet that Shabbat offers to those who cherish her. It is appropriate to quote the resounding words of Rabbi Abraham Joshua Heschel in his classic book, *The Sabbath*:

> To set apart one day a week for freedom, a day on which we would not use the instruments which have been so easily turned into weapons of destruction, a day for being with ourselves, a day of detachment from the vulgar, of independence of external obligations, a day on which we stop worshipping the idols of technical civilization, a

day on which we use no money ... is there any institution
that holds out a greater hope for our progress than the
Sabbath?[224]

IV

SUMMARY AND HALAKHIC CONCLUSIONS

In this responsum, we have discussed the laws of Shabbat with
attention to specific forms of *melakhah* and *shvut*. These concepts
remind observers of God's gifts of life and liberty by requiring us to
act in distinctive patterns on the seventh day. *Melakhah* is understood
to refer primarily to actions that result in a durable physical change;
shvut overlaps with this category, but also includes actions and even
thoughts that compromise the tranquility of Shabbat and erode the
distinctiveness of the seventh day. By desisting from *melakhah*, we begin
to appreciate the natural resources of our remarkable world and become
able to resist the temptation to define life's value primarily in terms of
our own actions. By dedicating the day to tranquility, we dignify our
lives and are refreshed for the tasks awaiting us on the six days of labor.

We have learned that the operation of electrical and electronic
circuits may not be categorically banned as *melakhah*, but that many
specific actions involving such appliances violate the laws of Shabbat.
For example, any appliance used to cook food or heat air and water is
banned under the category of *toledat bishul*, a derivative form of cooking.
The operation of any appliance that records data—whether text, audio,
or images—is banned under the category of *toledat koteiv*, a derivative
form of writing. Most consumer electronics fall within this category
and are therefore incompatible with Shabbat observance.

While a comprehensive ban on all uses of electricity may be justified as a fence around the Torah, some uses are not only permissible but even positively indicated. Certainly, any action needed to save a life—even if it involves biblically banned forms of *melakhah*—may be permitted under the rubric of *pikuaḥ nefesh*. Actions that are forbidden under the authority of rabbinic law must be avoided unless they are required for the preservation of human dignity. In some cases, such actions may also be indicated to avoid waste and excessive exertion. The balancing of these norms is complex and requires consultation with halakhic experts based on the particulars of any given situation and appliance.

Having completed our review of *melakhah, shvut,* and other relevant halakhic principles, we may summarize our conclusions as follows:

PISKEI DIN

Considerations of Melakhah

1. The operation of electrical circuits is not inherently forbidden as either *melakhah* or *shvut*. However, the use of electricity to power an appliance that performs *melakhah* with the same mechanism and intent as the original manual labor is biblically forbidden on Shabbat. For example, grinding coffee, trimming trees, sewing, etc., are all forbidden with electrical appliances in the same way as they are forbidden without the use of electricity, as an *av melakhah*.

2. The use of electricity to perform an activity with a *different* mechanism but for the same purpose as a *melakhah* is forbidden to Jews on Shabbat as a derivative labor (*toledah*). Such prohibitions share with the primary forms the severe status of being biblically forbidden. Thus, cooking with an electric heating element or a microwave oven on Shabbat is forbidden as *toledat bishul*,²²⁵ though it is permitted on Yom Tov. Recording text, sound, images, or other data with an electronic device is forbidden as *toledat koteiv*, a derivative form of writing. Sabbath and Yom Tov operation of any electronic recording device, camera, computer, tablet, or cellular phone is forbidden by this standard. Moreover, the creation of a durable image, as with a printer, is also forbidden as a derivative form of writing. Automation may be employed prior to Shabbat to set some such processes in motion, but even here, one must be cautious about the temptation to adjust such devices, as well as their capacity to undermine the distinct atmosphere of Shabbat.

3. For the sake of protecting life, even biblical prohibitions are superseded. Thus, all electrical and electronic devices needed to administer medicine and medically necessary therapies or to summon medical assistance are permitted on Shabbat. If a health challenge is not life-threatening, then Jewish people should not perform *melakhot*, but it may be permissible to employ non-Jewish assistants or use automated systems to help the patient.

Considerations of Shvut

4. The positive commandment of *shvut*, to rest on Shabbat, demands a day of differentiation, in which one avoids commerce, the creation of loud sounds, and anything that would replicate the atmosphere of the work week. Electrical appliances like fans, light fixtures, and magnetic key cards and fobs may be used without violating either the law or the spirit of Shabbat. However, when it comes to electronic communication devices, even if some are not forbidden as a form of *melakhah*, the tranquility of Shabbat may be compromised by such activities. Rabbinical teachings indicate that Shabbat should be dedicated to prayer, Torah study, meals, and rest, not to weekday concerns. We ought to anchor our day in physical environments such as the synagogue and dinner table, that reinforce the holy nature of the day and allow its spiritual potential to be realized.[226] However, Sabbath-observant people can be trusted to decide what formally permitted activities are consonant with their Shabbat tranquility.

5. Positive halakhic values such as protecting human dignity, avoiding excessive strain, financial hardship, and

the squandering of natural resources may supersede the *rabbinic* restraint on using electricity as indicated by *shvut*. Calling an isolated or ill individual might be permitted as an act of *ḥesed* and an expression of honoring parents. The use of electrical motors to assist frail and disabled people to move around, and the use of assistive devices to enhance hearing, speech, and vision, may be justified based on the imperative to protect human dignity, despite the possibility that such tools might lead one to an activity that is rabbinically banned. The use of elevators to reduce strain on Shabbat is likewise permitted. Turning off electrical appliances is permissible to avoid financial hardship and the wasting of natural resources (in contrast to extinguishing a fire, which is not permitted to save fuel). In such cases, halakhic imperatives such as protecting human dignity, avoiding excessive strain, and conserving resources may supersede rabbinic restrictions (*shvut*), but not biblical prohibitions (*melakhah*).

6. Refraining from operating lights and other permitted electrical appliances is a pious behavior that can prevent inadvertent transgression and reinforce the distinctiveness of Shabbat. In many of our communities, a ban on operating all appliances, including lights, has become the operative practice, and should therefore be maintained. Those who do make limited use of electricity must be attentive to the distinctions explained in this responsum, avoiding any activities that would result in cooking, recording, or other labors on Shabbat. They also would be well-advised to be sensitive to the practice of visitors who seek to avoid any operation of circuits, and they may wish to defer to the more stringent practice of much of the observant community. In this way, Shabbat may provide

its observers with a distinctive day of delight, dedicated to prayer, Torah study and fellowship. Then Shabbat will continue its powerful role as a sign of the covenant between God and Israel, transmitting holiness from generation to generation, and supporting the creation of sacred communities.

APPENDIX

TABLE OF RULINGS FOR COMMON ELECTRONICS

The variety of electrical appliances and electronic applications is vast and growing by the day. It is impossible to discuss every form available today or to anticipate what innovations will be introduced in the coming years. For this reason, I have focused on broad principles and applied them in the table below to some of the more common devices from which other applications may be extrapolated. There will certainly be a need for further studies as technology and its surrounding culture continue to develop. Recall that even permitted activities may be avoided to further differentiate Shabbat from the weekday; and even forbidden activities may be permitted, as discussed above, when overridden by countervailing halakhic values such as *pikuaḥ nefesh*, saving a life.

We designate activities that are biblically forbidden except to protect life as A for *assur* "forbidden"). Activities that are rabbinically forbidden unless superseded by a countervailing halakhic value are categorized as P for *patur aval assur* "forbidden but exempt"). Activities that we consider to be permitted outright are categorized as M for *mutar l'khatḥilah*.

KEY: *A=Assur (forbidden); P=Patur (exempt); M=Mutar (permitted)*

Appliance	Halakhic Concern(s)	Shabbat	Yom Tov	Comments
Computer (desktop, laptop, hand-held, tablet)	Derivative writing; resting	A	A	Captures user data; downloads and saves files
Digital Camera, Voice Recorder	Derivative writing; resting	A	A	Unless automated
Electric vehicle	Carrying; may need repair	P	P	Permitted for disabled people to preserve dignity; and in dangerous situations
Electric Dishwasher	Derivative cooking	A	M	Heats water; timer operation permissible
Elevator	Resting	M	M	Helps avoid Shabbat exertion
E-reader	Derivative writing	P	P	Permitted for disabled people for dignity.
Fan (air)	Final blow (completion)	M	M	
Heating element	Derivative cooking	A	M	

Inserting batteries, cords	Repairing	A	A	
Intercom	Resting	M	M	Possible danger overrides *shvut*
Lighting fixture	Various	M	M	
Magnetic stripe card Type I (credit, debit, fare cards)	Derivative writing; resting	A	A	
Magnetic stripe Type II	Resting	M	M	Possible danger overrides *shvut*
Microwave oven	Derivative cooking	A	M	
Playing music	Resting	P	P	
Phone call (audio)	Resting	P	P	Permitted for ill people even absent danger

SECTION II

SAVING SANCTITY WHEN FACING DISEASE AND DEATH

CHAPTER 5:
VIRTUAL MINYAN WHEN PHYSICAL GATHERINGS ARE UNSAFE

By March of 2020, the coronavirus known as COVID-19 had spread rapidly across the world, leading many governments to impose severe restrictions on travel and public gatherings and, in some cases, near-total lockdowns. During the early days of the pandemic, much of communal life—social, educational, cultural, spiritual, and more—rapidly shifted online. In one sense, the timing was good, since video conferencing software platforms had recently improved and proliferated. Eventually, communities developed safe ways to gather physically again—praying outside (even in the bitter cold), and then indoors with masks and distancing.

As immunity rose and infections became milder and less common over the next two years, communities returned to normal public worship. Such returns were uneven, however, with some community members reluctant to return in person out of health concerns, while others had established meaningful gatherings online that they preferred to their local options. The crisis was destabilizing to synagogues, some of which flourished as never before, while others struggled or failed.

Questions of halakhic practice during the pandemic focused initially on the constitution of a minyan online, the ability to complete specific liturgical elements that are generally restricted to a quorum, and then other ritual questions, such as the permissibility of video-witnessing ritual acts related to conversion, marriage, and divorce. Halakhists also debated triage ethics, the subject of the next chapter.

Unfortunately, I was one of the earlier people in New York to become infected with COVID-19, and self-quarantined starting on Erev Purim, March 9, 2020. Still, as *mara d'atra* (the local authority for deciding Jewish practice) for JTS, I quickly had to decide how we would handle daily minyan when it suddenly shifted online.

On March 18, I taught a virtual shiur at JTS Rabbinical School Community Time, followed by a written version in my "Tachlis and Torah" message the next day. While I did not submit a written responsum for the CJLS on this subject, I participated in the discussions surrounding the official statements issued by the co-chairs, Pamela Barmash and Elliot Dorff, and voted in favor of a responsum written by Joshua Heller, "Streaming Services on Shabbat and Yom Tov." All these essays were built on the prescient work of Avram Reisner in 2001. I have composed a brief responsum for this volume to address the core question of virtual minyan, distilling the difficult experiences of the pandemic for application to other, hopefully less frightening, circumstances.

QUESTIONS:

May a minyan be constituted entirely online? If only as an emergency accommodation, then under what circumstances? Are there rituals that always require an in-person minyan? Must participants in an online minyan display their video and unmute their audio? What modifications are required for Shabbat and Yom Tov?

RESPONSE:

Jews who have reached the age of mitzvot bear an individual obligation to pray each day, whether a minyan is available or not. Still, public prayer is important, given the Talmud's understanding of the verse in Psalms, "I offer my prayer to You at a propitious hour" (69:14). At Brakhot 8a, the Bavli asks, "When is a propitious hour? When the community prays."

The Shulḥan Arukh states at OH 90:9, *Yishtadeil adam lehitpaleil b'beit ha-knesset im ha-tzibbur*, "a person should attempt to pray in synagogue with the community," but recognizes that sometimes this is not possible. In such cases, Rabbi Karo instructs people to pray alone, but at the same time as their congregation, so that the communal aspect of prayer is not lost entirely. Just as Jews orient towards Jerusalem when praying anywhere in the world, so, too, do we orient to the time of prayer in our community. In this way, we combat isolation in time and space, connecting to public worship even when alone.

Among the many lessons of the pandemic was its demonstration of the broad desire to pray with community, even within the limitations of virtual gatherings. We never learned how to sing together in real time, and we missed the social aspects of prayer. Yet many Jews, including those who seldom showed up in person for daily minyan previously, began to make a practice of logging on to services, transcending the loneliness and boredom of life in lockdown. Still, the question remained of whether a minyan could be constituted entirely online.

This question had already been answered in the negative by the CJLS twenty years earlier, when it approved a 2001 responsum called, "Wired to the *Kadosh Barukh Hu*: Minyan via Internet" by Avram Reisner (I voted in favor). He reviewed many relevant sources from the Talmud and Codes, especially from SA OH 55 (dealing with *kedushah*, prayers that require a minyan) and sections 197 and 198 (dealing with *zimmun*, the invitation to recite grace after meals). The general sense of these materials is that a minyan requires ten members to gather in one location, even though some physical barrier, such as a pillar, separates them. If they can hear one another and be seen by some members of the minyan, they can form the required quorum. Others who are standing outside can attach themselves to the minyan, but not constitute it.

In accord with these ancient precedents, Rabbi Reisner decided that a minyan must be formed in person, but that remote participants can attach themselves to it and share the experience of public prayer. For example, if a family gathers for a shiva minyan, but one of the mourners is too ill to attend, they may join in an audio or video conference and say Kaddish together with those who are present. However, writing in 2001, Rabbi Reisner concluded that an online community with no physical nucleus could not form a minyan. The physical presence of a core ten was essential. Rabbi Reisner addressed additional concerns such as the need to pray in one's own time zone. His arguments were well grounded in classical sources that have stood the test of time remarkably well.

Rabbi Reisner did not, however, address a situation in which physical gatherings are deemed unsafe, and in some jurisdictions, illegal. In such extreme situations, could a minyan ever be constituted online? The urgent conditions of the COVID-19 pandemic in spring 2020 led me, like others, to go back to the sources.

I found a relevant halakhic precedent in the 18th-century writings of Ḥid"a, Rabbi Ḥaim Yosef David Azulai (1724-1806). Rabbi Azulai was born and based in Jerusalem, but he often traveled in Europe as an emissary to raise funds for his impoverished community, as described in his travelogue, *Ma'agal Tov*. As such, he was sensitive to rules in which travelers to Venice and other Italian port cities, arriving from distant lands such as Alexandria, would be required to isolate for forty days (*quaranta giorni*), or quarantine. There were colonies set up for this purpose, and travelers would be grouped in houses by their date of arrival and guarded to prevent them from mingling or departing early.

This is the situation that Rabbi Azulai describes in *Maḥazik Berakhah*, one of his commentaries to the Shulḥan Arukh (OH 55:11), regarding an enforced stay in a *lazzaretto*, or quarantine facility:[1]

In a *lazzaretto* that they maintain in these cities,[2] if there are two groups there who are not permitted to contact one another, with six in one house and four in another, and they are separated in their numbers by law—I heard from a rabbi whom I regard highly, may his light increase, that he wondered if while there, the four could stand at the entrance of their house and join together [with the six standing at the entrance of the other house] to form ten, since they could see each other, or perhaps they are not allowed to join together. As a simple person, I think, based on what they reported, that they may join together [to form a minyan]. For they are unable to be in one house, and a guard stands outside the entrance, and they are not allowed to exit, and the space outside is tight, and is also a public pathway. In such a situation where they are not allowed by the king and local authorities to be together, and the four have attempted to stand by the door and show them their faces, then this is like the case [in the Talmud] of showing one's face through a window to join a minyan. So here, and even more so, because they are unable to be together, and not even near each other. And since there are numerous halakhic authorities upon whom to depend it seems we should lean on them and not allow forty days to pass without public prayer, of not hearing Kaddish or Kedushah. Likewise with a veranda [here he references a situation where a man is not allowed to enter the synagogue but can stand and be seen from the balcony—even the women's section] we have humbly offered that he should try to go down as much as he can [to the level of the minyan] and they can be seen—that we can depend on those above to rule that he may join the minyan, all the more so in such circumstances.[3]

While the situation described by Ḥid"a is different from the home-quarantine experienced by hundreds of millions of people during COVID, it is nevertheless a good model for the salient halakhic issues. Note that the two groups of Jews are prevented from gathering by government decree, and that they have developed a system to show each other their faces, even if they cannot be physically close. Given that there is a pathway between them, it seems unlikely that they can hear each other clearly. Indeed, Rabbi Karo had previously mentioned this concern about the Talmudic source in SA OH 195:2. And yet, somehow, these Jews can coordinate and hear well enough to respond to prompts found in Kaddish and other prayers.

Rabbi Azulai's concern that forty days (quarantine) not pass without the people joining in *kedushah* prayers that require a minyan resonates with our experience in the pandemic. Mourners were especially distraught by their inability to recite Kaddish, a precious practice that sanctifies the divine name and expresses continued loving dedication to the memory of relatives. Forty days is a typological number in Judaism—the days of revelation at Mt. Sinai as well as darker events such as the flood and the tour of the spies in the land. Rabbi Azulai is sensitive to the deep need for Jews to gather and praise God, an activity that sustains individuals, communities, and perhaps even the world.

Rabbi Ḥaim Mordecai Margulies cites Rabbi Azulai approvingly in his Shulḥan Arukh commentary, *Shaarei Teshuvah* (OH 55:15).[4] Later commentaries, such as Rabbi Yisrael Meir Kagen's *Mishnah Berurah*, cite the concept of "showing one's face" to allow the combination of groups that are unable to gather in one space to form a minyan. However, all sources emphasize the importance of making maximal effort to draw as close as possible.

Recent responsa have addressed the challenges of forming a minyan at the cemetery, where numerous families may be gathered in small groups, and Jewish grave diggers may also be in the area. May the mourners in one group of less than ten say Kaddish if other Jews nearby are in their line of sight and can respond to the prayer? In his commentary *Hashukei Ḥemed* to B. Brakhot 21b, Rabbi Yitzḥak Zilberstein (b. Poland, 1934; Israel) writes that the pathways found in cemeteries do not constitute a thoroughfare that divides the mourners, and therefore, they may be allowed to form a minyan, even from different sections of the cemetery.[5]

Early in the COVID-19 pandemic, some rabbis argued that a virtual minyan could be formed for the recitation of the Mourner's Kaddish alone, while other prayers, such as Barkhu and Kedushah, should remain limited to situations when ten adult Jews could gather in one place. Reciting the Mourner's Kaddish fulfills the mitzvah of honoring one's parents and showing love (*ḥesed*) to all relatives. Moreover, it is a strong motivation for many Jews to join and make minyan for others. As such, it is understandable that some rabbis who were otherwise uncomfortable with virtual minyan agreed to extend this leniency only to the Mourner's Kaddish.

Given what we have learned from earlier generations of Jews contending with enforced quarantine and relying on the opinion of

Rabbi Azulai and later authorities, I decided that the permission should be broader, to allow the recitation of Barkhu, Kaddish, and Kedushah for all services. That said, I required that no fewer than ten people "show their faces" by turning on the video. I also instructed participants to unmute for the responsive prayers that required a minyan, so that we could approximate the experience of being together in prayer.

Once virtual minyan had been permitted, the question arose whether Torah could be chanted without ten Jews present. This question was felt most keenly in congregations, as the initial weeks of seclusion stretched into months and then years. Many children became *b'nai mitzvah* during this period, and other important life cycle events normally connected to the Torah service were likewise observed. In some cases, the video conference was hosted by one clergy person alone in the sanctuary with the Torah scroll, with all others online.

I was not faced with this question directly and felt awe-struck admiration for rabbis and cantors who handled such challenging circumstances with integrity and sensitivity. In the daily minyan that I supervised, we decided not to chant Torah with its blessings unless we were able to gather a minyan by the Torah. Otherwise, we would chant the Torah text without its special liturgy, just as if we were reading from a printed book. However, as the technology continues to improve, it may be possible for the ten people to see the scroll directly, and for the remote reader to chant "from the writing" (*min ha-ketav*) as the Talmud instructs.

What about forming a virtual minyan on Shabbat and Yom Tov? During the pandemic, many congregations that had resisted live streaming their services on these holy days made emergency accommodations, and relatively few have discontinued them. As I discuss in my responsum on the use of electronics on Shabbat, there are numerous challenges to using computers on Shabbat, from the creation of ephemeral screen views to the recording of more durable images and texts. The use of chat features within video conferencing platforms was especially problematic on Shabbat since it involved typing text messages which were recorded and preserved by the platform.

The best practice, to my understanding, is for congregations in such circumstances to set up their livestream before Shabbat, to keep the equipment as hidden as possible, to avoid setting up screens in the sanctuary, and to ensure that viewers online have access with minimal input. "Set and forget" became the watchword of more observant communities, but this wasn't always possible. Emergency circumstances were grounds for leniency, but when it became safe for ten or more Jews to gather in person, they became the primary congregation, and it became appropriate to minimize remote participation to passive observation.

Just as it was urgent and appropriate for Jewish communities to accommodate the needs of Jews isolated from one another in the most dangerous phases of the pandemic, it was also urgent and appropriate to reassert the primacy of in-person gathering when the danger had passed. Yes, there are substantial benefits to providing remote access even in normal times—relatives who are unable to make a journey to participate in a family celebration may at least witness the event from afar. Likewise, with congregants who are disabled or immunocompromised and unable to enter public spaces safely, virtual participation can be deeply important. Such situations always deserve sensitive accommodations, whether the situation is a global pandemic or a very local and personal condition.

While COVID-19 was the most extensive and extended cause of social disruption in a century, we have subsequently experienced many other disruptions to physical gathering, from blizzards and floods to fires, hazardous air quality days and wars. We have learned valuable lessons about the importance of maintaining Jewish prayer communities even when we cannot cluster safely in person. And we have also learned how precious it is to gather once more when the danger has passed. With gratitude to God for ending the plague of COVID-19, we pray for good health and joyous gatherings. As we read in Proverbs 14:28, *be-rov am hadrat melekh*, "when many people gather, the Sovereign is sublime."

CHAPTER 6: TRIAGE AND THE SANCTITY OF LIFE

I n March 2020, as I recovered from an early case of COVID, I was asked by a physician friend to address questions related to triage—the sorting and assigning of treatment to patients based on an agreed system of priorities—that I normally associate with battlefields and similar sudden calamities. Of course, the novel coronavirus pandemic was a sudden calamity on a global level, and doctors, other health professionals, and researchers raced to find solutions to keep infected patients alive. In many places, the greatest challenge was the lack of needed supplies, from basic items like masks and gloves to ventilators. Just as challenging was the lack of medical staff, especially as many of them were themselves infected, and all were physically and emotionally exhausted by this sudden outbreak. The creativity, resilience and dedication of these professionals was heroic. The ethical dilemmas that they faced challenged those of us on the sidelines to look closely at the issues, and to offer the best guidance available.

Rabbi Elliot Dorff and I each wrote a responsum about the same time. As has so often been the case, I found myself agreeing with Rabbi Dorff in conclusion, but approaching some of the presenting issues differently. As such, it was appropriate for the CJLS to consider each of our papers independently, even while we took the unusual step of co-authoring a shared conclusion. This responsum was approved by CJLS on May 13, 2020.

Although the COVID-19 crisis has passed, it is unlikely that COVID-19 will be the last pandemic or the final experience of medical scarcity in this generation, and so the ethical and halakhic challenges it brought up will remain relevant in the years ahead.

QUESTION:

On what basis should medical professionals determine which patient gets lifesaving treatment in a pandemic emergency setting?

RESPONSE:[1]

The COVID-19 pandemic caused extraordinary levels of illness, disruption, and death around the world. As I began to write this responsum in late March 2020, having survived my own mild bout with this disease, we did not know how much more destructive the novel coronavirus would be. Medical systems were quickly overwhelmed, and the world responded with unprecedented efforts to isolate people and slow the spread of this virus. These efforts included rationing of medical supplies and triaging patients in need of intensive medical care.[2] Some early afflicted regions, such as northern Italy, faced dreadful decisions to determine which patients to treat intensively, if at all, and which must be left to die.[3]

Unfortunately, this was not the first period in which bioethicists or *poskim* (rabbis who decide questions of halakhah) contended with the allocation of scarce medical resources. Ethical discourse in each crisis builds on the experience and lessons learned previously. Most contemporary medical policy is based on secular understandings of ethics, especially utilitarian approaches intended to produce the greatest benefit for the largest number of people.

In contrast, Jewish ethics begins with theological beliefs in divine creation, the fashioning of humans in the divine image, the Torah's record of commandments designed to sanctify the people Israel, and the efforts of rabbis in the past two millennia to apply these beliefs and practices to contemporary life. Halakhah is a normative literature that is primarily deontological, or rule-based, though Jewish teachers have always believed that a consequence of Jewish normative practice is ultimately to bring blessing to the world. Still, halakhic sources are not generally consequentialist or utilitarian in the sense of deciding actions based on the actor's assessment of what will yield the greatest immediate and quantifiable good.

During the COVID-19 pandemic, medical authorities boldly declared the need for utilitarian approaches to triage. For example, doctors Douglas White and Benjamin Lo established a rating system for the allocation of resources.[4] Over the course of fifteen years, Ezekiel Emanuel developed bioethical foundations for such ratings, with a 2020 update to address the COVID-19 pandemic published in the *New England Journal of Medicine* (NEJM).[5] I will present a summary of these articles—both of which are utilitarian in their results—before offering a different perspective based on Jewish legal texts and practice, with their emphasis on the sanctity of life.

My intended audience for this responsum is threefold. I hope that it will prove useful to medical clinicians, ethicists, and public health officials, whatever their personal faith identity, as they contend with morally challenging realities and formulate triage policies for a religiously diverse population. This responsum is also addressed to rabbis, chaplains, and others tasked with providing spiritual support for patients and their loved ones in such disturbing circumstances. Finally, I acknowledge and address some of the challenges for families contending with painful decisions and losses while forced to remain isolated from one another.

Utilitarianism: From Theory to Practice

Dr. Emanuel and his colleagues identify four fundamental values that they consider essential to developing a fair distribution of resources:[6]

a) Maximizing the benefits produced by scarce resources

b) Treating people equally

c) Promoting and rewarding instrumental value

d) Giving priority to the worst off

These fundamental values are not easily reconciled with one another. What follows is my synopsis of their explanations, which should be read in full.

The first value, *maximizing benefit*, is essentially a utilitarian determination that emphasizes saving the most lives, or even the most life-years possible. *Equal treatment* is based on an egalitarian account of justice and would assign resources to people without discrimination, perhaps by use of a random lottery, even if this method would not yield the best results on the macro level (most lives saved). *Instrumental value* brings us back to utilitarianism. It acknowledges the popular conviction that especially in a crisis, people are not truly equal. Some people are more useful—for example, medical clinicians who can save the lives of others. Saving one doctor might allow for the saving of multiple lives, which would not be the case when saving a person in a "non-essential" field of work.[7] Their fourth value, *giving priority to the worst off*, returns us to a justice basis, helping people who are already most vulnerable, or perhaps those who have benefited least in life, even if this allocation does not yield the greatest "utility."

We have here a seesaw between what appears to be the greatest good, and what seems most just or fair. Yet Emanuel, et al., are not stymied. In their view, the first fundamental value they promote, *maximizing benefits*, is "paramount in a pandemic," and overrides considerations of justice or fairness. They say, "saving more lives and more years of life is a consensus value across expert reports." Their essentially utilitarian outlook drives the six policy recommendations of their article, from which I will excerpt (these words are theirs; readers are urged to consult their NEJM article for fuller explanations).

Synopsis of Emanuel, et al., policy recommendations for triage in a pandemic:

1) Operationalizing the value of maximizing benefits means that people who are sick but could recover if treated are given priority over those who are unlikely to recover[8] if treated as well as those who are likely to recover without treatment.

2) Critical COVID-19 interventions — testing, PPE, ICU beds, ventilators, therapeutics, and vaccines—should go first to front-line health care workers and others who care for ill patients and who keep critical infrastructure operating, particularly workers who face a high risk of infection and whose training makes them difficult to replace.[9]

3) For patients with similar prognoses, equality should be invoked and implemented through random allocation, such as a lottery, rather than a first-come, first-served allocation process.

4) Maximizing benefits requires consideration of prognosis—how long the patient is likely to live if treated— which may mean giving priority to younger patients and those with fewer coexisting conditions.

5) People who participate in research to prove the safety and effectiveness of vaccines and therapeutics should receive some priority to receive COVID-19 interventions.

6)   There should be no difference in allocating scarce resources between patients with COVID-19 and those with other medical conditions.[10]

Each of these policy recommendations is justified within the realm of the authors' fundamental values, and they are certainly correct that it is best to establish consistent ethical practices rather than leaving life and death determinations to spur-of-the-moment decisions by clinicians at the bedside.

Still, Emanuel, et al., acknowledge that implementing some of their recommendations would be "extremely psychologically traumatic for clinicians—and some clinicians might refuse to do so." For example, they state, "we believe that removing a patient from a ventilator or an ICU bed to provide it to others in need is also justifiable and that patients should be made aware of this possibility at admission."[11]

If the previous sentence did not catch your attention, it should. Removing a viable patient from a ventilator or an ICU bed, sometimes without their consent, and perhaps over their desperate objections, will often result directly in their death. Furthermore, the authors do not limit this permission to end the life of a patient to one who is actively dying or even terminally ill.

Their fourth policy recommendation uses age as a factor, with younger patients given priority even over viable older patients. If patients have similar prognoses, then, "equality should be invoked and operationalized through random allocation." Understand their position: priority should not be given to those first to arrive at the hospital, since that policy would discriminate against people who live farther from treatment centers and might hurt people whose "strict adherence to recommended public health measures" delayed onset of their own illness.

These recommendations accord with the fundamental values that

Emanuel, et al., have established, and they sound reasonable. However, they would have the following radical results:

1) Patients living with disability or chronic health conditions might be denied intensive care in the presence of other patients with better overall health, or younger patients.

2) Patients already being treated would not have priority over those newly arrived but could be bumped from beneficial therapy in place of someone who could benefit even more.

3) Triage officers or committees would be empowered to decide to terminate life-sustaining treatment for a patient who is not terminally ill, directly leading to their death, without the consent or over the protests of the patient and their family or health care proxy.

Clinicians engaged in direct patient care would be spared the moral burden of making these decisions, but they would nevertheless be required to implement them. This requirement could also cause moral injury, as journalist Jennifer Senior has argued.[12]

Moreover, in the name of efficiency, important principles of justice would be abandoned. Disability rights scholars and activists have rightly sounded the alarm over the devaluation of such lives in a crisis. Ari Ne'eman writes, "Even in a crisis, authorities should not abandon nondiscrimination. By permitting clinicians to discriminate against those who require more resources, perhaps more lives would be saved. But the ranks of the survivors would look very different, biased toward those who lacked disabilities before the pandemic. Equity would have been sacrificed in the name of efficiency."[13] Likewise, the utilitarian perspective is often functionally ageist, since older patients and neonates tend to experience significant medical complications. This calls to mind the Torah's threat that a nation that does not show mercy to the elderly and the young might conquer and torment Israel (Deut. 28:50).[14]

The most fully articulated guide to triage is found in the work of Douglas White and Benjamin Lo. In pursuit of fairness, and to relieve frontline clinicians of the moral burden of decision-making, they call for the designation of triage officers: "The separation of the triage role from the clinical role is intended to promote objectivity, avoid conflicts of commitments, and minimize moral distress. The triage officer will also be involved in patient or family appeals of triage decisions, and in collaborating with the attending physician to disclose triage decisions to patients and families." These arguments are all valid, and indeed, the triage officer might also have greater expertise and sensitivity to various cultural and religious norms than does any given clinician. Still, the use of a triage officer would not resolve the ethical dilemmas of these decisions, nor would it prevent clinicians from experiencing moral distress when asked to reallocate medical resources away from their own patient, causing them to die.

Triage decisions would, in White and Lo's proposal, be based on a scoring system whose core component is SOFA, the Sequential Organ Failure Assessment score, which "is used to determine patients' prognoses for hospital survival." "In addition," they write, "the presence of life-limiting comorbid conditions, as determined by the triage team, is used to characterize patients' longer-term prognosis." Only if there is a tie between two patients on their prognosis to survive their hospitalization and the presence of life-limiting co-morbid conditions, are other criteria such as age or profession considered. In this regard, they are "soft utilitarian."

To their credit, White and Lo reject the use of "exclusion criteria" in their multi-principle priority score, and do not include disability—other than dementia—in their table of "Examples of Severely Life Limiting Comorbidities (Commonly associated with survival <1 year).[15] Still, their utilitarian analysis means that some patients would be denied treatment based on an assessment of their life prospects (including age bands), and some viable patients who very much want to live could be forcibly removed from ventilation, causing them to die.

The COVID-19 crisis illustrated the unequal and unjust treatment and health outcomes of many populations, especially people of color, people living with disability, and people forced to live in congregate environments, such as nursing facilities and prisons. Triage presents another opportunity for injustice, even if exclusion criteria are phrased carefully to avoid explicit bias.[16] Before even "soft" utilitarian recommendations for the allocation of scarce medical resources are accepted and implemented, we must pause and ask whether other ethical and religious values deserve consideration.

From Utilitarianism to Sanctity

Halakhic norms used to inform discussions of triage of medical resources are extrapolated from different contexts, such as the redemption of captives, the allocation of water, prioritization in the giving of charity, negotiations during a siege, and the final Mishnayot in Tractate Horayot (3:7-8) that establish now generally defunct hierarchies in lifesaving.[17]

Rabbi Elliot Dorff provides an excellent overview of five Jewish discourses relevant to triage in chapter 12 of his 1998 book, *Matters of Life and Death*, and in his new responsum addressing the COVID-19 pandemic, "Triage in the Time of a Pandemic" (CJLS, rev. May 1, 2020).[18]

As Rabbi Dorff has written, there is little discussion of medical triage in classical Jewish sources, perhaps because pre-modern medicine was so ineffective. Nevertheless, Rabbi Dorff derives significant guidance on medical triage from these classical sources, ultimately endorsing a policy proposal that matches that of the medical utilitarians. Rabbi Dorff writes,

> This will mean that some patients who would ordinarily receive and benefit from treatment may either not receive treatment, have the initiation of treatment postponed, or have treatment discontinued and, as a result, may die or suffer some other adverse health-related consequence. This is the tragedy of the necessity to triage.

He states that the underlying principle is to "maximize the number of lives saved," but denies that this analysis is utilitarian, basing it instead on a quantitative interpretation of the obligation to save life (*pikuaḥ nefesh*). Rabbi Dorff understands saving *numerous* lives as a more complete expression of the commandment than saving only one life.[19] There is considerable ambiguity about the precise formula to be used for prioritizing patients in Rabbi Dorff's view. If a viable patient currently receiving treatment is to be disconnected in favor of another with a better diagnosis, then there is great risk of violating the cardinal halakhic rule: "one life may not be sacrificed for another" (*ein doḥin nefesh mipnei nefesh*).[20]

In the vast rabbinic canon, there is almost nothing to suggest Rabbi Dorff's quantitative approach to *pikuaḥ nefesh*. Almost—but not quite—nothing. As he shows, early rabbinic sources recount the biblical story of Sheva b. Bikhri, in which a group of bandits demands the life of one person, or else they will massacre the entire group.[21] Although the primary position prohibits sacrificing one to save the many, and this is normative practice, there are some phrases and some positions within these stories that imply that one person may be sacrificed lest the entire population perish. Yet, these same stories can be read differently, that only if the one person was already sentenced to death, or actively dying, or specified by the attackers, or certain to die with the rest of the group, and only in the context of a war, could one be sacrificed to save the many. The sages do not justify the surrender of Sheva b. Bikhri as an act of *pikuaḥ nefesh*. Rather, his status as a "marked man" strips him of the standard shield of *pikuaḥ nefesh* protection.

From this story, it is hard to conclude that one patient who is currently receiving lifesaving treatment—who is not terminally ill, and who has not requested or authorized discontinuation of a treatment that is causing them anguish—that such a person could nevertheless be forcibly extubated to give another person a chance to live. Even the "lenient" authorities, such as Rabbi Yehudah, permit the sacrifice of a specified group member only if the entire group, including this person, would otherwise be killed. This is far removed from the COVID-19 triage scenario in which the person using the ventilator can be sustained and even healed, even if their long-term prognosis is worse than that of a younger or otherwise healthier patient.

Maimonides limits the possibility of sacrificing one to spare the many to a person who is already condemned to death, and he hesitates to share this information, even in such a case.[22] In the responsa literature, this passage is used to confirm the prohibition on killing one to save the many, and a refusal to quantify the value of life. Yeḥiel Yaakov Weinberg, who survived the Shoah and understood the terrible moral calculus forced on communal leaders in crisis, writes in his responsa collection, *Seridei Aish*, of the supreme value of each individual life:

> Rather the interpretation [of the Sheva b. Bikhri story] is that [saving] life is the highest value, and it is not given to quantification or assessment [of value], even if many lives can be saved only by the killing of one person. Murder is absolutely forbidden with no limit or condition.[23]

Rabbi Dorff offers the rabbinic retellings of Sheva b. Bikhri's story as a basis for instituting a policy in the extreme situation of a pandemic, in which one viable patient could be denied scarce medical resources, or even have them removed, to treat one or more other patients. I would need to see more support in the halakhic literature to reach the same conclusion.

As it happens, halakhic literature is not entirely silent on the question of the allocation of scarce medical resources. In the eighteenth century, Yosef b. Meir Teomim (1727-1792, Lemberg, known for his collection, *Pri Megadim*) established a general principle of medical triage in Jewish law: "If there are two patients, one in greater danger than the other, and resources sufficient for only one of them, then the patient in certain danger has priority over one in possible danger."[24] This principle is cited and applied to bioethics scenarios by twentieth century Orthodox *poskim* Moshe Feinstein, Shlomo Zalman Auerbach, and Menashe Klein.

In the coronavirus pandemic, it was not always been immediately apparent which patient was in greatest danger since some of the classic symptoms of respiratory distress did not present before the patient's oxygen level crashed. This, however, was a diagnostic challenge, not an ethical one. Once a patient's dire condition was understood, the obligation to prioritize saving their life was immediately activated.

Regarding the prioritization of medical care (*din kedimah bi-ripui*) between two needy patients, Rabbi Feinstein rules in a pre-treatment scenario that if one patient is not expected to live out the year (*tereifah*) due to other medical impairments (comorbidities), then a second patient with a better prognosis may be given priority, for he has not relinquished "his presumption of life." If both are likely to live a year with treatment, then whoever arrives first claims the required resource. If it is not known which patient has made prior claim, then he suggests the conflict be settled by lottery.[25] While the one-year standard mentioned in halakhic sources may seem archaic given medical advances, White and Lo also use likelihood of above-one-year survival in their triage criteria, which have been adopted by many hospitals.

Rabbi Auerbach cites Pri Megadim to justify allocating resources to the patient with the greatest medical need. However, he then questions whether it would be permissible to remove a ventilator from one patient and attach it to another who is in greater immediate danger, or to one who has greater chances of recovery. He suggests that the first patient has "claimed" the resource and is not obligated to relinquish their claim. Yet Rabbi Auerbach concludes his discussion with great trepidation: "I have not nailed down what I have written, for the questions are very serious, and there are no clear prooftexts [in halakhic literature].[26]

Rabbi Menashe Klein responds to a question from an observant physician serving in a hospital with only one ventilator. If the first patient in need is terminally ill, may they be treated, even to preserve a brief life of less than a year? And what if an otherwise healthy patient with better chances of survival arrives later —may the ventilator now be removed from the dying patient to save the life of the newcomer? In contrast to Rabbi Auerbach, Rabbi Klein responds with unambiguous permission:

> Nevertheless, what emerges in my humble option is that the proper path according to all, and according to the halakhah and practice that have been established is that as long as there is no viable patient, they may use this machine [i.e., the ventilator] for whoever needs it, even for a terminal patient, but if a viable patient comes, then they should transfer this machine and give it to the viable patient.[27]

The basis of Rabbi Klein's analysis is not that saving multiple lives has greater priority than saving one, but simply that a dying patient has a limited claim to equipment that can be used to save the life of a person who is not otherwise dying. This is not an argument of one-versus-many, but rather of one against one. All lives are of equal value, but courses of therapy are not equally effective for all patients. While every breath of life has value, Jewish law has long established that a person who is dying may be treated differently from a person whose life can be saved. Rabbi Klein takes this principle to its logical conclusion—one may remove the ventilator from a dying patient to save a stable patient, sacrificing the already departing life of one to save the other. This is not the same as taking the resource from one viable patient to transfer to another.

These sages write with trepidation and doubt, and I share the same emotions. Nevertheless, I would make the following general statements with reference to medical triage in halakhah:

1.   In general, there is an egalitarian approach to lifesaving, with all human life treated as equally sacred. The rabbis famously state, "Whoever saves one life is as if they saved an entire world."[28]

2.   A person may never intentionally end the life of another, except in self-defense, justified war, and in very narrow and largely theoretical forms of capital punishment. Even if our intention is to save a different life, we may not intentionally end an innocent person's life. To do so would violate the cardinal rule of halakhah, "we do not sacrifice one life to save another."

3.   If an action does not endanger one's own life, then they are obligated to save the lives of others, even at a financial loss. This idea is taught in the story of two villages that are watered by one meager stream. The residents of the upstream village may use all the drinking water they need to survive, even if this does not leave enough for

the second village. However, the upstream village may not use all the water for their animals; rather, they should leave enough to sustain the people in the second village (B. Nedarim 80b). This idea derives from the command, "Do not stand [idly] over the [endangered] blood of your companion" (Levit. 19:16).[29]

4.   A person may endanger themselves to rescue others who are in mortal danger, for example in confronting a terrorist or volunteering to serve in the army. Yet a person is not *required* to sacrifice themselves to save others. As Rabbi Akiva teaches in the famous canteen story, one may prioritize saving their own life over the life of their companion (B. Bava Metzia 62a, see discussion above in Chapter 1). The background principle to these stories may be that the burden of proof lies on the one who "does not have current possession of the goods" (*ha-motzi mi-ḥaveiro alav ha-ra'ayah*). One's own life is a "good" over which one has been assigned responsibility. This perspective justifies providing frontline medical workers with extra protections, such as scarce PPE and vaccines, so that they are not forced to endanger themselves when helping others (and so that they might extend their abilities to continue lifesaving work).

5.   *Pre-Treatment triage:* If it comes to rescuing either Person A or Person B, and only one can be saved, several factors may be considered:

a. A patient in immediate and grave danger has priority over one whose condition is stable without this therapy.

b. A patient who is expected to recover and live an

indefinite period has priority over a terminally ill patient. Jewish law differentiates between brief survival and long-term recovery, meaning one year or more of expected survival.

c. If two patients arrive on the same day with similar need for treatment, and similar prognosis, then a transparent and fair process that avoids any possibility of bias should be implemented to determine which patient to treat first.

d. A new arrival may not requisition medical equipment already being used to sustain the life of another patient, unless the first patient no longer requires the therapy, or is declared to be terminally ill.

6.   *Post-treatment triage:* "Current possession" implies that it is forbidden to take away a life-sustaining resource from one person to give it to another. However:

a. If the current possessor is suffering from the therapy and in their own estimation is not benefiting, then they or their authorized representative may choose to discontinue the therapy to focus on palliative care.

b. If Patient A is determined by the physician to be terminally ill, then their ventilator may be reassigned to Patient B who is not terminally ill.[30]

c. A vital medical resource may not be taken from one person and given to another on the ground that the latter is younger, generally healthier, expected to live a greater number of years, or somehow more valuable to society, including their occupation as a medical professional. Such criteria would undermine our foundational belief that all people are created in the divine image, and that life has infinite worth. It would run counter to the cardinal rule of halakhah, "we do not take one life to save another." Only if the current user of the ventilator is determined to be terminally ill, or requests termination of the therapy because of suffering, may the scarce resource be reallocated to save another life.

These findings apply beyond the COVID-19 pandemic to the allocation of scarce medical equipment such as ventilators and dialysis machines, and to other medical resources such as donated organs, and specialized staff. It seems to me that Jewish law does not permit the removal of lifesaving therapy from Patient A to save the life of Patient B unless Patient A or their medical proxy requests cessation of treatment due to the suffering caused by their extended illness, or in the event that Patient A is determined to be terminally ill (expected to die within a year), with or without use of the equipment. In this regard, I respectfully disagree with the conclusions of Drs. Emanuel, et al., White, and Lo, and with my senior colleague and friend Rabbi Elliot Dorff (who calls such a case tragic).

One of the most painful experiences at the height of the COVID-19 pandemic was the imperative to isolate afflicted individuals, to restrict travel, and to avoid even small gatherings. Until an effective vaccine or therapy became available in 2021, social distancing was the only way to slow the spread of infection and prevent the caseload from overwhelming medical systems. But this meant that many seriously ill and dying patients were deprived of the comfort of close family and friends, except by video conferencing, which was often inadequate or unavailable.

Momentous decisions such as shifting from curative to palliative care are challenging in the best circumstances and are far harder when there is limited or no ability to spend time at the side of the patient, to consult directly with their medical team, and to assess what course of action best fulfills the patient's values and needs. Adding to this the pressure to reallocate scarce resources such as ventilators only aggravated the family's moral burden and the possibility of subsequent regret.

Given this painful reality, our paper was intended to help families retain their sense of the dignity and worth of their loved one, to bolster their resolve to advocate for full access to even scarce medical resources, as long as there was a prospect of recovery, and to transition to palliation when it became evident that while the dying process could be slowed, death within a year remained inevitable. At that point, physicians, nurses, chaplains, and other caregivers could gently inform the patient and family of this reality and state that palliative care is likely the more comfortable, and religiously appropriate course of action.

In normal circumstances when adequate medical resources are available, it is appropriate to give the patient and their advocates extra time to adjust to this sad reality. But in a pandemic setting when every hour of delay in reallocating resources to patients whose lives can be saved can have deadly consequences, the family should soon be informed that continued intensive care would be futile and is contraindicated by hospital—and even by Jewish—policy.

CONCLUSION

In the throes of a pandemic or other health emergency, clinicians might need to choose among patients (or have a triage officer choose for them) to receive intensive medical treatment. The utilitarian ethics favored by many clinicians may sometimes overlap in practice, but they are fundamentally divergent from the halakhic approach. Jewish law provides several criteria for the prioritization of care, based on the sacred obligation to heal those who are ill. Patients who have the most urgent need should be the first to receive treatment, unless they are unlikely to survive, in which case patients who are expected to survive with intensive therapy should receive priority. After that, the first patient to request the resource has priority.

If a patient who is currently being sustained through artificial means decides (themselves, through advanced directive, or through proxy) to discontinue this therapy due to their experience of futile suffering, then it may be reallocated to another patient based on the above criteria. Likewise, if a ventilator- or dialysis-dependent patient is deemed terminal, the scarce resource may be reallocated to a viable patient.

However, it is forbidden to remove a patient from a ventilator, causing their death, based only on the utilitarian assessment that another patient has a better long-term prognosis, or meets some other socially valued criterion. Even physicians who advocate such actions concede that they would cause clinicians "moral distress" (White and Lo) or be "extremely psychologically traumatic for clinicians" (Emanuel, et al.). Clinicians and ethics committees should refuse such orders and focus instead on healing and saving all viable patients equally with all available resources.

PISKEI DIN

CONSENSUS HALAKHIC CONCLUSION
BY RABBIS DORFF AND NEVINS

Our respective responsa addressed many of the medical, logistical, moral, and spiritual challenges of medical triage in a crisis such as the COVID-19 pandemic. While our presentations differ in approach and presentation, and we reach some incompatible positions, we agree on the following practical conclusions:

1. Equal access to medical care is a moral and halakhic imperative. Triage decisions must not be based on criteria other than the best chance to save lives.

2. Scarce resources used to prevent infection, such as personal protection equipment and vaccines, may be assigned on a priority basis to medical professionals and other emergency responders to support them in their lifesaving efforts.

3. Jewish law differentiates between brief respite and recovery. Scarce medical resources may be directed toward patients who are expected with current therapy to recover over those who are not expected to recover, even with current therapy. Diagnostic tools such as the Sequential Organ Failure Assessment, may be used to prioritize allocation of scarce medical resources towards patients who may be rescued, and away from those who are not expected to survive hospital discharge.

4. If a patient is already receiving medical therapy and

is responding positively, they may not be removed from the equipment prematurely to rescue the life of another person based on comparison of the two patients' age, ability, general health, or social status. The only criterion for removing a person from therapy is the determination that they cannot survive to discharge, or their own request to shift to palliative care.

5. If the triage officer determines that a patient cannot be saved, and that their medical resources must be reallocated to another patient in urgent need, the basis for this decision must be explained fully and sensitively to the patient or their representative, and the hospital must continue to support the patient with appropriate palliative and pastoral care, maintaining the respect and dignity of the patient until the end.

CHAPTER 7:
EARLY CIRCUMCISION FROM
MEDICAL NECESSITY

In the spring of 2020, Jewish ritual life was seriously disrupted due to rapid spread of the COVID-19 virus, soaring mortality rates, and consequent government decrees to enforce social distancing and ban public gatherings. In addition to the impact on synagogue life, these new protocols disrupted Jewish family life, including one of the most sacred and specific of rituals, the circumcision of healthy Jewish boys on the eighth day of their lives.

While there have always been exceptions made to delay brit milah (ritual circumcision) if a child is unhealthy, here families were opting to advance the ceremony so that it could be performed in the hospital before discharge. In fact, there had already been a trend in this direction unrelated to COVID. Some Jewish families were inclined to complete this minor surgery in the hospital, not the home, even if the *mohel* was as experienced and competent as a physician (some *mohelim* are also physicians). I was asked by a couple at whose wedding I had officiated what Jewish law had to say about this decision both before the fact (l'khathilah) and afterwards (b'di'avad) if the child had been circumcised prior to the eighth day. This responsum is a more complete version of my initial oral response.

QUESTION:

In times of public danger such as a pandemic, is it permissible to circumcise a baby boy in the hospital prior to the eighth day after his birth? If so, would this satisfy the mitzvah of brit milah, or is *hatafat dam brit* (the production of a drop of blood by pin prick, also referenced as HDB) required on or after the eighth day? If not, then what is the status of a child who was circumcised prematurely? Either way, what if any elements of the brit milah liturgy may be recited at a later point?

RESPONSE:[1]

During peak infection periods of the novel coronavirus pandemic, it was forbidden in many jurisdictions to gather even in small groups. Israel and some other nations imposed periodic lockdowns when citizens were mostly forbidden to venture from their homes at all. Some families sought to limit the risk of viral transmission by circumcising their newborns in the hospital, and then convening family and friends by video conference to recite the appropriate liturgy at a later point.

Their concern was understandable, but it was generally possible for a professional *mohel* to observe the same protective protocols as in a hospital to prevent spreading infection. Indeed, extraordinary precautions were common in the months following the COVID-19 outbreak, with *mohalim* and parents clad in personal protective equipment during the ceremony.

There is no requirement for guests to attend brit milah in person, nor for it to be held in a private residence, and so the preferred response to our challenge was simply to limit attendance on the eighth day to the baby, *mohel*, and parents, in the safest location possible (such as a covered open-air setting), with others witnessing the event by video.

This form of limiting gatherings became our default policy. Clergy would approach such families with sensitivity, listen to their concerns, and work with them to find a solution that protected the safety of their child and family, while fulfilling the mitzvah of brit milah on day eight. Nevertheless, during a general lockdown, it was not always possible to obtain the services of a qualified *mohel* on the eighth day.

In cases of physical danger, brit milah may always be delayed until it is safe (as we often do in cases of jaundice or hypospadias, for example), at which point the mitzvah of brit milah is already active. Mishnah Shabbat 19:5 states, "we do not circumcise an ill child until he recovers," and this has remained universal halakhic practice.

Yet the child of our question is not currently ill and delaying the circumcision by more than a few weeks would introduce new levels of medical complexity. It might require that the later procedure be performed by a urologist; after the first few weeks, the procedure might require use of anesthesia and an operating room. Aside from additional risk and expense, it might be impossible to complete the ritual requirements of brit milah in a medical center: the surgeon might not be Jewish, the ceremony might not be held during daylight, the parents would likely not be present in the operating room, the prayers would not be said as part of the procedure. Moreover, we must also consider the possibility that for some parents, once the traditional period for brit milah has passed, they may hesitate to circumcise their son altogether. Given these concerns, we again emphasize that the proper response in a pandemic is to arrange for a socially distanced but otherwise traditional brit milah by a trained *mohel* on the eighth day.

Still, the question has been asked: what if the parents have already circumcised their son in the hospital earlier than the eighth day? Let us assume that the question emerges from a difficult scenario in which parents and their physicians have decided that the only way to assure the health of the newborn and their family is to conduct a medical circumcision in the hospital prior to discharge, and before the eighth day.[2] What next?

There are some examples of urologic emergency such as paraphimosis, in which the foreskin gets stuck behind the glans, causing liquid to build up; an effective resolution is to circumcise such a male without delay. Another medical condition is phimosis, unusual tightness of the foreskin, which is usually uncomplicated but could prevent a newborn from urinating, elevating risk of urinary tract infection, which could also justify an early circumcision.[3]

If there is a true medical justification for early circumcision, then the broad principle of *pikuaḥ nefesh*, avoiding life-threatening conditions, would permit the circumcision during the first week of life. But the mitzvah of brit milah does not take effect until the child's eighth day. This leads to the second question. To complete the mitzvah of brit milah, would such a child later require *ḥatafat dam brit* (HDB), the drawing of a drop of blood from the foreskin site? Or could it be that fulfilling this important mitzvah is made impossible by the early medical circumcision?

Beginning with Shlomo ben Aderet (Rashba, Barcelona, 1235-1310), rabbis have addressed the implications of circumcision that expert physicians insist be performed prior to the child's eighth day of life due to an unnamed medical danger, *mipnei ha-sakanah*. From the context, it appears that their primary concern was with the health of the child, and without exception, rabbis have permitted an early procedure based on *pikuaḥ nefesh*, the obligation to save life. However, they have shared Rashba's view that such an early procedure does not fulfill the mitzvah of brit milah, the covenant of flesh, but is mere surgery. This determination raised the question of what, if anything, could be done to complete the mitzvah for a Jewish child circumcised before the eighth day. This second question was not resolved unambiguously by our predecessors and requires broader review of the halakhic record.

The Babylonian Talmud at Shabbat 137a discusses the case of a *mohel* who has been given two boys to circumcise, one on Saturday, and the other on Sunday. If he accidentally switches them and circumcises the Sunday boy on Saturday, namely the 7ᵗʰ day since his birth, is the *mohel* liable for violating Shabbat (not to mention upsetting the parents)? After all, he will have performed surgery on a boy who is not yet commanded to be circumcised, and on Shabbat!

We generally say that the mitzvah of brit milah is so great that it supersedes Shabbat (M. *Nedarim* 3:11), but that is when the mitzvah is active (*be-kum mol*). In this case, the surgery was done prior to when commanded. Rabbi Eliezer holds that the *mohel* is guilty of violating Shabbat, but Rabbi Yehoshua exempts him.⁴ Neither sage would permit an intentionally early circumcision, and neither claims that the *mohel* has completed the mitzvah of brit milah on the seventh day. This Talmudic passage implies that an early circumcision is not considered to have fulfilled the mitzvah of brit milah, though it does not offer guidance on a subsequent remedy.

A millennium after the Mishnah was edited, Rashba addressed a case of medical need for early circumcision.⁵ This text is the basis for all subsequent discussion, and so it bears full citation:

> *Question:* Regarding an infant whom the expert physicians require that he be circumcised within the eight days because of danger: There is available a Jewish *mohel*, and also a gentile—who should circumcise him, and if the gentile did it, what is the status of his circumcision?

> *Response:* Anything to avoid danger is permitted, for nothing stands in the way of saving a life. However, anyone who was circumcised prior to the eighth day, this is not *milah* [the covenant of flesh] but only surgery, and there is no difference if [the surgeon] was gentile or Jewish. But if they didn't complete the circumcision, for example if bits of connective tissue remain attached, or they did not peel back the inner foreskin, they should go back after the

wound heals, and have a Jewish *mohel* remove the bits of connective tissue and peel back the inner foreskin, for it is established that one whose foreskin has been removed but not peeled is as if they had not been circumcised.

Several things are evident from Rashba, and several are not. Clearly, he recognizes medical danger (whatever it may be) as adequate motivation to permit an early circumcision. Also clear is that such an early procedure is not considered brit milah (covenant of the flesh) but merely surgery. For this reason, the religious identity of the surgeon is immaterial.

Unclear is what, if anything, should be done to fulfill the mitzvah of brit milah. Rashba mentions a case where the initial surgery was incomplete; in such a case, a Jewish *mohel* could later finish the job, on or after the eighth day, and thereby complete the mitzvah of brit milah. But what if the surgery was completed entirely *before* the eighth day? What becomes of the mitzvah? Rashba does not say, and this ambiguity is preserved by the major codifiers, Rabbi Yosef Karo and Rabbi Moshe Isserles.

In his Beit Yosef commentary to Tur (YD 264), Rabbi Karo quotes the responsum of Rashba. In Shulḥan Arukh (YD 262), Rabbi Karo emphasizes the importance of conducting circumcision during the day, even if not on the eighth day, and requires that a nighttime circumcision be followed by HDB during the day. But it is not clear that Rabbi Karo means to include early circumcision in this ruling. Much more common is a brit milah that has been *delayed* for medical necessity. His point is that even if the procedure is not held on the eighth day, it should still be during the daytime, based on a ruling in Tosefta Shabbat 15:9.

In his comments to SA YD 262:1, Rabbi Isserles says that if a child is circumcised early, within the eight days, *yatza*, "[the obligation is] completed." This one-word ruling of Rabbi Isserles might imply that he reads Rashba to mean that if a child was, from medical necessity, circumcised early, then the mitzvah of brit milah has been discharged, with no further action required. However, the text continues, "See below, section 264."[6]

Two sections later, at YD 264, Rabbi Isserles cites the continuation of Rashba's responsum to indicate that any boy circumcised before his eighth day is not considered to have fulfilled brit milah. As the Vilna Gaon and others note, Rema's second statement seems to contradict the first one; perhaps, as Rabbi Hillel Hirtz suggests in his Shulḥan Arukh commentary, Beit Hillel, Rema at 262 was merely reporting a minority view.[7]

In his commentary, Be'er Ha-golah, Rabbi Moshe Rivkes (b. Prague, 1600) seeks to harmonize the two statements of Rabbi Isserles, beginning with his words at 264:

> "Circumcision before eight days is not called milah." Meaning—to require that he be circumcised by a Jew, but if a Jew circumcised him completely within the eight days then he has satisfied the obligation of brit milah as Rabbi Moshe Isserles wrote in section 262:1. But if a gentile circumcised him completely within the eight days, according to Rabbi Isserles then they would need to take from [the baby] a drop of covenantal blood.

This attempt at reconciliation argues that Rabbi Isserles would require HDB only if the person who performed the early circumcision was a gentile. If he was a Jew, then there would be no further need. This harmonization is attractive, but it is not supported by any specific words in Rabbi Isserles, and it goes against his primary source, Rashba, who emphasized that it makes no difference if the early surgery was done by Jew or gentile. The matter is insufficiently explained by medieval and early modern sources. As Beit Hillel states, "when a biblical command is in question, we rule stringently." This indicates the need for HDB.

Still, we must ascertain if HDB itself satisfies the mitzvah of brit milah. Ambiguity on this point goes back to the Tannaitic period, starting with the report of Tosefta Shabbat 15:9:

> Rabbi Shimon b. Lazar reports that Beit Shamai and Beit Hillel did not disagree regarding a child born without a foreskin, that it is necessary to take from him a drop of covenantal blood, because it is a hidden foreskin. On what then did they disagree? Regarding a (male) convert who is already circumcised when he comes to convert. Beit Shamai say that one must take from him a drop of covenantal blood, but Beit Hillel says there is no need to take from him a drop of covenantal blood.[8]

The rationale for HDB in a child "born circumcised" is that there is nevertheless some vestigial foreskin left, to which the mitzvah of brit milah can be attached by means of HDB. It is hard to know what these sages meant by the "vestigial foreskin" (orlah kevusha) and whether this accords with human anatomy. In any event, for a male convert who had a prior medical circumcision, there is no such vestigial foreskin, and so, according to Rabbi Hirtz, HDB has no effect. Nevertheless, it is established halakhah that a male convert to Judaism who was previously circumcised should undergo HDB prior to immersion in the mikveh (SA YD 265:3).

In section 264 of Yoreh De'ah, we learn that other deficiencies in the circumstances of circumcision, such as it being performed at night, or by a gentile, must be "fixed" later by the ritual of HDB. But this option is not mentioned by Rashba or the codifiers with reference to the child circumcised early for medical need, even if by a gentile surgeon. Why not?

One possibility is that once the foreskin has been cut and peeled back during the day, even the wrong day, there is no further ritual allowed. The Vilna Gaon understands Rashba's silence on the matter to indicate that our case resembles that of a child born without a foreskin (*nolad mahul*), and there is no need for HDB (YD 264 #10). It is a case of "that which is crooked cannot be straightened" (Kohelet 1:15).[9]

We might compare this situation to a sacrifice required on a specific day: once the date has passed, the mitzvah can no longer be fulfilled.[10] By the time the eighth day of this child's life arrives and the mitzvah of brit milah becomes active, there will be no foreskin to cut, and the mitzvah opportunity will have been lost.[11]

However, David Ha-Levi (Poland, 1586-1667) writes in *Turei Zahav* at YD 264:4 that Rema was needlessly confusing here, and that HDB is certainly required for a child circumcised early. Shabbetai ben Meir HaKohen (Lithuania, 1621-1662) writes in his *Siftei Kohen* (Sha"kh) commentary on Shulḥan Arukh YD 262 #2, and again at YD 264, #6, that a child who was circumcised for medical need prior to eight days should certainly have a subsequent HDB. Otherwise, why wouldn't Rashba have required a Jewish surgeon for the early circumcision? It is true that a Jew should not violate Shabbat to perform an early brit milah for no medical reason (as in the Talmud's case of the absentminded *mohel*), or a subsequent HDB, but this does not mean that the mitzvah of brit milah can be abandoned.

This position is restated forcefully by Yeḥiel Michael Epstein in Arukh HaShulḥan at YD 262:5, and confirmed by Menashe Klein (Slovakia, New York, Jerusalem, 1924-2011) in his responsa, *Mishneh Halakhot* 16:127. Since Rashba stated clearly that circumcision prior to day eight is not called *milah*, but merely surgery, it is obvious to these rabbis that, unless there is more work to be done on the circumcision, the child should undergo *hatafat dam brit* to fulfill the commandment of brit milah. Isaac Klein (Hungary, New York, 1905-1979) reaches the same conclusion, ruling, "If a child was circumcised before the eighth day, *hatafat dam* is required." This position was confirmed by the CJLS.[12]

Halakhic practice likewise establishes that male converts who were circumcised as gentiles should undergo HDB as part of entering the covenant of Abraham. There may not be any foreskin left to remove, but Jewish males bear an obligation of "covenantal blood," (*dam b'rit*) and so HDB is required of them.

In our case too, it seems that this is the most appropriate course of action. If a family is convinced by the expert opinion of their physician(s) that medical circumstances—whether of their specific child or of public health—make it impossible to safely circumcise their child on the eighth day, and they are likewise concerned about the health risks of delaying until a later date, then they may have the medical procedure performed in hospital prior to discharge.

However, they will not have satisfied their son's requirement for brit milah. Therefore, they should convene a subsequent ceremony including *hatafat dam brit* and the liturgy of brit milah. True, we have a one-word ruling by Rabbi Moshe Isserles that implies the opposite, but even there, the SA refers to his statement two sections later that clarifies the continuing obligation, and the arguments of Ta"Z, Sha"kh, Arukh HaShulḥan, *Mishneh Halakhot*, and Rabbi Isaac Klein requiring subsequent HDB are more convincing than those of *Be'er Ha-golah* that limit the requirement to cases where the surgeon was not Jewish.

Of course, once we have established the necessity of HDB on day eight, we come back to the same situation of a *mohel* or Jewish physician visiting the home during a pandemic, raising the same possibility of viral transmission as brit milah. Unless there is a true medical emergency that justifies early circumcision such as those offered above, our recommendation remains that brit milah for a healthy child should be completed by a *mohel* on the boy's eighth day of life.

It is true that *hatafat dam brit* does not require specialized training and could theoretically be performed by the child's parents.[13] Such a ceremony should not be held on Shabbat or Yom Tov but otherwise at the earliest date possible for the safety of the child. Yet this is only after the fact, following a medical emergency, or for a family that went ahead and had their child circumcised, and now wants to complete the mitzvah of brit milah. Before the fact, families should be counseled to wait until the eighth day to conduct brit milah with a *mohel*.

Some have argued that this requirement of HDB may discourage families from gathering to name their medically circumcised son with appropriate prayers; given this possibility, they would like to rely on the one-word apparent permission of Rabbi Isserles in YD 262. I am unable to reach this conclusion for four reasons:

1)   Rabbi Isserles clarifies his statement at YD 264, saying (together with Rashba) that early circumcision does not fulfill the commandment of brit milah.

2)   We have a general halakhic principle that when in doubt about a biblical command, we follow the stringent position, *safeik d'oraita le-ḥumrah*.[14]

3)   If the family chooses a ceremony without HDB, then none of the blessings of brit milah can be said, since the mitzvah is not fulfilled.

4)If we drop the requirement of HDB following early medical circumcision during a pandemic, then this may set a popular precedent even in ordinary circumstances, eroding support for traditional brit milah on the eighth day of a boy's life, which is already under pressure in some circles. Many Jewish men will therefore fail to fulfill the commandment of brit milah, given by God to Abraham (Gen. 17:10): "You shall guard this covenant between Me and you and your descendants after you: every male among you shall be circumcised."

LITURGY FOR COMPLETION OF BRIT MILAH

Our third question relates to the liturgy appropriate for a ceremony of HDB and naming following early circumcision for medical necessity. The first blessing recited at a standard brit milah, *ve-tzivanu al ha-milah* ("...who has commanded us about circumcision"), is said just before the foreskin is removed, and is associated with that surgical act. Tosefta Brakhot (6:12) and both Talmuds assign this blessing to the *mohel*, whereas the second blessing, *ve-tzivanu le-hakhniso be-verito shel Avraham avinu* ("...who has commanded us to enter him into the covenant of Father Abraham") is to be said by the parent.

In a case where the surgical removal of the foreskin preceded the eighth day, it is not appropriate to recite the first blessing *al ha-milah* in the hospital, when the mitzvah has not yet become active. Should this blessing be pronounced later during the HDB? On the one hand, we do not say this blessing in cases of a child "born circumcised" or of a male convert, but in those cases, there was no point when this person was both Jewish and uncircumcised, so this mitzvah simply never applied to him. In our case, the child was born Jewish and with a foreskin, and so even if it was removed early for medical necessity, the mitzvah of brit milah still applies to the child starting on his eighth day and can be fulfilled by HDB. True, we have a general rule that "we are lenient in not requiring blessings of doubtful obligation" (*safeik brakhot le-hakeil*), but in this case the child's obligation of brit milah is biblical and unambiguous, and so it makes sense to include this blessing just prior to HDB.[15]

In Bavli Shabbat 137b, Shmuel emphasizes that blessings associated with mitzvot be followed immediately by the commanded act (*kol ha-mitzvot te'unot berakhah bi-sha'at asiyatan*). However, the second blessing, *lehakhniso bi-vrito shel Avraham avinu* ("to enter him into the covenant of Father Abraham"), is assigned to the parent(s) (or the *sandek*), not to the *mohel*, and so it is customarily said *after* the act.[16]

Tosefot explains that the second blessing, recited by the parent, can follow the circumcision, since it is not said by the person who performed the mitzvah, i.e., the *mohel*.[17] Rabbi Asher b. Yeḥiel (Rosh) agrees with Rabbenu Tam's position that this second blessing is not linked specifically to this act of brit milah, but refers to the general concept and our dedication to God.[18] But may it be said on a different day altogether?

It seems to me that if the family convenes on the eighth day or shortly afterwards with the intention of completing the mitzvah of brit milah for their already circumcised child through the procedure of HDB, that the second blessing—the parents' blessing—may indeed be said at that point. This blessing, "to enter him into the covenant of Abraham," implies future action, as Ta"Z observes (*ki le-hakhniso mashma le-ha-ba*), echoing Rosh and other earlier authorities. It anticipates a process that goes back to Abraham, and then extends far beyond the moment of circumcision, requiring years of education and modeling Jewish faith and observance. It is true that HDB in other cases such as conversion does not require either blessing, but in this case, the family's intention from the birth of this Jewish child was to complete his obligation in the safest and earliest way possible.

With this in mind, the second blessing may be said by the parent(s) in the subsequent ceremony following the procedure of HDB, which could be done privately, prior to the entrance of other guests to the physical or virtual room. As we saw in the comments of Shakh, the moment of HDB can be considered fulfillment of brit milah, and it certainly indicates the intention to enter the child into the covenant of Abraham. Indeed, the medical circumcision will likely have occurred in a hospital operating room, without the presence of parents and their circle of family and friends, possibly without the presence of any Jews at all.

The subsequent gathering is the moment when the parents formally commit to enter the child into the covenant, and therefore this blessing is appropriate then. Likewise, the communal response, "as he has entered the covenant, so may he enter a life of Torah, marriage, and good deeds!" is appropriate at this point.

What of the third blessing, *asher kideish yedid mi-beten*, ("who has sanctified the beloved one from the womb")? This blessing is somewhat mysterious. According to Rashi, it refers to Isaac, who is named by God and declared part of the covenant while still *in utero* (Gen. 17:19; see b. Shabbat 137b, and Beit Yosef YD 265). The later procedure of his brit milah on the eighth day confirms Isaac's prior designation. Likewise, in our case, the child is designated for brit milah from birth; the later ceremony confirms this covenant.

If so, then the ceremony for a child who was circumcised early for medical necessity fulfills the mitzvah of brit milah through the ritual of HDB, and the entire brit milah liturgy follows (see a siddur or rabbi's manual for the full texts):

1)   The ceremony begins with *barukh ha-ba*, "blessed is the boy who has arrived," followed by the verses and protective prayers about Elijah and the placing of the child on his throne.

2)   The *mohel*, a Jewish physician or one of the parents or relatives, recites the blessing *al ha-milah*, "for the covenant of flesh," followed by *hatafat dam brit*.

The first steps described above could be conducted publicly, followed immediately by steps 3-5, or privately a few minutes before other guests enter the physical or virtual room. If so, the second stage of the ceremony could open with a song such as *Eliyahu ha-navi*, followed by the following steps:

3)   The parents recite their blessing, *l'hakhniso*, "to enter him into the covenant," to which the witnesses respond, *k'sheim she-nikhnas*, "as he has entered ...."

4)   The rabbi or other leader raises a glass of wine and says the blessing *borei pri ha-gafen*, "who creates the fruit of the vine," continues with the final blessing, *asher kideish yedid mi-beten*, "who sanctified the beloved one from the womb," and then pronounces the child's name with the established liturgy, *kayyeim et ha-yeled ha-zeh*, "sustain this child ...."

5)   A festive meal followed by *birkat ha-mazon* with the special additions for a brit milah is appropriate since this is considered to complete the process that began with the early circumcision for medical necessity.

We again emphasize that this responsum applies narrowly to a situation in which physicians deem it dangerous to the child and/or his family to wait until the eighth day and conduct brit milah outside of a hospital.

As with any emergency accommodation, it may be tempting to apply this ruling more broadly. After all, many contemporary parents prefer to have their child circumcised in the hospital, and to convene family later for a baby naming celebration without surgery. However, medical circumcision alone does not complete the great mitzvah of brit milah. The Torah states (Gen. 17:14) that males who have not entered the covenant of *milah* are "cut off from their people." Jewish law and popular practice have for millennia emphasized the importance of brit milah on the eighth day for healthy babies. Any Jewish child who has undergone a medical circumcision that was not performed by a Jewish *mohel* on the eighth day should therefore undergo *hatafat dam brit* to complete the mitzvah of brit milah.

What if a family not only insists on an early medical circumcision, but also refuses to allow HDB, and requests that their son be named in a synagogue or home ritual comparable to that done for girls? Some rabbis might be inclined to disconnect the two rituals—one to complete brit milah, and the other to name the child—and agree to name the child as requested while urging the parents to attend to the mitzvah of brit milah at a later date. In such a case, there would be no brit milah blessings said, not at the baby naming, and not at a later HDB.

Other rabbis would not participate in or permit a synagogue naming ceremony for a child whose parents refuse to complete the mitzvah of brit milah—even through the minor ritual of HDB. They would argue that naming a child in such circumstances would remove a motivation for HDB, and potentially lead the family into error.[19]

The second position accords better with the precedents we have cited, but there may be exceptional circumstances that call for a different rabbinic decision. This situation of brit milah hesitancy, which was common in American synagogues even prior to the pandemic, is a classic challenge for rabbinic leadership. Rabbis are expected to uphold the practice of mitzvot and must not do anything that undermines the practice of brit milah. Yet they are also expected to draw our people closer to Jewish community and should not shame or push a child away from receiving a Jewish name and education.

A compromise here might be to require such parents to sign a letter acknowledging that their medically circumcised son has not fulfilled the mitzvah of brit milah, and that they agree to explain to him the need for *hatafat dam brit* and help him fulfill it prior to his bar mitzvah. Following this, the clergy may agree to conduct a naming ceremony for the child. Such a ceremony would not include any of the three blessings of the brit milah ceremony.

PISKEI DIN

Circumcision of a Jewish boy should not precede his eighth day since the mitzvah of brit milah does not become active until that point. In the unusual circumstance that a medical emergency justifies early circumcision, or after the fact, if a family has already circumcised their child before the eighth day, then the family should convene on the eighth day or the earliest subsequent opportunity authorized by their physician, other than on Shabbat or Yom Tov, and proceed with *hatafat dam brit* and the relevant liturgy.

CHAPTER 8:
CONTEMPORARY CRITERIA
FOR THE DECLARATION OF
DEATH

Note: This responsum contains graphic descriptions of illness and injury.

My first foray into bioethics was when, as a college student, I received an internship at the Hastings Center for Bioethical Research. During that summer, I studied Jewish, Catholic, and Protestant perspectives on the termination of life support for terminally ill patients. The resulting article, "Knocking on Heaven's Door," was published in *Mosaic*, the student journal of Harvard-Radcliffe Hillel, in 1986, and was included by Professor Harvey Cox in the sourcebook for his course, "Jesus and the Moral Life."

Writing that paper also gave me the opportunity to interview Rabbi Seymour Siegel, and to learn about his work as a scholar of the theory and practice of halakhah. He was the chair of the CJLS in the 1970s, followed by my teacher, Rabbi Joel Roth, who also advised me on this project. This experience was influential in my decision to apply to JTS and become a rabbi.

Even earlier, I had begun to discuss dilemmas of Jewish bioethics with my father and teacher, Michael A. Nevins, M.D. As governor of the New Jersey chapter of the American College of Physicians and a member of the New Jersey bioethics commission in the 1980s, he advocated for legal and medical policies that combined "common sense, compassion, and conscience." He advised the CJLS as a medical expert in the early

1990s, when Rabbis Elliot Dorff and Avram Reisner were writing their respective responsa on end-stage medical care, arguing that "dying with all the tubes attached" was not necessarily indicated on either medical or moral grounds.

This specific project rose from a shudder of concern that I felt when reading a *New Yorker* article, "As Good as Dead: Is there really such a thing as brain death?" by Gary Greenberg (August 13, 2001). I wondered whether the Conservative and Orthodox rabbis who came to accept the theory of brain death in the 1970s and 1980s had acted too precipitously. As I researched the topic, my concern shifted to the lack of uniformity in medical protocol for declaring death based on neurological criteria. My responsum, which was approved by the CJLS on September 8, 2004, confirmed the decisions of earlier rabbis with the caveat that specific protocols demonstrating the inability to breathe had been completed.

In 2018, the Jewish Theological Seminary presented a conference on brain death featuring neurologist Alan Shewmon, MD, who has argued that even the "gold standard" protocol for determining brain death can lead to false-positive readings when, for example, there is upper spinal cord injury. He furthermore questioned the entire premise of brain function as the sole criterion for distinguishing between life and death. As a result, I added an update to the conclusion of the responsum.

QUESTION:

What is the precise moment of death according to halakhah?

RESPONSE:[1]

> "O Lord, what is humanity that you should care about mortals, that You should think of them? Humans are like a breath; their days are a passing shadow."
>
> (Psalm 144:3-4, JPS translation, modified for gender)

The Process of Dying

The time of death is perhaps the most mysterious of all human transitions. In halakhic literature, much attention has been focused on the treatment of the person up until the moment of death, and of their body and survivors after that point. But when, precisely, does a person die?

The prominent medical writer and surgeon, Sherwin Nuland, writes that, "Every one of death's diverse appearances is as distinctive as that singular face we each show the world during the days of life."[2] The Bavli in Tractate Brakhot (8a) cites a *baraita* claiming there to be 903 forms of death. The most painful separation of soul from body is described as croup; the gentlest is death by a kiss, likened to the withdrawal of a hair from milk.[3] Some deaths are sudden, but often the final passage is a gradual transition. Contemporary medical discussions of death describe a *process* in which the body shuts down its vital functions until the person is declared dead. Jewish mystical sources likewise discuss a transition, three days in duration, during which the soul gradually separates from the body.[4]

Therefore, it may not be accurate from a physiological or a spiritual perspective to speak of a single moment of death. Some bioethicists, such as Norman Fost, question both the accuracy and the purpose of identifying a uniform standard.[5] Others, like Baruch Brody, argue that it is most useful to choose different definitions of death for different courses of action.[6]

Nevertheless, there is a halakhic need to identify a point of transition between life and death. One set of obligations—to heal or at least to comfort the dying person—is exchanged at the time of death for a new set of obligations: to prepare the body for burial, to mourn the deceased, and to comfort the bereaved. The declaration of death may be necessary for terminating treatment, especially for patients who lack relatives to authorize such a change.[7] Defining a moment of death is also necessary to establish the date of *yahrzeit*. Yet it is the issue of organ donation that has lent the greatest urgency to this question. Lives can be saved by harvesting vital organs from a person who has died. But it is impossible to remove vital organs such as the heart and liver without raising the prospect of murder, unless clear and defensible criteria have been established for the declaration of death.

In ordinary circumstances, breathlessness (apnea) can be verified directly, and is accompanied by other signs of death, such as cardiac arrest. In the extraordinary circumstance that a ventilator-dependent patient with heartbeat has been shown to have no upper or lower brain function, and is a candidate for organ donation, precise medical and halakhic criteria of death are required. The definition of these criteria is the focus of our study. We shall argue in this paper that Judaism has historically defined life and death in terms of respiration. In our day, the absence of respiration is likewise the single most significant criterion in the determination of death.

The Evolution of Death

For much of Jewish and general history, the permanent cessation of breathing was the standard for determining death. By the nineteenth century (with the invention of the stethoscope), physicians began to emphasize lack of pulse rather than absence of respiration in the declaration of death, though there remained difficulties in establishing either in some cases. Until the last few decades, physicians used the following methods to determine death: the observation of fixed, dilated pupils after some defined time had passed, auscultation (listening for presence of heartbeat and respiration), and eventually, *rigor mortis* and putrefaction.[8]

In the late 1960s, two technological developments inspired the search for an additional method for the diagnosis of death. The first was the improvement in and profusion of ventilators that could allow a patient, while incapable of spontaneous respiration, to remain alive. Many patients used such ventilators on a temporary basis, yet it had become evident by 1968 that a significant number of people being kept alive in this fashion had no prospects of recovery. Margaret Lock described the resultant "living cadaver" as a machine-human hybrid.[9]

The second development was the introduction of anti-rejection medications, such as cyclosporine, that allowed far greater success in the transplantation of whole organs. By 1968, an *ad hoc* committee of Harvard Medical School proposed a new definition of "brain death" to allow for the removal of ventilators in certain cases, and for the harvesting of healthy organs from brain-dead patients for transplantation to human recipients. This process became particularly important for the harvesting of the liver and heart, which lose viability rapidly upon traditional cardiorespiratory death.

The story of the Harvard Medical School committee and the subsequent 13 years of medical and legislative activity to clarify and standardize the brain death diagnosis is beyond the scope of our study.[10] One ambiguity that was quickly clarified was the equation of brain death with what came to be called "whole brain death," defined by the destruction of the cerebrum *and* the brain stem, rather than "higher brain death," which describes the destruction of the cerebrum and results in the permanent loss of consciousness.

Today, "brain death" refers to the complete loss of function of all areas of the brain. Still, the term "brain death" remains confusing, since the issue is *human* death defined by neurological criteria. This term is also often misapplied in common parlance to refer to prolonged and apparently permanent cases of coma. For example, family members sometimes refer to a comatose patient as "brain-dead" even though he is breathing spontaneously.

Technically, brain death is defined as "the irreversible cessation of all functions of the entire brain, including the brain stem."[11] Patients in a persistent vegetative state may have lost *higher* brain functions, but they still respond to certain stimuli, may breathe without ventilators, and are not considered by rabbinical or medical authorities to be dead.

The notion of brain death was first proposed in 1968 and gained currency and legal status starting in the 1970s. Nonetheless, the definition of death has grown more complicated and controversial.[12] In recent years, the medical literature has produced numerous critical evaluations of the brain death diagnosis.[13]

There are detailed protocols available for the diagnosis of brain death,[14] yet such careful methods may not be consistently employed by physicians before calling in the transplant team. Protocols may vary from the emergency room to the critical care units, from hospital to hospital, and from doctor to doctor.[15] Neurosurgeons Michael Wang and J. Peter Gruen and nurse Pamela Wallace documented the variety of tests used in the diagnosis of brain death in one California hospital, and called for greater uniformity in how this diagnosis is made.[16] They concluded that, "Physicians are trusted to rigorously apply accepted standards and practices when making the diagnosis of brain death. Failure to strictly adhere to the whole-brain guidelines jeopardizes the public's trust in the clinical diagnosis of brain death."

Bioethicists initially raised concerns that the new definition of death was driven simply by the desire for donated organs, and some physicians pointed to the continuation of minimal brain function even in cases of "whole brain death."[17] Nonetheless, Western societies quickly adapted to the new standard.

Yet in Japan, a society with comparable levels of education and medical resources, the new standard of death was not so readily accepted. Despite concern for saving the lives of potential organ recipients, Japanese society declined to view the patient who appears alive—if not lively—to be a "living cadaver." As a result, donor cards in Japan ask people to select either a traditional cardiopulmonary definition of death or brain death before authorizing removal of their organs.[18]

Even in America, where the acceptance of brain death is presumed to be widespread, physicians are wary of the presence of relatives during the administration of clinical tests for brain death.[19] Brain-dead patients may continue to exhibit spinal reflexes, including the "Lazarus sign," in which the body briefly sits up and raises its arms when the ventilator is shut off, making it appear as if the patient had been more "living" than "cadaver."[20]

Nevertheless, a broad American consensus in support of accepting brain death as a new standard has taken hold in recent decades, driven, no doubt, by the prospect of saving lives through the harvesting of vital organs from people who "no longer need them" and avoiding futile treatment. The standard definition of death was clarified by the Uniform Declaration of Death Act (1981), which "has been upheld by statute or judicial opinion in each of the 50 states and has been at least partially adopted in most of the world's industrialized nations"[21]

> An individual who has sustained either (1) irreversible cessation of circulatory and respiratory functions, or (2) irreversible cessation of all functions of the entire brain, including the brain stem, is dead.[22]

Differences remain between American states in the required form of diagnosis; New Jersey and New York are distinct for granting a religious exemption from the diagnosis of brain death.[23] In a comprehensive survey of brain death legislation across the world, Dr. Eelco F.M. Wijdicks found that 70 of 80 countries surveyed had guidelines or codes of practice governing the declaration of brain death, although the standards for diagnosis varied widely.[24] The variety of diagnostic procedures among medical professionals lends greater urgency for clarity among practitioners of halakhah. Our purpose in this responsum is to review the current medical standards for brain death diagnosis and to determine whether these can satisfy the requirements of Jewish law.

Within the halakhic community, the acceptance of the status of brain death remains unsettled. As we shall see, Conservative rabbis have generally accepted the idea of whole brain death, while Orthodox rabbis are divided on the subject. Many of the articles from the 1970s and 1980s employed now-obsolete criteria, such as a flat electro-encephalogram (EEG); this is now considered an unreliable indicator of brain death.[25]

The development of neurological criteria for the declaration of death has challenged halakhic authorities either to adopt or to reject the new standards. While much has been written on both sides of the issue, the crucial question of *what specific diagnostic criteria are required for a halakhic declaration of death* has received relatively little attention. Although diagnostic procedures may be constantly evolving, it is incumbent upon the local *poseik* to become familiar with contemporary criteria for death, to guide families faced with difficult decisions at the end of life. This paper aims to apply classical rabbinic sources to contemporary medical norms, to establish a working halakhic definition of death for our time.

THE DEFINITION OF DEATH IN CLASSICAL RABBINIC TEXTS

Respiratory Death

The primary rabbinic text to define physical criteria of death is from Talmud Tractate Yoma. The relevant Mishnah, Yoma 8:7 (on Bavli 83a), states:

> If a building collapsed [on Shabbat], and it is unknown if a person is [trapped] there or not, whether he is alive or dead, gentile or Jew, they should clear the rubble off him. If they find him alive, they should extricate him; if he is already dead, they should leave him [until after Shabbat].[26]

The Gemara at 85a seeks to clarify how the rescuers are to determine whether the victim is dead or alive:

> The rabbis taught: How far [into the rubble] should they check [to determine if he is alive]? Until his nose. Some say: until his heart.

Rashi explains that this question applies when the victim is found to be absolutely still, like a corpse:

"How far should they check?" If he appears dead, for he
is not moving his limbs, how far should they excavate to
learn the truth?

In such a case, which criteria are necessary to verify that the victim
is dead—cardiac or respiratory?[27] Although it might be expected that
clearing rubble off the chest would allow the victim to breathe, the
halakhah assumes that respiration can be checked even if only the head
is exposed. What, then, is the dispute about? After a short digression in
the Gemara, Rav Papa explains that this dispute relates only to a case in
which the victim is uncovered feet (and thus chest) first—some would
accept evidence of asystole [cardiac standstill] as conclusive; others
would insist on digging further until the head is uncovered to confirm
the lack of respiration:

> Rav Papa says, the dispute is from the bottom [of the
> victim's body] upward; but if [he was found] top to bottom,
> once his nose had been checked [for signs of respiration],
> nothing further is required, for it is written, "all in whose
> nose is the breath of life (Genesis 7:22)."

Therefore, the primary criterion of death is respiratory, although
some would accept cardiac criteria as conclusive in cases where the
person could not be checked for respiration. This latter view is rejected
by the codes of halakhah.

Rashi explains Rav Papa's analysis with diagnostic precision:

> One opinion is to inspect the heart—if it is alive—that his
> spirit is beating there; the other opinion is to continue to
> the nose, for at times life is not discernible at the heart,
> but it is discernible at the nose.

Rashi's gloss indicates that cardiac arrest is harder to discern than the absence of respiration. Yet from the Gemara, it is evident that the absence of respiration is not merely easier to verify than cardiac standstill; it also accords with the Biblical concept of the "breath of life." In other words, the Gemara indicates that respiratory failure bears more *significance* than does asystole.

The Gemara's respiratory standard of death is codified in the medieval codes of Jewish law. Maimonides states that the absence of respiration discernible at the nose is sufficient evidence of death:[28]

> If they examined his nostrils and found no breath there, they leave him there, *for he is already dead.*

Rabbi Karo makes the same ruling in the Shulḥan Arukh:

> Even if a person were discovered crushed, who cannot live for more than a moment, they should continue excavating and checking him until his nostrils; *if they detect no life* [i.e., respiration] *at his nostrils, then he is certainly dead,* and it matters not whether they first found his head or his legs.[29]

The *Mishnah Berurah* explains the final phrase to mean that absence of heartbeat alone does not prove death, but absence of respiration alone *is* conclusive.[30] The Talmud and codes of Jewish law view lack of respiration, not cardiac arrest, as the primary criterion for the declaration of death.[31]

Although the rabbis considered absence of respiration to be sufficient evidence of death, they clearly meant the *permanent* absence of respiration. Maimonides warns to wait for some time to verify permanent cessation of respiration in case the person had merely fainted.[32] Of course, people who faint continue to breathe, but it can be difficult to detect their respiration. Rambam's ruling is confirmed by Rabbi Karo in Beit Yosef.[33] Rabbi Isserles makes a similar statement regarding a pregnant woman who has apparently died—a caesarean section should not be attempted in case she is merely comatose and now would be killed by the surgery.[34]

Such fears about premature declarations of death became greatly pronounced in both general and Jewish society in the late eighteenth and nineteenth centuries. In Germany, the fear of "apparent death" (*Scheintod*) leading to live burial became a sensation, prompting civil legislation in 1772 to mandate a three-day waiting period before burial. This law impinged upon the Jewish custom of burying, when possible, within a day of death. The Jewish community, led by Rabbi Jacob Emden and philosopher Moses Mendelssohn, successfully secured a Jewish exemption from this law. Yet many Jews, agitated by radical *maskilim* who dismissed rabbinic authority, were shaken in their confidence to diagnose death and proceed with burial within 24 hours.[35] Permanent lack of pulse and breath can be hard to verify, particularly in cases involving hypothermia and drowning.

In our day, the extraordinary adjustment being proposed is to view a patient who is apparently breathing (albeit via a ventilator) and maintaining a heartbeat as nevertheless dead. To be blunt, this means removing functioning vital organs from one person and giving them to another. Based on the texts reviewed above, such an adjustment would seem unthinkable. Indeed, one might expect a horrified reaction in our day, like the *Scheintod* panic of earlier generations. Surprisingly, this has not been the case in Western societies, and it has also not typified the responses of many halakhic authorities. The measured Jewish response may be motivated by the prospect of saving lives, but it is also grounded in classical halakhic examples of an additional set of texts used for the diagnosis of death.

Alternative Evidence of Death: Fatal Neck and Back Injuries

So far, we have dealt with the diagnosis of death in a person whose body appears completely inert and lifeless. The rabbis also discussed cases in which death could be declared, despite continued convulsions of the body, based on the observation of mortal injury. Although the respiratory criteria discussed above have been the primary means for determining death in Jewish texts, there is an alternative criterion for death even in the classical literature: destruction or severance of the spinal cord. The biblical story of the death by neck injury of the priest Eli after the Holy Ark had been captured in battle by the Philistines (I Samuel 4:18) is studied by the rabbis at Ḥullin 21a to understand the significance of fatal neck injuries:

> Rav Yehudah said in the name of Shmuel: if a person's spine was broken and most of the surrounding neck severed, he defiles in a tent [i.e., he is considered dead and conveys ritual impurity]. But you may object—what about the case of Eli, whose spine was broken, but not most of his neck [and yet he was considered dead]? The elderly are different, for it is written, "When he [the messenger] mentioned [the capture of] God's ark, he [Eli] fell backwards off his chair by the side of the gate, breaking his spine, and he died, for he was an old man and also heavy."

According to Rav Yehudah, citing Shmuel, the observation that a person's neck is broken and mostly severed is by itself sufficient evidence of death. Yet because Eli was elderly, he was considered dead even without his neck being severed.[36] That is, injuries do not occur in isolation from other causes of frailty or illness in a person.

The Ḥullin text continues to describe other types of spinal cord

injuries that would leave a person legally dead, even should his body
continue to convulse:

> Rav Shmuel bar Naḥmani said in the name of Rabbi
> Yoḥanan, if he were torn like a fish, he defiles in a tent.
> Said Rav bar Yitzḥak, provided his back [were sundered].

Rashi explains that such a mortally wounded person "defiles in a tent"
even if his body continues to convulse. The Shulḥan Arukh[37] restates
this Gemara, claiming that some people are so grievously wounded as
to be considered dead even while displaying signs of life:

> Someone whose spine is broken, and most of whose neck
> is severed, or one whose backbone is ripped out like a fish,
> even if he is still alive [i.e., moving], is *considered as if dead*,
> and renders [others present] ritually impure.

In addition to these sources, which detail spinal injuries, several
rabbinic sources equate the decapitation of animals with death, despite
persistent signs of life. The most often cited source is Mishnah Ohalot
1:6:

> A person does not render others impure [i.e., die] until
> his soul departs. Even if he is severely lacerated or nearly
> dead, he is still considered alive to fulfill or seek exemption
> from leviritic marriage, to entitle [his mother or wife] to
> eat priestly tithes or to deprive her. So too cattle and
> beasts do not render unclean until their life departs. If
> their heads are severed, even if their bodies continue to
> convulse, they are already impure, just like the severed tail

of a newt twitches [even after it has been cut off].

Maimonides explains the convulsions of a decapitated animal, saying: The movement of the limbs *after death* is called *pirkus*.[38] In Hilkhot Tuma'at Meit, he codifies the distinction evident in the Mishnah between a terminally ill person, who is considered alive, and a mortally wounded person, who is considered dead despite the continued convulsions.[39]

In Tractate Gittin (70b), Rav Yehudah in the name of Shmuel describes the case of a man whose esophagus and trachea have been severed, but who is nevertheless allowed to execute a bill of divorce for his wife. Jewish law requires the husband to be not only alive but lucid while the *gett* is written, witnessed, and then delivered to his wife! If he cannot breathe, why isn't he considered to be legally dead?

Perhaps some air could still get to the man's lungs through the severed windpipe, or maybe he was simply holding his final breath, and he had a very speedy scribe at his side. Surely, a person with a severed trachea and esophagus could not remain conscious for more than a few brief moments. Later in the Gemara, this case is challenged, since Rav Yehudah also spoke in the name of Shmuel of a man who had his trachea and esophagus slit *and ran away*, that observers could testify that he had died. Indeed, Rambam cites this as halakhah in Hilkhot Gerushin 13:17. This may not mean that he was considered dead from the moment that he was last seen running, but his death is deemed by halakhah to be unavoidable and imminent, due to his inability to breathe.

These strange cases are comparable to an animal that has been ritually slaughtered—its trachea and esophagus are severed but it may retain consciousness for a few moments. Nevertheless, the animal's imminent death is considered inexorable.[40] It is noteworthy that *shehitah* does not involve severing the carotid artery. Rabbi Yehudah does differ from this position (Ḥullin 27a), requiring severing the artery, but the Gemara on

28b clarifies that Rabbi Yehudah's opinion applies only to birds that will be roasted whole, and that his purpose is to expel the blood, not to qualify the slit of the artery as an integral part of slaughter.[41] As Rashi says there, "life does not depend on the blood vessels, and they needn't be mentioned except in regard to [expelling] the blood."[42] This confirms that halakhah employs respiratory, not circulatory, criteria in the determination of death.

Another text that clarifies the legal consequences of decapitation comes from the laws of Shabbat. A significant halakhic concept is that if an action is generally permitted on Shabbat, but it has a forbidden and unavoidable consequence, then the first action is not allowed. This theory is known by the expression, "If you cut off [a chicken's] head, will it not die?"[43] In other words, decapitation leads inexorably to death, even if temporary bodily signs of life persist. The heart may be beating, and the limbs may be moving, but the chicken cannot breathe, and it therefore is considered dead.

Synthesis of the Classical Halakhic Sources

Despite the ambiguities that result from the Talmud's diverse descriptions of death, an underlying principle may be deduced. The key to the halakhic understanding of death comes from the words, "until his life departs." The word *nefesh* ("life") is explicitly connected to breath by the Torah: "[God] breathed the breath of life in his nostrils; and the human became a living creature" (Genesis 2:7). Other words that describe the animating spirit that defines life, *neshamah* and *ruah*, likewise relate to respiration.

The grievously injured people mentioned in our Mishnah are nearly dead, *but they are still breathing*, and are therefore considered alive. One who is decapitated, or whose trachea is slit, *is no longer able to breathe* and is therefore considered dead within moments of the injury. The

Yoma text describes a motionless person who is declared dead based on respiratory failure. The Ḥullin and Ohalot texts describe humans (and animals) who, *though still moving,* are declared dead due to catastrophic injury to the neck or chest. Such injuries prevent the victim from breathing. Movement of the body implies continued cardiac activity— but the victim's inability to breathe means that death is imminent. Indeed, Rambam's definition of *pirkus* captures this state precisely—*the movements made after death.*

Similarly, the Gittin text allows that a person may remain alive for a few moments after his trachea is slit, but it still considers him to be dead, with no further inspection required after that. Severe neck and torso injury make respiration impossible and death inevitable. The case of Eli, whose neck was broken but not severed, and yet who was considered dead without verifying lack of respiration, is presented as an exception to the general practice.

At the other end of life, the heart of a human embryo begins to pump fluid through blood vessels on day twenty of gestation.[44] Nevertheless, it is not deemed a true life until many months later, "when it exits [the womb] into the air of the world."[45] The fetus has a special status as part of the mother's body, but it is not considered an independent life until it is born and *begins to breathe.*

Thus, it is not movement or even pulse that ultimately defines life and death, but the ability to breathe. This interpretation harmonizes the Talmudic and later halakhic materials, yielding a consistent respiratory standard for the start and end of life.

While some have argued that the decapitation texts constitute an *alternative* to the respiratory standard, there is no reason to assume that the ancient Rabbis or their gentile contemporaries ascribed particular significance to the functioning of the nervous system in determining death. The spinal cord is ignored in *sheḥitah,* and all the neck injury cases except for that of Eli require that the neck be mostly severed for death to be declared without testing directly for respiration. Our synthesis of the disparate rabbinic sources integrates the legal and linguistic data into a coherent halakhic approach that will guide us as we explore the medical literature.

CURRENT MEDICAL CRITERIA FOR THE DIAGNOSIS OF DEATH[46]

In the *New England Journal of Medicine*, Dr. Eelco F.M. Wijdicks provides a protocol detailing a neurological examination used to declare brain death.[47] The priority is to assess whether the patient's condition is permanent or is, rather, the temporary result of reversible factors. Before an examination for brain death can proceed,

> the following prerequisites [must be] met: the ruling out of complicated medical conditions that may confound the clinical assessment, particularly severe electrolyte, acid-base, or endocrine disturbances; the absence of severe hypothermia, defined as a core temperature of 32°C or lower; hypotension; and the absence of evidence of drug intoxication, poisoning, or neuromuscular blocking agents.

Once these confounding factors have been ruled out, the clinical exam for brain death commences. Wijdicks describes in detail a three-part clinical exam, which tests for the lack of spontaneous or responsive cranial nerve activity, the absence of brain-stem reflexes, and apnea. The latter is tested by turning off the ventilator for several minutes and measuring the rise of CO_2 in the bloodstream. These tests are typically repeated between six and 24 hours after the first exam.[48]

The brain death protocol for pediatric cases differs from the standards described for adults.[49] Because most pediatric cases of brain death are caused by severe asphyxial injury (which may injure organ systems other than the brain), organ procurement from pediatric donors is rare.

The apnea test—which measures the presence or absence of effective respiration—is typically the final and conclusive clinical examination for brain death. Dr. Plum writes,

> The apneic test represents the ultimate physiological-clinical test to diagnose brain death. I know of no personal observation of a responsibly conducted, positive apnea test that has been reversed by subsequent recovery. Conversely, instances of omission of the apnea test have led to potentially unfortunate errors or premature assumptions of brain death.[50]

Thus, after confounding factors have been ruled out and the patient has demonstrated no response to painful stimuli in the higher brain nor to the examination of brain-stem reflexes, the apnea test confirms the brain death diagnosis.

Although the patient might move during the test, the absence of any breathing efforts, confirmed by a rise of carbon dioxide levels in the blood, shows that the patient is not breathing spontaneously. This test is repeated and, if it confirms the total lack of respiration, death is declared. Bodily movements during the exam are understood as spinal cord and not brain stem reflexes. These spinal cord reflexes are consistent with the rabbinic literature's description of *pirkus*, spasmodic motion *after* death.

In very rare cases[51] when the apnea test cannot be administered due to confounding factors (such as the presence of barbiturates that cannot be cleared or initial CO_2 levels that are too high or too low), radionuclide brain perfusion and other imaging techniques are used to verify a diagnosis of brain death. Such diagnosis depends upon measurement of "the complete absence of [blood] flow throughout the brain and the internal carotid arteries."[52] This exam is rarely used, since it is much more complicated and is not as conclusive as the protocol described above.

A simpler option is transcranial doppler ultrasonography (TCD), "a noninvasive monitoring tool which allows imaging of blood flow velocities in intracranial blood vessels."[53] Such tests may play an important ancillary role in the diagnosis of brain death, but they do not alone suffice for medical purposes. In a study of cerebral blood flow after brain death, doctors W. Mel Flowers and Bharti R. Patel conclude that, "visualization of arterial flow does not exclude brain death, but the diagnosis should be confirmed by repeat studies and other means."[54] Wijdicks cautions that, "absent flow intracranially may be due to transmission difficulties and in itself is not a criterion for death."[55]

If there is no blood flow in the brain, does this not prove the patient's inability to breathe, albeit less directly than the apnea test? In fact, intracranial blood flow exams measure the carotid arteries, but the medulla, which directly controls the respiratory impulse, is supplied by the vertebral artery.[56] Thus, it is possible that a patient could show no intracranial blood flow, but still be capable of spontaneous respiration.

From the perspective of halakhah, neither radionuclide brain perfusion imaging nor TCD measures respiration, and therefore these tests do not suffice to prove death. In contrast, the clinical neurological examination culminating in the apnea test has been proven effective over time as a verification of the complete absence of respiration and of brain death. Should a future test for total respiratory failure be developed, it would apparently satisfy the halakhic definition of death. Meanwhile, apnea is the best halakhic measurement of death in a ventilator-dependent patient who has met all the other criteria of brain death.

HALAKHIC RESPONSES TO BRAIN DEATH CRITERIA

Soon after the discussion of brain death standards entered American legal discourse, halakhic authorities here and then in Israel began to review traditional texts such as those mentioned in the previous section, to determine how halakhic analysis would understand brain death. Dozens of articles have been published to date, and it will not be possible to review them here. We will rather focus on specific rationales and guidelines offered by the defenders and critics of using brain death criteria to declare death.

Although saving a life is one of the highest of all Jewish values, avoiding homicide supersedes even this commandment. As the rabbis said, "one life cannot be disposed of in favor of another."[57] Nevertheless, halakhic authorities have been willing to examine new criteria for death to see if additional lives might be saved, either by transplantation of vital organs, or by making scarce medical resources available to other patients. Concerns for not desecrating the body (nivul ha-meit), not delaying burial (halanat ha-meit), not profiting from the dead (ein hana'ah min ha-meit), and for maintaining the general dignity of the dead (k'vod ha-meit) remain operative, but do not outweigh the requirement to save a life. The first task, of course, is to determine if the potential donor is truly dead.

In 1976, the journal Conservative Judaism published articles by Daniel C. Goldfarb and Seymour Siegel, each of whom reviewed the relevant rabbinic sources and contemporary medical information, and found grounds for "updating the criteria of death."[58] Since that time, numerous Conservative rabbis have touched upon the subject, including David Feldman,[59] David Golinkin,[60] Avram Reisner,[61] Elliot Dorff,[62] Joseph Prouser,[63] and Aaron Mackler.[64] All of these authors accepted the theory of brain death, though only Golinkin and Reisner specified clinical tests necessary for this diagnosis to be halakhically accepted.

The Reform Movement's Central Conference of American Rabbis published a responsum on the harvesting and storage of organs for transplantation that approved the use of brain death criteria accepted by the medical profession but did not stipulate its own standards.[65] Moshe Zemer reviewed the relevant literature and observed that, "the halakhic test for death, the cessation of breathing, parallels the modern medical test for brain death." Although he did not endorse any specific diagnostic test, Rabbi Zemer accepted the finality of the brain death diagnosis for the purpose of organ donation and saving a life.[66]

A great deal has been published on this subject by Orthodox rabbis, with two distinct camps emerging. One side was led by J. David Bleich, who argued that unless the complete lysis (liquefaction) of the brain can be proven (which it can't without autopsy), the diagnosis of brain death has no halakhic standing.[67] Prominent Ḥaredi *poskim* adopted this position as well. On the other side are Moshe Tendler, Fred Rosner,[68] and the Israeli Chief Rabbinate,[69] who argued that brain death is comparable to the descriptions of spinal cord destruction or decapitation made in early rabbinic sources.

A central drama of this debate was determining the final opinion of the late Rabbi Moshe Feinstein, whose authority is accepted by all these rabbis, but whose thoughts on brain death evolved and ultimately remained subject to dispute. A neutral review of these positions was written by Yitzhok A. Breitowitz.[70]

Many of these articles focus on intracranial blood flow tests, with rabbis such as Shlomo Zalman Auerbach warning that injecting substances for the radionuclide test into a dying patient may hasten his death and is therefore forbidden.[71] Nevertheless, these *poskim* contemplate the significance of such tests done *after the fact*—can they be used to prove death?

Dr. Rosner uses the decapitation texts (particularly from the Shulḥan Arukh) to make the case that any injury that effectively severs communication between body and brain is tantamount to death, even if cardiopulmonary signs of life persist.[72] Rabbi Bleich argues strenuously against the equation of brain death with decapitation, claiming that only the complete lysis of the brain (and perhaps not even that) could be considered tantamount to physical decapitation.[73]

In an extensive footnote contained within his CJLS-approved paper on end-of-life medical care, Rabbi Reisner cogently defends the position of Rabbi Tendler and Dr. Rosner against Rabbi Bleich's requirement of the complete destruction of the brain to declare death:

> Decapitation does not signal total destruction of the tissue of the brain, but only its loss of contact with the organism. Destruction of the brain tissue will surely follow, but only at some unspecified later time. It is precisely the irreversible cessation of the integrated function of brain and body that is modeled by decapitation.[74]

Based on this argument of integrated function, Reisner finds the Uniform Declaration of Death Act acceptable under halakhah, provided that the appropriate diagnostic tests have been completed. Despite continued opposition by prominent Israeli *poskim* such as Rabbi Yosef Shalom Elyashiv, the Israeli Chief Rabbinate has issued a similar finding, which has been the basis of successful heart transplant programs in Israeli hospitals.

THE HEART OF THE MATTER

However, Rabbi Bleich's fundamental objection to the concept of brain death rests not on any claims regarding the integrated functioning of the brain. The cornerstone of his argument is that *heartbeat* is the primary criterion of life.[75] To make this argument, he must set aside the clear meaning of the standard texts found in Yoma, Ḥullin, Gittin, Ohalot, and the codes of Maimonides and Rabbi Karo.

Rabbi Bleich bases his argument primarily on Rashi's comments on *Yoma* 85a. Bleich claims that the heart itself is to be considered one of the limbs. Although the heart is indeed counted by the rabbis among the 248 body parts (*eivarim*), in this context, such a reading is unpersuasive. Rashi's phrase, "he doesn't move his limbs," clearly refers to voluntary movement. If Rashi meant to include the heart in this phrase, then the Gemara's question would be rendered nonsensical. We would have to understand it: "If the person appears dead, for he is not moving his limbs, [not even his heart], then how far should we excavate—up to his heart, or up to his nose—to know the truth?"

Rabbi Bleich also cites Rashi's explanation of the position in the Gemara that lack of heartbeat would suffice to declare death. Rashi explains this position with the words, "for it is there that the soul beats" (his translation). Bleich takes this as Rashi's own position, and neglects to mention that this gloss is simply Rashi's explanation of the opinion that was rejected by all codes of Jewish law. He acknowledges that Rashi's commentary is not viewed as a halakhic code but persists in using it to build an untenable position.

Rabbi Bleich also argues against the halakhic significance of spontaneous respiration. He notes that victims of polio epidemics in the twentieth century often suffered respiratory paralysis, and yet were conscious and able to converse with the assistance of an iron lung. By the standard of spontaneous respiration, he asserts, they would absurdly have to be considered dead. He further cites the example from Gittin 70b to prove that a man who cannot breathe is still considered alive enough to execute a writ of divorce.

Rabbi Bleich's examples are interesting, but are the cases indeed comparable? The polio victims exhibited other tangible indications of life, including the ability to talk. The Gittin case, which is frankly difficult to imagine, describes a man who is able, via pantomime, to execute a complicated document despite his slit trachea. The brain-dead individual, in contrast, is permanently unconscious, unresponsive to stimuli, and unable to breathe on their own. They are, to use Rashi's earlier phrase, "like dead, for they don't move their limbs." Bleich argues that the halakhah pays no heed to consciousness in the diagnosis of death. This may be true, but he himself argues that bodily movement has significance.

From the case of Eli, discussed in Ḥullin 21a, we learn that the context of an observation is significant. Normally, the neck would need to be nearly severed, making respiration impossible, if the person was to be declared dead without further examination. Because of Eli's advanced age, he was declared dead even without his neck being severed. Based on the Talmudic sources, we can say that a person who lies still, appears dead, and is not breathing, as would be true in cases of brain death—is dead.

Even Rabbi Bleich's prooftexts work against his argument for a cardiac, rather than a respiratory standard. He cites out of context a responsum of Ḥatam Sofer[76] that purportedly proves that cardiac activity is more important than respiration. This responsum[77] is a polemic against those secular authorities and *maskilim* who wished to delay burial until the body began to decompose. Ḥatam Sofer vigorously asserts the adequacy of respiratory arrest in proving death.

Referring to the story of Elijah's miraculous resuscitation of a boy who had stopped breathing (I Kings 17:17), Sofer mentions a condition in which a pulse could be felt at the neck even though the person was apparently not breathing. Some would say, therefore, that Elijah merely restored breath to the boy, but Sofer sees the boy's respiratory arrest (even with continued heartbeat!) as a true death, and Elijah's act of resuscitation as a true resurrection of the dead.

In normal cases, Sofer continues (addressing the skeptical *maskilim*), when a body is still as a stone, and there is no heartbeat, and there is no breath, then the person is surely dead and can be buried without further delay. Bleich seizes upon this sentence as proof that Sofer requires stillness, cardiac arrest, *and* respiratory failure to certify death. Once again, a careful reading belies Bleich's claim. To skeptics who would require waiting until putrefaction before burial, Sofer cites every possible proof of death—*rigor mortis*, asystole, and apnea—to prove the finality of the diagnosis. But as far as the halakhah is concerned, *respiration is the sole criterion*. In a passage that Bleich does not quote, Ḥatam Sofer endorses the respiratory standard of death in the strongest possible terms:

> Once his breathing ceases, one should no longer violate Shabbat [to rescue him]. This is the general principle for all who die, and this has been the accepted criterion in our hands ever since God's congregation became a holy nation. Should all the winds in the world fill their sails with wind, they would not budge us from the place of our holy Torah!

Bleich has tried very hard, but Ḥatam Sofer will not be budged from the traditional halakhic definition of death: permanent respiratory arrest. Indeed, Rabbi Auerbach reaffirms the respiratory standard in his early responsum on the topic:[78]

> For it seems, in my humble opinion, that the truth of the matter is that anyone who has ceased breathing, and in whose nostrils we have not succeeded in restoring breath, is dead. He should be considered to have died from the very moment when the breath of life departed his nostrils and his breathing ceased.

Yet Rabbi Bleich remains convinced of the cardiac standard. He summons non-halakhic sources such as Rabbenu Baḥya's homiletical comment about the need to love God "with all your heart," for that is the final organ to die. He also cites a responsum of Tzvi Ashkenazi,[79] regarding whether a chicken whose heart could not be located should be deemed *tereifah*.[80] Based on his understanding of anatomy and kabbalistic notions,[81] Tzvi proclaims the heart to be essential to all life. This may or may not be the case—mechanical hearts are no longer theoretical—but it does not displace the clear halakhic definition of death: respiratory failure.

Another prominent halakhic authority, Ahron Soloveichik, has advanced an even more restrictive definition of death.[82] He argues that the halakhah requires *three* criteria for the declaration of death: respiratory, cardiac, *and* neurological.

> The process of death begins with cessation of respiration, and it ends with the total termination of all the three vital functions in life—respiration, cardiac activity, and brain activity .... A person who becomes devoid of respiration but who still has cardiac activity is considered semi-alive and semi-dead. Consequently, if someone will kill him, he will be considered a murderer. Hence, it is absolutely forbidden to cut out the heart of that person even though the removal of the heart of the donor is indispensable to the preservation of the life of that one.

This argument is powerful, but on what is it based? None of the halakhic texts present these three criteria of death—respiratory, cardiac, and neurological—as a unified set. The category of being "semi-alive" is apparently Rabbi Soloveichik's own invention. He bases the cardiac criterion upon the same philosophical, homiletical, and kabbalistic texts

about the heart cited by Rabbi Bleich from *Moreh Nevuhim*,[83] Rabbenu
Bahye, and Ḥakham Tzvi's citation of Rabbi Yitzhak Luria. These texts
do not relate to the Talmudic criteria of death, nor are they presented
as halakhic rulings. Soloveichik goes so far as to claim that brain waves
registered on an EEG constitute bodily "movement," but even Bleich
finds this difficult to accept.[84] *As we have seen, the Talmud and codes of law
focus on lack of respiration, not cardiac activity, and certainly not brain activity,
for the diagnosis of death.*

Within the Ḥaredi community, statements made by prominent
poskim against the concept of brain death continue to carry great
influence. Like Rabbi Feinstein, Rabbi Auerbach's position seems to
have vacillated based on continued medical updates (and lobbying).
His writing assumes that the blood flow test is the final determination
of brain death, but even if that test is met, he considers the patient
to be *goses* (actively dying) until the heart has permanently stopped.
Rabbi Auerbach ultimately rejects the brain death standard, apparently
without realizing that brain death today establishes the complete and
permanent cessation of respiration.[85]

Nevertheless, Orthodox support for the donation of vital organs is
growing, as evidenced by the advocacy organization H.O.D.S. (Halachic
Organ Donor Society).[86] Avraham Steinberg's article in *The Encyclopedia
of Jewish Medical Ethics* reviews the primary halakhic approaches to brain
death, and concludes that permanent cessation of spontaneous respiration
is the halakhically significant criterion for death in these circumstances:

> Based on the above-mentioned criteria, the establishment
> of the moment of death as being defined as the complete
> and irreversible cessation of spontaneous respiration is *not
> a change in the halakhah*. What has changed is the medical
> technology to establish that the cessation of respiration is
> absolute and irreversible.[87]

Heart and liver donations are accepted by observant Jews; they may also be donated by observant Jews to save the lives of other people, so long as the appropriate halakhic criteria are met for the donor to be declared dead. To accept organs donated by gentiles but to refuse to donate them would be a particularly galling example of the desecration of God's holy name.[88]

CONCLUSION

Jewish law has consistently favored the respiratory standard for the determination of death. Although Rashi on Yoma 85a implies that the respiratory standard was adopted due to ease of diagnosis, the Gemara states that breath is the essence of life. The sources that we have cited from Ḥullin 21a, Mishnah Ohalot 1:6 and Gittin 70b view severe neck injury, destruction of the spinal cord, or decapitation as tantamount to death. We have concluded that these cases are distinguished by the inability of the victim to breathe. Because the protocol for ascertaining brain death currently includes verification of the complete cessation of respiration, it suffices to prove halakhic death.

This understanding differs from that advanced by previous advocates of accepting brain death as the proof of death, such as Rosner, Tendler, and Reisner, who view the neurological injury suffered to the brain stem as halakhically significant in and of itself. Our position focuses on the respiratory failure caused by brain death as the halakhically significant criterion.

A diagnosis of brain death, according to its rigorous protocol, is required for halakhic purposes only when contemplating an action such as the harvesting of vital organs.[89] It may be possible one day to transplant the hearts and livers of non-heartbeating donors, thereby avoiding this ambiguous situation.[90] Meanwhile, the brain death protocol, with its test of apnea, satisfies the traditional definition of death established in Yoma 85a and the codes that follow it.

We must remain clear that the stringent criteria proposed by Wijdicks and Plum, et al., to rule out any temporary or reversible factors, followed by careful clinical examination, are *prerequisites* to the diagnosis of halakhic death. The brain-reflex clinical examination should indicate whether the components of the brain stem—midbrain, cerebellum, pons, and medulla oblongonta—have indeed ceased to function. These examinations are also *preliminary* to the halakhic diagnosis of death. They accord with Rashi's explanation of Yoma 85a, that the patient is utterly unresponsive. These tests also can dissuade medical staff from performing an apnea test which could be dangerous for a patient who *does* retain brain function, and whose death could be hastened by a premature apnea test.

What about the continued heartbeat? It seems counterintuitive to dismiss this rhythmic function as *pirkus*, or generally spasmodic movement after death. Yet the heart is a muscle that can continue to beat even outside of the body (as it often does during heart transplant operations). We do not consider a heart transplant recipient to have died and been reborn. Asystole alone does not define death, and continued heartbeat may indeed qualify as *pirkus*.

Heartbeat alone does not constitute a living person, either in the womb or in the ICU. The brief persistence of cardiac activity in cases where there is no consciousness, no movement in response to any neurological examination, nor any spontaneous respiration as demonstrated by the apnea test, is consistent with a halakhic declaration of death. The cardiac standard has clearly been rejected by the Gemara and codes in cases where the person is found to be "like dead."

The apnea test confirms that the brain stem has ceased to function and meets the traditional respiratory criterion of death. This is the halakhically significant and final determination of death. Indeed, a patient who fails to breathe during the apnea test, showing no signs of spontaneous respiration after all the preliminary confounding factors and brain reflex exams have been accounted for, is dead by both classical Jewish and contemporary medical criteria. The moment that this test is completed can serve as the official moment of halakhic death.

Because of claims made by some neurologists that the apnea test might cause the very necrosis of the brain stem that it seeks to discover, physicians must always determine if there are any confounding factors, including injuries to the upper spinal cord, or other illnesses which might mimic the symptoms of brain death while leaving brain function intact. Prior to the apnea test, physicians must use the most conclusive and least harmful clinical examinations and tests to determine if the patient retains any brain function. If such exams indicate continued function, then the apnea test should not be performed.

Even if the patient is incapable of spontaneous respiration, if they exhibit other brain functions, even in a minimally conscious state, then they are not considered to be dead. However, in a verifiably brain-dead person, spinal cord reflexes, local cellular functions, and continued heartbeat and circulation may be considered as *pirkus*, spasmodic movements after death.

These conclusions are based upon our halakhic understanding informed by contemporary medical research. We remain humbled by the rapidly evolving technology, and sensitive to the religious and cultural differences that may lead some patients and their families to reject the declaration of death based on neurological criteria.

Of necessity, this paper has focused on the technical aspects of medical practice and halakhic precedent. This should not obscure the fact that each incidence of such death is tragic for the patient and for his or her family. Indeed, the declaration of death based on neurological criteria, despite continued heartbeat, can be particularly troubling for relatives who are not fully convinced that their loved one has died. Medical literature is likewise concerned with this problem. Clergy who are properly sensitive to both the halakhic and the pastoral challenges of this moment can be an invaluable resource for the grieving family. They may explain the spiritual significance of the "breath of life" and its connection to familiar Hebrew terms such as *nefesh, neshama,* and *ruaḥ* It would be appropriate to tear a garment at the time that death is declared, to recite Psalms, to ask forgiveness from the deceased, and to follow all the other sensitive customs taught by our holy Torah.

PISKEI DIN

1. A ventilator-dependent patient with heartbeat but no apparent brain function may be declared dead according to halakhah, based on the following criteria:

2. If, after the established waiting period, confirmatory tests and brain-reflex exams show there to be no brain function, the patient shall be tested for apnea.

3. Failure to breathe during the apnea test (or any future procedure that verifies the absence of spontaneous respiration) proves that the patient is considered dead based on the traditional standard of Jewish law—the permanent cessation of respiration.

4. After the apnea test is concluded, ventilation shall be continued until the results are known, death is declared, and the family has had an opportunity to consider donation of vital organs to save another person's life. The donor's body should be treated with the utmost dignity and be prepared for Jewish burial at the earliest possible opportunity.

CHAPTER 9: AFTERWORD – AMONG THE MOURNERS OF ZION

T his final chapter departs from our primary theme of Torah and Technology but relates to the themes of illness and mortality in the second section of the book. Given the mystery of life after death, this chapter also relates to the questions of personhood and identity found in the first section. There we discussed the status of bodies that have been modified or substituted by machines. Here we wonder how the living can relate to the dead, transitioning from bereavement to consolation while working to retain the memory of our loved ones. My main purpose here is to honor the memory of my beloved mother and teacher, Phyllis B. Nevins, *Pesya bat Yitzḥak Ha-levi v'Raḥel*, may God's peace be upon her. She was a great advocate of my journey in Torah and mitzvot, and I am forever grateful to her for giving me life and guiding me in this sweet and satisfying path.

I

Stepping back from the grave of my mother, who died of lymphoma at age 66 in 2005, I accepted words that I had often offered to others:

*Ha-makom   yinaḥeim   etkḥem   b'tokḥ   sha'ar   aveilei   tzion
virushalaim.*

May God [literally, the Place] comfort you among the other
mourners of Zion and Jerusalem.

Over the course of shiva, as this curious statement was repeated, I
began to wonder about its origins. I knew that it wasn't a biblical verse,
nor was the expression found in the Talmud or Midrash. A comprehensive
search revealed that this common expression of comfort is not found
even in medieval codes or commentaries. Reference books on mourning
rituals such as *Gesher Ha-Ḥaim* and *Kol Bo Al Aveilut* do not address its
origins. Daniel Sperber's seven-volume study of Jewish customs is silent
about the phrase, and it is not part of Sephardic custom at all. Where
does it come from, and what does it mean?

The closest we get to a biblical source is Isaiah 61:2. Here, the
prophet announces his mission "to comfort all who mourn, to provide
for the mourners of Zion, to give them a turban instead of ashes ...." In
this message of national restoration, the prophet of exile envisions a
return to Zion and the rebuilding of her ruined cities. Isaiah's image of
redemption is comforting in the grand scheme of history, but what does
it offer to a bereaved person who mourns for a parent, spouse, sibling,
or child? In the raw moments of burial and then shiva, what comfort
is there in a millennial hope for the rebuilding of Zion? Moreover, why
was this sentiment transformed and expanded into our familiar words
of condolence?

In Mishnah Middot (2:2), we learn about an ancient Temple-era
custom of comforting the mourners:

All who entered the Temple Mount came in on the right side, circled, and exited on the left side, except for one who had suffered a loss, who circled from the left. [Others] would ask him, "Why are you circling from the left?" "I am bereaved," [he would reply. They then said,] "May the One Who dwells in this house comfort you."

This custom is explained with variations in two other rabbinic texts, Midrash Pirke D'Rabbi Eliezer (17), and the minor tractate of the Talmud, *Sofrim* (19:9). In both places, King Solomon is credited with having had Temple gates designated specially for grooms and mourners. On Shabbat, people would sit between these gates to congratulate the former and to comfort the latter. Thus, was kindness integrated into the very architecture of God's house.

The Midrash concludes, "Once the Temple was destroyed, the sages decreed that bridegrooms and mourners should go to synagogues and houses of study. The local people would see the groom and rejoice with him. Seeing the mourner, they would sit on the ground with him so that all Israel would fulfill the obligation of kindness."[1] Yet, what would the people say to mourners in the synagogue? Could the Temple-period expression, "May the One who dwells in this house comfort you," be employed in the synagogue or study hall? Does God dwell in our local sanctuaries?

This question is addressed in the fifteenth century *Sefer Maharil: Minhagim*, a compendium of German-Jewish customs written by Yaakov Moelin.[2] He relates a debate within German Jewry about whether it is appropriate in synagogue to use this Temple-era expression, as some apparently continued to do. Interpreting Deuteronomy 33:12, Moelin states that ever since the Temple was destroyed, God's presence has never dwelled anywhere else. If so, then it would seem inappropriate to say in synagogue, "May the One who dwells in this house comfort you."[3]

What then shall we say to the mourner? Rabbi Moelin cites in the name of his father, Rabbi Moshe Moelin, that we say, *Hashem yinaḥemkha im sha'ar aveilei tzion*, "God shall comfort you with the other mourners of Zion."

While this expression is not identical to ours, it is quite close. Jacob ben Moses[4] refers to God as *ba'al haneḥamot*, "the Master of consolation." At some point, the phrase evolved further, opening with the divine appellation, *Ha-makom* ("the place"), perhaps influenced by the Talmudic *Ha-makom yimalei ḥesronkha*, "May God fill your void."[5] To Zion was added its twin, Jerusalem, yielding our current usage.

Eleazar ben David Fleckeles, in a responsum written after the death of his father, prays that God "Shall comfort me among the mourners of Zion and Jerusalem."[6] Thus, by the early nineteenth century, our standard expression of comfort has taken shape and become prevalent in Ashkenazi circles. But what, precisely, does it mean?

II

The few discussions of our phrase in rabbinic literature have addressed a technical problem with this practice. Following the example set by Job, Jewish law forbids one to speak to a mourner until he or she opens conversation. This allows the mourner to set the tone for the visit and prevents visitors from rushing to fill the painful silence with inappropriate patter. Yet Jewish custom encourages us to offer this standard expression already as the mourners file between us at the grave. How come?

One unsatisfying answer is that the very act of walking away from the grave between two lines of friends may be viewed as an act of dialogue initiated by the mourner, thereby liberating their friends to start engaging them with words of comfort. Yet Moshe Feinstein argues that walking from the grave is not a statement, nor is the expression in question the substance of comforting the bereaved, any more than is the Talmudic era, "may you be comforted from heaven."[7] Rabbi Feinstein states that none of these formulae fulfill the mitzvah of *niḥum aveilim*, "comforting the bereaved." That mitzvah requires patience, to wait for the mourner to break the silence, and only then to speak to the heart until his spirit is stilled.[8]

If the expression, *Ha-makom yinaḥeim etkhem*, is not even fulfillment of the mitzvah of comforting the bereaved, then why do we offer it? One possibility is the power of the opening appellation for God, *Ha-makom*, "the place." Jeremiah 13:17 makes an opaque statement that there is a hidden place of weeping due to the pride of Israel. In Bavli Ḥagigah 5b, Rav Shmuel ben Inya explains in the name of Rav that this is a hidden place within God. Rav Shmuel bar Yitzhak adds that there is weeping in this place over the lost glory of Israel. In a recent responsum, Eliezer Waldenberg expands this thought, saying that hidden within God is a place of sorrow for the suffering and dispersion of the people Israel. Only when the exiles return, and the pride of Israel is restored, will God be comforted.[9] Michael Graetz suggests that *yinaḥeim* could plausibly be read as a passive *nifal*, and *etkhem* could be vocalized *itkhem*, yielding, "God shall be comforted together with you among the other mourners of Zion and Jerusalem."[10]

As it were, God projects a joyous exterior; yet within, God shares fully in the pain of Israel and refuses to be comforted until the time of redemption. In a similar fashion, the mourner harbors a secret place of sorrow in the heart, even when presenting a happy exterior to the world. This expression validates the enduring place of pain over a loss and assures the mourner that God shares in their sorrow. This explanation is beautiful and compelling. It indicates that the mourner is joined in sorrow not only by the community of other human mourners, but even by God. If so, then our expression is not so much the substance of *niḥum aveilim*, the comforting of mourners, as a *heiter aveilut*, permission to join the company of sorrow in heaven and on earth.

Having explored the origins and current explanations of our standard expression of consolation, I would like to offer several additional interpretations.

Ha-makom—The Place

In Exodus 20:20, God instructs Moses that an earthen altar may be built "in the place (*ha-makom*) where I shall mention my name." Rashi explains that God gives the priests permission to enunciate God's explicit name only at the altar, i.e., the place where the Shekhinah, or divine presence, hovers. If so, "the place" refers not only to the locus of human worship but also to the divine presence summoned by our service.

"The place" is frequently cited by the rabbis in contexts where God's *presence* is keenly felt. As a name for God, "the Place" is invoked to console a person for the loss of property (Brakhot 16b), in thanksgiving for delectable food (B. Brakhot 40b), and to ask mercy for a patient to recover (B. Shabbat 12b). In the latter context, the Hebrew term *Ha-makom* is equated by Rabbi Elazar with the Aramaic *Raḥmana*, meaning "Merciful One." Perhaps there is something particularly merciful about this description of God? It seems that to describe God as "the place" is to say that despite God's transcendence and eternity, there is nevertheless a point of access at which a mortal, dependent, vulnerable human can address and even reach God. In other words, "the Place" is God's portal of prayer.

When the rabbis claim that Abraham established the morning service, they cite Genesis 19:27 for support: "Avraham rose early in the place (*ha-makom*) where he stood facing God." Something about the place allows Abraham to connect with God. For Abraham, the place is not merely a physical site, but a point of connection to God.

This brings us back to the grave. The rabbis are concerned that mourners will be tempted at the grave to deny the justice of God. For this reason, we fill the cemetery with special prayers. We recite *tzidduk ha-din* (the justification of God's justice), tear a garment, and praise God as the true judge (if we haven't already), and of course, recite the Kaddish, the ultimate affirmation of God's greatness.

Yet perhaps this anxiety is misplaced. Perhaps the grave is "the place" where people become most aware of their dependence upon God. There in the cemetery, surrounded by mute testimony to human mortality, we are startled into recognition of our limited term on earth. Our prayers are intensified by this awareness, allowing us finally to recognize the words: *lekha Adonai ha-gedulah v'ha-gevurah vha-tiferet v'ha-netzah v'ha-hod*, "Yours, O Lord, are greatness, might and glory, and triumph and beauty!"[11] This place, the cemetery, is a place of terrible power, and we have no alternative but to turn to God for comfort.

Yinaheim etkhem—"*shall comfort you*"

What does it mean to comfort a person? A beautiful demonstration is given by Joseph in the closing lines of Genesis. After the death of Jacob, his other sons fear that Joseph will exact revenge for their earlier betrayal. Joseph reassures his brothers, telling them not to fear, that he will provide for them and their children. "And he comforted them and spoke to their hearts" (50:21). The act of comforting requires recognition of the source of sorrow as well as an alternative emotional path.

This is a lesson that the brothers urgently require. Earlier in Genesis,

Jacob's sons presented their father with false evidence of Joseph's death, and he refused to be comforted. His children offered superficial and self-serving expressions of comfort, but he stated, "I will descend to the grave grieving for my son" (37:35). For Jacob to have accepted their guilt-ridden expressions of sympathy would have been inappropriate, whether or not he divined that Joseph was truly alive.[12] To be comforted is to change one's thinking from denial to acceptance. What the children presented to their devastated father as comfort was incomplete and unacceptable.

True expressions of comfort demand understanding of the nature of the source of sorrow. One who accepts comfort must agree to let go of a measure of anguish and accept the previously unthinkable new reality. The activity of comforting requires change within both the comforter and the comforted.

The most curious case of comfort comes yet earlier in the book of Genesis, when God apparently regrets creating humanity. In Hebrew, God's regret is described strangely as comfort: *Vayinaḥeim Adonai ki asah et ha-adam ba'aretz, vayitatzeiv el libo*, "The Lord regretted having made Adam on earth, and it anguished His heart" (6:5). This sentence is problematic on several levels. Does God experience regret? And, if so, why is God's regret described as comfort? Rashi uses this verse to explain the phenomenon of comfort with great sensitivity:

> Another explanation of *vayinaḥeim*—the thoughts of God reversed from the attribute of mercy to the attribute of justice. It rose in thought before God what should be done with this Adam in the land. And so, whenever the language of *niḥum* is used, it refers to reconsideration of what to do.

Rashi conveys to us the essence of comfort. To be comforted is to accept a different perspective, to release some of the pain and denial, and to come to grips with the new reality. Even God experiences this dynamic of response to the reality of flawed people, shifting between mercy and justice depending upon the situation. To be comforted is to discover an alternative option for a disappointing situation. So, too, must humans modulate their emotions after death, from intensive grief to a form of sorrow that accepts memory in place of the physical presence of their loved one.

B'tokh sha'ar aveilei tzion viyrushalaim—"Among the other mourners of Zion and Jerusalem"

Now, who are they? Isaiah mentions them almost as if they are an organized group. Indeed, later in Jewish history, there emerged groups of mourners identified as *avelei tzion*. After the Second Temple was destroyed, pious Jews would engage in excessive fasting to demonstrate their yearning for the restoration of Zion.[13]

Throughout the Middle Ages, there were Jewish groups in Jerusalem and across the diaspora who established ascetic societies of mourners. This stance was controversial since the Talmud warns mourners not to grieve excessively. Moreover, some of these ascetics were apparently Karaites. Still, the practice persisted. There is a note of defensiveness in the 9th century Midrash, Pesikta Rabbati (35), that explains that while after Tisha b'Av, just like after a funeral, one is allowed to eat and drink again, nevertheless one must "keep sighing in the heart over [Jerusalem] until the Holy One rebuilds her." This Midrash may reflect the pressure felt by Avelei Zion to moderate their mourning for the destruction of the Temple. Like Jacob, they refused to be comforted, even as others encouraged them to acclimate to the new reality.

In the special version of *birkat ha-mazon* said in a shiva house, we alter the paragraph "rebuild Jerusalem," with an extended description of the mourners of Zion. Either these people who felt the national calamity so intensely came to be viewed as role models of what an ordinary mourner should experience, or perhaps our phrase developed as a warning to the mourner not to become like the "mourners of Zion," a group that grieved obsessively over the ancient destruction of Jerusalem. Jewish law viewed excessive mourning for the dead as unhealthy. Mourners returning from the cemetery are required to eat a *se'udat havra'ah*, a revival meal,[14] and to avoid the cemetery during the week of shiva. Rav Yehudah in the name of Rav warns not to mourn excessively. Three days were considered appropriate for intensive weeping, seven for eulogizing, and thirty for external signs of grief, such as not grooming or ironing clothes.[15]

Perhaps the juxtaposition of "the Place" comforting "the mourners of Zion" is itself a corrective: Do not focus your grief excessively on the physical site of the Temple. As Rav Ami teaches, God is the Place of the world; the world is not the place of God.[16] Likewise, you should not mourn without limit for the physical presence of the person you loved. The ultimate Place, God's *Shekhinah*, is the source of comfort at this very moment.

Betokh—"In the Midst"

Our expression of comfort reminds the mourner that they are *betokh*, "in the midst," of others who grieve. Perhaps a hint is embedded in this simple word. After all, it is this word that serves as the key for determining the number ten as our quorum for prayer. In Brakhot 21b, we learn by *gezera shava*, a decree of equivalence, that the passage in Leviticus 22:32, "I shall be sanctified in the midst of Israel," is to be read in light of Numbers 16:21, "separate from the midst of this evil group." Just as it was ten there, so is it ten here. Matters of holiness, including the Kaddish, require a minyan. While it is true that only the mourner knows their own grief, this microcosm of Israel, this community of comfort, will allow them to escape isolation.

The requirement of minyan for the recitation of Kaddish is a mechanism to combat depression and endless sorrow. Community comes to the mourner, and then the mourner must seek out community, identifying themselves as emotionally wounded by the loss. To stand in the midst of a congregation and recite Kaddish is to invite comfort and to embrace healing. If God is sanctified in the midst of Israel, then Israel is comforted in the presence of God.

Zion and Jerusalem

For much of the past twenty-five centuries, Jerusalem has been a symbol not of current glory, but of memory and yearning. While the city as we know it is beautiful, it is not the Jerusalem of today that brings us repeatedly to its walls. To enter Jerusalem is to escape the ordinary bounds of time. Here, the presence of past generations is keenly felt. Here, the future redemption is experienced not as idle fantasy but as urgent desire. Jerusalem is a place where the present moment feels just like that—a fleeting idyll between *ḥurban v'tekumah*, destruction and reconstruction.

To link one's loss with Jerusalem is to proclaim the enduring power of the life lived by one's relative. While their body may be buried, their presence persists among the living, just as David and Solomon and all the ancient prophets and pilgrims of Israel are still experienced in modern Jerusalem. But this linkage also reflects a millennial perspective. Just as Judaism views Jerusalem as destined for renewed glory, so, too, does it offer faith in bodily resurrection, in the ultimate renewal of life.

To be comforted among those who mourn for Zion and Jerusalem is to expand one's consciousness beyond the bounds of the current painful moment. Reality is not only what we see and experience today. Reality includes the past and future. Our loved ones may seem out of reach, but if equipped with the proper perspective, we may yet feel their continued power of anchoring our past and guiding us toward a better future.

As a rabbi, and as a son, I have found burial to be the emotional tipping point. It is then that the finality of death is felt most powerfully. At that moment, we are forced to accept the impermanence of our physical selves. Yet in the cemetery, we may perceive a greater place, an eternal presence that is not within the world, but which contains all that was, is, and will ever be. Lifting our gaze from the grave, walking between our friends, we are invited to join the company of all mourners in Zion, seeking solace in the infinite mystery of God.

ENDNOTES

NOTES TO CHAPTER 1

ARTIFICIAL INTELLIGENCE AND AUTONOMOUS MACHINES

1   Keith Abney, "Robotics, Ethical Theory, and Metaethics: A Guide for the Perplexed," in Patrick Lin, Keith Abney, George A. Bekey, editors, *Robot Ethics: The Ethical and Social Implications of Robotics* (MIT Press, 2012). See also Steve Torrance, "Artificial Agents and the Expanding Ethical Circle," *AI and Society* (2013) 28:399–414, and Wallach and Allen, below. The machine ethics conversation began in science fiction literature with Isaac Asimov's Three Rules of Robotics, first mentioned in his 1942 short story, "Runaround." These were: 1) A robot may not injure a human being or, through inaction, allow a human being to come to harm; 2) A robot must obey orders given it by human beings except where such orders would conflict with the First Law; 3) A robot must protect its own existence as long as such protection does not conflict with the First or Second Law. Asimov later added a fourth or Zeroth Law (so named because it superseded the other three): Zeroth: A robot may not harm humanity, or, by inaction, allow humanity to come to harm. Scholars (and Asimov himself) have noted the unworkability of these laws which, like other deontological systems, run aground in situations of contested rights, as when two people's interests are in conflict and the robot must help or harm one.

2   The edited volume *Robot Ethics* has 22 chapters, including one providing Buddhist reflections on the subject and another that models a "Divine-Command Approach," though there is no religious reasoning evident in the chapter. Artificial Intelligence has been mentioned by some scholars of halakhah, but without analysis of the field or substantial conclusions about the issues before us. There is an article regarding liability issues at stake with autonomous vehicles in Volume 38 of the Israeli journal, *Teḥumin*, that I discuss below. Nadav Berman Shifman graciously shared with me his forthcoming article, "Autonomous Weapon Systems and Jewish Law: Ethical-Political Perspectives," to which I refer below.

3   Text as approved available at: https://www.rabbinicalassembly.org/sites/default/files/nevins_ai_moral_machines_and_halakhah-final_1.pdf.

4   A transcript of Ezra Klein's July 11, 2023 interview with Demis Hassabis is available here: https://www.nytimes.com:2023:07:11:podcasts/transcript-ezra-klein-interviews-demis-hassabis.html.

5   https://www.whitehouse.gov/ostp/ai-bill-of-rights/

6   Torrance calls this the biocentric position. Nadav Berman Shifman writes (p.36 of v.27), "It is by the body that we sense the world and other beings and through it we come to understand what good and evil are. Ultimately, it is the body that makes us vulnerable and at the same time punishable. This dependence of morality on materiality and mortality, is neglected in the discussion about robot ethics, probably due to the aforementioned dominance of Cartesianism in Western philosophy, and to the predominance of the 'algorithm ethics.'"

7   Melanie Mitchell, "Artificial Intelligence Hits the Barrier of Meaning," *New York Times*, Nov. 5, 2018. Regarding current methods for training computers to discern the "meaning" of language, see the "Language as a Litmus Test," box within the article,

"Artificial Intelligence and Ethics," by Jonathan Shaw, *Harvard Magazine* (Feb. 2019) p.,47, and then Barbara J. Grosz, "Smart Enough to Talk With Us? Foundations and Challenges for Dialogue Capable AI Systems" in *Computational Linguistics*, 44:1 (March 2018) 1-15.

8   See below for discussion of Michael Graziano, *Consciousness and the Social Brain* (Oxford University Press, 2013).

9   I thank AI researcher and consultant, Sergey Feldman, for this and other insights (see below).

10   See OECD.AI's 2019 statement of AI Principles, Transparency, and Explainability (Principle 1.3): "AI Actors should commit to transparency and responsible disclosure regarding AI systems. To this end, they should provide meaningful information, appropriate to the context, and consistent with the state of art: to foster a general understanding of AI systems; to make stakeholders aware of their interactions with AI systems, including in the workplace; to enable those affected by an AI system to understand the outcome, and; to enable those adversely affected by an AI system to challenge its outcome based on plain and easy-to-understand information on the factors, and the logic that served as the basis for the prediction, recommendation or decision."

11   Amitai Etzioni, Oren Etzioni, "AI Assisted Ethics," *Ethics and Information Technology* (2016) 18:149–156.

12   Amitai Etzioni, Oren Etzioni, "Designing AI Systems that Obey Our Laws and Values," *Communications of the ACM*, (2016) Vol. 59 No. 9, pp. 29-31. See also, Oren Etzioni, "To Keep AI Safe—Use AI," *Recode*, Feb. 4, 2016.

13   Collective Constitutional AI: Aligning a Language Model with Public Input, ANTHROP\C. Oct 17, 2023. https://www.anthropic.com/index/collective-constitutional-ai-aligning-a-language-model-with-public-input

14   Cf. Etzioni ("AI Assisted Ethics"): "Autonomy in computer science refers to the ability of a computer to follow a complex algorithm in response to environmental inputs, independently of real-time human input."

15   Wendell Wallach, Colin Allen, *Moral Machines: Teaching Robots Right from Wrong* (Oxford University Press, 2009). See also their chapter, "Moral Machines: Contradiction in Terms or Moral Abdication?" in *Robot Ethics* (2012), where they update their argument and respond to some criticisms of their book. This chart is included in both texts.

16   The tragic crashes of Lion Air Flight 610 and Ethiopian Airlines Flight 302— Boeing 737 MAX 8 airplanes whose autopilot systems malfunctioned in 2018 and 2019, killing all aboard—remind us that even well-intentioned AI systems do not always produce moral results. Indeed, researchers discuss the "brittleness" of AI systems that lack contextual awareness to questions and contain incongruous data in the way that humans naturally do.

17   Waymo, the autonomous vehicle unit of Alphabet, claimed 10 million physical miles driven autonomously as of October 2018. Israeli competitor Intel Mobileye claims that safety can be demonstrated without such measures, which it deems wasteful, and indeed, Waymo uses computer simulations virtually to drive ten million miles every day. Nevertheless, there are many "edge cases" that cannot be anticipated, and also the danger of hacking, either of the systems directly, or of essential environmental cues such as stop signs, that can be compromised in ways discernible only to machines.

18   https://www.nhtsa.go/technology-innovation/automated-vehicles-safety#issue-road-self-driving

19   https://futureoflife.or/ai-principles: See FLI president Max Tegmark's account of

the history of this project in *Life 3.0: Being Human in the Age of Artificial Intelligence* (Alfred A. Knopf, 2017).

20 See David Edmonds, *Would You Kill the Fat Man? The Trolley Problem and What Your Answer Tells Us about Right and Wrong* (Princeton University Press, 2015). MIT has a "Moral Machine" website that introduces the topic and allows visitors to browse various scenarios and even play a related game: http://moralmachine.mit.edu:.

21 Ronald C. Arkin, *Governing Lethal Behavior in Autonomous Robots* (CRC Press, 2009). See also Paul Scharre, *Army of None: Autonomous Weapons and the Future of War* (WW Norton and Co, 2019), and his essay, "Killer Apps: The Real Dangers of an AI Arms Race" in *Foreign Affairs* (May/June 2019), pp. 135-144. Israel is a leader in the field of autonomous weapons, with its Harpy system capable of airborne loitering for hours, identifying and attacking enemy radar installations; the Guardium uninhabited ground vehicle patrolling the Gaza border; and the Trophy Merkava tank defense system capable of automatically returning fire.

22 See Scharre, *Army of None*, Chapter 3.

23 US Department of Defense Directive 3000.09 (2012; rev. 2017) addresses autonomy in weapon systems in guarded language. Although military planners profess not to intend to relinquish the authorization of lethal force to AI, this could change in response to enemies acting without such scruples. See discussion in Scharre, Chapter 6.

24 See the DARPA video on "three waves of AI" by John Launchbury, for a sense of what is envisioned in future AI: https://youtu.be:-Oo1G3tSYpU.

25 For a primer on AI that broaches concerns with LAWS, read the 2018 report of the United Nations Institute for Disarmament Research (UNIDIR), "The Weaponization of Increasingly Autonomous Weapons: Artificial Intelligence." As of April 2018, twenty-six countries had signed a call for the ban of fully autonomous weapons systems. Yet even some who signed the ban, such as China, were simultaneously announcing advances in technologies such as "swarms" of drones guided by AI. See Elsa Kania, "China's Strategic Ambiguity and Shifting Approach to Lethal Autonomous Weapons Systems," *Lawfare*, April 18, 2018.

26 The four basic principles of the Law of Armed Conflict (LOAC) are: distinction, proportionality, military necessity, and unnecessary suffering. See https://loacblog.com/loac-basics:4-basic-principles/. For much more (>1200 pages) see the US DoD Law of War Manual, and the IDF Code of Ethics and Mission. See, too, Moshe Halbertal's blog at the Shalom Hartman Institute website, "War and Ethics in the IDF Ethical Code."

27 According to the National Highway Traffic Safety Administration, in 2016 there were 37,461 traffic fatalities in the United States, with almost a third involving alcohol-impaired-driving crashes.

28 Scharre opens his book, *Army of None*, with an event in the USSR on Sept. 23, 1983 when sensors conveyed false information of five nuclear missiles incoming from the USA; a human operator sensed that something was amiss and sought additional radar confirmation before sending the alarm up the chain of command, possibly averting a nuclear apocalypse. Would an automated system have delayed responding in such a circumstance?

29 Thanks to Yoni Brafman for this argument, which applies equally to non-military applications.

30 Paul Scharre, *Army of None*, 282-3, reporting an interview with Arkin on June 8, 2016.

31   Harry Davies and Bethan McKernan, "'The Gospel': How Israel uses AI to select bombing targets in Gaza," *The Guardian*, December 1, 2023.

32   Marissa Newman, "Israel Quietly Places AI Systes at Center of Military," *Bloomberg News*, July 13, 2023.

33   For an alarming discussion of the potential social, economic, and political harms that artificial intelligence could enable, see Yuval Noah Harari, "Why Technology Favors Tyranny," *The Atlantic* (October 2018) and the chapter "Liberty" in his book, *21 Lessons for the 21st Century* (Spiegel & Grau, 2018). Shoshana Zuboff has dubbed this "The Age of Surveillance Capitalism." Yet more alarming is the 2017 Slaughterbots video, a fictional short film that illustrates the moral perils of LAWS and advocates halting the development of autonomous weapons.

34   See Jay Stanley, "The Dawn of Robot Surveillance: AI, Video Analytics and Privacy," published by the American Civil Liberties Union, June 13, 2019.

35   Paul Scharre, "Killer Apps," 138-9.

36   See M. Ryan Calo, "Robots and Privacy," chapter 12 in *Robot Ethics* (2014).

37   Leviticus 19:14. Rabbinic expansions are found at B. Avodah Zarah 6a-b and Sifra Kedoshim, 2:2.

38   See "Virtual Humans in Health-Related Interventions: A Meta-Analysis," by T Ma, H Sharifi, D Chattopadhyay, conference paper, May 2019. In "Managing Chronic Conditions with a Smartphone-based Conversational Virtual Agent," (IVA 18) Michael K. Paasche-Orlow, Jared W. Magnani, et al., conclude, "Given that chronic diseases affect such a large portion of the population, and the complexity of self-care management regimens—especially for patients with low health literacy— virtual agents represent an important tool for improving population health and decreasing healthcare costs." I thank Dr. Paasche-Orlow for explaining the use of virtual health agents.

39   I thank Toby Schonfeld for suggesting this analogy to proxy decision-making.

40   For a detailed (and in the second half, highly technical) introduction, see the 2017 video tutorial, "Fairness in Machine Learning," by Solon Barocas and Moritz Hardt, https://vimeo.com:248490141. I thank Sergey Feldman for the reference and for flagging this as a topic of moral concern.

41   For example, social biases may be anchored in fact patterns that are accurate, and yet those patterns are themselves reflections of bias, such as gender or racial discrimination. Barocas discusses two discourses in American discrimination law, disparate treatment, and disparate impact. The former relates to procedural fairness and equal opportunity, while the latter considers larger social structures that may lead to unequal outcomes and promotes options for distributive justice. We will discuss models of fairness in halakhic discourse and their implications for directing machine learning below. The question of which biases are erroneous, which are accurate but morally unacceptable, and which are defensible, is an endlessly contentious matter which plays out, for example, in discussions of affirmative action. Defensible bias has specific dimensions within halakhic discourse, with its manifold distinctions among actors and actions.

42   Cathy O'Neil, *Weapons of Math Destruction: How Big Data Increases Inequality and Threatens Democracy* (Broadway Books, 2017). See also Dhruv Khullar, "AI Could Worsen Health Disparities," *New York Times*, Jan. 31, 2019. Regarding loan applications, see this discussion of "threshold classifiers" and how they can be made less biased: https://research.google.com/bigpicture/attacking-discrimination-in-ml/.

43   While we frequently describe halakhah as "Jewish law," it is quite rare for

halakhic rulings to be enforced with means comparable to the law enforcement methods of governments and their police forces, even in Israel. That said, it is not uncommon for religious discourse to influence the development of civil law, especially in areas that are unsettled or controversial. Of course, for observant Jews, halakhic guidance plays an even more direct role in their interaction with these new technologies.

44   See Mira Beth Wasserman, *Jews, Gentiles, and Other Animals: The Talmud after the Humanities* (Penn University Press, 2017), pp. 33, 166, 234-235.

45   לסקירה רחבה של הנושא ראו נחום רקוב, השליחות וההרשאה במשפט העברי (מוסד הרב קוק, 1972: תשל"ב).

For a comparison to *mandatum* in Roman law, see Barry Nicholas, *An Introduction to Roman Law* (Clarendon Press, 1962, rev. 2008), pp.187-89.

46   בבלי קידושין דף מא עמוד א. האיש מקדש את בתו כשהיא נערה. כשהיא נערה אין, כשהיא קטנה לא: מסייע ליה לרב, דאמר רב יהודה אמר רב, ואיתימא רבי אלעזר: אסור לאדם שיקדש את בתו כשהיא קטנה, עד שתגדל ותאמר בפלוני אני רוצה.

47   שם, עמוד ב.

48   משנה מסכת ברכות פרק ה, משנה ה. המתפלל וטעה סימן רע לו ואם שליח צבור הוא סימן רע לשולחיו מפני ששלוחו של אדם כמותו. תוספתא מסכת תענית (ליברמן) פרק ג. צו את בני ישראל ואמרת אליהו את קרבני לחמי' לא איפשר לומ' כל ישראל אלא מלמד ששלוחו של אדם כמותו. מכילתא דרבי ישמעאל בא - מסכתא דפסחא פרשה ג. ויקחו להם. וכי כלן היו לוקחין אלא לעשות שלוחו של אדם מכאן אמרו שלוחו של אדם כמותו:

49   מכילתא דרבי ישמעאל משפטים - מסכתא דנזיקין פרשה ב. ורצע אדוניו את אזנו. למה נאמר, לפי שמצינו בכל מקום ששלוחו של אדם כמותן, אבל כאן הוא ולא שלוחו. ספרא מצורע פרשה ה. אשר לו הבית שלא ישלח ביד שליח יכול אפילו זקן, ואפילו חולה, תלמוד לומר ובא והגיד הכהן, ידקדק הכהן כיצד בא הנגע לביתו. ספרי במדבר פרשת מטות פיסקא קנג. אמר לאפוטרופוס כל נדרים שתהא בתי נודרת מיכן ועד שאבוא ממקום פלוני הפר לה והפר לה שומע אני יהיה מופר ת"ל ואם הניא אביה אותה והם היפר אביה מופר ואם לאו אינו מופר דברי ר' יאשיה, ר' יונתן אומר מצינו בכל מקום ששלוחו של אדם כמותו.

50   במדבר פרק יח פסוק כח. כֵּן תָּרִימוּ גַם אַתֶּם תְּרוּמַת ה' מִכֹּל מַעְשְׂרֹתֵיכֶם אֲשֶׁר תִּקְחוּ מֵאֵת בְּנֵי יִשְׂרָאֵל וּנְתַתֶּם מִמֶּנּוּ אֶת תְּרוּמַת ה' לְאַהֲרֹן הַכֹּהֵן:

51   רמב"ם הלכות תרומות פרק ד הלכה א. עושה אדם שליח להפריש לו תרומות ומעשרות שנאמר כן תרימו גם אתם לרבות שלוחכם ואין עושין שליח עכו"ם שנאמר גם אתם מה אתם בני ברית אף שלוחכם בני ברית.

52   טור חושן משפט הלכות גביית מלוה סימן צז. כ"כ רב אלפס בתשובה שאם הלוה אלם ורוע מעללים ומעיז פניו מלפרוע חובו מותר ליכנס לביתו לדעת מצפונו אפי' ע"י שליח עכו"ם.

53   טור חושן משפט הלכות שלוחין סימן קפח. א אין שליחות לעובד כוכבים לא שיעשה הוא שליח לישראל ולא שיעשנו ישראל שליח אבל אשה ועבד ושפחה בני שליחות הן כיון שחייבין בקצת מצות ויש להן דעת אבל חרש שוטה וקטן כיון שאין להן דעת לאו בני שליחות הן לא שיעשו הם שלוחין ולא שאחרים יעשנום שליח: וראו בדרכי משה שם, אות (א).

54   הד משנה הלכות זכיה ומתנה פרק ד. ולכאורה יש סברא לחלק בין עכו"ם ובין חשו"ק בדין שליחות לחומרא משום דבעכו"ם איתא בהו דין שליחות בעלמא בין בהממשלה ובין בהשליח היינו בשליח עכו"ם עבור ישראל דבהממשלה הישראל איתא ביה דין שליחות וגם בעכו"ם השליח יש בו דין שליחות היינו בעכו"ם לעכו"ם רק דעכו"ם לישראל ליתא דין שליחות מדאורייתא אבל כל חד אפי נפשיה יש בהם דין שליחות.

55   Ḥatam Sofer writes in a responsum (#90) that if one used a gentile agent to lead an animal and thus acquire it, this is effective (מועיל) since they have similar laws of agency (his word קאמיסיאנע seems to come from "commission" and mean a type of appointment):

שו"ת חתם סופר קובץ תשובות סימן צ. ומטעם זה נ"ל לקיים לדינא איד דתשובת

משאת בנימין דבמשך על ידי שליח עכו"ם מועיל משום דבדיניהם הוה קאמיסיאנע כמותו, אף על גב דמשאת בנימין בעצמו לא נחית לכך.

56 ע' שו"ת להורות נתן חלק ו סימן צו. בזה י"ל דאע"ג דאין עכו"ם נעשה שליח לישראל מ"מ פועל עכו"ם של ישראל שפיר נעשה שליח, דהרי הא דאין העכו"ם נעשה שליח לישראל אין החסרון בישראל המשלח, שהרי הישראל בעצמו היה יכול לעשות מעשה זה, אלא שהחסרון הוא משום שאין העכו"ם יכול לקבל כחו של ישראל המשלח, דהתורה לא ריבתה דין שליחות בעכו"ם, ואשר מהאי טעמא אין העכו"ם יכול לעשות זה עבור הישראל.

57 תורת חסד אורח חיים סימן מה. ואמנם כבר ביארנו לעיל דאף אם נימא לדינא סברת המח"א הנ"ל דבפועל עכו"ם יש שליחות משום דידו בידו מ"מ כ"ז לענין ממון ולא לענין מצות ואיסורין. וכד' הראב"ד והתוס' לענין יד עבד כיד רבו וכו'. ואין לברך כשנעשה מעקה ע"י פועל נכרי. וע"ע שו"ת ציץ אליעזר חלק יט סימן סד. ומכח האי טעמא דפועל יום שאני דגופו קנוי לבעה"ב לגמרי וידו כיד בעה"ב ממש. ס"ל להמח"א שם לפני כן בדבריו דאפילו אם עשה את המעקה ע"י פועל יום עכו"ם דג"כ הבעה"ב מברך עליו מפני דחשיב כאילו הוא בעצמו עשאה. ואליבא דהפר"ח ס"ל להמח"א שם דבכל גוונא בעה"ב מברך ואפילו אם עכו"ם שלוחו (ולא פועל יום) עשה את המעקה כדיעו"ש.

58 שולחן ערוך אבן העזר הלכות גיטין סימן קמא סעיף לה. וראו ברא"ש מסכת גיטין פרק ה...אבל הכא כיון דלא עשה העובד כוכבים אלא מעשה קוף בעלמא ומינה הבעל בכתבו את ישראל שבאותו מקום שליח למה יפסל הגט וכן נהגין באשכנז ובצרפת ע"פ דברי ר"ת לשלוח גט וקידושין על ידי עובד כוכבים וממנה בכתבו ישראל שבאותו מקום שליח. וע"ע ברבינו ירוחם - תולדות אדם וחוה נתיב כד חלק ג דף רו טור ד, מסירה לא תנשא לכתחלה משום דגוי לאו בר כריתה הוא ואם נשאת לא תצא משום דרבי שמעון דאמר במתניתין כלם כשרים ואמר ירד רבי שמעון לשטתו שטל רבי אליעזר דאמר עדי מסירה כרתי וקיימא לן כרבי אליעזר ע"כ. ורבי' תמהו על דברי הגאון כי אינו פסול אלא כשמינהו ישראל שליח במקומו אבל כשהגוי לא עשה אלא מעשה קוף בעלמא ומינה הבעל בכתבו את ישראל שליח ליתן לה גט ושולח הגוי ליתן לישראל שבאותו מקום מה שהוא שולח לו לא יפסל הגט וכן נהגו באשכנז וצרפ' על פי ר"ת לשלוח גט וקידושין ביד גוי וממנה שליח בכתבו לישראל שבאותו מקום.

59 בבלי קידושין דף מב עמוד ב. והא דתנן: השולח את הבעירה ביד חרש שוטה וקטן - פטור מדיני אדם וחייב בדיני שמים, שילח ביד פיקח - פיקח חייב; ואמאי? נימא: שלוחו של אדם כמותו! שאני התם, דאין שליח לדבר עבירה, דאמרינן: דברי הרב ודברי תלמיד - דברי מי שומעין?

60 רמב"ם חובל ומזיק פרק ה. האומר לחבירו שבר כליו של פלוני על מנת שאתה פטור הרי זה חייב לשלם, וכאילו אמר לו סמא לו עינו של פלוני על מנת שאתה פטור, ואף על פי שהעושה הוא החייב לשלם הרי זה האומר לו שותף בעון ורשע הוא שהרי הכשיל עור וחיזק ידי עוברי עבירה. ובדברי רמא בשולחן ערוך חושן משפט הלכות שלוחין סימן קפב סעיף א: הגה: בכל דבר שלוחו של אדם כמותו, חוץ מלדבר עבירה דקיימא לן אין שליח לדבר עבירה (טור). ודוקא שהשליח בר חיובא, אבל אם אינו בר חיובא הוי שליח אפילו לדבר עבירה (הגהות מיימוני פרק ה' דשלוחין).

61 The halakhah also permits serving a gett (writ of divorce) by throwing it at the feet of a woman, based on, "her four cubits acquire for her." This practice is not permitted, however, if the wife is a child. Why the child's personal space or courtyard doesn't acquire her divorce is the presenting issue of our sugya. There is tension between the tannaitic source, which assumes that a very young girl may be betrothed, and the amoraim, who follow Rav's dictate (discussed above) that the girl must be old enough to give informed consent.

62 רש"י מסכת בבא מציעא דף י עמוד ב. משום שליחות איתרבאי - מדרבי רחמנא שליחות לאדם, כדתניא (קידושין מא, א) ושלח - מלמד שהאיש עושה שליח, ושלחה - מלמד שהאשה עושה שליח, אתרבאי נמי חצרה, דהויא לה כשלוחה.

63 E. Benjamin Skinner, *A Crime So Monstrous: Face-to-Face with Modern-Day Slavery* (Free Press, 2008).

64 מכילתא דרבי ישמעאל משפטים - מסכתא דנזיקין פרשה יד. ועי' דברי התורה תמימה לשמות כב, ד הערה מה) כך משמע הלשון ושלח שעזבו לנפשו בלא השגחה ושמירה, ולכן אם מסרו לחרש שוטה וקטן הרי עזבו מרשותו לרשות הפקר שלא בהשגחה לכן חייב, משא"כ אם מסרו לפקח פטור הוא וחייב השליח, משום דהרי שמור הוא תחת יד הפקח ואפילו שלחו לא שייך לומר שהפקח עושה שליחותו של המשלח,

משום דקיי״ל אין שליח לדבר עבירה, וראו בסוגיא ב״ק נ״ו א׳:

65   This midrash may be harmonized with the Bavli source cited above, exempting slaves from the "double" fine for stealing; the slave is responsible not to steal but lacks independent financial resources to pay a fine. The designation of the deaf-mute (חרש) as legally incompetent has been studied and modified by Rabbi Pamela Barmash, "Status of the Ḥeresh and of Sign Language," (CJLS, approved May 24, 2011).

66   The emerging field of affective computing equips machines to identify the emotional state of human users and to respond in kind, either by modulating the tone of voice or suggesting appropriate actions. See for example, the MIT Media Lab. It seems that the interface shift—away from keyboards and screens toward voice and visual representations of virtual agents—leads people to interact with digital devices differently than with either mute machines or live persons. Judith Shulevitz discusses such potentially disturbing trends in AI design in, "Alexa, how will you change us?" *The Atlantic*, Nov. 2018. See also Nicholas A. Christakis, "How AI will rewire us," *The Atlantic*, April 2019.

67   Of course, free will is very much contested in contemporary studies of human behavior, much as בחירה חפשית was in ancient Jewish sources starting with Rabbi Akiva's claim in M. Avot 3:15, "All is foreseen, but choice is given," and on to Maimonides in his "Eight Chapters" (esp. Ch. 8). Neuroscientist Robert Sapolsky argues in *Behave: The Biology of Humans at our Best and Worst* (Penguin, 2017) that there is no independent part of us (a homunculus, or a soul) that makes decisions free from the influence of biology. In contrast, Michael Gazzaniga describes a complex decision-making process of mind, emerging from the biological structures of the brain and the social structures surrounding the person, to yield an "interpreter" that approximates autonomy. See *Who's in Charge? Free Will and the Science of the Brain* (Ecco, 2012). We certainly have the perception of human free will, and both religious and secular legal systems assign individuals responsibility based on that presumption. Michael Graziano discusses free will (200-202), concluding, "We frequently act without any conscious knowledge of why, and then make up false reasons to explain it. Consciousness is hardly the sole controller of behavior. But in [my] current theory, consciousness is at least one part of the control process."

68   See next section for discussion of limited liability for indirect damage.

69   רמב״ם נזקי ממון פרק ב, הלכה ו. בעטה בארץ ברשות הניזק והתיזה צרורות מחמת הבעיטה והזיקו שם חייב לשלם רביע נזק שזה שינוי הוא בהתזת הצרורות, ואם תפש הניזק חצי נזק אין מוציאין מידו, ואפילו היתה מהלכת במקום שאי אפשר לה שלא תתיז ובעטה והתיזה משלם רביע נזק, ואם תפש הניזק חצי נזק אין מוציאין מידו.

70   For a survey of these rules, see Rambam, MT Laws of Assault and Damage, chapter 6.

71   See Beth Berkowitz, *Animals and Animality in the Babylonian Talmud* (Cambridge University Press, 2018), esp. Ch.3, "Animal Morality" which explores the possibility of animals as subjects that bear moral culpability for their actions.

72   רמב״ם נזקי ממון פרק א. העושה מעשה שדרכו לעשותו תמיד כמנהג ברייתו הוא הנקרא מועד, והמשנה ועשה מעשה מעשים שאין דרך כל מינו לעשותו כן תמיד כגון שור שנגח או נשך הוא הנקרא תם, וזה המשנה אם הורגל בשינויו פעמים רבות נעשה מועד לאותו דבר שהורגל בו שני׳ (שמות כ״א ל״ו) או נודע כי שור נגח הוא.

73   אחריותו של הנהג ברכב אוטונומי על נזקים, מאת יוסף שפרונג וישראל מאיר מלכה, תחומין, כרך 38(2018) . הרב שפרונג גם מרצה על הנושא על סרטון רכב אוטונומי (2016) הנמצא באתר אוניברסיטת תל אביב.

74   חזון אי״ש לאו״ח לו.

75   תלמוד בבלי מסכת שבת דף קנג עמוד ב. אמר רב פפא: כל שבגופו חייב חטאת - בחברו פטור
אבל אסור. כל שחברו פטור אבל אסור - בחמורו מותר לכתחלה.

76   חידושי הרמב"ן מסכת שבת דף קנג עמוד ב.

77   The Amoraim, Rav Pappa and Rav Huna, debate whether the Torah's rule of
"half-damage" paid by the owner of an "innocent" ox that went wild implies shared
responsibility or is, rather, a fine. Rav Huna says the latter, which means that if the ox's
owner admits the damage, then they are exempt from paying the fine. The halakhah
follows Rav Huna, which would indicate that the owner of an autonomous vehicle that
causes damage, and who reports the accident to the authorities, might likewise be fully
exempt from payment. See b. Ketubot 41a.

78   ראו בבלי ב"ק ק ע"א, קונטרס הרמב"ן בדינא-דגרמי, רמב"ם פ"ז מהל' חובל ומזיק, טור ושו"ע חו"מ
שפו א', וגם הערך "גרמא בנזקין, גרמי" באנציקלופדיה תלמודית.

79   See Jeremy Kalmanofsky, "Participating in the American Death Penalty," (CJLS,
approved Oct. 15, 2013).

80   For a full account see David Edmonds, *Would You Kill the Fat Man?*

81   The size of the person matters, since otherwise the (presumably typical sized)
observer could sacrifice themselves, which would alter the ethical question.

82   "Doctrine of Double Effect," in Stanford Encyclopedia of Philosophy, 2004, rev.
2014.

83   Neil Levy, "Neuroethics: A New Way of Doing Ethics," *AJOB Neurosci.* 2011 Apr-
Jun; 2(2): 3–9.

84   Indeed, studies starting with Benjamin Libet's "Unconscious cerebral initiative
and the role of conscious will in voluntary action" in *Behavioral and Brain Sciences*, 1985;
8(4): 529-539, have shown that unconscious emotional responses are often quicker than
are consciously intellectual ones. This again raises the question of free will (see above),
and whether individuals "decide" how to act based on reasoning rather than instincts that
may be stimulated subconsciously. Still, the presence of such instincts does not deny any
role to the conscious mind.

85   Perhaps the text where the rabbis come closest to permitting the sacrifice of
one to save many is Tosefta Terumot 7:20 (and parallel in Yerushalmi Terumot Ch. 8,
halakhah 10), which describes a siege situation in which marauders demand one victim to
kill, or else they will kill the whole group (this is a rabbinic rendition of the biblical story
of Sheva ben Bichri told in II Samuel 20). The Tosefta prohibits such a sacrifice, unless
the invaders specify one target. In that case they may surrender the target rather than
allow themselves all to be killed. Rabbi Judah goes further—if all are in danger, then one
may be sacrificed. This seems to approximate a utilitarian calculus, but it could also be
understood as a form of self-defense. See comments of Saul Lieberman in *Tosefta Kifshuta*,
pp.420-421. I thank Noah Bickart for suggesting this source.

86   מהרש"א חידושי אגדות מסכת בבא מציעא דף סב עמוד ב. והי אחיך עמך חייך קודמין וכו'
דמלת עמך משמע שיהא הוא טפל לך ונראה לפי הדרש דרבי עקיבא דאם הוא היה הקיתון של מים של שניהם
דמודה רע"ק לבן פטורא דשניהם ימותו ואל יראה כו' ואפשר דהיינו טעמא כדאמרינן דמאי חזית דדמא
דידך סומק טפי מדמא דחברך וק"ל:

87   See Mishnah Bekhorot 2:6-8. In each of these three mishnayot, Rabbi Tarfon
rules that two equal claimants should divide property, whereas Rabbi Akiva insists that
the one in possession retains ownership:

רבי טרפון אומר יחלוקו רבי עקיבא אומר המוציא מחברו עליו הראיה.

88   תלמוד בבלי מסכת פסחים דף כה עמוד ב.

89   Ephraim Oshry, א :ה ממעמקים ת"שו, pp. 14-25 (esp. p.23). I thank Robert Scheinberg for bringing this source to my attention.

90   שולחן ערוך חושן משפט סימן שפח סעיף ב בדברי רמ"א. היה רואה נזק בא עליו, מותר להציל עצמו אף על פי שע"י זה בא הנזק לאחר.

91   I thank Yoni Brafman for this point.

92   I explain my approach to halakhic formalism and values-guided interpretation in a 2015 responsum, "Halakhic Perspectives on Genetic Engineering," pp. 29-38.

93   דברים פרק יב, כח. שְׁמֹר וְשָׁמַעְתָּ אֵת כָּל הַדְּבָרִים הָאֵלֶּה אֲשֶׁר אָנֹכִי מְצַוֶּךָּ לְמַעַן יִיטַב לְךָ וּלְבָנֶיךָ אַחֲרֶיךָ עַד עוֹלָם כִּי תַעֲשֶׂה הַטּוֹב וְהַיָּשָׁר בְּעֵינֵי ה' אֱלֹהֶיךָ:

94   רמב"ן ויקרא פרק כג. ...ונראה לי שהמדרש הזה לומר שנצטוינו מן התורה להיות לנו מנוחה בי"ט אפילו מדברים שאינן מלאכה, לא שיטרח כל היום למדוד התבואות ולשקול הפירות והמתנות ולמלא החביות יין, ולפנות הכלים וגם האבנים מבית לבית וממקום למקום, ואם היתה עיר מוקפת חומה ודלתות נעולות בלילה יהיו עומסים על החמורים ואף יין וענבים ותאנים וכל משא יביאו בי"ט ויהיה השוק מלא לכל מקח וממכר, ותהיה החנות פתוחה והחנוני מקיף והשלחנים על שלחנם והזהובים לפניהם, ויהיו הפועלים משכימין למלאכתן ומשכירין עצמם כחול לדברים אלו וכיוצא בהן, והותרו הימים הטובים האלו ואפילו השבת עצמה שבכל זה אין בהם משום מלאכה, לכך אמרה תורה "שבתון" שיהיה יום שביתה ומנוחה לא יום טורח. וזהו פירוש טוב ויפה:

95   See https://www.etzion.org.il/he/download/file/fid/11095, p.200. I thank Nadav Berman Shifman for directing my attention to this discussion. In a 2006 responsum with Elliot Dorff and Avram Reisner, we cited Rabbi Lichtenstein's discussion of human dignity as another example of the importance of values within halakhic discourse. See "Homosexuality, Human Dignity, and Halakhah," p.14 and n.90.

96   Hans Jonas, *The Imperative of Responsibility: In Search of an Ethics for the Technological Age* (University of Chicago, 1985). The original German edition was published in 1979.

97   תלמוד בבלי מסכת עירובין דף ק עמוד ב. אמר רבי יוחנן: אילמלא לא ניתנה תורה היינו למידין צניעות מחתול, וגזל מנמלה, ועריות מיונה. דרך ארץ מתרנגול - שמפייס ואחר כך בועל.

98   For example, Mishnah Sanhedrin 1:4 states that capital crimes are heard by a court of 23 judges and adds that this is true if the defendant is a person or a domesticated animal. The Mishnah says, "just as the owners are killed, so is the ox" כמיתת בעלים כך (מיתת השור). Rabbi Eliezer says that dangerous animals such as a wolf, bear, lion, tiger, leopard and snake should be killed on the spot, but Rabbi Akiva defends the equivalence of procedure between humans and animals (except for snakes), with each tried by a court of 23, and this becomes codified law. The rabbinic bestiary also includes animals that share certain human features such as sirens and the אדני השדה, as discussed in my paper, "Halakhic Perspectives on Genetically Modified Organisms," (CJLS, approved Nov. 10, 2015) n.40. See also Beth A. Berkowitz, *Animals and Animality in the Babylonian Talmud* (Cambridge University Press, 2018), especially chapter 3, "Animal Morality," and chapter 5, "Animal Danger."

99   ויקרא פרק יח, כה. וַתִּטְמָא הָאָרֶץ וָאֶפְקֹד עֲוֹנָהּ עָלֶיהָ וַתָּקִא הָאָרֶץ אֶת יֹשְׁבֶיהָ:

100   This is the core argument of David Mevorach Seidenberg's book, *Kabbalah and Ecology: God's Image in the More-than-Human World* (Cambridge University Press, 2015).

101   Gershom Scholem, "The Idea of the Golem," *On the Kabbalah and its Symbolism*, trans. R. Manheim (Schocken, 1965); Byron Sherwin, *The Golem Legend: Origins and Implications* (University Press of America, 1985); Moshe Idel, *Golem: Jewish Magical and Mystical Traditions on the Artificial Anthropoid* (State University of New York Press, 1990). At the end of his volume, Idel observes a distinction between Sephardic and Ashkenazic

mystical tendencies highlighted by the golem. Sephardic mystics (with some exceptions) ignored the topic. They tended to focus on philosophical contemplation of the *sefirot* (divine spheres), whereas Ashkenazi mystics were more interested in the use of letter combinations and divine names for magical purposes, with the golem serving as a proof of principle. Both forms of mysticism were pious exercises designed to demonstrate reverence for the divine creation. Idel discusses the early modern emergence of the golem, following the Renaissance reclamation of magical traditions as models of scientific exploration in Christian and Jewish circles. Of course, the golem has been used for many other agendas, Jewish and general, including this inquiry into AI and halakhah.

102   בראשית פרק ב, ד. אֵלֶּה תוֹלְדוֹת הַשָּׁמַיִם וְהָאָרֶץ בְּהִבָּרְאָם בְּיוֹם עֲשׂוֹת ה' אֱלֹהִים אֶרֶץ וְשָׁמָיִם:
בראשית רבה (תיאודור-אלבק) פרשת בראשית פרשה יב. אמר ר' יהושע בן קרחה בהבראם באברהם, בזכות אברהם (שהיה עתיד להעמיד).

103   The Hebrew text is copied from the Bar Ilan (26+) collection, taken from Judah Eizenstein in Otzar Midrashim. The English is Idel's translation in Golem, based on the text of Ithamar Gruenwald, "A Preliminary Critical Edition of Sefer Yezira," in *Israel Oriental Studies*, v.1 (1971), 174, par.61, which omits the words in brackets. I have translated these words from Eizenstein and interpolated them into Idel's translation [within brackets]. See citation below of B. Sanhedrin 99b, where Reish Lakish claims that whoever teaches Torah to another's child is כאילו עשאו "as if he made him," using the same prooftext about the souls "made" by Abraham in Ḥaran.

104   פירוש רש"י לבראשית פרק ב, ז. לנפש חיה - אף בהמה וחיה נקראו נפש חיה, אך זו של אדם חיה שבכולן, שנתוסף בו דעה ודבור:

105   See Idel, chapter 5, "Ashkenazi Ḥasidic Views on the Golem," Golem, 54-80. He notes that mystical commentators like Eleazar of Worms read the piyut's line הדעה והדבור לחי עולמים as proof of the limits of human creative power. Idel clarifies that the mystical meaning is unlikely to have been intended by the poet, though we note that this poem is first found in the mystical midrash היכלות רבתי, and the next text from the Bavli would likely have been well known to the author of this poem.

106   בבלי סנהדרין דף סה עמוד ב.

107   It seems to me that the Aramaic word חבריא alludes to Deut. 18:11, וְחֹבֵר חָבֶר, which JPS translates as "casts spells." Jeffrey Tigay, in *Jewish Publication Society Torah Commentary, Deuteronomy* (1996) p. 173, and n.31, p.375. suggests that the etymology may come from "murmuring" a spell, or perhaps from "joining" the spell to its target.

108   There are no explicit attestations of the creation of a golem by the Maharal of Prague, a contemporary of Eliyahu of Ḥelm, until the 1847 folkloric work of Leopold Weisel, *Der Golem*. See "How the Golem Came to Prague," by Edan Dekel and David Gantt Gurley, *Jewish Quarterly Review* 103:2 (Spring 2013), pp. 241-258. The 1909 book of fabrications, *Niflaot Maharal*, by Polish rabbi Judel Rosenberg, added a connection to blood libels.

109   Tzvi Hirsh ben Jacob Ashkenazi, the Ḥakham Tzvi, was born in Moravia in 1660, and died in Lemberg, Poland, in 1718. He was sent to study in Sephardic lands, hence the title, Ḥakham. Historians have puzzled over Ashkenazi's use of the signature ס"ט, generally understood as ספרדי טהור, which he obviously was not. Perhaps it means סיפיה טב or refers to a family miracle narrative. See ר' שלום משאאש, ספר שמ"ש ומגן ח"ד (ירושלים, תשס"ז).

110   שו"ת חכם צבי סימן צג. נסתפקתי אדם הנוצר ע"י ספר יצירה כאותה שאמרו בסנהדרין רבא ברא גברא וכן בן העידו על זקני הגאון מוהר"ר אליהו אבד"ק חעלם מי מצטרף לעשרה לדברים הצריכין עשרה כגון קדיש וקדושה מי אמרינן כיון דכתיב ונתקדשתי בתוך בני ישראל לא מיצטרף או דילמא כיון דקיי"ל בסנהדרין המגדל יתום בתוך ביתו מעה"כ כאילו ילדו מדכתיב חמשת בני מיכל כי וכי מיכל ילדה והלא מירב ילדה אלא מירב ילדה ומיכל גדלה כו' ה"נ כיון שמעשה ידיה של צדיק הוא הו"ל בכלל בנ"י שמע"י של צדיק הן הן תולדותם וני"ל דכיון דאשכחן לר' זירא דאמר מן חברי"י את תוב לעפרך הרי שהרגו ואי ס"ד שיש בו תועלת לצרפו לעשרה לעשרה לכל דבר

שבקדושה לא היה ר' זירא מעבירו מן העולם דאף שאין בו איסור שפיכת דמים דהכי דייק קרא (אף שיש בו
דרשות אחרות) שופך דם האדם באדם דמו ישפך דוקא אדם הנוצר תוך אדם דהיינו עובר הנוצר במעי אמו
הוא דחייב עליה משום שפכ"ד יצא ההוא גברא דברא רבא שלא נעשה במעי אשה מ"מ כיון שיש בו תועלת
לא היה לו להעבירו מן העולם א"ו שאינו מצטרף לעשרה לכל דבר שבקדושה כך נ"ל וכו'. צבי אשכנזי ס"ט:

111   תלמוד בבלי מסכת סנהדרין דף יט עמוד ב. ללמדך שכל המגדל יתום בתוך ביתו - מעלה עליו
הכתוב כאילו ילדו. ובמקביל ע' בבלי מגילה יג ע"א וכתובות נ ע"א. וע"ע סנהדרין דף צט עמוד ב. אמר ריש
לקיש: כל המלמד את בן חבירו תורה מעלה עליו הכתוב כאילו עשאו, שנאמר ואת הנפש אשר עשו בחרן.

112   בראשית פרק ט, ו. שֹׁפֵךְ דַּם הָאָדָם בָּאָדָם דָּמוֹ יִשָּׁפֵךְ כִּי בְּצֶלֶם אֱלֹהִים עָשָׂה אֶת־הָאָדָם:

113   This curious feature of the verse is also the basis for Rabbi Ishmael's claim at
b. Sanhedrin 57b that Noahides (i.e., non-Jews) have a special prohibition on performing
abortions. Yet a third application is proposed by Nadav Berman Shifman to ban
autonomous weapons systems, since it is only "by man" that human blood may be shed
(unpublished draft, 2018, p. 9).

114   Jacob ben Tzvi Emden was born in 1697 and died in 1776, in Germany.

115   שו"ת שאילת יעבץ חלק ב סימן פב. בהא דמספקא ליה למר אבא בספרו (סימן צ"ג) בונצר ע"י
ספר יצירה אם מצטרף לעשר'. קשיא לי מאי קמבעיא ליה אטו מי עדיף מחרש שוטה וקטן דאינן מצטרפין.
אף על גב דמבני ישראל הן ודאי וחשובין כשאר אדם מישראל לכל דבר חוץ מן המצות וההורגן חייב ואית
להו דעתא קלישתא מיהא וכ"ש הקטן דאתי דאחי לכלל דעת ואפ"ה לא מצטרף. האי גברא דלאו בר דעה הוא כלל
צריכא למימר מיהת בכלל חרש הוא דהא אשתני רבי זירא בהדיא ולא אהדר ליה הא ודאי גרע מניה אלא
שיש לדקדק. לכאורו' נרא' שהי' שומע דהא שומע דהא דהא אשתני לקמיה דר"ז אי הכי הוי ליה חרש השומע ואינו מדבר
דינו כפקח לכל דבר. אבל אין זה נרא' אמת כי אם הי' בו כח השמיע' הי' ראוי גם לכח הדבור בודאי ולא
הי' מהנמנע אצלו אלא מבין ברמיזות וקריצות הי' כמו שמלמדים את הכלב לילך בשליחות להוליך ולהביא
מאומ' מאדם אחר כן שלוחו לזה והלך. וכתוב בספר חס"ל שאין חיותו אלא כחיות הבהמ'. ולכן אין בהריגתו
שום עברה א"כ פשיטא דאינו אלא כבהמ' בצורת אדם ובעיגלא תילתא דמיברי להו לר"ח ולר"א. ואגב אזכיר
כאן מה ששמעתי מפה קדוש אמ"ה ז"ל מה שקרה באותו שנוצר ע"י זקנו הגראב"ש ז"ל כי אחר שראהו
הולך וגדל מאד נתיירא שלא יחריב העולם על כן לקח ונתק ממנו השם שהי' דבוק עדיין במצחו וע"י זה
נתבטל ושב לעפרו. אבל הזיקו הזיק ועשה בו שריט' בפניו בעוד שנתעסק בעתיקת השם ממנו בחוזק.

116   Idel links this idea to the early rabbinic concept that the divine creation
continued to grow in proportion until God curbed it, as found in B. Ḥagigah 12a. The
divine name שדי is said there by Reish Lakish to mean, אני הוא שאמרתי לעולם די, "I am the
One who said to the world, enough!" Likewise, with AI, the ultimate challenge may be not
in its creation, but in its restraint.

117   See Louis Jacobs, *Theology in the Responsa* (Littman, 1975, 2005), pp. 334-335.

118   Jacob Katz, *Halakhah and Kabbalah* [Hebrew] (Magnes Press, 1984); Moshe
Ḥallamish, *Kabbalah in Liturgy, Halakhah and Customs* [Hebrew] (Bar Ilan Press, 2000),
chapters 5-8, esp. 7, "Yosef Karo—Kabbalah in his halakhic decisions." As Ḥallamish writes,
תורה וקבלה סמוכות היו אצלם על שולחן אחד, "Torah and Kabbalah were placed together for
them on one table" (p.162). In 2003, Robbie Harris argued in a CJLS responsum about the
recitation of "Amen" to the leader's blessing גאל ישראל that one should not pay regard
to kabbalistic arguments in the determination of halakhah, even when made by a great
authority such as Yosef Karo. Although I voted for the paper (and follow its second
suggestion, the practice of Magen Avraham, of saying the blessing together with the
leader), I do not share his antipathy to considering mystical sources in the determination
of liturgical practice (which is itself a mystical activity).

119   Byron L. Sherwin, "Golems in the Biotech Century," *Zygon* 42:1 (March 2007).
He relates that Gershom Scholem attended the dedication of Israel's first computer
at the Weizmann Institute in 1965. Scholem dubbed it, "Golem I." David B. Ruderman
discusses the importance of the topic of creating life among Jewish and Christian
Renaissance thinkers in chapter 8 of *Jewish Thought and Scientific Discovery in Early Modern*

Europe (Yale University Press, 1995), pp. 138-9. A bit earlier (p. 132) he writes, "A general consensus among historians of science has emerged about the cultural complexity of the age in which modern science was born, about the coexistence of mystical and rational elements among scientific thinkers, and the need to view scientific thought in its broader intellectual, religious, and social context." The same can be said of halakhah: Context and complexity matter.

120   Yuval Noah Harari, "Why Technology Favors Tyranny," *The Atlantic* (October 2018). See Gary Kasparov's discussion of AlphaZero's style of chess play in comparison to his own, "Chess, a drosophila of reasoning," in *Science* (Dec. 7, 2018), Vol. 362, Issue 6419, p. 1087.

121   See "Integrated information theory: from consciousness to its physical substrate," by Giulio Tononi, Melanie Boly, Marcello Massimini, and Christof Koch. *Nature Reviews Neuroscience*, vol. 17, pp. 450–461 (2016).

122   Michael Graziano, *Consciousness and the Social Brain* (Oxford University Press, 2015), p. 25.

123   https://www.nytimes.com:2023:02:16:technology/bing-chatbot-microsoft-chatgpt.html.

124   See for example, "The Moral Status of Animals," in the *Stanford Encyclopedia of Philosophy.*

125   Beth Berkowitz, *Animals and Animality*, pp. 157-160.

126   Abraham Joshua Heschel, *The Insecurity of Freedom: Essays on Human Existence* (Jewish Publication Society, 1966), p. 26.

127   Please see further discussion of this topic in my responsum, "The Use of Electrical and Electronic Devices on Shabbat" (CJLS, approved May 31, 2012) p. 3ff and notes. See also David Hoffman's responsum, "Building at What Cost?" (CJLS, approved October 17, 2018).

128   ע' אנציקלופדיה תלמודית כרך ב, אמירה לנכרי שבת.

129   This explanation is offered by Rashi at B. Shabbat 153a, s.v. מאי טעמא. The context is that of a Jewish traveler who fails to reach their destination before Shabbat. They may hand their purse to a gentile to hold for Shabbat, since gentiles are not commanded to observe Shabbat. Rashi explains the objection— והרי הוא שלוחו לישאנו בשבת "this would turn the gentile into the Jew's agent to carry it on Shabbat." The Gemara provides a descending series of preferred actions designed to minimize transgression without tempting the Jew to ignore the laws and carry their own purse. In general, it is better to tie the purse onto a donkey than to hand it to a person. As the Gemara explains, "What is the reason? These are people; this [donkey] is not a person!" מאי טעמא - הני אדם, האי - לאו אדם. This suggests that asking even exempt classes of people to perform work on Shabbat is more problematic than causing an animal to do the task. How much more so for a machine! For much more on this topic, see Jacob Katz's classic study, *The Shabbes Goy: A Study in Halakhic Flexibility* (Jewish Publication Society, 1989).

130   See Rabbi Lichtenstein above. This line of thought seems to originate with M. Shabbat 22:3. See Bavli there at 146a, and comments of Rashba: וי"ל כיון דבעלמא במקלקל פטור אבל אסור הכא משום צורך שבת מותר לכתחילה.

131   Michael Saxon and Christopher Korpela, "Killing with Autonomous Weapons Systems," *War Room*, Jan. 17, 2018.

132   בבלי ברכות דף סב עמוד ב. אמר רבי אלעזר, אמר לו דוד לשאול: מן התורה - בן הריגה אתה, שהרי רודף אתה, והתורה אמרה: בא להרגך השכם להרגו. וע"ע שם דף נח ע"א, וביומא דף פה ע"ב

ובמקבילות במדרש.

133   רמב״ם רוצח ושמירת הנפש פרק א. כל היכול להציל באבר מאיבריו ולא טרח בכך אלא הציל בנפשו של רודף והרגו הרי זה שופך דמים וחייב מיתה אבל אין בית דין ממיתין אותו. וע׳ בית יוסף חושן משפט סימן שפח. ובודאי מי שאינו מוחזק בכך אין ממיתין אותו אחר מעשה אבל מי שהוחזק בכך ממיתין אותו בין בשעת מעשה בין לאחר מעשה וכל הקודם זכה וכו׳.

NOTES TO CHAPTER 2

JEWISH PARAMETERS FOR GENETIC ENGINEERING

1   I have adapted this translation from the *Jewish Publication Society Tanakh* (1985), shifting from the singular "man" to the plural and gender-neutral "humans," etc. since that is clearly the verse's intention. In general, I employ gender-neutral language in my own writing, but maintain the gendered language found in direct quotations.

2   Adam Miklosi, *Dog Behavior, Evolution and Cognition* (Oxford University Press, 2007). Cited in Emily Anthes, *Frankenstein's Cat: Cuddling Up to Biotech's Brave New Beasts* (Scientific American/Farrar, Straus and Giroux, 2013) 184. Raymond Coppinger has also proposed that "flight distance," the tolerance animals have for interaction with humans, would have played a role, with advantage conferred upon those wolves that exhibited greater tolerance for human contact.

3   Anthes, 176, citing Chris T. Darimont, et al, "Human Predators Outpace Other Agents of Trait Change in the Wild," *PNAS* 106, no. 3 (2009), and Stephen Palumbi, "Humans as the World's Greatest Evolutionary Force," *Science* 293 (Sept. 7, 2001): pp. 1786-90. Most unfortunately, we are also causing the evolution of bacteria that are adapted to resist antibiotics, especially by using antibiotics to accelerate muscle growth in animals raised for their meat. See Pamela Barmash's responsum, "Veal Calves," (approved by CJLS on Dec. 12, 2007, by a vote of 9-5-7), esp. note 68.

4   Daniel Zohary and Maria Hopf, *Domestication of Plants in the Old World*, third edition (Oxford University Press, 2000).

5   Charles Darwin, *The Origin of Species* (Signet Classics, 2003), p. 76. On the failure of Darwin to discover the genetic mechanism of inheritance, see Brian Charlesworth and Deborah Charlesworth, "Darwin and Genetics," in *Genetics* (Nov. 2009, vol. 183, no. 3, pp. 757-766).

6   While this episode is generally read as a miracle narrative, some modern commentators have sought an epigenetic explanation in which the amino acids in the fungi of the exposed bark could theoretically have caused the development of brown coats in the sheep. See "Jacob and the Spotted Sheep: The Role of Prenatal Nutrition on Epigenetics of Fur Color," by Joshua Backon, a cardiologist and faculty member at the Hebrew University Medical School, in The *Jewish Bible Quarterly*, Vol. 36, no. 4, 2008, pp. 263-5. http://jbq.jewishbible.org/assets/uploads/364:364_sheep.pdf, as well as Nahum M. Sarna's comments in *Jewish Publication Society Torah Commentary: Genesis* (1989), p. 212. The late Midrash cited in our frontispiece claims that Jacob was engaged in something akin to genetic engineering, intentionally modifying the qualities of his herd.

7   Isaiah 11:6-9 and 65:25 (cf. Hosea 2:20). Rabbi David Kimhi (France, 1160-1235) comments on Isa. 11:7 that in the messianic era, carnivorous species will "return" to the vegetarian ways that had purportedly been their original practice on the ark, before they devolved into wild creatures.

8   Darwin's theory of evolution was dependent, as he explicitly acknowledged (p. 499), on the prior work of geologists such as Charles Lyell, in establishing the great antiquity of earth. Without this insight, there would not have been sufficient time for the small mutations described by Darwin to yield the enormous diversity of plant and animal life on earth. However, contemporary biologists have observed a much more rapid pace of evolution, as discussed below.

9   For an Orthodox approach, see Natan Slifkin, *The Challenge of Creation: Judaism's*

Encounter with Science, Cosmology and Evolution (Yashar Books, 2006). Arthur Green discusses the "sacred dimensions" of evolution in the first chapter of *Radical Judaism: Rethinking God and Creation* (Yale University Press, 2010). The most recent entry is by Alan L. Mittleman, *Human Nature & Jewish Thought: Judaism's Case for Why Persons Matter* (Library of Jewish Ideas, Princeton University Press, 2015).

10   Peter R. Grant and B. Rosemary Grant, *Forty Years of Evolution: Darwin's Finches on Daphne Major Island* (Princeton University Press, 2014), p. 245.

11   I thank Pamela Barmash for directing my attention to the remarkable work of Nobel-prize winning researcher Norman Borlaug and for sharing her general expertise in biblical, rabbinic, and horticultural matters. Borlaug is known as "the man who saved a billion lives."

12   Antithrombin is an anticoagulant made by the human liver that prevents blood clots from forming; lysozyme is an enzyme found abundantly in human breast milk that destroys harmful bacteria such as E. coli, protecting the child from dysentery, and allowing the development of a stronger immune system. Both products might be "pharmed" to produce medication for humans who have a deficiency of the requisite enzyme. These experiments are discussed by Anthes in *Frankenstein's Cat*.

13   I thank Mark Berger for alerting me to this company and the implications of its products.

14   See Wikipedia entries on Genetic Engineering, Horizontal Gene Transfer, Agrobacterium, and Hybrids.

15   Genetically modified rice has, it is claimed, the potential to alleviate global hunger, malnutrition, and poverty. See Dermont, M. and Stein, A.J., "Global Value of GM Rice: A Review of Expected Agronomic and Consumer Benefits," in *New Biotechnology* (2013). Still, there are unresolved controversies about the safety and the ethics of GM crops, since the GM products of agribusiness giants such as Monsanto are displacing the unmodified crops of subsistence farmers, requiring them to purchase new seed annually rather than simply reserving some of their traditionally grown crops for replanting. Organic farmers have likewise taken legal action out of concern that their crops would become contaminated by GM pollen, leading patent owners to sue farmers for unintentional copyright violation.

16   See the following USDA website for data on the adoption of genetically engineered crops by American farmers: http://www.ers.usda.gov/data-products/adoption-of-genetically-engineered-crops-in-the-us.aspx.

17   I realize, of course, that many causes of hunger are of a political, economic, and even cultural nature. If crops cultivated to feed animals for meat production were replaced with vegetables intended for human consumption, the farms of America alone could feed the world on a vegetarian diet. Still, we cannot assume that human appetites for meat, and for financial profit, will be eliminated. Perhaps the development of cultured (lab-grown) meat will address human appetites in a way that is more efficient, more ethical, and less polluting in the future.

18   Andrew Pollack, "U.S.D.A. Approves Modified Potato," *New York Times*, Nov. 7, 2014.

19   An article defending GMOs is found in Michael Specter, "Seeds of Doubt: An Activist's Controversial Crusade against Genetically Modified Crops," in *The New Yorker* (August 28, 2014). For a critical response, see "Rooted in Science," letter to the editor by Eric Chivian published in response to "Seeds of Doubt," *The New Yorker* (September 15, 2014), and Ramon J. Seidler's essay, "Pesticide Use on Genetically Engineered Plants," in *EWG AgMag* (September 2014).

20   See "Risks of Neonicotinoid Insecticides to Honeybees," by Anne Fairbrother, John Purdy, Troy Anderson, and Richard Fell in *Environmental Toxicology and Chemistry*, (Volume 33, Issue 4), April 2014, pp. 719–731. They conclude, "However, under field conditions and exposure levels, similar effects on honeybee colonies have not been documented. It is not reasonable, therefore, to conclude that crop-applied pesticides in general, or neonicotinoids in particular, are a major risk factor for honeybee colonies, given the current approved uses and beekeeping practices."

21   A FAQ document by the World Health Organization includes links to detailed documents such as *Principles for the risk analysis of foods derived from modern biotechnology.*

22   See "SemBioSys Bankruptcy," blog posted on May 24, 2012 by Paul Christensen.

23   See this page from Iowa Public Television for a graphic illustration of the process, and this YouTube instructional video.

24   FDA press release: https://www.fda.gov/news-events/press-announcements/ fda-approves-first-gene-therapies-treat-patients-sickle-cell-disease. European Medicines Agency announcement: https://www.ema.europa.eu/en/news/first-gene-editing-therapy-treat-beta-thalassemia-and-severe-sickle-cell-disease#/~/text=Casgevy%20 (exagamglogene%20autotemcel)%20is%20indicated,suitable%20donor%20is%20not%20 available.

25   See http://newlinkgenetics.com:. I thank Michael B. Weiss for informing me about this new technology and generally about the state of the field.

26   Article by Jiao JG, Li YN, Wang H, Liu Q, Cao JX, Bai RZ, Huang FY, in *Digestive and Liver Disease*, 2006 Aug; 38(8): pp. 578-87. Epub 2006 Jun 13, accessed via PubMed on July 16, 2014.

27   See *Hastings Center Report*, Volume 52: "Creating Chimeric Animals: Seeking Clarity on Ethics and Oversight" (Nov. 2022).

28   See "Protection without a Vaccine" by Carl Zimmer, published in *The New York Times*, March 9, 2015. Also, "Vector-Mediated Antibody Gene Transfer for Infectious Diseases" by Bruce C. Schnepp and Philip R. Johnson in *Gene Therapy for HIV and Chronic Infections*, Volume 848 of the series *Advances in Experimental Medicine and Biology*, published Feb. 12, 2015, pp. 149-167).

29   "Genetically Engineered Crops that Fly Under the US Regulatory Radar," by Alex Camecho, Allen Van Deynze, Cecilia Chi-Ham, and Alan B. Bennett in *Nature Biotechnology* (Nov. 2014) Vol. 32, No. 11, pp. 1087-1091. See also Andrew Pollack, "By 'Editing' Plant Genes, Companies Avoid Regulation" *New York Times*, January 1, 2015.

30   But see *Regenesis: How Synthetic Biology will Reinvent Nature and Ourselves*, by George Church and Ed Regis (Basic Books, 2014). Among their more radical notions is the development of a "posthuman" species, dubbed *Homo evolutis*: "It seems likely that legal, moral and ethical concerns will loom larger and sooner due more to selection than to speciation—and due more to mixing of species than to isolating one species from another," p. 248.

31   See "Expression of multiple horizontally acquired genes is a hallmark of both vertebrate and invertebrate genomes," by Alastair Crisp, Chiara Boschetti, Malcolm Perry, Alan Tunnacliffe, and Gos Micklem, published in *Genome Biology* 2015, 16:50, available at: http://genomebiology.com/2015/16/1/50, and also a popular review, "Genetically modified people," in *The Economist*, published Mar. 14, 2015, and available at http://www.economist.com/node/21646197/print. I thank Rabbi Philip Gibbs for directing me to this material.

32   See *Genes, Cells and Brains: The Promethean Promise of the New Biology* by Hilary Rose

and Steven Rose (Verso, 2014), esp. Ch.1, "From Little Genetics to Big Genomics."

33   See   http://www.ucsusa.org/food_and_agriculture/our-failing-food-system/ genetic-engineering:

34   http://www.genome.gov/els/:. In its 2011 strategic plan, published in *Nature* (Vol. 470, Feb.10, 2011), p. 210, box 5, NHGRI identified "broader social implications" as including "the implications of increasing genomic knowledge for conceptualizing health and disease; for understanding identity at the individual and group levels, including race and ethnicity; for gaining insights about human origins; and for considering genetic determinism, free will and individual responsibility."

35   Seymour Siegel, "Science and Ethics: A Creative Partnership," in *Conservative Judaism* 33:4 (1980) 56-60.

36   Kassel Abelson, "The Kashrut of Microbial Enzymes," approved by the CJLS on Dec. 14, 1994. Below we will also mention the work of Isaac Klein on the kashrut of rennet and of gelatin that are derived from animal sources, and then chemically transformed.

37   Avram Israel Reisner, "Curiouser and Curiouser: The Kashrut of Genetically Engineered Foodstuffs," approved by the CJLS on Dec. 10, 1997 (16-0-0). See discussion in Section IV below.

38   See esp. MT Shabbat 21:9, Rozeaḥ 13:13; Tur OH 305, and HM 272; SA HM 272:9. The question of what amount of expected human benefit may justify what extent of animal suffering resists any formulaic response. Some animal rights advocates, following in the footsteps of Peter Singer's *Animal Liberation* (New York Review of Books, 1975), claim that no amount of human benefit may justify any imposition of animal suffering. At the other extreme are those who hold that any human benefit, even in the development of cosmetics, can justify any level of animal suffering, based on dominion theology. The halakhic principle of צער בעלי חיים indicates a middle ground; humans are entitled to use the labor and the bodies of animals but must avoid causing them needless suffering. Many rules of the Torah reinforce the importance of compassionate behavior towards animals. See the CJLS responsum of Elliot Dorff and Joel Roth, "Shackling and Hoisting," (approved by CJLS on Sept. 20, 2000, by a vote of 21-0-0); the previously cited responsum, "Veal Calves" by Pamela Barmash; Zvi Kaplan's article, "Animals, Cruelty to" in the *Encyclopedia Judaica*, 2nd edition (Macmillan, 2006), Vol. 2, pp. 165-166; and Joshua Cahan's, "Tza'ar Ba'alei Hayim in the Marketplace of Values," in *Conservative Judaism* 65:4 (Summer 2014), pp. 30-48.

39   See, for example, "Gene Flow from Genetically Modified Rice to its Wild Relatives: Assessing Potential Ecological Consequences," by Bao-Rong Lu and Chao Yang in *Biotechnology Advances* (Nov.-Dec 2009), Vol. 27(6), pp. 1083-1091. As the authors write, "Pollen-mediated gene flow is the major pathway for transgene escape from GM rice to its wild relatives." Other studies report that insect-mediated gene transfer may be an even larger vector for contamination of non-GM crops. These authors raise many questions, including, "fitness changes brought to wild relatives by the transgenes." It would seem that similar questions are relevant to the modification of animal DNA, as for example, in the case of the Aquabounty transgenic salmon. See http://aquabounty.com:.

40   See Komesaroff, P.A., Dwyer, D.E. "The Question of the Origins of COVID-19 and the Ends of Science." *Bioethical Inquiry* (2023). https://doi.org:10.1007:s11673-023-10303-1.

41   בבלי ברכות לב ע"ב.

42   See discussion of the "siren" below. Mishnah Kilayim 8:5 mentions אדני השדה, "men of the field," human-like primates (according to the comments of Ḥanokh Albeck there, אדם=אדן), that Rabbi Yosi considered to be human enough to convey ritual impurity. In his Mishnah commentary, Rambam derides this as a creation of fable-tellers. I thank

Joshua Heller for drawing this text to my attention. See discussion in Refael Rachel Neis, *When a Human Gives Birth to a Raven: Rabbis and the Reproduction of Species* (University of California Press, 2023).

43   Mark Popovsky, "Choosing our Children's Genes: The Use of Preimplantation Genetic Diagnosis," approved by CJLS in 2008 (10-2-4).

44   Rabbi David Golinkin, *Responsa in a Moment*, Even HaEzer 2:7, "Does Jewish law permit genetic engineering on human beings?" This collection was published on 13 Sivan 5760 (June 16, 2000). It is noteworthy that Golinkin treats ethical and theological concerns as separate from "Jewish law," which he feels may nevertheless respond with a ban based on these external concerns.

45   An outstanding essay on this subject was written by Ronald M. Green, "Curing Disease and Enhancing Traits: A Philosophical (and Jewish) Perspective," in *Jews and Genes: The Genetic Future in Contemporary Jewish Thought*, ed. Elliot N. Dorff and Laurie Zoloth (University of Nebraska Press: Jewish Publication Society, 2015), pp. 257-273. On his first page, he provides Charles M. Culver's precise definition of what is meant by "disease" (though they prefer the somewhat archaic term "malady"): "A person has a malady if and only if he has a condition, other than his rational beliefs and desires, such that he is suffering, or is at increased risk of suffering, a harm or an evil—namely death, pain (physical or psychological), disability, loss of freedom or loss of pleasure—and there is no sustaining cause that is distinct from the person." Green provides an extended analysis of this definition and its utility in determining whether a proposed gene therapy should be considered to be for purposes of medicine or enhancement.

46   שולחן ערוך יורה דעה הלכות צדקה סימן רנ. כמה נותנין לעני, די מחסורו אשר יחסר לו. כיצד, אם היה רעב, יאכילוהו.

47   טור יורה דעה הלכות ביקור חולים ורפואה ונוטה למות וגוסס סימן שלו. ע"כ בא ללמדנו שנתנה לו רשות לרפאות ומצוה היא ובכלל פיקוח נפש הוא והזריז ה"ז משובח ואם מונע עצמו ה"ז שופך דמים.

48   רמב"ם הלכות דעות פרק ג. המנהיג עצמו על פי הרפואה, אם שם על לבו שיהיה כל גופו ואבריו שלמים בלבד ושיהיו לו בנים עושין מלאכתו ועמלין לצורכו אין זו דרך טובה, אלא ישים על לבו שיהא גופו שלם וחזק כדי שתהיה נפשו ישרה לדעת את ה', שאי אפשר שיבין וישתכל בחכמות והוא רעב וחולה או אחד מאיבריו כואב.

49   Israel Knohl argues in *The Sanctuary of Silence* (Fortress, 1995; Eisenbrauns, 2007), that the Holiness Source (HS or H) differs from the Priestly Source (PS or P) in extending the mandate to practice holiness beyond the realm of the priesthood and the sanctuary to extend to all of Israel. See esp. Chapter 4.

50   While verse 19 appears to be a complete non sequitur from verse 18, attention to the juxtaposition may clarify the meaning of כמוך, as yourself. Leviticus may be teaching that humans have a special responsibility towards members of their own species, and a related responsibility to preserve the distinction between other species of animals and plants.

51   Translations of this and the following text from Deut. 22 are from Jacob Milgrom, *The Anchor Bible, Leviticus 17-22: A New Translation with Introduction and Commentary* (Yale University Press, 2000), p. 1657. Remaining translations are mine unless otherwise indicated.

52   רמב"ן ויקרא פרק יט (יט) ...ואסור לחרוש בשור ובחמור, מפני שדרך כל עובד אדמתו להביא צמדו ברפת אחת ויבאו לידי הרכבה:

53   Milgrom, Leviticus 17-22, p.1658.

54   Midrash Sifra prohibits the crossbreeding not only of "pure" species but also of

"impure" species such as the horse and the donkey. This, Milgrom notes, contrasts with the Qumran sect which, in a reconstructed text of MMT (מקצת מעשי תורה) B 75-82, limits the prohibition to "pure" species.

55   Michael Fishbane, *Biblical Interpretation in Ancient Israel* (Clarendon Press, 1985) 59, n. 38, cited in Milgrom, Leviticus 17-22, p. 1658f.

56   Nevertheless, rabbinic sources prohibit the hitching of different animal types to one yoke (See M. Kilayim 8:2-6).

57   Ken Druse, *Making More Plants: The Science, Art and Joy of Propagation* (New York: Clarkson Potter Publishers, 2000), p. 173.

58   See http://en.wikipedia.org/wiki/Propagation_of_grapevines.

59   תלמוד ירושלמי (ונציה) מסכת כלאים פרק א דף כז טור א :ה"א.

60   The line of tradition here is rather confusing, and I thank Richard Kalmin of JTS for clarifying it for me. The amoraim R' Yonah and R' Lazar are here citing a Babylonian amora named Kahana (who was not ordained), who in turn cites the tanna, R' Lazar. R' Yossi cites Rabbi Hila to say that this statement was shared by all the tannaim. Still, the two versions of the expression diverge after מעתה אסור, making it seem that the tannaitic statement was limited to the first three words. That might explain why the Bavli cites this tradition in the name of Shmuel—he was expanding upon the three-word tannaitic statement that was "said by everyone." The opening question is also somewhat ambiguous; its three clauses could be read sequentially, or the third phrase could modify the second. I accept Jeremy Kalmanofsky's preference for the latter reading.

61   רמב"ם הלכות כלאים פרק א, הלכה ד.

62   כסף משנה הלכות כלאים פרק א. לכן נ"ל דלאו דוקא נקט רבינו מאכל אדם אלא כל דבר שרוצה בקיומו אסור זה בזה ואפי' אם רוצה בקיומו למאכל בהמה ולא נתכוון רבינו לשלול אלא העשבים המרים בלבד וכדדייק סיפא דלישניה ודין זה נ"ל שלמד רבינו ממה שאמרו בירושלמי בריש כלאים גבי זוני:

63   שולחן ערוך יורה דעה הלכות כלאי זרעים וכלאי בהמה סימן רצז. אין אסור משום כלאי זרעים אלא הזרעים הראויין למאכל אדם, אבל עשבים המרים וכיוצא בהם, מן העיקרים שאינם ראויים אלא לרפואה וכיוצא בהן, אין בהן משום כלאי זרעים.

64   בית יוסף יורה דעה סימן רצה אות ז ד"ה ואסור לקיים. ומותר ליקח ענף מן המורכב ולנטוע במקום אחר. כן כתב הרמב"ם והרא"ש (שם) והוא ירושלמי בפרק קמא דכלאים (ה"ד) תני גוי שהרכיב אגוז על גבי פרסק אף על פי שאין ישראל רשאי לעשות כן מותר ישראל ליטול ממנו יחור והולך ונוטע במקום אחר:

65   בית יוסף יורה דעה סימן רצה. וכתב הרא"ש (כלאים סי"ס א) נמצא דין כלאים עכשיו בחוצה לארץ נחלק לג' חלקים הרכבת אילן מדאורייתא כלאי הכרם מדרבנן כלאי זרעים מותר:

66   ראו אנציקלופדיה תלמודית, כרך ב, אסורי הנאה [עמוד צב טור 2].

67   רמב"ם הלכות כלאים פרק ג. יש מיני כלאים בזרעין שיהיה המין האחד נפרד לצורות הרבה מפני שינוי מקומות והעבודה שעובדין הארץ עד שיראה כשני מינין ואף על פי שאין דומין זה לזה הואיל והן מין אחד אינן כלאים זה בזה.

68   In the production of kosher wine in Israel, the ban on grafting is understood to apply only to the grafting of a grapevine onto the rootstock of a different species of tree, not to the grafting of one grape variety upon another.

69   See Rambam (MT Kilayim 1:1 and 1:5), and R' Karo (SA YD 295:1 and 296:1) with Levush and Biur HaGr"a.

70   R' Karo is impelled to start a second series of paragraphs within YD 297 to accommodate the great quantity of regulations for *kilayim*. This one appears at 297:9'.

71   As we have seen, Shmuel's saying is repeated in B. Sanhedrin 60b, but the

expression חוקים שחקקתי is stated in the name of a different chain of sages in Yerushalmi Kilayim; in his Torah commentary to Leviticus 19:19, Ramban ascribes the saying to R. Pinḥas in the name of R. Ḥanina, who do appear on the same page of the Yerushalmi, but regarding a different subject; perhaps Ramban was working from memory and misattributed the expression, or perhaps he had a different text of the Yerushalmi.

72 Shmuel's universal application of *kilayim* abroad is not accepted as the halakhah.

73 בראשית רבה (תיאודור-אלבק) פרשת בראשית פרשה י ד"ה וכל צבאם אמר.

74 ויקרא רבה (מרגליות) פרשת בחוקותי פרשה לה [ד]. ד"א אם בחוקותי תלכו, חוקים שחקקתי בהם את השמים ואת הארץ, אם לא בריתי יומם ולילה חוקות שמים וארץ לא שמתי (ירמיה לג, כה). חוקים שחקקתי בהן את השמש ואת הירח, שנ' כה אמר י"י נותן שמש לאור יומם חקות ירח וכוכבים לאור לילה (שם :ירמיהו: לא, לד). חוקים שחקקתי בהן את הים, בשומי לים חקו (משלי ח, כט). חוקים שחקקתי בהן את החול, אשר שמתי חול גבול לים חק עולם לא יעברנהו (ירמיה ה, כב). חוקים שחקקתי בהן את התהום, בחוקו חוג על פני תהום (משלי ח, כז), חוק וחוג לגזירה שוה.

75 Translation by Daniel Matt, *The Zohar: Pritzker Edition*, Volume 8 (Stanford University Press, 2014), pp. 39-40. See notes 115, 116, and 117.

76 והמרכיב שני מינין, משנה ומכחיש במעשית בראשית, כאילו יחשוב שלא השלים הקדוש ברוך הוא בעולמו כל הצורך, ויחפוץ הוא לעזור בבריאתו של עולם להוסיף בו בריות.

77 Ramban discusses his concern with species preservation elsewhere. See his comments to Genesis 1:11, and to Deut. 22:6, regarding the commandment to send away the mother bird which, like the ban on sacrificing two generations of an animal family in one day, he understands to be motivated in part by species preservation (in addition to avoiding cruelty):

רמב"ן דברים פרק כב פסוק ו (ו) כי יקרא קן צפור לפניך - גם זו מצוה מבוארת מן אותו ואת בנו לא תשחטו ביום אחד (ויקרא כב כח). כי הטעם בשניהם לבלתי היות לנו לב אכזרי ולא נרחם, או שלא יתיר הכתוב לעשות השחתה לעקור המין אף על פי שהתיר השחיטה במין ההוא, והנה ההורג האם והבנים ביום אחד או לוקח אותם בהיות להם דרור לעוף כאלו יכרית המין ההוא:

78 Midrash Bereshit Rabba, Parashat Bereshit, 11:6 and 12:1 in the Vilna edition. The first text also appears in a variant form in Theodore-Albeck, 11:2. I credit and thank Avram Reisner for noticing this dichotomy and its significance for our subject. See also the parallel text in Sifre Devarim, Ha'azinu, Piska 307.

79 These words, cited from the Vilna ed. of 12:1, are absent in Theodore-Albeck, who surmises (Vol. 1, p. 99, note 3) that they were an addition to the printed edition, influenced by Kohelet Rabba 2:1(11):

א"ר יצחק בר מריון כתיב (בראשית א) ויצר ה' אלהים את האדם מה ת"ל אשר יצר אלא הצור הוא צייר נאה כביכול מתגאה בעולמו ואומר ראו בריה שבראתי וצורה שצייירתי.

80 ספר באר הגולה באר השני פרק י.

81 תלמוד בבלי מסכת פסחים דף נד עמוד א. דתניא, רבי יוסי אומר: שני דברים עלו במחשבה ליבראות בערב שבת ולא נבראו עד מוצאי שבת, ובמוצאי שבת נתן הקדוש ברוך הוא דיעה באדם הראשון מעין דוגמא של מעלה, והביא שני אבנים וטחנן זו בזו ויצא מהן אור. והביא שתי בהמות והרכיב זו בזו ויצא מהן פרד.

82 Byron L. Sherwin, "Golems in the Biotech Century," in *Zygon: Journal of Religion and Science*, Vol. 42:1 (Mar. 2007), pp.133-144; J. David Bleich, "Genetic Engineering" in *Tradition: A Journal of Orthodox Jewish Thought*, Vol. 37:2 (Summer 2003), pp.66-87. See esp. p.70. Bleich cites Maharal at Be'er Ha'Golah 2:3, but the relevant text is found at 2:10 in the Bar Ilan collection (Version 21). We return to Bleich's understanding below. Avram Reisner (1997, n.24) cites this text by way of Michael Broyde, writing in *The Journal of Halacha and Contemporary Society* #34, p. 64.

83   See *The Origin of Species*, p. 499.

84   The establishment of species extinction as a fact of natural history is credited to the French naturalist Georges Cuvier (1769-1832). For an overview of historical and contemporary extinction events, see Elizabeth Kolbert, *The Sixth Extinction: An Unnatural History* (Henry Holt and Co., 2014).

85   Again, see Peter R. Grant and B. Rosemary Grant, *Forty Years of Evolution: Darwin's Finches on Daphne Major Island* (Princeton University Press, 2014), esp. chapters 8-10. This subject is discussed by Moises Velasquez-Manoff in "Should You Fear the Pizzly Bear?" *The New York Times Magazine* (August 14, 2014). He attributes the characterization of species orthodoxy as informed by racial sentiment to Michael Arnold, who in turn faulted Darwin himself for denigrating "mixed-race" humans. See Jon Cohen, *Almost Chimpanzee: Redrawing the Lines That Separate Us from Them* (Macmillan, 2010), p. 37.

86   "Reticulate Evolution and Marine Organisms: The Final Frontier?" by Michael L. Arnold and Nicole D. Fogarty. Int J Mol Sci. 2009 Sep; 10(9): pp. 3836–3860. Published online, Sep 3, 2009. doi: 10.3390:ijms10093836.

87   For an introduction, see this Wikipedia article: http://en.wikipedia.org/wiki/DNAmethylation, and also, "Unique epigenomic code identified during human brain development," published on July 3, 2013, at *Science Daily*: http://www.sciencedaily.com/releases/2013/07:130705102037.htm.

88   For example, see Frances A. Champagne, "Interplay Between Social Experiences and the Genome: Epigenetic Consequences for Behavior," in *Advances in Genetics* 77 (2012), and also, "Transgenerational Inheritance in Mammals," by Isabelle M. Mansuy, Rahia Mashoodh, and Frances A. Champagne, chapter 13 in *Epigenetic Regulation in the Nervous System* (Elsevier Inc, 2013). I thank Robert Pollack of Columbia University for sharing these articles with me.

89   For the unsettled definition of "species" among biologists, see, "Quantifying the use of species concepts" by Sean Stankowski and Mark Ravinet in *Current Biology* (May 10, 2021), https://doi.org/10.1016/j.cub.2021.03.060. For discussion of the philosophical problem defining species, see "Species," in the *Stanford Encyclopedia of Philosophy*. I thank Alan Mittleman of the Jewish Theological Seminary for sharing this latter source and discussing it with me.

90   Maimonides, *The Guide for the Perplexed*, trans. Shlomo Pines (University of Chicago Press, 1963), Section III, chapter 18. I thank Jeremy Kalmanofsky for pointing me to this text and explaining its significance within Rambam's theory of individual providence.

91   See discussion in Benjamin Sommer, *The Bodies of God and the World of Ancient Israel* (Cambridge University Press, 2009), pp. 87-88, 156-158.

92   Many ancient cultures discussed fantastical hybrid creatures such as the Assyrian lamasu—giant statues of a beast with a bull or lion's body, eagle's wings, and a human head—that guarded the entrances to cities and palaces. Homer's sirens featured a woman's upper body and voice, but had the feet of birds, and posed mortal danger to men (*The Odyssey*, 12:52). The scene of Odysseus lashed to his ship's mast in order to safely encounter the sirens is surprisingly depicted in the famous mosaic floor of the ancient Beit Shean synagogue, as Columbia historian Seth Schwartz reminds me. Rabbinic literature refers to mermaids in several locations, such as Sifra to Shmini, Par. 3 (according to Ravad's commentary), and especially in Rashi's explanation of the "dolphinum" on B. Bekhorot 8a, which he identifies with the siren (despite it being half fish rather than half bird):

רש"י מסכת בכורות דף ח עמוד א ה"ג הדולפנין פרים ורבים מבני אדם שאם בא אדם עליהם מתעברות

הימנו. בני ימא דגים יש בים שחציין צורת אדם וחציין צורת דג ובלע"ז שריינ"א.

93 Note, however, Ezekiel 44:17, which commands that when the priests enter the inner court, they shall be clothed in linen garments, with no wool upon them. Rada"k notices the contradiction with Leviticus, and concludes that this must be an "innovation for the future" (ḥidush l'atid). Metzudat David seeks to harmonize the texts, claiming that Ezekiel is describing a non-officiating setting.

94 דברים פרק כב, יא-יב (יא) לֹא תִלְבַּשׁ שַׁעַטְנֵז צֶמֶר וּפִשְׁתִּים יַחְדָּו: ס (יב) גְּדִלִים תַּעֲשֶׂה-לָּךְ עַל-אַרְבַּע כַּנְפוֹת כְּסוּתְךָ אֲשֶׁר תְּכַסֶּה-בָּהּ: ראו רש"י שם על סמך בבלי יבמות דף ד עמוד א.

95 See Israel Knohl's discussion of the tztitzit as symbolic of the expansion of holiness regulations to all of Israel in the Holiness Source (HS) in The Sanctuary of Silence, p. 186. It may be that wool was the only fabric that could be permanently dyed in ancient Israel, whereas linen was the whitest available fabric. Indeed, B. Yevamot 4b indicates that tekhelet is always to be made of wool: תכלת עמרא הוא.

96 http://learn.jtsa.edu/content/commentary/noah/5774/why-did-god-flood-world

97 ראו תלמוד בבלי מסכת סנהדרין דף קח עמוד א. כי השחית כל בשר את דרכו על הארץ, אמר רבי יוחנן: מלמד שהרביעו בהמה על חיה, וחיה על בהמה, והכל על אדם, ואדם על הכל. בראשית רבה (תיאודור-אלבק) פרשת בראשית פרשה כח ד"ה [מאדם עד בהמה. ר' עזריה בשם ר' יהודה הכל קילקלו מעשיהם בדור המבול, הכלב עם הזאב תרנגול עם הטווס ה"ה כי השחית כל בשר וגו' (בראשית י יב). ובמיוחד מדרש תנחומא (בובר) פרשת נח סימן יא. כשם שפרעו מן האדם שחטאו, כך פרע מן הבהמה והחיה והעוף, ומנין שנפרעו מהם, שנאמר ויאמר ה' אמחה וגו' (שם :בראשית: ו ז), וכל כך למה, ללמדך שאף הם ערבו משפחותיהם, והיו הולכין על מין שאינן שלהן, כל מין ומין על מין שאינו שלו, וקרא הקדש ברוך הוא לנח ויאמר לו בחר לך בהמה וחיה ועוף [מאותן] שלא ערבבו את משפחותיהן, שנאמר מכל הבהמה הטהורה (שם :בראשית: ז ב), טהורה כשם שנבראת, וכיון שיצאו מן התבה העיד עליהן הקדש ברוך הוא שלא ערבבו משפחותם, שנא' למשפחותיהם יצאו (שם :בראשית: ח יט).

98 For a survey of contemporary theories of halakhah, see Elliot Dorff's, The Unfolding Tradition: Jewish Law After Sinai (Aviv Press, 2005). On pp. 212-221, Dorff introduces Joel Roth's halakhic approach, which he deems deductive and positivist, with attendant strengths and weaknesses, and then provides a self-critical discussion of his own philosophical approach to halakhah, pp. 327-337. These examples accord with what we are calling formalism vs. values-informed analysis. In legal theory, see Aharon Barak, Purposive Interpretation in Law, trans. Sari Bashi (Princeton University Press, 2005), which presents a universal theory for the role of self-conscious interpretation in secular law, and then Frederick Schauer, "Formalism," in Yale Law Journal 97:4 (March 1988) pp. 509-548. I thank Yoni Braffman for these sources.

99 Tamar Ross, Expanding the Palace of Torah: Orthodoxy and Feminism (Brandeis University Press, 2004) p. 64-66.

100 Ḥaym Soloveitchik argues in an influential article, "Rupture and Reconstruction: The Transformation of Contemporary Orthodoxy," Tradition 28:4 (1994), that since about 1950, non-Ḥasidic Orthodoxy has shifted from a mimetic to a textual model of religious transmission, in the process losing the sense of divine intimacy ("the touch of His presence") and replacing it with strict obedience ("the pressure of His yoke"). This shift may be related to the primarily formalist halakhic responses to technology among Orthodox authorities observed in this section and their reluctance to engage in theological and moral reasoning in response to genetic engineering.

101 An example of the former result is the responsum that I co-authored with Elliot Dorff and Avram Reisner on homosexuality; the latter result includes my responsum on electricity and Shabbat.

102 Avraham Steinberg, Encyclopedia of Jewish Medical Ethics (Feldheim, 2003), Volume II, "Human Cloning," p. 513.

103 Steinberg, p. 514. Emphasis in original. He is discussing cloning here, not transgenics.

104 J. David Bleich, "Survey of Recent Halakhic Periodical Literature: Genetic Engineering," *Tradition: A Journal of Orthodox Jewish Thought*, 37:2 (Summer 2003) pp. 66-84. See discussion above in Section II. Avram Reisner cites this source at pp. 107-108 and comes to similar conclusions.

105 See, for example, Isaac Klein's chapter 6 on the kashrut of cheeses, and chapter 7 on the kashrut of gelatin, in his volume, *Responsa and Halakhic Studies* (Ktav Publishing House, 1975), pp. 43-83. Klein cites, among other sources, the Rema's comments at SA YD 87:10, עור הקיבה, לפעמים מולחים אותו ומייבשין אותו, ונעשה כעץ, וממלאים אותו חלב, מותר; דמאחר (ב״י בשם שבולי לקט) שנתייבש הוי כעץ בעלמא, ואין בו לחלוחית בשר, and the responsum of R' Ḥayim Ozer Grozinsky, 3:33 שו״ת אחיעזר, and 4:11.

106 ערוך השולחן יורה דעה סימן פד סעיף ל.

I thank Jeremy Kalmanofsky for directing my attention to this source, which is also discussed by Avram Reisner on p. 103.

107 שו״ת מנחת שלמה תנינא (ב - ג) סימן ק, אות ד.

108 I thank Avram Reisner for directing me to this source. Auerbach continues in the next paragraph to make the case that the offspring of an impure species remains impure, even if it is raised somehow by a pure species.

109 Influential practitioners of values-informed halakhic interpretation include Eliezer Berkowitz, Daniel Sperber, Elliot Dorff and Gordon Tucker. See, for example, Elliot Dorff's essay, "The Philosophical Foundations of My Approach to Bioethics," an appendix to his book, *Matters of Life and Death: A Jewish Approach to Modern Medical Ethics* (Philadelphia: Jewish Publication Society, 1998), pp. 395-417, cited above in The Unfolding Tradition.

110 Yet, in his Talmud commentary to Bavli Kiddushin 39a, Rashi's explanation of the law is not so distant from Ramban's formulation:

רש״י מסכת קידושין דף לט עמוד א . חקתי תשמרו - מדלא כתיב ושמרתם את חקתי משמע את חקתי אשר מעולם תשמרו מלמד שהזהיר את נח ובניו עליהן ואלו הן החקים בהמתך לא תרביע שדך לא תזרע ואיזו זריעת כלאים שאני אומר שחקקתים לך כבר דומיא דבהמה דבר המסויים והיינו הרכבה ומהכא נפקא לן בסנהדרין (דף ס) דבני נח הוזהרו עליהן והכא אתה מוסיף ללמוד מהיקש זה דומיא דבהמה אפי׳ בח״ל דהא חובת הגוף היא אף שדך בח״ל.

111 Avram Reisner, however, cites (p. 107) Radbaz's commentary to MT Kilayim 1:6 as proof that not all *poskim* have maintained the traditional ban on hiring a non-Jew to crossbreed species.

112 תלמוד בבלי מסכת סנהדרין דף נו עמוד ב. רבי אלעזר אומר: אף על הכלאים. מותרין בני נח ללבוש כלאים, ולזרוע כלאים, ואין אסורין אלא בהרבעת בהמה ובהרכבת האילן. רמב״ם הלכות מלכים פרק י הלכה ו. מפי הקבלה שבני נח אסורין בהרבעת בהמה ובהרכבת אילן בלבד, ואין נהרגין עליהן.

113 בית הבחירה למאירי מסכת סנהדרין דף נו עמוד ב. בני נח אסורים בהרבעת בהמה בשאינה מינה וכן בהרכבת אילן בשאינו מינו אלא שאין אלו משבע מצוות ואינו נהרג עליהן ושאר מיני הכלאים מותרין בהן:

114 As the Bavli considers, this logic might indicate that gentiles are therefore liable for all laws that God has decreed. The distinction is made based on word order in the verse, את חקתי תשמרו; *kilayim* are part of the statutes established from the beginning of creation and are thus applicable to all people.

115 שו״ת יביע אומר חלק ה - אורח חיים סימן יט. גבי ז׳ מצות שנצטוו עליהם בני נח, ר׳ אליעזר אומר אף על הכלאים, ומותרים בני נח ללבוש כלאים ולזרוע כלאים, ואינם אסורים אלא בהרבעת בהמה ובהרכבת

האילן, וס״ל לרבינו דאע״ג שאין הלכה כר״א משום דא״כ הו״ל ח׳ מצות לב״נ שנהרג עליהם, ואנן קי״ל שרק על ד׳ מצות ב״נ נהרג, מ״מ כיון דשמואל מפרש לה בגמ׳ (סנהדרין ס), משום דאמר קרא את חקותי תשמורו, חוקים שחקקתי לך כבר (לבני נח), בהמתך לא תרביע כלאים שדך לא תזרע כלאים, מה בהמתך בהרבעה אף שדך בהרכבה. אלמא דס״ל לשמואל שב״נ אסורים בכלאים אף על פי שאין נהרגים עליהם.

116   שו״ת מהרי״ל החדשות סימן קכב. ולהושיב עוף על ביצים שאין מינו כגון תרנגולת ואווזות אמ׳ שהוא אסור משום צער ב״חא.

117   See this policy page from the National Institutes of Health OLAWS (Office of Laboratory Animal Welfare) website: http://grants.nih.gov/grants/policy/air/NIH_ensure_welfare.htm

118   See Burcin Ekser and David KC Cooper, "Overcoming the barriers to xenotransplantation: prospects for the future," in *Expert Review of Clinical Immunology* 2010 March; 6(2): pp. 219–230. They write, "The most significant advances to date have been the production of pigs expressing a human complement-regulatory protein (e.g., human decay accelerating factor [CD55], membrane cofactor protein [CD46] or CD59 [44-48]) and pigs in which the gene for α1,3-galactosyltransferase has been knocked out (α1,3-galactosyltransferase gene-knockout [GTKO] pigs) [49-52]." I thank patent judge Jeff Fredman for bringing this source to my attention.

119   The genetic difference between humans is estimated to be on average .1%, whereas the genetic difference between humans and chimpanzees and bonobos is about 1.2%. Counted a different way, with missing sequences included, the human-chimp gap is considerably larger, more like 4-5%.

See also, this June 28, 2012 letter in *Nature*: "The Bonobo Genome Compared with the Chimpanzee and the Human Genomes."

120   In September 2015, the National Institutes of Health proclaimed a moratorium on "Research Involving Introduction of Human Pluripotent Cells into Non-Human Vertebrate Animal Pre-Gastrulation Embryos." See http://grants.nih.gov/grants/guide/notice-files/NOT-OD-15-158.html. On Nov. 6, 2015, it conducted a workshop on this subject, which is of intense interest to biomedical researchers eager to grow human-compatible tissue, and has raised deep concerns among bioethicists. In this paper, we endorse such concerns, which do meet the standard of *kilayim* as we understand it.

121   See Daniel J. Keeves, *In the Name of Eugenics* (Harvard University Press, 1995), and Michael Sandel's chapter 4, "The Old Eugenics and the New," in *The Case Against Perfection* (Harvard University Press, 2007).

122   For a disturbing history of eugenics in New Jersey, see the work of my father, Michael A. Nevins, M.D., *A Tale of Two Villages: Vineland and Skillman, NJ* (iUniverse, 2005). Some of these institutions remained active until the 1970s.

123   Mark Popovsky's 2008 CJLS responsum, "Choosing our Children's Genes: The Use of Preimplantation Genetic Diagnosis," argued against using PGD for the purpose of selecting embryos based not only on aesthetic traits but also on genetic health (with a narrow exception for severe disability) on grounds similar to those of Sandel (see below). However, Avram Reisner and Marilyn Wind filed a persuasive dissent defending the consideration of avoiding disease (but not selecting for the sex or other traits) in choosing which embryo to implant. Popovsky's concerns over the arrogance of PGD strike me as weaker than the arguments for health (even though I did vote for his responsum).

124   George Church and Ed Regis describe a speculative approach to modifying the human genome to impart multi-virus resistance or even complete immunity in chapter 5 of their book, *Regenesis*, "-60 MYR, Paleocene: Emergence of Mammalian Immune System. Solving the Health Care Crisis Through Genome Engineering." Recent reports of IGT, immunoprophylaxis by gene transfer, cited above, indicate clinical progress in this

field. See also, "Synthetic biology devices and circuits for RNA-based 'smart vaccines': a propositional review," by Oliwia Andries, Tasuku Kitada, Katie Bodner, Niek N Sanders, and Ron Weiss in *Informa*, February 2015, Vol. 14, No. 2 , pp. 313-331.

125   I thank Isaac Zentner, a PhD candidate in genetics at Drexel University, for providing these examples. Biogen Idec is developing a drug to reverse MS damage known as anti-LINGO. See "Drug-based modulation of endogenous stem cells promotes functional remyelination in vivo," letter published in *Nature* Vol 522, p. 216, June 11, 2015. Doi:10.1038:nature14335.

126   See subheading "Human Genetic Engineering" in the Wikipedia article, "Gene Therapy." (8.31.15)

127   See "CRISPR/Cas9-mediated gene editing in human tripronuclear zygotes" by Puping Liang, et al., in *Protein and Cell*, April 18, 2015. Reported by Gina Kolata, "Chinese Scientists Edit Genes of Human Embryos, Raising Concerns," in *The New York Times*, April 24, 2015. The acronym CRISPR stands for "clustered regularly interspaced short palindromic repeat."

128   See article by David Baltimore, et al., "A prudent path forward for genomic engineering and germline gene modification," in *Science* (3 April 2015: Vol. 348 no. 6230), pp. 36-38.

129   דברי הימים ב פרק טו, יב. (יב) וַיַּחֲלָא אָסָא בִּשְׁנַת שְׁלוֹשִׁים וָתֵשַׁע לְמַלְכוּתוֹ בְּרַגְלָיו עַד-לְמַעְלָה חָלְיוֹ וְגַם-בְּחָלְיוֹ לֹא- דָרַשׁ אֶת-יְקֹוָק כִּי בָּרֹפְאִים:

130   אבל ראו שו"ת הרשב"א חלק א סימן תיח ד"ה וחכמת הרפואה. וגם כי יש בה בהתרפאות מחכמי בני האדם קצת מבוא להסרת הבטחון מהאלהים כמו שנתפש מלך ישראל בזה הענין (ד"ה ב' ט"ז) וגם בחליו לא דרש את ה' כי אם ברופאים. ולזאת הסבה שובה חזקיה מאנשי דורו כשגנז ספר רפואות לחולשת אמונות אותו הדור. עם רוב הספר ההוא באותה חכמה ואמתתו וקלות השגת התועלת ממנו עד שהיה מביא לה הסרת בטחונם. ואם תהיה התשובה כי באלו תכונות תתחזק אמונת האל בלבבות ולא נחוש להסרת הבטחון עם הצורך הגדול להתרפאות הגופות אשר הוא הכרחי לנו. הנה לא נמלט בשום פנים מהמשיך התשובה הזאת בעצמה בכל הענינים שנרצה. והוא שכבר נתפרסמו אמונת התורה האמתיות בחדוש העולם והשגחה והגמול והתחזקו בהם הלבבר'. ואין ראוי שנחוש' על שום אדם שיפקפק עליהם בעבור החכמות עם הצודק גם כן להשיג מתועלת החכמה התרפאות נפשותינו. כי איך תהיה רפואת הגופות עלינו יותר חביבה מרפואת הנפשות?

131   Deuteronomy 8:17, JPS trans. of וְאָמַרְתָּ בִּלְבָבֶךָ כֹּחִי וְעֹצֶם יָדִי עָשָׂה לִי אֶת-הַחַיִל הַזֶּה.

132   Jeffrey H. Burack, "Jewish Reflections on Genetic Enhancement," in *Jews and Genes: The Genetic Future in Contemporary Jewish Thought*, ed. Elliot N. Dorff and Laurie Zoloth (University of Nebraska Press: Jewish Publication Society, 2015), pp. 310-341.

133   Burack discusses this on p. 334: "With present technology there is no absolute guarantee that a somatic gene therapy intervention will not inadvertently result in germ line changes." Jeff Fredman called my attention to an article by Masanori Takehashi that provides evidence for Burack's concern by demonstrating that adenovirus, a standard gene therapy viral vector, "may inadvertently integrate into a patient's germ line." Masanori Takehashi, et al. "Adenovirus-mediated gene delivery into mouse spermatogonial stem cells," in *Proceedings of the National Academy of Sciences* (104:8, Nov. 2007). The abstract concludes, "These results suggest that adenovirus may inadvertently integrate into the patient's germ line and indicate that there is no barrier to adenovirus infection in spermatogonial stem cells."

134   Alan Mittleman, *Human Nature and Jewish Thought: Judaism's Case for Why Persons Matter* (Library of Jewish Ideas; Princeton University Press, 2015) p. 184.

135   Aaron Mackler, "Genetic Enhancement and the Image of God," in *Jews and Genes*, pp. 274-284.

NOTES TO CHAPTER 3

THE KASHRUT OF CULTURED MEAT

1   See "Building a $325,000 Burger," by Henry Fountain, published on May 12, 2013 in the *New York Times*. Dr. Mark J. Post graciously reviewed a draft of this responsum and offered helpful comments and corrections for which I am deeply grateful. I have also benefited from the advice of Dr. Robert Pollack of Columbia University.

2   For an introduction to the technology and history of developing cultured meat, see the Wikipedia article, "Cultured Meat," https://en.wikipedia.org/wiki/Cultured_meat. The *Journal of Integrative Agriculture* published a special issue (14:2) on cultured meat in 2015. New scholarly and news articles are being published each month. See too the commercial websites of the Good Food Institute, http://www.gfi.org/why, and New Harvest, http://www.new-harvest.org/faq. Jeff Bercovici gives a thorough profile of Memphis Meats in the webzine Inc.

3   See   http://www.theatlantic.com/health/archive/2016/09/is-lab-grown-meat-kosher/500300/ .

4   "The State of Global Policy on Alternative Proteins," Good Food Institute,

5   "U.S. Approves Sale of Lab-Grown Chicken" by Linday Qiu, *New York Times*, June 21, 2023. More precisely, the USDA issued "grants of inspection" to two companies, UPSIDE Foods and GOOD Meat, signaling its intention to eventually approve their products. See USDA website article, "Human Food Made with Cultured Animal Cells for early regulatory concerns identified prior to any products being introduced into the American market.

6   Text as approved by CJLS available at:

https://www.rabbinicalassembly.org/sites/default/files/public/halakhah/cjls/kashrut_of_cultured_meat_responsum_final_version_march_2018.pdf.

7   See the July 29, 2016 report of The Nature Conservancy, "U.S. Beef Supply Chain: Opportunities in Fresh Water, Wildlife Habitat, and Greenhouse Gas Reduction," p. 50.

8   In 2011, Hanna L. Tuomisto and M. Joost Teixeira de Mattos predicted that the environmental impact of cultured meat production would be far lower than any conventional forms of meat production: "Despite high uncertainty, it is concluded that the overall environmental impacts of cultured meat production are substantially lower than those of conventionally produced meat." See *Environmental Science & Technology*, 2011, 45 (14), pp. 6117–6123. A more cautious subsequent assessment from *Environmental Science & Technology*, 2015, 49 (19), pp. 11941–11949 is available here. See, too, Carolyn S. Mattick, et al, "A Case for Systemic Environmental Analysis of Cultured Meat," *Journal of Integrative Agriculture* 2015, 14(2): pp. 234–240. They argue that a systematic energy-use comparison should take account of the non-meat uses made of animal carcasses—feathers, skins, etc., that would need to be replaced by other synthetic products. Nevertheless, Memphis Meats claims in its Feb. 1, 2016 press release, "While generating one calorie from beef requires 23 calories in feed, Memphis Meats plans to produce a calorie of meat from just three calories in inputs. The company's products will be free of antibiotics, fecal matter, pathogens, and other contaminants found in conventional meat." It has been suggested that cultured meat might become a critical component of feeding the rapidly growing human population, but it is too early to verify such a claim.

9   For halakhic sources and discussion of these concepts, please see the prior chapter, "Halakhic Perspectives on Genetically Modified Organisms."

10   The Israeli Zomet Institute's journal *Teḥumin* published a series of halakhic studies, critiques, and rejoinders in volumes 34-36. To start, see Zvi Ryzman: צבי רייזמן, בשר מתאי גזע, תחומין לד (תשע"ה), ע' 99-112. For subsequent *Teḥumin* articles and a study by J. David Bleich in *Tradition*, see below.

11   For an overview of epigenetics, see the Wikipedia article, and citations in notes 85-86 of my GMO responsum. Siddhartha Mukherjee offers an excellent presentation on the significance of epigenetics in *The Gene: An Intimate History* (New York: Scribner, 2016), pp. 392-410. I discuss the implications of gene editing systems such as CRISPR/Cas9 briefly below. See Jennifer A. Doudna and Samuel H. Sternberg, *A Crack in Creation: Gene Editing and the Unthinkable Power to Control Evolution* (Houghton Mifflin Harcourt, 2017).

12   Dr. Post explained (personal communication, Sept. 9, 2016) that patients who undergo an autologous transplant—that is, they have bone marrow or even an organ removed and then returned to their body—may experience organ rejection of their own cells. When cells are removed from a body, they change and are not necessarily recognized by the immune system when they "come home." He writes, "A possible explanation is that epigenetic changes occur that alter the phenotype of the cells. There may be other reasons that we do not know of right now."

13   Dr. Post described the process as follows (personal communication, Sept. 9, 2016): "The cells that we are using for cultured meat are designated stem cells, meaning that they are already somewhat differentiated towards muscle cells, yet they are still sufficiently undifferentiated to be able to proliferate. Once they stop proliferating (because we starve them), they will differentiate into mature muscle fibers. The first step in that process is that they merge to become multinucleated myotubes. The myotubes, when given sufficient biochemical and mechanical cues, will then mature into muscle fibers usually after performing some form of labor. It is our intention to make muscle fibers that are biochemically and microscopically indistinguishable from real muscle, so that they likely also have the same taste and mouthfeel. Still, if you would implant this muscle fiber back in the same cow that donated the stem cells, it would probably be recognized as being 'foreign.'"

For now, the focus is on creating thin strips of muscle tissue, which are then layered to form a product resembling ground beef. It would also be possible to culture a multilayered product comparable to a steak, but that would require a synthetic circulatory system to deliver nutrients and oxygen and to remove waste. There is also preliminary discussion of using 3-D printing to create complex tissue.

14   David Lau, "Halakhic Inquiry: Cultured Meat as Manufactured in Your Company," letter to Didya Tuvia, CEO of Alef Farma, Rehovot, Jan. 17, 2023 [11 pages, Hebrew].

15   A parallel midrash in Pesikta Zutrata to Shmini (31a), emphasizes that this applies to all impure species of bird:

ואת בת היענה. בת זו ביצת היענה. יצאת זו ללמד על כל הביצים של עופות הטמאים "And the daughter of the ostrich–This "daughter" is the ostrich's egg. This variant comes to teach that the eggs of all impure birds [are not kosher]."

16   The rabbis at b. Bekhorot 6b derive from the Torah's repetition of the ban on eating camels that not only their flesh but also their milk is forbidden. See also SA YD 81:5. Only infants are permitted directly to nurse human breast milk, but if a woman expresses milk into a cup it may be drunk by an adult. It is not considered to be truly "dairy," but still may not be eaten with meat because of misleading appearances (מראית עין). Bee honey is permitted because it is considered by halakhic sources to be a secretion

not of the animal, but rather of the flowers, and because bee parts like legs that break into the honey are deemed detrimental to taste, and also because the permission to eat bee honey is deemed a biblically mandated exception. See Tosafot to Avodah Zarah 69a, s.v. ההוא.

17   רמב"ם הלכות מאכלות אסורות פרק ג, הלכה א.

18   The culinary use of urine, though not from donkeys, is still practiced in China. See Dan Levin's article, "Recipe for a Ritual Chinese Dish: Eggs, Time and Plenty of Urine," *New York Times*, July 22, 2016.

19   רמב"ם הלכות מאכלות אסורות פרק ד הלכה כ. עור הבא כנגד פניו של חמור מותר באכילה מפני שהוא כמו הפרש ומי רגלים שהן מותרין, יש עורות שהן כבשר והאוכל מהן כזית כאוכל מן הבשר, והוא כשיאכל אותן כשהן רכים. +:השגת הראב"ד: עור הבא כנגד פניו. כתב הראב"ד ז"ל :א"א: רב ששת פשט להו לאיסורא במסכת בכורות ממתני', עכ"ל. ובשולחן ערוך יורה דעה הלכות בהמה וחיה טהורה סימן פא סעיף א. חלב בהמה וחיה טמאה או טריפה, וציצרה ומי רגליה אסורים כבשרה. ויש מי שמתיר במי רגליה (רמב"ם פ"ד ד"כ). אבל מי רגלים דאדם, לדברי הכל, מותרים.

20   J. David Bleich, "Stem Cell Burgers," in *Tradition* 46:4 (2013) 56-58. Rabbi Chaim Soloveitchik of Brisk, Ḥiddushei ha-Grah al ha-Rambam, Hilkhot Ma'akhalot Assurot 3:11. This theory is also discussed by R' Yehudah Bezalel Spitz at the beginning of his *Teḥumin* (v. 35, p. 193) rebuttal to Rabbi Ryzman in *Teḥumin* v.34. See also Rabbi Spitz's English article, "The Halachic Status of Genetically Engineered Meat," in *Tradition* #72 (2016), pp.56-80 (on this point, p.66f).

21   רמב"ם הלכות מאכלות אסורות פרק ג הלכה ו. אף על פי שחלב בהמה טמאה וביצי עוף טמא אסורין מן התורה אין לוקין עליהם שנאמר מבשרם לא תאכלו על הבשר הוא לוקה ואינו לוקה על הביצה ועל החלב, והרי האוכל אותן כאוכל חצי שיעור שהוא אסור מן התורה ואינו לוקה אבל מכין אותו מכת מרדות.

22   תלמוד בבלי מסכת פסחים דף פד עמוד א. איתמר, גידין שסופן להקשות. רבי יוחנן אמר: נמנין עליהן בפסח, ריש לקיש אמר: אין נמנין עליהן בפסחא. רבי יוחנן אמר: נמנין עליהן, בתר השתא אזלינן. ריש לקיש אמר: אין נמנין עליהן, בתר בסוף אזלינן.

23   תלמוד בבלי מסכת חולין דף קב עמוד ב. אמר ר' יוחנן: לא תאכל הנפש עם הבשר – זה אבר מן החי, ובשר בשדה טרפה לא תאכלו – זה בשר מן החי ובשר מן הטרפה, ור"ש בן לקיש אמר: לא תאכל הנפש עם הבשר – זה אבר מן החי ובשר מן החי, ובשר בשדה טרפה לא תאכלו – זה בשר מן הטרפה. אבל אבר מן החי ובשר מן החי, לר' יוחנן – חייב שתים, לר"ש בן לקיש – אינו חייב אלא אחת; אבל בשר מן החי ובשר מן הטרפה, לר"ש בן לקיש – חייב שתים, לר' יוחנן – אינו חייב אלא אחת; אבל אבר מן החי ובשר מן הטרפה – לדברי הכל חייב שתים.

24   שולחן ערוך יורה דעה הלכות שחיטה סימן יג. בהמה, חיה ועוף טעונין שחיטה; דגים וחגבים אין טעונין שחיטה. הגה: ומותר לאוכלם מתים או לחתוך מהם אבר ולאכלו, אבל אסור לאכלן חיים משום: בל תשקצו.

25   Nevertheless, on this basis, Rabbi Yaakov Ariel recommends that cultured meat be taken only from fish, thereby removing from consideration both the limb ban and the ban on mixing meat and dairy products. See *Teḥumin* v. 36, p.454.

26   תלמוד בבלי מסכת נזיר דף נג עמוד ב. דתניא: וכל אשר יגע על פני השדה בחלל חרב או במת – על פני השדה – זה המאהיל על פני המת, בחלל – זה אבר מן החי ויש לו להעלות ארוכה...

27   Translation taken from *Sifre: A Tannaitic Commentary on the Book of Deuteronomy*, translated from the Hebrew by Reuven Hammer (Yale University Press, 1983), pp.130-131. In note 5, Rabbi Hammer refers to b. San. 56a and t. AZ 8:4ff for sources on the "woman of goodly form" being sexually permitted only to the initial Israelite conquerors of Canaan, not to Jewish soldiers generally. This biblical "leniency" of allowing the rape of captives was in any event restricted by the rabbis to that generation, and forbidden to gentiles and all later Jewish soldiers.

28   Christine Hayes discusses the Bavli's use of the Noahide laws to intensify the differentiation between Jews and non-Jews towards the end of her book, *What's Divine About Divine Law?* (Princeton University Press, 2015), pp. 361-365. See, too, her discussion of the Sifre Devarim source and other parallels.

29   See m. Eduyot 6:3. T. Eduyot 2:10, b. Ḥullin 102a, et al.

30   It has been suggested that this might be an instance of the principle קים ליה בדרבה מיניה, whereby a person who is found liable to receive a severe punishment is relieved of liability for a more lenient category. Still, it is not evident to me that the limb ban is less severe than the pork ban. Both are biblically forbidden to Jews, with full liability triggered by consumption of a *kezayit*. Another possibility, אין איסור חל על איסור, will be addressed below.

31   רמב״ם הלכות מלכים פרק ט. וכן חייב על אבר מן החי, ועל בשר מן החי בכל שהוא, שלא ניתנו השיעורין אלא לישראל בלבד, ומותר הוא בדם מן החי.

32   This principle appears in many places in the Bavli. For example, Pesaḥim 35b, Yevamot 13b and 32a, Ḥullin 100-101, and 113-114. In Rambam MT, see Hilkhot Ma'akhalot Asurot, 14:18, and Hilkhot Issurei Biah, 17:8.

33   תלמוד בבלי מסכת פסחים דף כב עמוד ב. והרי אבר מן החי, דכתיב לא תאכל הנפש עם הבשר, ותניא, רבי נתן אומר: מנין שלא יושיט אדם כוס יין לנזיר, ואבר מן החי לבני נח - תלמוד לומר ולפני עור לא תתן מכשול. הא לכלבים - שרי! - שאני אבר מן החי, דאיתקש לדם. דכתיב רק חזק לבלתי אכל הדם כי הדם הוא הנפש. רש״י שם. מה אבר מן החי אסור - באיסור האמור בו, אף דם מן החי - אסור באיסור האמור בו, כלומר: כרת משום דם גמור, מהו דתימא: רק חזק לבלתי אכול הדם - אוזהבת מבכרך ומצאנך דכתיב לעיל קאי, ודם זביחה הוא דאסור, אבל דם הקזה מותר.

34   אנציקלופדיה תלמודית כרך א, אבר מן החי [המתחיל בטור קב] אבמה״ח מותר בהנאה, ואפילו להסוברים שכל מקום שנאמר "לא תאכל" איסור הנאה בכלל, מכל מקום אבמה״ח למדים בהיקש מדם: רק חזק לבלתי אכל הדם וגו' ולא תאכל הנפש עם הבשר, מה דם מותר בהנאה, אף אבמה״ח כן. ולהסוברים שאבמה״ח למדנו מובשר בשדה טרפה, למדין היתר הנאתו מהכתוב בו: לכלב תשליכון אתו.

35   רש״י מסכת חולין דף קב עמוד א. במשהו בשר וגידין ועצמות - משלימין לכזית דמשום טומאה לא מחייב דאין בגידין ועצמות טעם ומשום אבר מחייב דלהכי פלגינהו קרא לאבר מן החי ובשר מן החי דמיחייב אאבר אף על גב דאין שיעור בשר ואבשר אף על פי שאינו אבר.

36   In his Drishah commentary [#3], Rabbi Yehoshua Volk questions why the Tur seems to dismiss the Talmud's measure of a *kezayit* found at the bottom of Ḥullin 102a (see Rashi there, and Rambam, MT Hilkhot Ma'akhalot Asurot, 5:3). Drishah's explanation is reasonable: any amount is forbidden, but liability for corporal punishment is limited to transgressors who eat a *kezayit*.

37   See sources in *Encyclopedia Talmudit*, v. 23, column 306, esp. b. Bekhorot 7b, and Tosfot, Ḥullin 64a-b, s.v. שאם ריקמה ואכלה and discussion below regarding Rabbi Sha'ar Yashuv Cohen on *d'var ḥadash*.

38   תלמוד בבלי מסכת יבמות דף סט עמוד ב. והתניא: בת כהן שנישאת לישראל ומת - טובלת ואוכלת בתרומה לערב! אמר רב חסדא: טובלת ואוכלת עד ארבעים, דאי לא מיעברא - הא לא מיעברא, ואי מיעברא - עד ארבעים מיא בעלמא היא.

39   שו״ת חוות-יאיר, ס' לא, ושו״ת ציץ אליעזר, חלק ד' ס' מח, א, ח.

See Rabbi Susan Grossman's 2001 responsum, "Partial Birth Abortion and the Question of When Life Begins", p. 16.

40   תחומין שם, ע' 103.

41   Dr. Post confirms this characterization: "They are adult stem cells and already have undergone differentiation towards mature cells, although they still maintain their

proliferative capacity. It is also true that we inevitably harvest more cells than just the stem cells. Collateral catch consists primarily of mature skeletal muscle cells and they will die rapidly and thus are NOT used for growth. Other cells in the collateral catch, such as fibroblasts will have a function in the culture and can grow and mature (forming sinewy stuff)." Personal communication, August 30, 2016.

42   Rabbi Yaakov Ariel (*Teḥumin* v. 36, pp. 452-3) says דינם כבשר רגיל, "their status is like ordinary meat," but Rabbi Ryzman reiterates his claim starting at p. 455. Even Rabbi Ze'ev Weitman, who is receptive to Rabbi Ryzman's conclusions, declines to defend this most bold of his arguments (v. 36, p. 458f).

43   ראו שו"ת משנה הלכות חלק טו סימן קז. וכל שאין הנאת גרון לא מקרי אבילה ללקות עליו.

44   http://www.dailymail.co.uk/sciencetech/article-2087837:Test-tube-meat-reality-year-scientists-work-make-profitable.html.

45   A novel approach for in vitro meat production, *Applied Microbiology and Biotechnology*, July 2015, Volume 99, Issue 13, pp. 5391-5395.

46   משנה מסכת מכשירין פרק ב. מצא בה בשר הולכין אחר רוב הטבחים אם היתה מבושל הולכים אחר רוב אוכלי בשר מבושל:

47   ערוך השולחן יורה דעה סימן פד סעיף לו.

The reference to angels is, in turn, derived from the Talmud, e.g. b. Brakhot 25b. See further discussion of this source in my responsum on genetic engineering, p. 32. Rabbi Auerbach makes a similar argument in permitting drinking from the Kineret on Pesaḥ, even if there is bound to be a microscopic amount of *ḥametz* present in the water.

48   The principle of nullification is meant for "after the fact" application, בדיעבד, not as an initial plan, לכתחילה. The *Teḥumin* authors give extensive attention to the implications for the nullification process of non-Jews performing this act, with the awareness that Jews may benefit from it (and even offer kosher certification). Rabbi Bleich closes with the paradox that cultured meat might be considered kosher only if it lacks kosher certification. Rabbi Ryzman argues that because there is only a doubt of forbidden meat (since he believes the stem cells are not meat), therefore nullification may be invoked even beforehand. His critics have their stringent responses. However, these arguments seem quite unnecessary, since my understanding is that the original cells, which were taken from a live specimen, will not survive into the final product, and the descendant cells created in a lab are not considered to be live limb meat. If such a cell were to survive, it would be unexpected, בדיעבד and therefore subject to nullification after the fact.

49   ראו שו"ת מנחת שלמה תנינא (ב - ג) סימן ק ד"ה בענין שאלתו: כיון שאנשים מטפלים בחלקיקים האלה ומעבירים אותם ממין אחד לשני הרי זה חשיב ממש כבראה לעינים ולא דמי כלל לתולעים שאינם נראים.

50   J. David Bleich, "Stem Cell Hamburgers" in *Tradition*, 46:4 (2013), pp. 48-62.

51   See, for example, the entry in the *Talmudic Encyclopedia*:

מושגים תלמודיים. אחשביה. דבר שאין לו חשיבות עצמית, ומקבל חשיבות על ידי מעשה האדם או מחשבתו. לדוגמא: המוציא בשבת מרשות לרשות, אינו חייב אלא אם כן הוציא כשיעור שקבעו חכמים לכל דבר ודבר לפי חשיבותו. ברם, אם הוציא, למשל, מין ממיני הזרעים שהצניעו קודם השבת לשם זריעה, או שהוציא דבר שהצניעו כדי להראותו כדוגמא, או לרפואה - חייב אפילו אם אין בו כשיעור שקבעו חכמים, מפני שהחשיבו. דוגמא נוספת: דם שנקפא מאליו - אין חייבים על אכילתו, משום שאכילה שלא כדרכה היא, שהרי דם אינו עומד לאכילה אלא לשתיה, אבל אם הוא הקפיא את הדם, החשיבו, וחייב על אכילתו.

We will return to אחשביה below regarding gelatin.

52 הרב יעקב אריאל, בשרותו של בשר מתורבת, תחומין לו (תשע"ו) ע' 447.

53 ראו דברי רמ"א בשו"ע יו"ד ס"ס פ"ז.

54 אנציקלופדיה תלמודית כרך ו, דבר המעמיד [המתחיל בטור תקס]. כחו של דבר המעמיד הוא שניכרת פעולתו בדבר שניתן לתוכו, וכאילו בכל חלק מן התערובת הוא ניכר, ולכן הוא חשוב כאילו ישנו בעין.

55   "Rudimentary egg and sperm cells made from stem cells: A feat achieved for the first time in humans could be a step towards a cure for infertility" by David Cyranoski, published in *Nature*, December 24, 2014. See: http://www.nature.com/news/rudimentary-egg-and-sperm-cells-made-from-stem-cells-1.16636.

56   The field of epigenetics studies the heritability of genomic change by means of DNA methylation and histone modifications. Yet the fundamental biological fact of variation down the generations remains intact. Siddhartha Mukherjee summarizes this reality in *The Gene*, p. 407: "Genomes and epigenomes exist to record and transmit likeness, legacy, memory, and history across cells and generations. Mutations, the reassortment of genes, and the erasure of memories counterbalance these forces, enabling unlikeness, variation, monstrosity, genius, and reinvention—and the refulgent possibility of new beginnings, generation upon generation."

57   See Jennifer Doudna and Samuel Sternberg, *A Crack in Creation*, pp. 130-34.

58   The CJLS passed and published a series of responsa on the definition of *davar ḥadash* in the 1980s. See Kassel Abelson, "The Kashrut of Mono- and Di-Glycerides" and again, with Mayer Rabinowitz, "Definition of a Davar Hadash," where the standard of forming new chemical compounds is the accepted threshold.

59   Personal communication, June 27, 2017. It will be interesting to see if researchers based in the United States, China, Israel, etc., will likewise refrain from editing the genes of cells to be used to manufacture cultured meat.

60   Christine Hayes provides a fascinating treatment of the relationship between realism and nominalism in rabbinic literature in chapter 5 of, *What's Divine about Divine Law*, "The 'Truth' About Torah." In the Bavli, the sages seem sensitive to criticisms and even mockery that their rulings are not "reality-based," but rather built on a foundation of fictitious assumptions. At times, they make accommodations to observed reality instead of asserting their authority to declare that "left is right." Still, legal systems do ultimately depend upon precedent, and so, we seek early sources in which to ground our approach to novel phenomena such as our subject.

61   On this important halakhic principle, see b. Pesaḥim 26-27, Sanhedrin 80b, et al, and in the codes, MT Avodah Zarah 7:14 and SA YD 142:11. For example, vegetables planted beneath an Asherah (idolized tree) benefit from the forbidden shade of the Asherah, but also depend on the permitted soil. Without the soil, there would be no vegetables, and so the vegetables are completely permitted, even though they have benefitted from illicit shade. Likewise with our case—even if the source cells could transmit their limb ban to descendant cells, the medium is what allows those cells to grow, and (assuming a kosher growth medium), the final product should be permitted.

62   Dr. Mark Post reports that fetal bovine serum is "usually 5-20% of the medium, the rest of the medium consisting of 300 defined components such as water, amino acids, sugar, minerals and vitamins." Personal communication, August 30, 2016.

63   Many kosher species such as larger fish may eat non-kosher species before themselves being captured and consumed. This does not affect the kosher status of the predator (though if one finds a forbidden animal within the stomach of a permitted animal, the forbidden item may not be eaten). See:

תלמוד ירושלמי (וילנא) מסכת תרומות פרק ח: בן ר' חייא בשם ר' יוחנן השוחט בהמה ומצא בה שקץ
אסור באכילה מה טעמא [דברים יד ו] בהמה בבהמה תאכלו ולא שקץ בבהמה תאכלו.

One might argue that here, too, the bovine fetal serum is like a food for the cultured meat, in that it is metabolized by the muscle tissues, and not retained as a distinct ingredient in the final product. However, the growth medium is *intentionally* added by the producer as part of the production process, and it seems, therefore, that it might be considered an ingredient. Moreover, as Rabbi Spitz argues in *Tehumin* v. 35, כבוש הרי זה כמבושל, soaking kosher food in a forbidden substance (or vice versa) is like cooking them together, leaving both items non-kosher; the non-kosher serum would thus taint even kosher cells. (See b. Pesaḥim 76a, b. Ḥullin 97b, 111b et al; according to Rishonim, the soaking must be for 24 hours for the taste transfer to occur, unless the liquid is salt, brine, or vinegar, in which case the transfer takes only six minutes) Given this concern, and that there are plant-based alternatives, and that animal sourced media may introduce health risks, it is clearly preferable to insist on vegetarian growth media.

64   It has also been noted that milk, leather, and other animal products may likewise become less available should fewer animals be raised for meat. See Mattick, et al (2015).

65   http://www.haaretz.com/science-and-health/premium-1.786281.

66   In his 1985 responsum, "The Use of all Wines," Rabbi Elliot Dorff cites an 18th century responsum of Rabbi Ezekiel b. Yehudah Landau (YD #26), who ruled that the bladder of a non-kosher fish could be used to clarify mead, and that this would not be considered בטל בששים לכתחילה, since the intention is not to enhance taste but to remove lees. This would be an additional precedent for allowing the use of non-kosher growth medium since the purpose is to allow the growth of the permitted product, and not for it to be consumed on its own.

67   הרב שאר ישוב כהן, הגדרת מושגי החמץ מבחינה מדעית והלכתית, ארחות 29, 10 – 5.

68   He refers here to the bizarre rabbinic theory of דם נעכר ונעשה חלב, that milk is a derivative of curdled maternal blood that has been transformed by the mother's body from one substance to another. Milk should therefore be categorically forbidden, since it originates with a forbidden substance (blood), but it is permitted by biblical inference. Likewise, with honey—it is a secretion from forbidden animals (bees) that has been rendered permitted only by biblical reference to its permitted consumption.

69   The starting point is a reference at b. Brakhot 43a to a musk (מושק), whose gland was burned for incense. Medieval commentators Ba'al Ha'Meor and Rabbeinu Yonah debate whether the substance may not only be burned but also added to foods as an aromatic, concluding leniently that the secretion should no longer be viewed as a derivative of forbidden blood. See discussion there in Rosh, #35.

70   ראו רמב"ם הלבות מאכלות אסורות פרק ד הלכה י. וכן החותך בשר מן החי מן הטהורים הרי
אותו הבשר טריפה והאוכל ממנו כזית לוקה משום אוכל טריפה, שהרי בשר זה מבהמה שלא נשחטה ולא
מתה, מה לי טרפה אותו חיה מה לי חתבה בסכין מה לי בכולה מה לי במקצתה הרי הוא אומר בשדה
טרפה לא תאכלו כיון שנעשית הבהמה בשר בשדה הרי היא טריפה.

71   Rabbi Isaac Klein addressed these subjects in chapters 6 and 7 of his book, *Responsa and Halakhic Studies* (Ktav Publishing House, Inc., 1975), pp. 43-74. See sources in the first Ryzman *Tehumin* article, v. 34, pp. 107-108.

72   בשו"ת גינת ורדים חלק יורה דעה חלק א סימן ד דין זה על סמך הבית יוסף [אבל כנראה לא
מדויק בציטוט]: אבל לענין אכילה כיון שנתיבש הרבה פקע ממנו איסור אכילה כיון דהא מיהא לא חזי למיכל
כשנתיבש הרבה וכבר כתבו הפוסקים דין זה וראו בב"י טי"ד ס"ס ע"ז שכתב וז"ל כתוב בשבלי הלקט וז"ל עור
קיבה שמולחין ומייבשין אותו ונעשה כעץ וממלאין אותו חלב מותר מאחר שנתייבש הוי כעץ בעלמא ואין
בו לחלוחית בשר עכ"ל. וראו עוד בשו"ת רבי עקיבא איגר מהדורא קמא סימן רו: אמנם בנ"ד כח דהתתירא
עדיף, כיון דמיבשים העור תחילה עד שנעשה כעץ. ליכא איסור בב"ח כלל.

73   Once again, this principle applies only to after-the-fact cases, not to intentional use.

74   This paragraph paraphrases Klein, p. 57. For a rather disturbing video documenting the process of turning pig skins into jelly candies, search for 'Gelatine' video by Belgian filmmaker Alina Kneepkens.

75   שו"ת משנת רבי אהרן סוף סי' טז. ראו ר' יהודה בצלאל שפיץ בתחומין כרך לה, ע' 196 שמצטט בטעות סי' טז.

76   See Rabbi Kassel Abelson's 1994 CJLS responsum, "The Kashrut of Microbial Enzymes."

77   טור יורה דעה הלכות שחיטה סימן יג. השוחט בהמה ומצא בה עובר בין אם הוא בן שמונה או בן תשעה בין חי בין מת מותר ואין טעון שחיטה וחלבו מותר ודמו אסור. וה"מ דבן תשעה חי אין טעון שחיטה שלא הפריס ע"ג קרקע אבל הפריס ע"ג קרקע טעון שחיטה ראויה וכל שפוסל בשאר שחיטות פוסל בו וחלבו אסור וכו'. וראה בשו"ע יג סעיף ג, דברי ט"ז, וגם בסימן סד.

78   I thank Philip Gibbs for suggesting this source.

79   See, for example: "Orthodox Groups Debate the Kashrut of Lab-Grown Meat," by Sam Sokol, *Jewish Telegraphic Agency*, August 10, 2013: http://www.jpost.com/Jewish-World/Jewish-News/Orthodox-groups-debate-kashrut-of-lab-grown-meat-32264/; הרב צבי שכטר, השתמשות בעניימו להכנת מאכלים כשרים. מסורה, גליון א' (1989), ע' מד-סג; "Is the Lab-Created Burger Kosher?" by Yehudah Shurpin, published at Chabad.org: http://www.chabad.org/library/article_cdo/aid/2293219/jewish/Is-the-Lab-Created-Burger-Kosher.htm; "Lab Grown Beef: But Is It Kosher?" by Yehuda Spitz, published in *Vos Iz Neias?* August 30th, 2013: http://www.vosizneias.com/140201/2013/08/30/new-york-lab-grown-beef-but-is-it-kosher/; as well as the *Teḥumin* articles and R' Bleich's "Stem-Cell Burgers."

80   תלמוד בבלי מסכת סנהדרין דף נט עמוד ב. מי איכא בשר היורד מן השמים? - אין, כי הא דרבי שמעון בן חלפתא הוה קאזיל באורחא, פגעו בו הנך אריותא דהוו קא נהמי לאפיה, אמר: הכפירים שאגים לטרף. נחיתו ליה תרתי אטמתא, חדא אכלוהו וחדא שבקוה. איתיה ואתא לבי מדרשא, בעי עלה: דבר טמא הוא זה או דבר טהור? - אמרו ליה: אין דבר טמא יורד מן השמים.

81   תלמוד בבלי מסכת סנהדרין דף סז עמוד ב. אמר אביי: הלכות כשפים כהלכות שבת, יש מהן בסקילה, ויש מהן פטור אבל אסור, ויש מהן מותר לכתחלה. העושה מעשה - בסקילה, האוחז את העינים - פטור אבל אסור, מותר לכתחלה - כדרב חנינא ורב אושעיא. כל מעלי שבתא הוו עסקי בהלכות יצירה, ומיברי להו עיגלא תילתא ואכלי ליה.

82   I translate עיגלא תילתא as "third-grown," not "three-year-old calf" since there is no such thing. After a year, a calf is called a heifer, and after three years it is called a cow even if it hasn't given birth to its own calf.

83   של"ה פרשת וישב מקץ ויגש דרך חיים תוכחת מוסר. והנה מצינו בגמרא (סנהדרין סה ב) דברא עגלא תלתא בכל ערב שבת על ידי עסק ספר יצירה בצירוף השמות, ובודאי זה הנברא על פי השמות ולא מצד התולדה אין צריך שחיטה, וניתר לאוכלו בעדיו חי, וכך עשו השבטים. ויוסף לא ידע והיה סבור שהוא הנולד מאב ואם, הביא דבה זו אל אביו שהם אוכלים אבר מן החי, והם כנים היו וכדין עשו.

84   בראשית פרק יח, ו-ח. (ו) וַיְמַהֵר אַבְרָהָם הָאֹהֱלָה אֶל שָׂרָה וַיֹּאמֶר מַהֲרִי שְׁלֹשׁ סְאִים קֶמַח סֹלֶת לוּשִׁי וַעֲשִׂי עֻגוֹת: (ז) וְאֶל הַבָּקָר רָץ אַבְרָהָם וַיִּקַּח בֶּן בָּקָר רַךְ וָטוֹב וַיִּתֵּן אֶל הַנַּעַר וַיְמַהֵר לַעֲשׂוֹת אֹתוֹ: (ח) וַיִּקַּח חֶמְאָה וְחָלָב וּבֶן הַבָּקָר אֲשֶׁר עָשָׂה וַיִּתֵּן לִפְנֵיהֶם וְהוּא עֹמֵד עֲלֵיהֶם תַּחַת הָעֵץ וַיֹּאכֵלוּ. ובמלבי"ם בראשית פרק יח פסוק ז. וימהר לעשות אתו שעשאו ע"י ספר יצירה. נראה שרצה לתרץ בזה איך האכיל להמלאכים בב"ח, ואמרו שהיה בשר שנברא ע"י ספר יצירה שאין לו דין בשר, וז"ש שלקח חמאה וחלב ובן הבקר אשר עשה, ר"ל יען שעשאו ע"י ספר יצירה היו יכולים לאכלו עם חלב.

85   ראו חולין קד ע"ב. וברמב"ם הלכות מאכלות אסורות פרק ט הלכה כ. אסור להעלות העוף עם הגבינה על השלחן שהוא אוכל עליו גזירה משום הרגל עבירה שמא יאכל זה עם זה, אף על פי שהעוף בחלב אסור מדברי סופרים.

86 David Lau, "Halakhic Inquiry: Cultured Meat as Manufactured in Your Company," letter to Didya Tuvia, CEO of Alef Farma, Rehovot, Jan. 17, 2023 [11 pages, Hebrew].

87 תלמוד בבלי מסכת פסחים דף קט עמוד א. תניא, רבי יהודה בן בתירא אומר: בזמן שבית המקדש קיים - אין שמחה אלא בבשר, שנאמר וזבחת שלמים ואכלת שם ושמחת לפני ה' אלהיך. ועכשיו שאין בית המקדש קיים - אין שמחה אלא ביין, שנאמר ויין ישמח לבב אנוש.

88 רמב"ם הלכות יום טוב פרק ו הלכה יח. והאנשים אוכלין בשר ושותין יין שאין שמחה אלא בבשר ואין שמחה אלא ביין.

89 ע"פ תלמוד בבלי מסכת ביצה דף ג עמוד ב, וכל ספיקא דאורייתא לחומרא.

NOTES TO CHAPTER 4

THE USE OF ELECTRICAL AND ELECTRONIC DEVICES ON SHABBAT

1 Prior studies regarding electricity and Shabbat within the Conservative Movement begin with Arthur Neulander's 1950 CJLS responsum, "The Use of Electricity on the Sabbath." He argues that the use of electricity cannot be compared to lighting fire on either halakhic or scientific grounds, and that the use of electrical appliances should be banned only in those instances when the result is *melakhah* or the action is not "in consonance with the spirit of Shabbat." Much has changed in the subsequent decades, both in the scholarship regarding this subject and in the ever-expanding uses of electricity, but Rabbi Neulander's basic observations are sound. Other responsa and the published discussion regarding Shabbat in the 1950 *Proceedings of The Rabbinical Assembly* (and republished in several places, including *Tradition and Change*, ed. Mordecai Waxman, Rabbinical Assembly, 1958, 1994) also touch upon the use of electricity. Joel Roth addresses this subject briefly in his article, "*Melakhah U'Shevut*: A Theoretical Framework," in *Conservative Judaism* (Spring 1982), pp. 15-16. In 1982 and 1989, the CJLS issued various responsa regarding the use of audio and video recording equipment on Shabbat that addressed the question of whether recording onto magnetic tape can be compared to the "writing" forbidden as *melakhah* on Shabbat. These are available on the RA website, and are published within *Proceedings of the CJLS, 1980-1985* (The Rabbinical Assembly, 1988). Michael Katz and Gershon Schwartz, discuss this subject in their chapter "Shabbat," in *The Observant Life: The Wisdom of Conservative Judaism for Contemporary Jews*, edited by Martin S. Cohen and Michael Katz (The Rabbinical Assembly, 2012), pp.133-135. Other essential resources regarding the conceptual framework of Shabbat, though not electricity, include the masterful essay on *shvut* by Boaz Cohen in *The Proceedings of the Rabbinical Assembly* (1945), and chapters on *melakhah* and *shvut* in Yitzhak Gilat's Hebrew book, פרקים בהשתלשלות ההלכה. Abraham Joshua Heschel's classic, *The Sabbath: Its Meaning for Modern Man* (Farrar, Straus, Giroux, LLC, 1951; republished by Shambhala Publications, 2003), provides a profound meditation on the role of Shabbat in modern civilization. The rapid spread of technology in the subsequent six decades has underscored many of Heschel's points.

Many studies regarding the use of electricity on Shabbat and Yom Tov have been published by Orthodox scholars. The entry חשמל in the *Talmudic Encyclopedia* [Hebrew] is supplemented with a lengthy (60 page) appendix in volume 18 that deals with many of these issues in great depth (while avoiding making a *p'sak din*). Whereas the main entry deals with basic questions about the use of electronics, the appendix considers specific types of appliances and the halakhic issues they raise. The book, *Electricity and Shabbat* [Hebrew] and several responsa by Shlomo Zalman Auerbach in his collection, *Minḥat Shlomo*, give comprehensive overviews. Rabbi Auerbach also wrote a monograph on electricity and halakhah called מאורי אש. The volume קונטרס קדושת שבת: הלכות כלי חשמל בשבת וביום טוב is encyclopedic in scope. קונטרס חשמל בשבת ולחולה by Yirmiahu Ben Asher (1992) deals in depth with accommodations for disabled and ill persons. The Israeli Zomet Institute has relevant articles on its website, http://www.zomet.org.il:. In English, several reviews of the halakhic literature have also been published: "The Use of Electricity on Shabbat and Yom Tov" by Michael Broyde and Howard Jachter in *The Journal of Halacha and Contemporary Society* (XXI, Spring 1991) generally supports Rabbi Auerbach's position:

http://www.daat.ac.il/DAAT/english/Journal/broyde_1.htm. *Shabbat and Electricity* by L.Y. Halperin (Jerusalem: Institute for Science and Halacha, 1993) combines all of the stringencies. These Orthodox works all consider the operation of electrical appliances to be biblically forbidden as *melakhah* though not without disagreements about which labor is involved. One of the many surveys of Shabbat law is by Shimon D. Eider, *The Halachos of Shabbos* (Lakewood, New Jersey, 1970).

2   Text as approved available at: https://www.rabbinicalassembly.org/sites/default/files/2020-05/ElectricSabbathSpring2012.pdf

3   Cited from p. 20 in Shambhala Library's 2003 edition. I have modified Heschel's language for gender neutrality, changing "man" to "one," and "his" to "their."

4   Electrical switches are no longer limited to structures of metal and plastic, but now include microscopic transistors that may be controlled by motions such as the tap of a finger on a touch screen or through touchless technologies that track sounds, gestures, and eye movements in order to control an application. There are even neural interface systems that allow the control of electronics through the use of electrodes inserted in the brain or placed on its surface. See "Reach and grasp by people with tetraplegia using a neurally controlled robotic arm," in *Nature* 485, pp. 372-375, May 16, 2012. The progression of such technologies from science fiction to practical application in recent years has been rapid and remarkable.

5   See the Wikipedia article on electric motors, especially the section regarding sparking in brushed DC motors: http://en.wikipedia.org/wiki/Electric_motor.

6   Smart home technologies are already altering the way that household appliances operate and interact with one another and with the occupants of the home. There is a vast online literature on this subject. Here is one survey article: http://articles.castelarhost.com/smart_home_technology.ht. In the foreseeable future, it may become impossible to use necessary appliances like toilets without triggering some sort of electronic monitoring of the device.

7   Already in the 1960s, Arthur Neulander pointed out that simply by being alive and moving, we constantly create electrical impulses and that our motions inevitably affect thermostats and other electrical appliances in our vicinity. As we shall discuss below, the halakhic codes have banned as פסיק רישיה any activity that inevitably results in *melakhah* unless the result is ולא ניחא ליה (detrimental); this strict standard, if taken literally, would prevent a Sabbath observer from opening a refrigerator or even an external window or door, since these actions change the temperature and trigger responses from heating and cooling systems. Indeed, the use of water taps, toilets, and drains eventually causes pumps to operate and should arguably be banned by the same reasoning. Yet the application of such a strict standard has proven to be unpalatable and indeed unfeasible for even the most strictly observant. These actions are often justified as grama, only indirectly causing the appliance to respond, but the line between direct and indirect causation is not always easily identified.

8   See "Tools of Entry, No Need for a Key Chain," by Matt Richtel and Verne G. Kopytoff, *New York Times* (July 4, 2011).

9   See "E-Books Top Hardcovers at Amazon," by Claire Cain Miller, *New York Times* (July 19, 2010). http://www.nytimes.com:2010:07:20:technology:20kindle.html?_r=1&ref=claire_cain_miller.

10   According to the Wikipedia article, "Transistor," sixty million transistors were manufactured for each person on earth in 2002. This number has presumably increased in the subsequent years. What if it all shut down? What if we were suddenly cast into a total blackout? While we may romanticize the supposedly natural state that preceded modernity, few of us would relinquish the electrical devices that have come to pervade and define our lives. Some people who are ill or disabled could be endangered by even

a brief power outage. Many people would be inconvenienced by going off the grid, and a prolonged blackout would quickly imperil everything from our food supply to public health and information services. Safety concerns aside, recent studies have shown that the human mind can become addicted to the torrent of electronically delivered data that stimulates the brain with dopamine. Public anticipation surrounding the launch of new electronic devices has become a dominant feature of our culture. As electronic media push aside older data delivery mechanisms, the change in comfortable habits has become inevitable. At some point in the foreseeable future, digital devices may be our only medium for reading new content.

11   This phenomenon has been labeled in the social science literature as "The Internet Paradox" by Robert Kraut and his collaborators. See their initial article, "Internet paradox: A social technology that reduces social involvement and psychological well-being?" Kraut, Robert; Patterson, Michael; Lundmark, Vicki; Kiesler, Sara; Mukophadhyay, Tridas; Scherlis, William, *American Psychologist*, Vol 53 (9), Sep. 1998, pp. 1017-1031, and the 2002 follow-up, "Internet Paradox Revisited" in the *Journal of Social Issues* 58:1 (2002), pp. 49-74. This phenomenon is also discussed in the May 2012 cover story of *The Atlantic*, "Is Facebook Making Us Lonely?" by Stephen Marche. He quotes MIT researcher Shelly Turkle's 2011 book, *Alone Together*: "These days, insecure in our relationships and anxious about intimacy, we look to technology for ways to be in relationships and protect ourselves from them at the same time." The problem with digital intimacy is that it is ultimately incomplete: "The ties we form through the Internet are not, in the end, the ties that bind. But they are the ties that preoccupy," she writes. "We don't want to intrude on each other, so instead we constantly intrude on each other, but not in 'real time.'" Marche concludes his essay with this sentence, "Facebook denies us a pleasure whose profundity we had underestimated: the chance to forget about ourselves for a while, the chance to disconnect." In Jewish terms, we might call this chance "Shabbat."

12   This is also largely true of any Jewish festival defined as Yom Tov, although its rules are more lenient regarding food preparation and carrying. See below.

13   Exodus 20:9 states, וְיוֹם הַשְּׁבִיעִי שַׁבָּת לַיקֹוָק אֱלֹהֶיךָ לֹא תַעֲשֶׂה כָל מְלָאכָה אַתָּה וּבִנְךָ וּבִתֶּךָ עַבְדְּךָ וַאֲמָתְךָ וּבְהֶמְתֶּךָ וְגֵרְךָ אֲשֶׁר בִּשְׁעָרֶיךָ. The classic works of halakhah are extremely protective of the Sabbath rest of non-Jews, but this value eroded dramatically with time, as documented by Jacob Katz in *The Shabbos Goy: A Study in Halakhic Flexibility* (Jewish Publication Society, 1989).

14   On שביתת כלים see Bavli Shabbat 18a, based on Exodus 23:12-13, which requires Sabbath rest for animals, and is understood by some rabbis to imply that even machines should be rested based on the words ובכל אשר אמרתי אליכם תשמרו. See Mekhilta D'Rabbi Yishmael, Massekhta D'kaspa 20 on the verse and discussion of this passage in Section II. In the Bavli, Beit Shammai is reported to forbid automatic labor, whereas Beit Hillel permits it, even if it has a lasting result, לבית הלל, אף על גב דקעביד מעשה - שרי. This subject is of intense interest to the Rishonim but is resolved according to the lenient view of Beit Hillel. See Shulḥan Arukh, OH 246:1.מותר להשאיל או להשכיר כליו לאינו יהודי, ואע"פ שהוא עושה בהם מלאכה בשבת, מפני שאין אנו מצווים על שביתת כלים. While devices set in motion prior to Shabbat are generally permitted (an exception being a flour mill, which makes excessive noise and may lead the public to assume that the owner is actively milling on Shabbat), there remains debate about setting timers to commence labor on Shabbat. However, dominant practice is lenient in this regard as well.

15   This contemporary practice recalls the classic debate between medieval Karaites and mainstream Jews (Rabbanites) regarding Exodus 35:3, "Do not burn fire in all your dwellings on the Sabbath day." The early Karaites claimed that the Torah here requires Jews to sit in the cold and dark on Shabbat (Eshkol Ha-kofer, No. 146), while the Rabbanites interpreted the verse only to prohibit kindling and tending fires on Shabbat,

but to permit the use of fires lit before Shabbat. The Rabbinic position, which yielded an increasingly sophisticated set of technological strategies to augment ענג שבת, Sabbath joy, is first described in Midrash Mekhilta D'Rabbi Yishmael, Massechta D'Shabta, Vayakhel, 1: ת"ל לא תבערו אש בכל מושבותיכם ביום השבת, ביום השבת אי אתה מבעיר, אבל אתה מבעיר מערב שבת לשבת "The verse, do not kindle fire in all your dwellings on the Sabbath day, means, on the Sabbath day you may not kindle, but you may kindle on the eve of the Sabbath for the Sabbath." Indeed, the custom of lighting candles to start Shabbat may have originated as a demonstrative separation from the Karaite practice. For a review of these sources, see Chancellor Ismar Schorsch's Torah commentary to Shabbat Beha'alotekha 5762 (2002): http://www.jtsa.edu/PreBuilt/ParashahArchives/5762/behaalothekha.shtml.

16   Under the theocratic government understood by early rabbinic literature to have been operative during the Second Temple and earlier periods, intentional (במזיד) violation of the ban on Sabbath labor could be punished by stoning (סקילה) if the violator had been forewarned (בהתראה), or otherwise by the divine punishment called כרת (literally, being "cut off," this may refer to a premature death or to some sort of spiritual destruction). The rules for unintentional violation (בשוגג) would have required the offender to bring a purification offering (קרבן חטאת), to be restored to good standing before God and the community. See Rambam, MT, Hilkhot Shabbat 7:1. On the cessation of the death penalty, see Bavli Sanhedrin 41a and 52b. There is some evidence during medieval times of emergency applications of the death penalty for protection of the Jewish community against informers but not, as far as I am aware, for Sabbath violations. See Menachem Elon, *Jewish Law: History, Sources and Principles* (Phildelphia: Jewish Publication Society, 1994), V. 1, p. 11, esp. note 25, and V. 2, pp. 696-7. There are social ramifications for those who violate Sabbath laws in observant communities, and of course, כרת may remain in effect, though there is no evidence of truncated lifespans for Sabbath violaters.

17   See "The Sabbath Manifesto" website: http://www.sabbathmanifesto.org/about. They sell a "cellphone sleeping bag" and have declared an annual "National Day of Unplugging."

18   Judith Shulevitz writes of the utility of Shabbat to prevent the complete breakdown of "universal time" as electronic communication makes individualized "mobile time" the norm. See *The Sabbath World: Glimpses of a Different Order of Time* (Random House, 2010), chapter 7, esp. pp. 197-8.

19   There is also a documented phenomenon of otherwise-Shabbat-observant youth using hand-held computers for texting and then describing themselves as keeping "half-Shabbos." See Steve Lipman, "For Many Orthodox Teens, 'Half Shabbos' Is A Way Of Life" in *The Jewish Week*, June 22, 2011. For such people, there is no attempt made to regulate the use of electronics in light of halakhah. In contrast, our project seeks to apply halakhic categories to the use of electronics, whether the result is permission or prohibition.

20   http://www.kosherlightswitch.com/ There is a lengthy responsum available on this site, justifying the use of this switch based on a patented technology in which the switch increases the probability of completion of the circuit but does not directly close it.

21   See http://www.timesofisrael.com/new-smart-shabbatphone-is-kosher-even-on-the-weekend/.

22   See http://www.israelhayom.com/site/newsletter_article.php?id=3653.

23   Rav Avraham Yitzhak Ha-Kohen Kuk permitted asking a non-Jew to milk Jewish-owned cows on Shabbat since the rabbinic ban on אמירה לנכרי is superseded by the biblical ban on צער בעלי חיים. From this precedent, permission has been extrapolated to use automated milking devices for Jewish-owned dairy cows on Shabbat. See Howard Jachter and Ezra Frazer, *Gray Matter*, volume 1, p. 202.

24   See Rambam's discussion of these categories at the beginning of the Laws of Shabbat, Chapter 1:2-4.

25   שֵׁשֶׁת יָמִים תַּעֲבֹד וּבַיּוֹם הַשְּׁבִיעִי תִּשְׁבֹּת בֶּחָרִישׁ וּבַקָּצִיר תִּשְׁבֹּת, "Six days shall you work, but on the seventh day shall you rest—from plowing and reaping shall you rest."

26   ירמיהו פרק יז (כא) כֹּה אָמַר יְקֹוָק הִשָּׁמְרוּ בְּנַפְשׁוֹתֵיכֶם וְאַל תִּשְׂאוּ מַשָּׂא בְּיוֹם הַשַּׁבָּת וַהֲבֵאתֶם בְּשַׁעֲרֵי יְרוּשָׁלִָם: (כב) וְלֹא תוֹצִיאוּ מַשָּׂא מִבָּתֵּיכֶם בְּיוֹם הַשַּׁבָּת וְכָל מְלָאכָה לֹא תַעֲשׂוּ וְקִדַּשְׁתֶּם אֶת יוֹם הַשַּׁבָּת כַּאֲשֶׁר צִוִּיתִי אֶת אֲבוֹתֵיכֶם

See Moshe Greenberg's essay:

משה גרינברג, פרשת השבת בירמיהו, דברי החוג העיון בתנ"ך בבית נשיא המדינה, עיונים בספר ירמיהו חלק ב' (1971), ע' 37-26. העורך בן ציון לוריא.

27   נחמיה פרק יג. (טו) בַּיָּמִים הָהֵמָּה רָאִיתִי בִיהוּדָה דֹרְכִים גִּתּוֹת בַּשַּׁבָּת וּמְבִיאִים הָעֲרֵמוֹת וְעֹמְסִים עַל הַחֲמֹרִים וְאַף יַיִן עֲנָבִים וּתְאֵנִים וְכָל מַשָּׂא וּמְבִיאִים יְרוּשָׁלִַם בְּיוֹם הַשַּׁבָּת וָאָעִיד בְּיוֹם מִכְרָם צָיִד: (טז) וְהַצֹּרִים יָשְׁבוּ בָהּ מְבִיאִים דָּאג וְכָל מֶכֶר וּמֹכְרִים בַּשַּׁבָּת לִבְנֵי יְהוּדָה וּבִירוּשָׁלִָם: (יז) וָאָרִיבָה אֵת חֹרֵי יְהוּדָה וָאֹמְרָה לָהֶם מָה הַדָּבָר הָרָע הַזֶּה אֲשֶׁר אַתֶּם עֹשִׂים וּמְחַלְּלִים אֶת יוֹם הַשַּׁבָּת: (יח) הֲלוֹא כֹה עָשׂוּ אֲבֹתֵיכֶם וַיָּבֵא אֱלֹהֵינוּ עָלֵינוּ אֵת כָּל הָרָעָה הַזֹּאת וְעַל הָעִיר הַזֹּאת וְאַתֶּם מוֹסִיפִים חָרוֹן עַל יִשְׂרָאֵל לְחַלֵּל אֶת הַשַּׁבָּת:

28   Jeffrey Tigay, article שבת in אנציקלופדיה מקראית, 7:504-517 (Jerusalem, 1976), see esp. section 3.

29   Baruch Schwartz, "Sabbath in Torah Sources," address to the Society of Biblical Literature (2007). It is available at: www.biblicallaw.net/2007/schwartz.pdf. Schwartz gives a novel explanation for the juxtaposition of Shabbat to the tabernacle narrative in the priestly source. The idea is that Shabbat is a holy day dedicated solely to the Lord, and that the act of dedication cannot be completed until the tabernacle is in place.

30   See Jubilees 50:6-13 and Damascus Document, Section 10. For the text of Jubilees 50, see http://www.pseudepigrapha.com/jubilees50.htm. In verse 8, the author announces a ban on marital sex on the Sabbath (the rabbis also considered such a ban, especially regarding the initial act of intercourse with a virgin, since it likely creates a wound or opening in the hymen, but ultimately permitted and indeed encouraged Shabbat intercourse. See B. Ketubot 5b, 62b and Y. Ketubot 5:11 30b). The Damascus Document's list is quite extensive. See Geza Vermes, *The Complete Dead Sea Scrolls in English* (New York: Penguin Books, 1995), pp. 139-40. An English translation is also available online:

http://www.bibliotecapleyades.net/scrolls_deadsea/deadseascrolls_english/05.htm. More recent studies consider the evidence of Qumran halakhah in texts such as MMT (מקצת מעשי תורה). See "Halakhah at Qumran: Genre and Authority," by Aharon Shemesh and Cana Werman, in *Dead Sea Discoveries*, Vol. 10, No. 1, *Authorizing Texts, Interpretations, and Laws at Qumran* (2003), pp. 104-129. Lawrence Schiffman's book, *The Halakhah at Qumran* (Leiden: E.J. Brill, 1975) provides an extended study on Sabbath law in Qumran, especially in Section III.

31   To give just a few examples, rabbinic law allowed for food preparation so long as it did not involve cooking or fine chopping; the Qumran sect apparently prohibited even the peeling of vegetables; rabbinic law allowed one to carry four cubits in the public domain on Shabbat; the Qumran sect did not allow any carrying at all; rabbinic law allowed one to walk 2,000 cubits out of town on Shabbat; the Qumran community capped such journeys at 1,000 cubits, and some sources indicate remaining within the home for the duration of Shabbat in literal compliance with Ex. 16:29. It seems possible that the Qumran sect either rejected the doctrine of *pikuah nefesh* or severely limited it (CDC 11:16f). See Schiffman for these and further examples. In his conclusion, he speculates that the medieval Karaites might have had access to some of the Qumran sect's documents (which we know from the Cairo Genizo to have been in circulation) and been influenced by these in their attempt to "turn back the clock" and purge Judaism of

rabbinic influence.

For a comprehensive study of Shabbat during the Roman period, see Robert Goldenberg's chapter, "The Jewish Sabbath in the Roman World Up to the Time of Constantine the Great" in *Aufstieg und Niedergang der Römischen Welt: Geschichte Und Kultur Roms Im Spiegel Der Neueren Forschung*, ed. Hildegard Temporini and Wolfgang Haase (Berlin) II.19.1 (1979), pp. 414-447. His comparison of rabbinic Sabbath law considering the evidence from Jubilees, Qumran, Philo, Josephus, and the New Testament, is found at pp. 422-23. See also E.P. Sanders, *Judaism: Practice and Belief, 63 BCE-66 CE* (Trinity Press International, 1993), chapter 11; this subject is discussed in several of the essays in *The Jewish Annotated New Testament*, edited by Amy-Jill Levine and Marc Zvi Brettler (Oxford University Press, 2011). See especially the notes to Matthew 12:1-14. Surviving evidence of ancient Jewish Sabbath observance from external sources focuses on issues such as the unwillingness of Jews to appear in court on Saturday but preserves little about the details of ritual observance.

32   As many have noted, the Torah seems to link these two narratives. For example, Genesis 2:2 states ויכל אלהים ביום השביעי מלאכתו אשר עשה, "on the seventh day God completed all the work which He had done;" similarly, Exodus 40:33 reads, ויכל משה את המלאכה, "Moses completed the work" (emphases mine) The tabernacle thus functions as a microcosm—a human approximation of the divine creation. See Midrash BeMidbar Rabba #12:

...בשביעי כתיב (שם :בראשית: ב) ויכולו השמים וגו' ובמשכן ותכל כל עבודת משכן וגו', בבריאת עולם כתיב ויברך אלהים, ובמשכן ויברך אותם, בשביעי ויכל אלהים, ובמשכן ויהי ביום כלות משה, בשביעי ויקדש אותו ובמשכן ויקדש אותו הוי את המשכן.

33   New Jewish Publication Society (NJPS) translation.

34   B. Beitza 16a דאמר רבי שמעון בן לקיש: נשמה יתירה נותן הקדוש ברוך הוא באדם ערב שבת. See also ולמוצאי שבת נוטלין אותה הימנו, שנאמר שמות לא+ שבת וינפש, כיון ששבת ווי אבדה נפש comments of Ramban to 31:13 at ועל דרך האמת. Rabbeinu Baḥya (Gen 7.22) likewise reads this verse as an allusion to the "additional soul" of Shabbat, which he calls "the well of blessing and the foundation of life," והוא מעין הברכות ויסוד החיים.

35   ראו מדרש תנחומא (ורשא) פרשת כי תשא סימן לג, אמר להם הקב"ה לישראל הוו זהירין בכבוד שבת שבו נחתי ממלאכת העולם שנאמר כי בו שבת.

36   Bernard Goldstein and Alan Cooper, "The Festivals of Israel and Judah and the Literary History of the Pentateuch" in *The Journal of the American Oriental Society*, Vol. 110, No. 1 (1990), esp. pp. 28-29, http://www.jstor.org/stable:603907?seq=10.

37   Seth Schwartz discusses the function of *zikkaron* in Josephus's use of biblical sources, in *Were the Jews a Mediterranean Society? Reciprocity and Solidarity in Ancient Israel* (Princeton University Press, 2010), pp. 93-94: "What Josephus repeatedly calls on his readers to remember is the evidence of God's *euergesiai* (benefactions) to Israel, and Israel's obligation to reciprocate these benefactions with gratitude and loyalty." In this sense, observing Shabbat is a weekly reminder of God's gifts; desisting from labor is thus an expression of loyalty—by imitating divine rest, one acknowledges dependence on God's provision of life and liberty.

On a more mystical level, Eitan Fishbane explains the dual format of Sabbath memory as follows: "For on Shabbat we are aware of the mystery and wonder of Divinity that brings this world into being anew each and every day; the beauty that reminds us of the divine Source and our never-ending capacity for spiritual renewal and rebirth. And we are also always aware of how our experience of Shabbat is a *yetzi'at mitzrayim*, an exodus from Egypt. For on Shabbat, we are liberated from our enslavement to our physical selves—to our greed, our pride, our lust. On Shabbat we are reminded that deep down we are soul and spirit, the breath of divine speech, the song of divine yearning. And we must lift these two dimensions—renewal and freedom—to the gaze of a mind transformed, an awareness of the divine anchor that gives meaning and substance to our all-too-ephemeral time in this world." Eitan Fishbane, *The Sabbath Soul: Mystical Reflections on the Transformative Power of Holy Time* (Jewish Lights, 2011), p. 4.

38   Rabbi Eliezer, son of Rabbi Shimon (bar Yoḥai), claims that this was the only Sabbath observed by Israel during their forty-year period in the desert:

ספרי זוטא פרק ט ד"ה ד. וידבר. כיוצא בו ר' אליעזר ביר' שמעון אומר וישבתו העם ביום השביעי (שם
שמות: טז ל) מלמד שלא עשו ישראל שבת כל ארבעים שנה שהיו במדבר אלא שבת הראשונה בלבד:

In contrast, Midrash Tehillim to Psalm 92 claims that Israel kept two Sabbaths prior to the revelation at Sinai, and that for the entire forty-year period, the Sabbath was a shared experience of God and Israel. God rested from manna production while Israel rested from manna collection. In this way, it became ביני ובין בני ישראל אות הוא לעלם, "an eternal sign between Me and Israel" (Ex. 31:17):

מדרש תהלים (בובר) מזמור צב ד"ה [ב] דבר אחר. תדע לך שכן הוא, שכל ארבעים שנה שהיו ישראל
במדבר, בששת ימי המעשה היה נותן להם את המן, ובשבת לא היה יורד, לא מפני שלא היה בו כח ליתן,
אלא מפני ששבת לפניו, כיון שראו העם בן, שבתו גם הם, שנאמר וישבתו העם ביום השביעי (שמות טז ל).
אמר הקב"ה השבת הזה נתתי לישראל אות ביני לבינם, בששת ימי המעשה פעלתי את העולם, ובשבת נחתי,
לפיכך נאמר ביני ובין בני ישראל [אות היא לעולם] (שם :שמות: לא יז).

39   Stephen A. Geller, "Manna and Sabbath: A Literary-Theological Reading of Exodus 16" in *Interpretation*, 59:1 (Jan. 2005), pp. 5-16.

40   מכילתא דרבי ישמעאל ויקהל - מסכתא דשבתא פרשה א. פרשה ויקהל ויקהל משה וגו'. למה
נאמרה פרשה זו, לפי שהוא אומר +שמות כה ח+ ועשו לי מקדש, שומע אני בין בחול בין בשבת, ומה אני
מקיים מחלליה מות יומת, בשאר כל מלאכות חוץ ממלאכת המשכן; במלאכת המשכן, ומה אני מקיים, ועשו
לי מקדש, בשאר כל הימים חוץ מן השבת; או אף בשבת, והדין נותן, ומה עבודה שאינה באה אלא מכח
המכשירין הרי היא דוחה חוץ מן השבת, מכשירי עבודה שאין עבודה באה אלא מכהן, אינו דין שידחו את השבת,
כגון שניטלה קרנו של מזבח או שנפגמה הסכין, שומע אני יתקנם בשבת, תלמוד לומר ויקהל משה, בחול
ולא בשבת.

41   מלאכת מחשבת. See especially Tosfot on Hagigah 10b, s.v. Melekhet Maḥshevet:

תוספות מסכת חגיגה דף י עמוד ב. מלאכת מחשבת אסרה תורה - פרש"י שאינה צריכה לגופה במין
מלאכה זאת שברצונו לא היה בנין זה בעולם ולא יתכן דאם כן בכל מלאכות נמי כגון סותר ע"מ לבנות
במקומו למה מיחייב דהא לא ניחא ליה שהיה הבנין בעולם וכן בקורע ע"מ לתפור ג"כ לא ניחא ליה בקרע זה
מעולם וקורע הבא באבלו או מחמת טרדא וקורע בחמתו למרמי אימתיה לכן נראה להר"י לפרש שאינו צריך
לעיקר שורש האיסור כגון הכא שאינו צריך לגומא שהיא המלאכה וכן מוציא מת במטה והרבה דחשיב פ'
המצניע (שבת דף צג:) ולא דמו למלאכת המשכן שהיו צריכים לעיקר המלאכה מכבה משום צורך הפחמין
וציידת תחשים וחלזון וכן כולם כיוצא בהן.

42   As many have noted, no biblical figure in the period of judges, prophets, and kings is described as having rested from labor on Shabbat. In addition to Moshe Greenberg's essay on Jeremiah cited above (note 26), see his article in *The Encyclopedia Judaica* (First edition, Jerusalem, 1971), vol. 14, pp. 558-562. Michael Fishbane studies the phenomenon of intra-biblical legal exegesis regarding Shabbat and Jeremiah's expansion of the Deuteronomic rendition in *Biblical Interpretation in Ancient Israel* (Clarendon Press, 1985), pp. 132-134.

43   Michael Fishbane, *Biblical Interpretation in Ancient Israel*, p. 479f.

44   Perhaps there is a theological message to the curious formulation of "forty less one;" 40 is a numerical indicator of creation and destruction (the Sinai theophany and Noah's flood). God uses 40 to create and destroy; the human capacity for creation and destruction is little less than divine, as Psalm 8 puts it. It is also interesting that creation

and destruction are linked in the *melakhah* pairs: מבעיר/מכבה, בונה/סותר, כותב/מוחק, קושר/
מתיר. The rabbis explain that the latter acts of destruction are required for the former acts of construction, but there is also an acknowledgement that these two modalities of change (+/-) are hinged together, like poles of an electric circuit.

45 Translation: D. A. Sola and M. J. Raphall.

46 Avraham Goldberg, in פירוש למשנה מסכת שבת [*Tractate Shabbat Mishnah Commentary*] (Jerusalem: Jewish Theological Seminary Press, 1976), p. 234, provides a complex analysis of the structure of this list and of the entire volume of Mishnah Shabbat. The book examines the 39 categories in reverse order, starting with הוצאה, but it treats each cluster of *melakhot* in forward order. Even this complicated scheme is not observed consistently. Sometimes, the tanna associates *melakhot* that share a characteristic, such as the use of doubles, to quantify the prohibited activity of writing, sewing, etc.

47 Goldberg argues that the word "on Shabbat" refers to the action of "does labor" rather than on the resulting "enduring work." See notes to 12:1. The standard of "durable change" is at minimum for a day, and more likely for several days.

48 We will consider the issue of durable impact below in asking whether recording data to a non-volatile digital memory device is to be deemed a permanent act, such as writing with ink on paper, or rather, is comparable to one of the non-durable forms of writing which are excluded from biblical labor, or כותב.

49 See Tur and S.A. OH 318:4 and sources cited there (and our discussion of בישול below). The rules regarding reheating wet vs. dry foods on Shabbat are complex and somewhat subjective, since the issue is at what point the food becomes edible, and what amount of reheating improves its quality.

50 שבכל מלאכת שבת בעין דבר המתקיים. Maggid Mishnah to MT Shabbat 11:15. See also Tur, OH 340, SA there 340:5, and esp. the extended comments of Mishnah B'rurah there, s.k. 22.

51 Goldberg, p. 153, citing B. Shabbat 96b and Y. Shabbat 3:2.

52 תלמוד בבלי מסכת שבת דף ע ע עמוד א. לפי שנאמר שמות לה ויקהל משה את כל עדת בני ישראל
אלה הדברים וגו' ששת ימים תעשה מלאכה. דברים, הדברים - אלה הדברים - אלו שלשים ותשע מלאכות
שנאמרו למשה בסיני.

53 תלמוד ירושלמי מסכת שבת פרק ז דף ט טור ב :ה"ב. רבנין דקיסרין אמרין מן אתרה לא חסרה
כלום אל"ף חד למ"ד תלתין ח' תמניא לא מתמנעין רבנן דרשין בין ה"א לחי"ת

54 According to the Bavli, the word אלה indicates the letter-values of 1+30+5, whereas the plural noun דברים adds a concept value of 2; the definite article ה adds 1 to reach the sum of 39. According to the Caesarean rabbis cited in the Yerushalmi, the entire sum of 39 is contained within the letter values of the word אלה since they allowed themselves to substitute (8) ח for (5) ה. Thus, אלה means 1+30+8 (!).

55 פרקים בהשתלשלות ההלכה: שלשים ותשעה אבות מלאכה ותולדותיהם See Yitzhak Gilat, p. 35, note 16, citing the struggles of Ḥatam Sofer, Nishmat Adam, and Pnei Yehoshua to resolve this conundrum.

56 תלמוד ירושלמי מסכת שבת פרק ז דף ט טור ד :ה"ב.

57 תלמוד בבלי מסכת שבת דף מט עמוד ב. תניא כמאן דאמר כנגד עבודות המשכן, דתניא: אין
חייבין אלא על מלאכה שכיוצא בה היתה במשכן, הם זרעו - ואתם לא תזרעו, הם קצרו - ואתם לא תקצרו
וכו'.

58 See Yerushalmi Brakhot 3c, Y. Nedarim 38b, Mekhilta DRY, BiShalaḥ, Vayisa #5 (p.170 in Hurwitz ed.), and especially, Shmot Rabbah 25:12:

א"ר לוי אם משמרים ישראל את השבת כראוי אפילו יום אחד בן דוד בא, למה שהיא שקולה כנגד כל
המצות, וכה"א (תהלים צה) כי הוא אלהינו ואנחנו עם מרעיתו וצאן ידו היום אם בקולו תשמעו, א"ר
יוחנן אמר הקב"ה לישראל אע"פ שנתתי קצבה לקץ שיבא בין עושין תשובה בין שאין עושין בעונתה היא
באה, אם עושין תשובה אפילו יום אחד אני מביא אותה שלא בעונתה, הוי היום אם בקולו תשמעו, וכשם
שמצינו שעל כל המצות בן דוד בא, על שמירת יום אחד של שבת בן דוד בא, לפי שהשבת שקולה כנגד כל
המצות, א"ר אלעזר בר אבינא מצינו בתורה ובנביאים ובכתובים ששקולה שבת כנגד כל המצות, בתורה
מנין שבשעה ששכח משה לומר להם מצות שבת אמר לו הקב"ה (שמות טז) עד אנה מאנתם לשמור
מצותי וגו', ומה כתיב אחריו ראו כי ה' נתן לכם את השבת, בנביאים מנין שנאמר (יחזקאל כ) וימרו בי
בית ישראל במדבר בחקותי לא הלכו, מה כתיב אחריו (שם :יחזקאל כ:) ואת שבתותי חללו, בכתובים
מנין שנאמר (נחמיה ט) ועל הר סיני ירדת ודברת עמהם, מה כתיב אחריו ואת שבת קדשך הודעת להם,
אמר להם הקב"ה לישראל אם תזכו לשמור שבת מעלה אני עליכם כאלו שמרתם כל המצות שבתורה ואם
חללתם אותה מעלה אני עליכם כאלו חללתם כל המצות, וכן הוא אומר (ישעיה נו) שומר שבת מחללו
ושומר ידו מעשות כל רע, בעת שאדם שומר את השבת גוזר גזירה והקב"ה מקיימה שנאמר (שם :ישעיה:
נח) אם תשיב משבת רגלך, מה כתיב אחריו אז תתענג על ה', כמה דתימא (תהלים לז) והתענג על ה' ויתן
לך משאלות לבך, ולא עוד אלא כל מה שאתה אוכל בעולם הזה אינו אלא מן הפירות, אבל הקרן קיימת לך
לעוה"ב שנאמר (ישעיה נח) והאכלתיך נחלת יעקב אביך כי פי ה' דבר.

59   See Elliot K. Ginsburg, *The Sabbath in the Classical Kabbalah* (State University of
New York Press, 1989), esp. chapter 2.

60   Yerushalmi Shabbat Ch. 7, Halakhah 1 (9b):

ר' יוחנ' ור"ש בן לקיש עבדין הווי בהדא פירקא תלת שנין ופלוג אפקון מיניה ארבעין חסר אחת תולדו' על
כל חדא וחדא. מן דאשכחון מיסמוך סמכין הא דלא אשכחון מיסמוך מיסמוך עבדוניה משום מכה בפטיש.

This reference to a three-and-a-half-year cycle is reminiscent of the Palestinian custom
of completing the Torah in three-and-a-half years. Perhaps the number is typological,
indicating that the observance of Shabbat is of equivalent importance or complexity to
the entire Torah. In any event, this claim of 1,521 *toledot melakhot* would seem to be a *guzma
b'alma*, a simple exaggeration.

61   See Joel Roth's discussion in *Melakhah U'Shevut*, pp. 6-18, as well as Yitzhak Gilat,
שלשים ותשעה אבות מלאכה ותולדותיהם, section 6, pp. 43-47. See note 1 for citations.

62   M. Bava Kama 1:1. See the opening discussion of Bavli Bava Kama for
a comparison and contrast between the various uses of *avot* and *toledot* in the three
contexts.

63   M. Kelim 1:1.

64   The main difference is the punishment of the multiple-act offender during
Temple times. If a person unintentionally performs several acts on Shabbat that are
forbidden under different primary categories of *melakhah*, then they would be liable for a
purification sacrifice (חטאת) for each discrete violation. However, if they were to violate
one primary category as well as one or more of its derivative prohibitions on a given
Shabbat, they would be liable only for one sacrifice.

65   Rambam has a distinctive theory of the *toledot* emphasizing their difference
from the labors involved in building the tabernacle. See Hil. Shabbat 7:4-7. From his
perspective, any activity that closely resembles an *av* is included within the *av*; *toledot*
only partially resemble the *avot*. See Magid Mishnah to Hil. Shabbat 7:4, and discussion
in Roth and Gilat.

66   As noted previously, אופה, baking, is said by some authorities not to have been
part of the tabernacle construction, but to be banned by association with בישול, cooking
(lit. boiling) of dyes. Why, then, did the Mishnah list baking rather than cooking? Because
it followed other labors involved with producing bread. Another explanation would be
that Mishnah Shabbat 7:2 originally had nothing to do with the tabernacle. Shimon Eider
writes of an in-between category in *The Halochos of Shabbos*, "If an act is similar both in

פעולה (action) and תכלית (purpose) to an Av Melacha that was in the Mishkan, it is a מעין מלאכה אחת." See *The Halachos of Shabbos* (Lakewood, New Jersey, 1970), V.1, pp. 7-9.

67   But see Joel Roth, pp. 9-10. "In sum, it is clear that not all *melakhot* involved in the *mishkan* are *avot*, and plausible that not all *avot* were involved in the *mishkan*."

68   משנה מסכת חגיגה פרק א משנה ח. הלכות שבת ...הרי הם כהררים התלויין בשערה שהן מקרא מועט והלכות מרובות.

69   רש"י מסכת חגיגה דף י עמוד ב. מלאכת מחשבת - שהמחשבה חשבה בדעתו ונתכוון לה, וזה לא נתכוון לה לבנין זה - לפיכך פטור, וזהו רמז מועט, דאילו מלאכת מחשבת בשבת לא כתיבא, אלא במשכן הוא דכתיב, ולפי שסמך בפרשת ויקהל פרשת שבת לפרשת משכן - אנו למדין מלאכת מחשבת לשבת.

70   *Talmud Ha-Igud*, edited by Shamma Friedman, BT *Shabbat Chapter VII with Comprehensive Commentary by Stephen G. Wald* (The Society for the Interpretation of the Talmud, 2007), English section, p. xi.

71   רמב"ם הלכות שבת פרק א הלכה ו. עשה מעשה ונעשית בגללו מלאכה שודאי תעשה בשביל אותו מעשה אע"פ שלא נתכוין לה חייב, שהדבר ידוע שאי אפשר שלא תעשה אותה מלאכה, כיצד הרי שצרך לראש עוף לשחוק בו לקטן וחתך ראשו בשבת אע"פ שאין סוף מגמתו ד להריגת העוף בלבד חייב שהדבר ידוע שאי אפשר שיחתוך ראש החי ויחיה אלא המות בא בשבילו וכן כל כיוצא בזה. וראו משנה ברורה סימן שכ ס"ק נב, כלי - דממילא היין הנסחט הולך לאיבוד כיון שהנקב בדופן החבית בצדה אבל אם היה תחתיו כלי שנוטף בה טיפת הנטיפה [נב] וכן אם היה הפקיקה בסתימת הנקב שלמעלה שהיין הנסחט יורד לתוך החבית בכל זה [נג] הוא איסור דאורייתא להדק או להסיר הפקיקה גם לשיטה זה:

72   See Bavli Shabbat 75a.

73   This is based on a case on Shabbat 103a. See Tosfot there, s.v. לא צריכא דעביד באראעא דחבריה. Furthermore, see SA OH 320:18, and summary comments of Mishnah Berurah to 314:1:11. See, too, the responsum of Eliezer Waldenberg, שו"ת ציץ אליעזר חלק ב, סימן טז ד"ה בעת, בנידוננו, who notes that Ashkenazi practice is to be stringent with *pesik reisheh d'lah niha leih*. However, if the prohibition is not biblical but rather rabbinic, then the rabbis rule leniently in permitting *pesik reisheh d'lah niha leih*. See comments in Magen Avraham to SA OH 314:5.

74   Rabbenu Ḥannanel, Ravad, Rashba, and then Rabbi Karo in the SA, all side with Rabbi Shimon, whereas Rambam follows the stricter position of Rabbi Yehudah. See comments of Ravad to MT, Hilkhot Shabbat 1:7.

75   It is also not evident that creating sparks alone constitutes the act of *mavir* — that may require a "completion" of the labor by the ignition of a combustible material with the sparks.

76   But see discussion of the Ḥazon Ish below. By his reasoning, creating such sparks may be rabbinically banned in the same way that it is rabbinically prohibited to generate sparks by tapping rocks together (presumably a piece of flint and a rock containing iron pyrites). The comparison is unconvincing, since the act of tapping rocks to create sparks is done intentionally and the result is immediately visible, which is not the case with any sparks in an electrical switch. The prevalence of solid-state switches reduces this consideration in any event.

77   I am indebted to the work of Shlomo Zalman Auerbach, *Minḥat Shlomo*, for many of these arguments, and to Michael Broyde and Howard Jachter for their review of 20th century Orthodox responsa in "The Use of Electricity on Shabbat and Yom Tov," *The Journal of Halacha and Contemporary Society* (XXI Spring 1991). The Israeli Zomet Institute also offers a brief article on the subject. Previous Conservative responsa have not offered a comprehensive review of these categories but see Isaac Klein's survey in *A Guide to Jewish Religious Practice* (Jewish Theological Seminary Press, 1979), chapter 5, esp. sections 5 and 11.

78   Unless, that is, the button is equipped as a grama switch that prevents the action from following directly upon the action. See discussion below.

79   See B. Yevamot 117a, Ketubot 52b, Bava Metzia 53b etc. and SA HM 117:3.

80   Lemberg/Lvov, 1828-1906, known by the title of his responsa, Beit Yitzḥak.

81   Beit Yitzḥak 2:31.

82   Minḥat Shlomo, pp. 71-74. Rabbi Auerbach was born, lived, and died in Jerusalem, 1910-1995, Jerusalem.

83   Tzitz Eliezer, 1:20:10. Rabbi Waldenberg was born, lived, and died in Jerusalem, 1915-2006, and was a prominent authority on halakhah and medical ethics.

84   The weakness of the *molid* argument can be readily demonstrated when comparing electricity to water. If one allows water to flow into a container like a pitcher or a glass, one has thereby transformed the container from empty to full and made it useful, even though it will revert to its prior empty state once the water is poured out. By this logic, one would never be allowed to transfer any substance from one container or another on Shabbat.

85   New appliances have often been tested prior to sale as documented on the outside package, though it is possible that any unit may indeed be used for the first time by the consumer. As such, it is better to avoid the initial use of an appliance on Shabbat.

86   Avrohom Yeshaya Karelitz, b. 1878 in Kosava, Belarus, d. 1953 in B'nei B'rak, Israel. His responsa were first published in 1911 (the title חזון איש—vision of a man—alludes to the letters of his name: אברהם ישעיה). His main discussion of electricity occurs in חזון איש לאורח חיים, סימן נ. After reviewing many topics in the Talmud and the medieval commentaries and codes, Rabbi Karelitz states (p. 74) that it is possible that heating the metal filament to the glowing point is a form of cooking, even though there is generally no "cooking after cooking" and the metal returns to its prior state. Even if this heating were considered unintentional and unproductive (*pesik reisha d'lah niḥa lei*), it would still be rabbinically banned, and he supposes that perhaps the heating of the filament is after all necessary for the flow of the current. He also considers the possibility that the generation of sparks would be forbidden as *shvut*, as in the classical case of knocking stones together. Having considered these possible rabbinic prohibitions, he focuses on the biblical ban on "building" as the most compelling argument against using electricity on Shabbat.

87   See Bavli Shabbat 47a, where assembling the whitewasher's pole is considered "forbidden but exempt." That is, this type of loose construction is not really considered to be complete building since the pole is constantly being adjusted but should nevertheless be avoided. מיתיבי: המחזיר קנה מנורה בשבת - חייב חטאת, קנה סיידין - לא יחזיר, ואם החזיר - פטור. אבל אסור. See Rashi's comments there.

88   According to Rabbis Broyde and Jachter, Moshe Tendler claimed during a lecture at Yeshivah University that Moshe Feinstein agreed with Rabbi Auerbach and rejected the Ḥazon Ish's view. See their article, p. 15, note 25.

89   In his volume, ירושלמי כפשוטו (Jewish Theological Seminary, 2008), pp. 138-139, Saul Lieberman observes that the Yerushalmi applies the category of מכה בפטיש to the final stage of any *melakhah*, even cooking, שהרי בכל אב מלאכה יש גם מכה בפטיש.

90   רש"י מסכת שבת דף קב עמוד ב. המכה בפטיש - גם הוא באבות מלאכות, והוא בלעז פי"ק +פטיש גדול+, שמפוצץ בו את האבן מן הסלע לאחר שחוצב את האבן סביב, ומבדיל מן ההר קצת - הוא מכה בפטיש מכה גדולה, והיא מתפרקת ונופלת, וזהו גמר מלאכה של חוצבי אבן, וכל הגומר בשבת מלאכה - תולדת מכה בפטיש היא.

91   תוספות מסכת שבת דף קב עמוד ב. מכה בפטיש - פי' בקונטרס שמפוצץ בו את הסלע לאחר
שחצבה ואין נראה לר"י דבמשכן לא הוה בנין אבנים ולא שביק תנא גמר מלאכה דכלים דהוה במשכן
ונקט מכה בפטיש דאבן דלא הוה במשכן אלא נראה לר"י דהאי מכה בפטיש היינו מכוש אחרון שמכה על
הכלי בשעת גמר מלאכה.

92   רמב"ם הלכות שבת פרק י הלכה טז. המכה בפטיש הכאה אחת חייב, וכל העושה דבר שהוא גמר
מלאכה הרי זה תולדת מכה בפטיש וחייב, כיצד המנפח בכלי זכוכית והצר בכלי צורה אפילו מקצת הצורה
והמגרד כל שהוא והעושה נקב כל שהוא בין בעץ בין בבנין בין במתכת בין בבלים הרי זה תולדת מכה בפטיש
וחייב, וכל פתח שאינו עשוי להכניס ולהוציא אין חייבין על עשייתו.

93   We shall return to this text below when considering Joel Roth's understanding
of it.

94   שו"ת ציץ אליעזר חלק ו סימן ג. איסור מתקן מנא, דבפתיחת הכפתור ועשיית החיבור בין
החשמל שבבטריה לבין הממברנה הוא מכניס רוח - חיים - זרמי בבל חלקי המכונה אשר מקודם לכך
נחשבה כגוף מת שכל רוח אין בה ובמכשיר בכך את המכונה שתהא ראויה למילוי תפקידה וא"כ אם מצינו
גבי הערכת שעון בשבת שהרבה מהפוס' אוסרים זה מדינא ולכמה מהם נוגע הדבר באיסור תורה משום
מתקן מנא.

95   Ben Ish Ḥai (Yosef Ḥaim of Baghdad, 1834-1909) permitted the use of a bicycle
within a *karmelit* on Shabbat for the sake of communal need, with the provision that the
tires not be filled or repaired on Shabbat. Within an *eruv*, he permits even the recreational
use of bicycles. See שו"ת רב פעלים חלק א - אורח חיים סימן כה.

96   I thank Joshua Heller for raising this question. Recharging batteries uses
electrical current to create a chemical reaction within the dry cell, which is a durable
change, and therefore could be considered a derivative form of *melakhah*. Discharging
batteries (by use of any battery-powered appliance) also causes a chemical change in
the cell, though this is, of course, not the goal of the user. We could consider the latter
activity to be a form of *kilkul*, a physical breakdown that is not productive and is therefore
not forbidden. In any event, recharging batteries would at least be forbidden under the
rabbinic category of *hakhanah*, preparing on Shabbat for use after Shabbat. See the
Wikipedia article, Battery (Electricity), especially the section on secondary batteries.

97   See the Wikipedia article, Electrical Resistance and Conductance. "Near room
temperature, the electric resistance of a typical metal increases linearly with rising
temperature, while the electrical resistance of a typical semiconductor decreases with
rising temperature .... At lower temperatures (less than the Debye temperature), the
resistance of a metal decreases as T_5 due to the electrons scattering off of phonons.
At even lower temperatures, the dominant scattering mechanism for electrons is other
electrons, and the resistance decreases as T_2."

98   See Bavli Shabbat 40b, אמר רב יהודה אמר שמואל: אחד שמן ואחד מים, ואחד סולדת בו
and .- אסור, אין יד סולדת בו - מותר. והיכי דמי יד סולדת בו? אמר רחבא: כל שכריסו של תינוק נכוית
Rashi there, s.v. סולדת.

99   See SA OH 318:4, and 253.

100   See SA OH 318:3.

101   Considered to be an entrance to *gehenna*-cooking with hellfire! See Bavli
Shabbat 39a. In this sense cooking with hot water really is *toledat ha-eish*, a derivative
form of cooking with fire.

102   See MT Hilkhot Shabbat 9:3, SA OH 318:3, and Magen Avraham there, SK 10.
These sources all permit putting food out to warm in the sun but forbid placing raw food
on a surface that has been heated by the sun to a temperature high enough to cook it.

103   Moshe Feinstein, Igros Moshe, OH 3:52. Born in Belarus in 1895, he immigrated

to the United States in 1936 and lived in New York City until his death in 1986.

104   Michael Pitkowsky has brought to my attention that Yitzhak Yosef (the son of Ovadia Yosef) writes in Yalkut Yosef, Shabbat, Vol. 3: 318 (p.150) that the use of a microwave oven should not be considered *toledat bishul* and is therefore permitted even for the sake of person who is ill but not in danger, חולה שאין בו סכנה. However, in his summary volume Kuntros Yalkut Yosef, Hilkhot Shabbat (B'ni Brak 5768), at 318:42 (pp. 201-2) Rabbi Yitzhak Yosef rules stringently that the microwave should be considered like *toledat eish* and be forbidden. Regarding חולה שאין בו סכנה see Bavli Shabbat 30a, and 61a-b.

105   Elliot Dorff explained (in personal correspondence) that the use of microwave ovens to warm solid, previously cooked foods on Shabbat might be permissible using the precedent of warming food in the sun. I understand this argument but am concerned that the distinction between liquid and solid foods is untenable, especially since such ovens heat foods unevenly, bringing some parts (especially with fat) to a boiling point (which for liquids is considered the biblically banned activity of *bishul* even if previously boiled) while leaving others relatively cool. To avoid error, I think it necessary to refrain from using microwave ovens on Shabbat even for warming foods. The same can be said of some stove covers (i.e., a *blech*) which have a flame beneath them and can get very hot. It is best on Shabbat to use a warming tray or oven that is designed for warming but not cooking food.

106   A brief note regarding the use of hot water taps is unavoidable here. Many appliances such as the Instant Hot tap, or a water cooler that draws water into a boiling chamber, cannot be used without directly boiling water, and are therefore probibited on Shabbat, but not Yom Tov. Much has been written about the various forms of residential and commercial boilers, and whether drawing hot tap water in a sink or shower necessarily causes cold water to flow into the boiler and there to be heated or cooked. The most prudent policy is to avoid drawing hot water through taps on Shabbat. Yet in most cases, the use of hot water will not immediately cause cold water to be heated. Rather, as with all cases of appliances equipped with thermostats (opening a refrigerator door or even an external house door, which accelerates termperature exchange), we may view these acts of heating as *grama*, or indirect, and therefore permissible.

107   Our primary focus is not on cooking food, but it is worth mentioning the question of whether the traditional restriction on מוליד אור, creating new fire on Yom Tov, is relevant to electrical appliances. Since we will argue below that electricity is not itself considered fire, there would seem to be no reason to limit Yom Tov use of electrical ovens to the adjustment of heat, and not permit turning such ovens and ranges on or off. There is no creation of charcoal when the element is turned off, as is indeed the case with gas ovens and ranges as well, nor is the metal improved by being "doused" as is the case in the Talmudic examples of צרוף. In his comments to Shabbat 42a, Rashi explains that dousing a metal ember is forbidden by the rabbis as a form of *shvut* but is permitted in order to eliminate a public hazard. This would seem even more so in our case, where there is no benefit to cooling the metal heating element. As such, it would seem to be permissible to turn off an electric oven or range, but if there is no danger to leaving the oven or range on, then it should be left undisturbed for the sake of differentiating between holy and profane times. Gas ranges should be lit on Yom Tov by the transfer of an existing flame. Turning off a gas burner on Yom Tov to avoid danger from an untended flame (or gas, should the flame go out) would seem to be permitted, since there is no creation of charcoal from the act of extinguishing. Still, if it can be left on safely, then the gas stove should not be extinguished even on Yom Tov, for the sake of emphasizing the sacred nature of the day. In general, the codes teach us to do whatever food preparation is possible prior to Yom Tov, in order to amplify the experience of rest on the holiday.

108   Abraham ben David (b. Narbonne 1120 – d. Posquieres 1198), pp. 1125-1198.

109   Compact fluorescent lights can achieve 75% greater efficiency than incandescent lamps, though the savings is somewhat reduced in colder climates, where the inadvertent heat by-product of ILBs needs to be replaced by furnaces or other heating systems. Many buildings today have no incandescent light bulbs. Federal legislation originally scheduled to go into effect in January 2012 (but subsequently delayed) would raise efficiency requirements for new light fixtures to the point that ILBs will be effectively banned. There is a backlash from political conservatives who resent government regulations promoting energy efficiency, as chronicled in this March 12, 2011 *New York Times* article. Still, it appears that the combined effect of energy savings, legislation, and improvements in lighting technology will end the dominance of the incandescent light bulb soon. CFLs are dropping in price and acquiring desirable qualities such as reduced size, dimmability, and warmer colors. LEDs are increasingly capable of replicating the warm spectrum of light favored by many consumers. See "Bulb In, Bulb Out," by Andrew Rice in *The New York Times Magazine* (June 3, 2011).

110   Some fluorescent lamps do employ a bi-metalic filament that is warmed as part of the starting mechanism, but the process and purpose are both distinct from the heating of metal for the purposes of softening and annealing, which are rabbinically prohibited as *bishul*. See again the Wikipedia article, Compact fluorescent lamp.

111   Goldberg notes that the four-step progression הבונה והסותר המכבה והמבעיר functions as a chiastic structure of A-B/B-A, or constructive-destructive-destructive-constructive.

112   This is apparently linked to one of the few other labors explicitly forbidden in the Torah, gathering firewood.

113   For example, there is no ban on opening or closing a window shade to brighten or darken a room. Likewise, it is not prohibited to use a mirror intentionally to control reflections of visible light.

114   In settings where it is unsafe or forbidden to light a fire, such as in hospitals and nursing homes where oxygen and other combustible gases are present, we allow patients to say candle-lighting blessings over electric lamps so that they not feel excluded from the experience of remembering Shabbat and other holidays. Still, this practice is clearly understood to be a concession to safety concerns and is not the ideal performance of the ritual.

115   At the end of the life of an incandescent bulb, the filament crumbles and leaves a powdery detritus. This is not comparable to charcoal, is not accessible, and is not likely to be generated in any given use since bulbs are designed to last for hundreds or even thousands of hours. As such, this creation would certainly be unintentional.

116   Translation by Philip Blackman.

117   In his comments to this Mishnah, Maimonides explains that it reflects the minority view of Rabbi Yehudah–that even if the person has no intention to harden the metal, but just to warm some water, it would be prohibited as an unintentional act.

פירוש המשנה לרמב"ם מסכת שבת פרק ג משנה ד. ומיחם שפינה ממנו מים לא יתן לתוכו מים כל עיקר מפני שהוא מצרף, ומשנה זו לר׳ יהודה ודבריו דחוין, אלא מותר לתת לתוכו מים ואפילו לא השאיר בו מן המים כלום דדבר שאין מתכוין הוא ומותר.

118   On annealing, see http://en.wikipedia.org/wiki/Annealing_%28metallurgy%29.

119   רמב"ם הלכות שבת פרק ט הלכה ו. המחמם את המתכת ב עד שתעשה גחלת הרי זה תולדת מבשל.

120   רמב"ם הלכות שבת פרק יב הלכה א. השגת הראב"ד: הרי זה תולדת מבעיר וחייב. א"א ולמה

לא משום מבשל כמו סיבתא לאתונא דמרפא רפי והדר קמיט (שבת עד), והמחמם את הגחלת והמצרפו במים אינו מכבה אבל הוא מכה בפטיש שגומר את חסומו מ"מ חיוב אין בו דצרוף דרבנן הוא.

121 Indeed, there may be no difference at all, since softening the metal is the first stage of the annealing process. More likely, it seems that Rambam is differentiating *melakhot* based upon the subsequent actions of the metalworker. See this Wikipedia article on annealing metals: http://en.wikipedia.org/wiki/Annealing_%28metallurgy%29

122 He even makes a pun on this, saying in a note that it is possibly מעביר ("transmitting" fire) rather than truly מבעיר (burning). Later in life, he admitted to doubts about the equation of incandescence with burning.

123 He tells a remarkable story in footnote 3 of a conversation he had as a young man with the Ḥazon Ish on the permissibility of heating water with an electrical coil, and how the Ḥazon Ish offered a new theory to prohibit the use of such an element because it is "pregnant" with fire, to which Rabbi Auerbach responded with shocked disbelief. Rabbi Auerbach returns to this subject in a later responsum, where he admits that his claim that electrical lighting is fire is not impregnable and suggests a much lower-level rabbinic prohibition on making light, based on a case in Bavli Beitza 33b of a person generating sparks by tapping rocks together. Yet even that was for the purpose of starting a real fire, which is not our case:

שו"ת מנחת שלמה תנינא (ב - ג) סימן כו. ואף אם נאמר שאין מבעיר במתכת כמו שאין בו כבוי מה"ת, אבל מדרבנן בודאי יש בו מבעיר כמו שבכבויו יש איסור דרבנן אם יעשה זה בשבת, וממילא אם נתחבר הזרם להמכונה מעט לבאורה דמי לטלטול נר הדולק דאפילו ר"ש מודה בזה, ולא מבעי בזה לצי"ג וצו"מ, ואף שיש בו גם שאר חלקים - הנה גם בנר יש בו חלקים שונים וכולם בסיס להאור (שבת מ"ז), ואם עושה זה בשבת יש בו ג"כ משום מוליד אור אם הברזל נתאדם וגרע ממוציא אור מעצים ואבנים (ביצה ל"ג ע"ב), דהתם הוצאת האור אינו בבלל מבעיר כיון שאין המלאכה מתקיימת עד שמדליק מזה קיסם או נייר והרי הדלקה ביו"ט מותרת והוצאת האור בעצם הוי רק מוליד ואחר כל הפלפול שהיי בזה פשוטו דהוא דרבנן, אבל הכא מוליד האש שיש בו קיום ותועלת מצד עצמו כי כח הזרם והלבן אחוזים ודבקים זב"ז.

124 Born February 3, 1918, in Poland, originally known as Shlomo Gorontzik (still at the time of this article), he immigrated to Palestine with his parents in 1925 and served as rabbi of the IDF and eventually as chief rabbi of Israel from 1973-1983. He died on October 29, 1994. See his biography in *Encyclopedia of Founders and Builders of Israel*, volume 3:1482 [Hebrew]. I thank Michael Pitkowsky for directing me to this source.

125 סיני: ירחון לתורה, למדע ולספרות, כרך כד, חוברת א-ו, "הדלקת החשמל בשבת," ע' קמח-קנב וע' שכו-שכט.

126 תלמוד ירושלמי מסכת יומא פרק ג דף מ טור ג. ה"ה. תני אמר רבי יהודה עשתות של ברזל היו מרתיחין אותן מערב יום הכיפורים ומטילין לתוך הצונין כדי שתתפוג צינתן ולא נמצא מכבה ביום הכיפורים אלא מסבור סבר רבי יוסי ורבי שמעון שינהם אמרו דבר אחד נימר רבי יוסי ורבי יודה ורבי שמעון שלשתן אמרו דבר אחד אלא אלא מיסבור סבר רבי יודה שאין תולדת האש כאש אלא כאש כיני רבי יודה סבר מימר שאין תולדת אש כאש ורבנן סברין מימר תולדת אש כאש ויחם לו חמין

127 תלמוד בבלי מסכת פסחים דף עה עמוד א. אמר ליה גחלת של עץ לא עץ אי איצטריך קרא לרבוי. כי איצטריך קרא - לגחלת של מתכת. וגחלים של מתכת לאו אש הוא? והא גבי בת כהן, דכתיב +ויקרא כא+ באש תשרף ואמר רב מתנה: פתילה של אבר היו עושין לה! - שאני התם, דאמר קרא באש תשרף תשרף לרבות כל שריפות הבאות מן האש, וכל שכן אש עצמה.

128 See above for Rabbi Auerbach's explanation of this rabbinic prohibition.

129 Avram Israel Reisner, personal communication, April 4, 2011.

130 רמב"ן שמות פרק לה (ג) לא תבערו אש בכל מושבותיכם ביום השבת - ענין הכתוב הזה ודאי לאסור בשבת גם מלאכת אוכל נפש, כי אמר כל העושה בו מלאכה יומת, ופירש שלא יבערו גם אש לאפות לחם ולבשל בשר כי האש צורך כל מאכל. והוצרך לומר כן מפני שלא אמר "העושה בו כל מלאכה" כאשר

אמר בעשרת הדברות (לעיל כ ט) לא תעשה כל מלאכה, ואמר מלאכה סתם, והיה אפשר שנוציא מן הכלל מלאכת אוכל נפש, כי כן נאמר בחג המצות (דברים טז ח) לא תעשה מלאכה ואין אוכל נפש בכלל, ולכך הזכיר בפירוש שאף אוכל נפש אסור בו: וכלשון הזה מצאתי במדרש (מכילתא כאן) רבי נתן אומר לא תבערו אש בכל מושבותיכם ביום השבת למה נאמר, לפי שהוא אומר ויקהל משה את כל עדת בני ישראל, שומע אני יהא רשאי להדליק לו את הנר, להטמין לו את החמין, ולעשות לו מדורה בשבת, ת״ל לא תבערו אש בכל מושבותיכם ביום השבת. וזה קרוב למה שאמרנו, שלא היו מלאכות הללו שהן הנאה לגופו בכלל איסור הראשון. ורצה רבי נתן לומר שלא הוצרך הכתוב לאסור אפייה ובשול ושאר צרכי אוכל נפש, שכבר אמר להם את אשר תאפו אפו ואת אשר תבשלו בשלו (לעיל טז כג), אבל עדיין כל מלאכות שאדם נהנה בהן ואינן עושין אלא הנאה לגוף כגון הדלקת הנר ומדורה ורחיצת גופו בחמין יהיו מותרות כי זה מעונג שבת, לכך נאמר לא תבערו אש לאסור הכל:

131   For the former explanation see Rashi on M. Shabbat 7:2 at Bavli 73a, s.v. *Mikhabeh u-mavir;* for the latter explanation see Tosfot at 94a, s.v. Rabbi Shimon. See Eider, *Halachos of Shabbos,* V. 1, p. 1, note 42.

132   See again, Andrew Rice, "Bulb in, Bulb Out," in *The New York Times Magazine,* June 3, 2011 (mentioned above in note 84): "What we term 'light' does not exist without the human eye—it's just radiation," says Nadarajah Narendran, a professor at the Lighting Research Center at Rensselaer Polytechnic Institute. "Your eye is a detector that senses this energy coming to it at different wavelengths." Those wavelengths are perceived as colors. Natural light combines all the colors of the visual spectrum. When people complain that fluorescent light is cold, what they're really describing is an overload of radiation at the bluish wavelengths." Of course, the same could be said of sound—that it does not exist without an ear to translate the sound waves into discernible noise, and the brain to interpret this noise so that it resolves into speech, music, etc.

133   In their 2023 CJLS responsum regarding transportation on Shabbat, Mordecai Schwartz and Chaim Weiner discuss Mishnah Beitza 4:7, which prohibits producing fire from wood, stones, *or water*—a puzzling detail that has occupied interpreters for centuries. The consensus follows Rambam, that the Mishnah refers to a technique of bottling water in glass and using it as a lens to concentrate sunlight and ignite wood. Rabbis Schwartz and Weiner have an alternative suggestion—that the Mishnah may refer here to capturing biolumiscent sea creatures in a bottle and using it as a kind of lamp, a method apparently mentioned in medieval Mediterranean contexts. This seems quite speculative, and the standard interpretation of this Mishnah reinforces our understanding that the rabbis were concerned with igniting fire on Shabbat, generally for the purpose of cooking.

134   http://faculty.biu.ac.il/~fixeled/

135   http://www.shaalvim.co.il/torah/maayan-article.asp?id=491 הדלקת נורות לד בשבת (LED)

136   לפי כל האמור לעיל נראה לכאורה שאין איסור מהתורה או מדברי חכמים בהפעלת נורת LED בשבת. ברם הטכנולוגיה שנורות אלו מבוססות עליה אינה מצטמצמת בתחום התאורה. גם מסכי מחשב, מקרנים, ערוצי תקשורת, מכשירי טלפון נייד ומכשירי חשמל נוספים עושים שימוש במוליכים למחצה להעברת אותות חשמליים ולהדלקת צגים. נראה שהדילמה שעמדה בפני חכמי הספרדים לפני שישים שנה עומדת ביום בפנינו בבואנו לדון בשאלת הדלקת LED בשבת.

137   If light is caused to shine on a photo-sensitive surface such as a plant, a photographic film, or a digital light sensor, then there would be a resultant derivative *melakhah* such as *zorea* or *koteiv*, but not *mavir*.

138   See this article from the Zomet Institute: http://www.zomet.org.il/Eng/?Category ID=198&ArticleID=409&SearchParam=grama. Such devices have been integrated into products such as the Amigo, an electric scooter used for frail or disabled individuals to get around on Shabbat.

139   Grama is a solution to mitigate other potential violations of *melakhah* as

well. Indeed, the use of thermostats to control the temperature of refrigerators, ovens, etc. means that one need not assume that they are directly responsible for causing the heating or cooling mechanism to operate each time the door is opened.

140   See Wikipedia articles, "Cathode Ray Tube," and "Liquid Crystal Display." See also the article, "Refresh Rate." The newest display technology is organic light emitting diodes (OLED), which are already in commercial production. These displays have many benefits, such as their ability to project darker blacks, their low energy consumption, and the fact they can be embedded in materials that are extremely thin, pliable and shatterproof. See the Wikipedia article, "Organic Light-Emitting Diode."

141   For an overview on digital memory, see the Wikipedia article, "Computer Memory."

142   See comments of Saul Lieberman, *Tosefta Kifeshutah*, Shabbat, p. 173, note 25, citing Rambam, R' Hai Gaon and Maggid Mishneh. This apparently means סימנים, namely a symbol such as א to indicate 1, ב to indicate 2, etc.

143   תלמוד ירושלמי מסכת שבת פרק יב דף יג טור ג :ה"ג.

144   ראבי"ה ח"א - הלכות עירובין סימן שצא ד"ה ומה שדימה. See discussion by Boaz Cohen, op cit., p.142.

145   Joshua Heller notes other places in rabbinic literature such as B. Megillah 9a and Gittin 19b where Greek is listed with Hebrew as one of the two languages of significance. He reasons that this was either due to the influence of the Septuagint or to the general hegemony of Greek as the legal language of the Eastern Mediterranean (personal communication).

146   Mishnah Shabbat 12:4 lists כתב בדיו, בסם, בסיקרא, בקומוס, ובקנקנתום, ובכל דבר שהוא רושם, "Whether he wrote in ink or in orpiment or in red paint or in gum ink or in vitriol-ink or with anything whatsoever that marks..." (Translation by Philip Blackman, V. 2, p. 61).

147   Blackman translation, V.2, p. 62.

148   See comments of Saul Lieberman, *Tosefta Kifeshutah*, Shabbat, pp. 173f and note 27, citing Tanḥuma (Warsaw) Ki Tissa #33. Rabbi Lieberman considers whether the primary labor is not restricted to רושם, inscribing letters, and whether כותב, writing, is not a derivative labor. In his Mishneh Commentary (12:3), Rambam says that according to Rabbi Yose, רושם and כותב are discrete categories of labor, with the former including the inscription of a solitary letter on the first ten and the twentieth of the planks in the tabernacle, whereas writing requires two letters (planks 11-19, יא-ט).

149   אין הכותב חייב עד שיכתוב בדבר הרושם ועומד כגון דיו ושחור וסקרא וקומוס וקלקנתוס וכיוצא בהם, ויכתוב על דבר שמתקיים הכתב עליו כגון עור וקלף וניר ועץ וכיוצא בהם, אבל הכותב בדבר שאין רישומו עומד כגון משקין ומי פירות, או שכתב בדיו וכיוצא בו על עלי ירקות ועל כל דבר שאינו עומד פטור, אינו חייב עד שיכתוב בדבר העומד על דבר העומד, וכן אין המוחק חייב עד שימחוק כתב העומד מעל דבר העומד.

150   Still, this labor is forbidden by the rabbis and therefore may not be performed ab initio, לכתחילה.

151   Arnold Goodman, "May a Shabbat Service be Taped?" passed by the CJLS on September 13, 1989, with 9 in favor, 11 opposed, 1 abstaining. Published in *Proceedings of the CJLS, 1986-1990*. I have been unable to find Rabbi Goodman's expression כדרך עשייתן in halakhic literature except in Beit Yosef, OH 475, in reference to making *shmurah matzah*. The sole usage in reference to Shabbat (according to the Bar Ilan Responsa Project 16+) is from the entry in the *Encyclopedia Talmudit* entry on "Koteiv." But the distinction here is that writing כלאחר יד demonstrates inferior intention—if you really wanted to write, you'd

do it the normal way, with your dominant hand. These sources do not imply that writing with a new and superior technology is כלאחר יד. In any event, even such secondary writing methods are considered אסור דרבנן, rabbinically forbidden.

אנציקלופדיה תלמודית כרך כו, כותב [טור תקפח] ב. הכתיבה. הכותב בשבת שחייב, הרי זה דווקא אם כתב כדרך הכותבים- כשאר [טור תקצה] מלאכות שבת, שאין חייב עליהן אם עשאן שלא כדרך עשייתן אלא כלאחר-יד* - שאין חייבים בשבת אלא על "מלאכת-מחשבת*", וכתיבה שלא כדרך הכותבים - כשאר מלאכות הנעשות שלא כדרכן - אינה "מלאכת מחשבת".

152   Mayer Rabinowitz and Dvora Weisberg, "Tape Recording and Photography on Shabbat," approved by the CJLS on Nov. 7, 1984, 7-7-3, printed in *PCJLS 1980-85*, p. 247, and also Gordon Tucker's responsum, "The Use of a Remote Audio/Video Monitor on Shabbat," which was approved on February 8, 1989, 16-1-2. Rabbi Tucker and Rabbi Dorff also filed a concurring opinion to Rabbi Goodman, agreeing with his conclusions (restricting permission to cases where non-Jews operated the camera), but not with his substantive arguments: "On Recording Shabbat and Yom Tov Services."

153   Many synagogues have installed automated audio and video recording devices for bar and bat mitzvah services, or trained non-Jewish staff to turn on this equipment on Shabbat. These activities are somewhat problematic. Congregations that have this practice should take special caution to avoid instructing the staff about the recording on Shabbat itself, and the equipment should be hidden from view, lest the congregation come to think that it is permissible to operate recording devices on Shabbat.

154   We cannot here address the extremely complicated subject of אמירה לנכרי\ אינו יהודי that has evolved in a radically more lenient direction than evidenced in early rabbinic literature. See Jacob Katz, *The Shabbos Goy: A Study in Halakhic Flexibility*, (Jewish Publication Society, 1989).

155   Avram I. Reisner, "On the Exodus (and Genesis) of Shemot" approved by the CJLS on December 5, 2003, 14-3-4. See esp., pp.13-14.

156   Joel Roth, "*Melakhah U'Shevut*," p. 15.

157   See the Wikipedia article, Electronic Paper. I am intentionally avoiding discussion of specific products such as the Kindle, Nook, iPad etc. since the technology is rapidly evolving. Rather I am focusing on halakhic issues which will hopefully remain relevant even for the next generation of consumer products.

158   For such a suggestion see Rabbi Gil Student's blog, http://torahmusings. com:2010:12:e-readers-and-shabbos:.

159   This finding would apply to the current market leaders, Apple's iPad and Amazon's Kindle, as well as similar products.

160   Wikipedia article, "Magnetic Stripe Card."

161   May the New York Metropolitan Authority's unlimited Metrocards and OMNY cards be used on Shabbat? On the one hand, each swipe does not result in a reduction in account value, and thus is not the equivalent of a cash transaction. On the other hand, the system does make a notation of the time and location of each swipe and the serial number of the card, since it does not permit repeated swipes in quick succession (there is an eighteen-minute interval imposed between uses). See http://www.mta.info/metrocard/ easyuse.htm#sub. There is also an issue with carrying the card unless the entire route is within the *eruvim*. Moreover, the use of a Metrocard involves a commercial transaction of the sort associated with the workweek, and therefore seems inconsistent with *shvut*, the obligation to rest, as discussed in Section II. Should use of the transportation system become permitted, the experience of resting in place on Shabbat as declared by the Torah, אל יצא איש ממקמו ביום השביע would quickly be forfeited. Certain cities, such as

Berlin, have train systems that do not require users to handle a fare card (though they are supposed to be kept on one's person and presented upon demand by an official). Some Shabbat-observant people use the Berlin system without any activity that could be deemed *melakhah*, justifying the use of transportation as a necessity for maintaining a Jewish community. Rabbi Gesa Ederberg of the Oranienburger Strasse Synagogue wrote a 2002 responsum on this subject for the Schechter Institute in Jerusalem, titled נסיעה בתחבורה ציבורית בשבת בעיר ברלין, and found grounds for permission to use the Berlin system because of its particular features. The halakhic issues involved in using public transportation on Shabbat are less severe than those pertaining to operating private automobiles with internal combustion engines. We discuss a possible exception for the use of public transportation by disabled people on Shabbat in Section III below.

162   There has been substantial public controversy about precisely what types of data are kept by hotels on their key cards. Generally, these are encoded with the guest's name, check-in and check-out date, and access permission for their room and other areas of the property. Some hotels allow guests to use the key card to charge services to their room bill, although the key merely verifies that a valid credit card authorization is on file with the hotel. From the 2011 incident regarding Dominique Strauss-Kahn at the Sofitel Hotel in New York, we learned that key cards are also capable of recording times of entry. See the *New York Times* article: http://www.nytimes.com:2011:05:18:nyregion/strauss-kahns-hotel-key-may-tell-tale-in-sex-case.html?_r=2&hp. If so, swiping key cards could be considered a form of writing; however, the time-stamp data is not available to the user, and is not necessarily done in each case. As such, we can rule leniently and consider such a recording to be an unintentional act, דבר שאינו מתכוון. In fact, hotel doors are programmed to record information about each entry, the times a door is left ajar, etc.; if key cards are banned, then so, too, might be the opening of a door altogether, even to exit.

לא גזרו שבות במקום סכנה.   163

164   I thank Aaron Alexander for encouraging me to add reference to this important concept. See, among many others, Hiddushei Ha-Ramban, Ha-Rashba and Ha-Ritba to B. Shabbat 130b. In the codes, see Rambam, Hilkhot Shabbat 6:9-10, Tur OH 586, Beit Yosef OH 307:5,

165   Joel Roth, "*Melakhah U'Shevut*: A Theoretical Framework," p. 5f, and Isaac Klein, p. 79 of *A Guide to Jewish Religious Practice* (see note 3 for bibliographic information). Rabbi Roth cites Israel Lipshitz (1782-1860) as the first proponent of this theory in his Mishnah commentary, Tiferet Yisrael.

166   I thank Rabbi Roth for correcting my use of the common pronunciation, *makeh b'patish*. There should not be a *dagesh* in the *peh* following the prefix. Regarding the use of this category for general acts of "labor," see the aggadah found at Yerushalmi Shabbat 7:2, 9b-c. It seems to me, based on this source's phrasing, "for whatever *melakhah* they could not find an *av*," that these Tannaim were depending upon an oral tradition that identified certain actions as *melakhah*, without specifying which of the 39 categories was involved. They used *makeh b'fatish* as their general category. However, we do not have an authoritative oral tradition defining electricity as *melakhah*, so Rabbi Roth's declaration requires an external argument about the nature of *melakhah*. Moreover, *makeh b'fatish* involves an action that leaves a permanent result (i.e., a hammer blow), which is not the case in shining a light. See Rambam's commentary on Mishnah Shabbat 12:1 and our discussion above.

167   It is notable that this text does not even refer to *melakhah*, but speaks instead of *ma'asekha*, "your acts."

168   Interestingly, the motive clause that begins למען, "so that," focuses not on the Israelites' experience of rest and reflection, but on those subservient to their control—

servants, foreigners, and beasts of burden. If Shabbat is, as Deuteronomy 5:14 claims, a "reminder of the Exodus from Egypt," here it serves to break not our memory of enslavement, but our taste for power over others. Of course, the Exodus association may be completely foreign to this biblical author, for whom Shabbat is purely a day of rest.

169   In reference to Shabbat: Ex. 16:23, 31:15; 35:2, and Lev. 23:3. In reference to Yom Kippurim, Lev. 16:31 and 23:32; with reference to New Year Lev. 23:24 (see discussion below), and regarding Sukkot, Lev. 23:39.

170   Rambam lists it as positive command, 154 in his *Book of Mitzvot*:

והמצוה הקנ"ד היא שצונו שנשבות בשבת והוא אמרו ית' (משפטי' כג) וביום השביעי תשבות. והנה נכפל צווי מצוה זו פעמים (נרשם בעמ' קנז). ובאר לנו יתעלה (עשה"ד) שהשביתה מן המלאכות היא חובה עלינו ועל בהמתנו ועבדינו. והנה התבארו משפטי מצוה זו במסכת שבת ובמסכת יום טוב:

See also *Sefer Mitzvot Gadol*, at Negative Mitzvah 75, and in *Sefer Ha-Ḥinukh*, Command 85 (he lists it separately for each of the festivals as well).

171   *Proceedings of The Rabbinical Assembly*, 1945.

172   מכילתא דרבי ישמעאל, בא - מסכתא דפסחא פרשה ט.

173   Translation by Jacob Lauterbach, *Mekhilta D'Rabbi Yishmael* (Jewish Publication Society, 1983).

174   ספרא אחרי מות, פרשה ה. (ט) אין לי אלא מלאכה שחייבים על מינה כרת מלאכה שאין חייבין על מינה כרת מנין שלא יעלה באילן ושלא ירכב על גבי בהמה ולא ישוט על המים, ולא יספוק ולא יטפיח ולא ירקד תלמוד לומר שבתון שבות, אין לי אלא שביתת רשות, שביתת מצוה מנין לא יקדיש ולא יעריך ולא ולא יחרים ולא יגביה ולא יתרום ולא יעשר ולא יקדיש ולא יגרש ולא ימאן ולא יחלוץ ולא ייבם ולא יפדה נטע רביעי ומעשר שני, תלמוד לומר שבתון שבות.

175   מכילתא דרבי שמעון בר יוחאי, פרק לה. אין לי אלא מלאכות ותולדות שהן אסורין מנין לאיסור שבות ת"ל כל מלאכה יכול יהו חייבין חטאת על איסור שבות ת"ל מלאכה המלאכה המיוחדת חייבין עליה ואין חייבין על איסור שבות. מנין למקח וממכר והלואה ופקדונות שנקראו מלאכה ת"ל אם לא שלח ידו במלאכת רעהו (שמ' כב י). מנין לדינין ולטעגות ולערעורין ולכל מעשה בית דין שנקראו מלאכה ת"ל כניניהו ובניו למלאכה החיצונה על ישראל לשוטרים ולשופטים (דה"א כו כט). מנין לקדושין ולגטין שנקראו מלאכה ת"ל אבל העם רב והעת גשמים והמלאכה לא ליום אחד ולא לשנים (עז' י יג). מנין לחשבונות שנקראו מלאכה ת"ל ויבא הביתה לעשות מלאכתו (בר' לט יא).

176   See Gilat, פרקים בהשתלשלות ההלכה, pp. 94-97. Ramban's sermon is found in *Kitvei Ramban*, ed. Ḥaim Dov Chavel (Mosad HaRav Kuk, 5742), V. 1, p. 211.

177   This dynamic is particularly challenging for congregational rabbis, who are frequently approached by congregants on Shabbat to discuss synagogue business, lifecycle events, and many other matters. The standard reply of "this is far too important to discuss informally; please call the office on Monday to make an appointment," can be amplified by reference to Shabbat, and in this way, to reinforce the value of *shvut* for the rabbi and for the congregation.

178   Rambam, MT Laws of Shabbat 23:4; Shulḥan Arukh, OH 338:1. See, too, Ethan Tucker's essay on this subject, accessible at: http://www.scribd.com/doc:23861930:Instruments-on-Shabbat-Full-Paper.

179   MT Shabbat 24:4. See the story of Rabbi Shimon bar Yohai chiding his mother for talking too much on Shabbat:

תלמוד ירושלמי מסכת שבת, פרק טו דף טו טור ב :ה"ג. רבי חנינא מדוחק התירו לשאול שלום בשבת אמר רבי חייב בר בא רבי שמעון בן יוחי כד הוה חמי לאימיה משתעיא סגין הוה אמר לה אימא שובתא היא....

180   שם, תלמוד ירושלמי מסכת שבת פרק טו דף טו טור א :ה"ג.

181 תלמוד בבלי מסכת שבת, דף קיג עמוד ב. בשלמא כולהו - לחיי, אלא שלא יהא הילוכך של שבת כהילוכך של חול מאי היא? כי הא דאמר רב הונא אמר רב, ואמרי ליה אמר רבי אבא אמר רב הונא: היה מהלך בשבת ופגע באמת המים, אם יכול להניח את רגלו ראשונה קודם שתעקר שניה - מותר, ואם לאו - אסור. מתקיף לה רבא: היכי ליעביד? ליקף - קמפיש בהילוכא, ליעבר - זימנין דמיתווסן מאני מיא, ואתי לידי סחיטה! אלא: בהא, כיון דלא אפשר - שפיר דמי. אלא: כדבעא מיניה רבי מרבי ישמעאל ברבי יוסי: מהו לפסוע פסיעה גסה בשבת? אמר לו: וכי בחול מי הותרה? שאני אומר: פסיעה גסה נוטלת אחד מחמש מאות ממאור עיניו של אדם. ומהדר ליה בקידושא דבי שמשי.

182 Pesikta Rabbati 116b and Y. Shabbat 15b.

183 הרהורים מותרים. See Bavli Shabbat 113b and 150a, among many other places, including the Shabbat song, מה ידידות.

184 The rabbis came to understand a "public domain" as a large but bordered location that could hold the entire population of Israel as it was in the desert. See Rashi on Shabbat 5a: לדגלי מדבר - וכל מלאכות דבשבת ממשכן גמרי לקמן, מדנסמכה פרשת שבת לפרשת משכן בויקהל. Since there are few such locations, most places where one might carry do not invoke the biblical prohibition, but rather a rabbinic ban on carrying in a כרמלית, an intermediary domain that is neither private nor fully "public." This narrow definition of the public domain is not fully evident in the Bavli (see Shabbat 5a-6a and 98a-99b) or the early codes such as MT Shabbat 14:1. See comments of Maggid Mishnah there, and Ritba, חידושי הריטב"א מסכת שבת דף ו עמוד א. וי"ל שלא אמר רבי יוחנן אלא במקום שאין בוקעים בו ששים רבוא כדגלי המדבר, and Tur OH 345 with comments of Beit Yosef at 345:7. For a full exposition of the understanding of רשות הרבים in contemporary society, see the responsum of Mishneh Halakhot 15:126.

185 As Gordon Tucker has pointed out, the common dichotomy of דאורייתא and דרבנן, biblical and rabbinic law, is misleading since so many of the rules declared "biblical" by the rabbis are not, in fact, clearly stated in the Bible. That is to say, "biblical" law is actually rabbinic! And, we would add, "rabbinic" law is, in a sense, biblical—since the rabbis understood Deuteronomy 17:11 to be a biblical foundation for their own authority: עַל פִּי הַתּוֹרָה אֲשֶׁר יוֹרוּךָ וְעַל הַמִּשְׁפָּט אֲשֶׁר יֹאמְרוּ לְךָ תַּעֲשֶׂה לֹא תָסוּר מִן הַדָּבָר אֲשֶׁר יַגִּידוּ לְךָ יָמִין וּשְׂמֹאל: On this verse, see Bavli Berakhot 19b, and our discussion of the principle in Elliot Dorff, Daniel Nevins, and Avram Reisner, "Homosexuality, Human Dignity, and Halakhah," approved by the CJLS on December 6, 2006. Nevertheless, the two categories of "biblical" and "rabbinic" do have significance within the halakhic system. Whether the rabbis believed that their understanding of biblical law was original to the intent of the Torah, or whether they applied this category only to laws that they themselves considered to be essential, is immaterial for the result. Biblical law has greater authority than rabbinic law, even if it is the rabbis who declare and define these laws.

186 The extrapolation of a ban on business discussions is mentioned in the comments of David Kimḥi (1160-1235) to Isaiah 58:13. See also, Bavli Shabbat 113 a-b, and 150a.

187 B. Eruvin 104a.

188 See, for example, Mishnah Shabbat 22:6 regarding the ban on ancient spa treatments, which is explained in the comments of Bartenura and Tosfot Yom Tov as *uvdin d'ḥol*. In Bavli Beitza 28a, the rabbis discuss the ban on using a butcher's scale on Shabbat, even for a permitted purpose, and explain it under this rubric. Michael Pitkowsky alerted me to an extensive treatment of this concept, though I have not yet had the opportunity to examine it:

קוסמן, אדמיאל, תפקידה המרכזי של קטגוריית איסורי "עובדין דחול" בטיעוניו ההלכתיים של ה"חתם סופר" כנגד תקלות הרפורמה בשימוש במכשירי הטכנולוגיה המתפתחת בשבת וביום-טוב. משפט והיסטוריה, תשנ"ט, 101-75.

189 מדרש אגדה (בובר) שמות פרק לא. שבת וינפש. שבת ממלאכה וינפש ממחשבה:

190 For a similar example, electric carts and cars do not involve combustion, and indeed, may not directly involve any form of *melakhah*. Yet their operation can lead to the need for maintenance and may facilitate carrying in a public domain and traveling beyond the Sabbath limits (such concerns are far greater with an electric car than with a wheelchair). Operators may be required to carry a license and to engage in commercial activity as part of the operation, which involves the third category of *shvut* listed above. All these concerns would argue for a rabbinic ban on the use of electrical vehicles as שבות under the rubric of גזירה שמא, a protection against violating Shabbat, unless a countervailing halakhic imperative such as human dignity supersedes them, as discussed below. Those who accept the 1950 CJLS minority position permitting people to drive to synagogue in a gas-powered car would be justified extending this permission to electric cars.

191 See Mekhilta D' Rabbi Yishmael, Bishalaḥ, Vayisa # 5, ed. Hurwitz, p. 170.

192 On the general permissibility (not on Shabbat) of participating in a minyan through remote connection, see Avram I. Reisner's responsum, "Wired to the Kadosh Barukh Hu: Minyan Via Internet," which was approved by the CJLS on March 13, 2001, and the next chapter of this volume.

193 This subject is endlessly complex and subjective. Is watching a sporting event (either in person or projected) compatible with keeping Shabbat? What about listening to a free musical or dramatic performance in the park? Such questions resist straightforward answers from the legal literature. Aside from the objective matters of avoiding *melakhah*, it is up to individuals and their spiritual guides to determine how to balance sacred and secular pleasures on Shabbat.

194 See I Maccabees 2:40-41, Josephus, *Antiquities* 12:6:2, Tosefta Eruvin 3:7, Sifre Devarim 203, and discussion in Goldenberg, "The Jewish Sabbath..." pp. 431-33.

195 B. Yoma 85a. See also Mekhilta D' Rabbi Yishmael, Ki Tissa:

מכילתא דרבי ישמעאל, כי תשא - מס' דשבתא פרשה א ד"ה פרשת כי. כבר היה רבי ישמעאל ורבי אלעזר בן עזריה ורבי עקיבא מהלכין בדרך, ולוי הסדר ורבי ישמעאל בנו של רבי אלעזר בן עזריה מהלכין בדרך אחריהם, ונשאלה שאלה זו בפניהם, מנין לפיקוח נפש שדוחה את השבת; נענה רבי ישמעאל ואמר, הרי הוא אומר, +שמות כב א+ אם במחתרת ימצא הגנב, ומה זה הוא, ספק שבא לגנוב ספק שבא להרוג, והרי דברים קל וחומר, ומה שפיכות דמים, שמטמא את הארץ ומסלקת את השכינה, הרי היא דוחה שבת, קל וחומר לפיקוח נפש, שדוחה את השבת; נענה רבי אלעזר בן עזריה ואמר, מה מילה שאינה אלא אחד מאבריו של אדם דוחה שבת, קל וחומר לשאר כל גופו, אמרו לו, ממקום שבאת, מה להלן בודאי אף כאן בודאי; רבי עקיבא אומר, אם דוחה רציחה את העבודה שהיא דוחה שבת, קל וחומר לפיקוח נפש שדוחה השבת. - רבי יוסי הגלילי אומר, כשהוא אומר, אך את שבתותי תשמורו, אך חלק, יש שבתות שאתה דוחה, ויש שבתות שאתה שובח. - רבי שמעון בן מנסיא אומר, הרי הוא אומר, ושמרתם את השבת כי קדש היא לכם, לכם שבת מסורה, ואי אתם מסורין לשבת. - רבי נתן אומר, הרי הוא אומר, ושמרו בני ישראל את השבת לעשות את השבת לדורותם, חלל עליו שבת אחת, כדי שישמור שבתות הרבה.

196 Even ספק נפשות, avoiding risk to health, is a valid excuse for performing otherwise forbidden labor. See Bavli Shabbat 129a, Rambam MT Shabbat 2:1 and 2:15; SA OH 128:10 and YD 263:2 (and Rema considering and dismissing the idea that this leniency is limited to protecting women).

197 For a comparison to the New Testament's synoptic Gospels traditions justifying violating Shabbat to heal and to pick produce for immediate consumption, see discussion in Goldenberg, "The Jewish Sabbath..." pp. 423-24, esp. notes 53, 54.

198 The first evidence of this latitude is found in Mishnah Rosh HaShanah 2:5.

חצר גדולה היתה בירושלים ובית יעזק היתה נקראת ולשם כל העדים מתכנסים ובית דין בודקין אותם

שם וסעודות גדולות עושין להם בשביל שיהו רגילין לבא בראשונה לא היו זין משם כל היום התקין רבן גמליאל הזקן שיהו מהלכין אלפים אמה לכל רוח ולא אלו ולא בלבד אלא אף החכמה הבאה לילד להציל מן הדליקה ומן הגייס ומן הנהר ומן המפולת הרי אלו כאנשי העיר ויש להם אלפים אמה לכל רוח:

199   תלמוד בבלי מסכת יומא דף פה עמוד ב. אמר רב יהודה אמר שמואל: אי הואי התם הוה אמינא: דידי עדיפא מדידהו, +ויקרא יח+ וחי בהם - ולא שימות בהם.

200   See comments of Beit Yosef to Tur OH 307:

אבל התוספות כתבו שאסור לומר לו להביא שום דבר וכו'. בפרק קמא דגיטין (ח: ד"ה אע"ג) ובפרק מרובה (ב"ק פ: ד"ה אומר) וכן כתוב בהגהות פרק ו' (אות כ, ד"ק ה"י) בשם סה"ג (סמ"ג עשין כח, קטו ע"ג) שפסק רבינו יצחק דדוקא משום מילה התירו דחיא שבת התירו אמירה לגוי או משום ישוב ארץ ישראל דבר שאין בו אלא משום איסור שבות אבל משום מצוה אחרת כגון להביא ספר תורה דרך כרמלית וכה"ג אסור לומר לגוי לעשותו עכ"ל וזהו דעת רבינו שכתב בסימן של"ח (קיב) שאבי העזרי (ראבי"ה סי' תשצו) התיר לומר לגוי לנגן בבלי שיר בחתופת דאמירה לגוי במקום מצוה שרי ואני כתבתי למעלה שאין להתיר אמירה לגוי אלא אלא בדבר שהוא דוחה דוחה שבת כגון מילה עכ"לּ. וכן נראה שהוא דעת הרשב"א שכתב בתשובה (ח"א סי' רצז, תשט) שאין אומרים בשבותין זו דומה לזו ואין לנו בהם אלא מה שהתירו בפירוש שהרי לעיתים מתירין אותם מחמת דבר אחר שירארה קל שמעלה וכתבם בשבת בערכאות של גוים מפני קנייתו בית בארץ ישראל ולעיתים מעמידין אותם אפילו במקום כרת החמור כהזאה ואזמל (פסחים צב.) עכ"ל (וכ"כ בדרכי משה סימן של"א בשם הר"ן פרק חבית (סא. ד"ה ובמקום) ומגיד משנה פרק ו' דשבת (ה"ט)):

201   B. Brakhot 47b; Sukkah 30a; BK 94a. See esp. Tosfot to Sukkah 9a, s.v. ההוא מביעי ליה.

202   For a discussion of this concept, see the CJLS responsum by Elliot Dorff, Daniel Nevins, and Avram Reisner, "Homosexuality, Human Dignity, and Halakhah," esp. pp. 10-16.

203   שו"ת ציץ אליעזר חלק ו סימן ו. הפעלת מבונת חרשים לשבת.

204   Pamela Barmash mentioned audio induction loop equipment that is used to assist people with cochlear implants and hearing aids to hear more effectively in noisy settings, by transmitting the audio signal on an FM channel to a receiver worn on the body, which amplifies the desired audio. See http://en.wikipedia.org/wiki/Audio_induction_loop.

205   Much has been written about the use of elevators on Shabbat. There are many mechanical systems involved and increasingly sophisticated electronics as well. Even systems set up for Shabbat operation have been challenged on the grounds that the elevator weighs its occupants and includes other safety features such as electronic eyes to prevent passenger injury, and is, thus, not truly an automatic device. From our perspective, the elevator is a repetitive device that does not effect any durable change, nor does it transport occupants from one domain to another. As such, it does not generally involve *melakhah*. That said, there may be the generation of logs and the recording of video from security cameras in the elevator that could meet our standard of derivative writing. Because these processes are not intended by the passenger, are generally not even noticed, and because the data is not accessible to him or her, these actions may be considered permitted as *davar she'aino mitkavein*. Some might consider the use of elevators to be impermissible under the rubric of *shvut*, but such rabbinic limits would be subject to competing values, as discussed below.

206   See the discussion at B. Brakhot 31b, in which a person who observes a fast on Shabbat (in response to a bad dream according to Tosfot, citing Rabbeinu Ḥannanel and Midrash Tehillim) is held "liable" for ignoring Shabbat delight:

תלמוד בבלי מסכת ברכות דף לא עמוד ב. ואמר רבי אלעזר משום רבי יוסי בן זמרא: כל היושב בתענית בשבת - קורעין לו גזר דינו של שבעים שנה, ואף על פי כן חוזרין ונפרעין ממנו דין עונג שבת. מאי תקנתיה? אמר רב נחמן בר יצחק: ליתיב תעניתא לתעניתא.

207   ילקוט שמעוני ישעיהו רמז תצו. וקראת לשבת עונג, אמר רב יהודה אמר רב כל המעניג את
השבת נותנים לו משאלות לבו שנאמר והתענג על ה' ויתן לך משאלות לבך, עונג זה איני יודע מהו כשהוא
אומר וקראת לשבת עונג הוי אומר זה עונג שבת, במה מעניגו אמר רבי יהודה בריה דרבי שמואל בר שילת
משמיה דרב בתבשיל של תרדין ובדגים גדולים ובראשי שומין, ורב חייא בר אסי אמר רב אפילו בדבר מועט
ולכבוד השבת עשאהו הוי עונג.

208   See Responsa of the Rif, #317, and many others such as the Rashba, I: 127,
who minimizes the application of *oneg Shabbat* to modify even a minor violation such
as tithing at dusk: ואם איתא כדברי התוספות היכי דחי עונג שבת איסורא דאוריתא? והלא אפילו בין
השמשות לא התירו הפרשה גופא משום עונג שבת

209   The medieval sages debate whether the biblical prohibition of *bal tashḥit* refers
only to the destruction of fruit-bearing trees, or includes all forms of waste. If the former,
then the broader ban on *bal tashḥit* is of rabbinic origin. See the entry in the *Encyclopedia
Talmudit*:

אנציקלופדיה תלמודית כרך ג, [בל תשחית] עמוד שלו טור 1. ונחלקו ראשונים: יש סוברים שבכל דבר
עובר על בל תשחית מן התורה, וכן אמרו: מנין אף למשטר הימנו אמת המים, תלמוד לומר: לא תשחית
את עצה, בכל דבר, היינו שמושך את אמת המים מן העיר שלא יהיה להם מים לשתות. ויש סוברים שעל
שאר דברים שמלבד אילנות מאכל אינו לוקה אלא מכת-מרדות* מדבריהם, שמן התורה אין האיסור אלא
באילנות, וחכמים הם שאסרו להשחית כל דבר.

210   Obviously, walking also avoids all the *melakhot* involved in driving on Shabbat,
such as burning fuel, carrying, and traveling beyond the *teḥum*. Plus, it is a healthy activity.

211   I thank Miriam Berkowitz for reminding me of this text and its applicability
to our discussion.

212   See also this gloss of Meir ben Yekutiel of Rothenburg in *Hagahot Maimainiyot*:

הגהות מיימוניות הלכות יום טוב פרק א. שהרי הכבוי הוא הכנה מפני שגורם להם להיות טובים להדלק
ולאחוז בהן האור.

213   This concept is found frequently in the Talmud, starting with B. Pesaḥim
15b, 20b and 55b. Abbaye states, להפסד מרובה - חששו, להפסד מועט - לא חששו, "they were
considerate of a major financial loss, but not of a minor loss." The debate then regards
whether the sages didn't also consider a minor loss as cause for leniency in a variety of
halakhic restrictions. Yet there is a broad view that *shvut* prohibitions are not superseded
by concerns for financial loss. See citations in *Encyclopedia Talmudit* s.v. *ḥefsed merubah*,
note 20.

214   Rema, SA OH 339:4. As Baruch Frydman-Kohl pointed out to me, there were
other grounds for leniency in this case, such as the timing at dusk (בין השמשות) and the
concern that the couple be able to engage in the mitzvah of procreation.

215   הכנה, or preparation, is another established form of *shvut*. See the discussion in
B. Beitza 2b, Eruvin 38b-39a, the commentaries there, esp. Tosfot, and in the codes, e.g.,
SA OH 416:2. As Rabbah says,

אמר רבה: התם - משום הכנה. דתניא: +שמות ט"ז+ והיה ביום הששי והכינו - חול מכין לשבת, וחול
מכין ליום טוב, ואין יום טוב מכין לשבת, ואין שבת מכינה ליום טוב.

216   Mishnah Eruvin 10:13; Bavli Pesaḥim 65a, Beitza 11a; Rambam MT Shabbat
21:27; Korban Pesaḥ 1:16, 18 etc. See Tosfot to Eruvin 102b s.v. והעליון, and comments of
Arukh HaShulḥan to OH 306:7.

217   See Rambam MT Shabbat 6:9.

218   We should avoid asking non-Jewish guests and friends to perform Shabbat tasks
for us, since this is halakhically problematic and can become a חילול ה' or "desecration

of the divine Name," since it makes it appear that Jews don't really accept the limits of Shabbat and are prepared to use non-Jews to get their work done. These concerns are diminished when non-Jews are regularly employed for daily jobs that include tasks of *shvut*. The Torah's vision of a Sabbath that extends to non-Jewish employees should remain our ideal.

219   טור אורח חיים סימן שמב. כל שבות דרבנן מותר בין השמשות לצורך מצוה כגון כדי ליטול עירובו המונח בכרמלית או לעלות מאחריו באילן או ליטול ממנו לולב המונח עליו או שהיה טרוד ונחפז לעשר פירות בין השמשות וכ"ב הר"י שמותר לומר לעכו"ם ביהש"מ להדליק הנר:

220   See Bavli Shabbat 126b-127a. Tur (OH 333) suggests that if a large group of guests requires such accommodation that each person clear the space for himself:

טור אורח חיים סימן שלג. מי שיש לו אורחין בשבת ואין לו מקום להכניסם או שאין לו מקום לבה"מ ויש לו אוצר תבואה יכול לפנותו בשבת כדי להכניס האורחין או לפנות מקום לבה"מ אבל שלא לצורך מצוה אסור לפנותו וכיצד מפנהו היה האוצר גדול מפנה ממנו ה' קופות היה שם ה' קופות מפנה מהם ד' אבל כולו לא יפנה שמא יבא להשוות גומות וכשמפנה אלו ד' או ה' קופות לא יחלקם בקופות קטנות להוליכם בהרבה פעמים כדי להקל המשוי מפני שמרבה בהילוך ואוושא מלתא טפי ואלו ד' וה' קופות שמפנה היינו לאורח א' ואם באו לו הרבה מפנה בשיעור הזה לכל אורח ואורח ובלבד שלא יפנה אחד לכולם דאיכא טירחא יתירתא אלא כל אחד יפנה לעצמו:

221   See B. Shabbat 30a, 61a and Rambam MT Shabbat 2:10 with commentaries there. This concept is also invoked to justify leniency in other contexts, such as permission not to sleep in the Sukkah for a person who is ill but not endangered. See B. Sukkah 25a-26a.

222   For example, OH 254:7, and comments of MB at S.K. 44:

משנה ברורה סימן רנד ס«ק מד (מד) שיתחוב בו - וה"ה דיכול להוציא במקל דכ"ז הוא דרך שינוי ונראה [מג] דע"י א"י מותר להוציא אף ברחת [הוא הכלי שאנו מוציאין בו הפת בחול]:

223   Pamela Barmash raised such questions in the first reading of this paper at the CJLS session on May 24, 2011.

224   Abraham Joshua Heschel, *The Sabbath* (New York: Farrar, Straus and Young, 1951), p. 28. I have substituted the gender neutral "our" for the original "man" in "man's progress."

225   As noted above, I believe that this restriction applies also to reheating previously cooked foods with an electric heating element or microwave oven on Shabbat, since it is impossible to differentiate between "warming" and "cooking." In contrast, warming trays and drawers are designed specifically to warm food and do not raise food above about 180 degrees F. I recognize that some microwave ovens may make more precise warming possible, and that the matter is open to interpretation. Because cooking food is a biblical prohibition and the line between warming and cooking is very fine, I believe that caution is the wisest policy, ספק דאורייתא לחומרא.

226   I discuss the importance of physical presence without digital distraction in creating religious communities, in my *New York Times* contribution to "Room for Debate," published September 8, 2011: http://www.nytimes.com/roomfordebate/2011/09/08/will-online-faith-communities-replace-churches/seeing-god-in-others-faces.

NOTES TO CHAPTER 5

VIRTUAL MINYAN WHEN PHYSICAL GATHERINGS ARE UNSAFE

1   There are numerous responsa from the early modern period related to enforced stays in a *lazzaretto*, which was a common occurrence for Jewish travelers. Sample questions include whether one is obligated to place a *mezuzah* on the door, given that the stay is longer than 30 days; whether it is possible to establish an *eruv ḥatzerot* to allow carrying between buildings on Shabbat; whether goods stored during the term of quarantine may be presumed to remain kosher, despite being outside of Jewish supervision; and tragically, whether a parent may reinter a child who died during quarantine and was buried by the gentile authorities.

2   Historian Federica Francesconi speculated that this *lazzaretto* could have been in Corfu, an important port between Venice and the Ottoman Empire that contained two Jewish communities (Venetian and Greek) in the 18th century (personal email communication). Then again, it could have been at any Italian port. In his memoir, *Maagal HaTov*, Rabbi Azulai mentions his own quarantine in Livorno.

3   בלאזאריטו שנוהגים בעריים האל אם יש ב' כתות שם שאינם יכולים ליגע זה בזה ויש ששה בבית א' וד' בבית אחר והם חלוקים במספרם כמשפט שמעתי מרב אחד אהובינו נר"ו שנסתפק הן בעודנו שם עם הד' יכולים להיות לפני פתח הבית ויצטרפו לעשרה כיון שרואים זה את זה או אינם מצטרפים ולי ההדיוט נראה לפי מה שכתבנו דמצטרפים דהרי אלו אינם יכולים לבא בבית והשומר עמם בשדה לפני הפתח וגם אשר בבית לא יוכלו לצאת חוץ כי המקום צר בחוץ וגם הוא מעבר לרבים ובכי האי גונא דאינם יכולים להיות ביחד מטעם המלך ושרי המדינות וכבר השתדלו אלו הד' לבא נגד הפתח ומראים להם פניה' הוי"ל כמראה פניו דרך חלון דמצטרף והכא נמי דבוותא וכל שכן הוא כי לא אפשר בשום פנים להיות יחד ולא קרב זה אל זה וכיון דאיכא כמה פוסקים נראה לסמוך עליהם ולא יתבטלו מ' יום מלהתפלל בצבור ולא ישמעו קדיש וקדושה ומה וכו כי אפי' בוארנאדאדו ועזרת נשים כתבנו בעניותנו דכל שהוא טורח קצת לירד לבהכ"נ והם מראים להם פנים יש לסמוך לומר דמצטרפים וכמש"ל וכ"ש וק"ו בנדון זה.

4   שערי תשובה סימן נה. [טו] בית. עבה"ט וכ' בשיורי כנה"ג עליות סגורות בבותל גמור אלא כלונסאות גבוהות עשרה ולמטה יש חצר גדולה שפונים אלי עליות ורואין זא"ז אין מצטרפין והביאו הא"ר ובמטה יוסף ח"ב סי' י"ג כתב דמצטרפין וכן עמא דבר ובמלכי בקודש דחה דבריו ובמח"ב משמע דמסכים ג"כ להשכנה"ג וכתב שכ"כ בשו"ת זרע אמת ע"ש ומ"מ כתב שאם שעומדים שם בעליות או בעזרת נשים אינו בנקל לירד למטה לבה"כ ומשתדלי' להראות להם פניהם מלמעלה יש לסמוך להקל, וכתב עוד במח"ב בלאזירט"ו (ר"ל מקום ששומרים מפני עיפוש אויר ר"ל קורין קאנטרמן) שיש שם ב' כתות ששה בבית אחד וד' בבית אחר ואין יכולים ליגע זה בזה נסתפק חכם אחד אם הד' יכולים להיות לפני פתח הבית ויצטרפו לעשרה כיון שרואין זא"ז וכתב כיון דאלו אין רשאים ליכנס לפנים והשומר עמם בשדה לפני הפתח וגם אשר בבית לא יוכל לצאת חוץ כי המקום צר מבחוץ וגם מעבור לרבים ואלו הד' משתדלים לבא אל הפתח ומראים להם פניהם ה"ל כמראה פנים דרך חלון דמצטרף וכ"ש הוא כיון דא"א בשום פנים להיות יחד וק"ו הוא מדינא דלעיל לסמוך על הפוסקים שלא יתבטלו יום מלומר קדיש וקדושה ע"ש:

5   חשוקי חמד ברכות דף כא עמוד ב. כל דבר שבקדושה לא יהא פחות מעשרה לצרף ל"קדיש" בבית העלמין אנשים העומדים רחוק.

NOTES TO CHAPTER 6

TRIAGE AND THE SANCTITY OF LIFE

1   The following responsum reflects my approach to the question but is followed by a consensus *p'sak din* with Elliot Dorff. While our approaches differed, in the end we were able to agree on most major policies. In addition to Dorff, I acknowledge the help of my father and teacher, Michael A. Nevins, MD, Michael Paasche-Orlow, MD, JTS Chancellor Arnie Eisen, JTS Assistant Professor Yoni Brafman, and CJLS colleagues Toby Schonfeld, Jeremy Kalmanofsky, Avram Reisner, and Pamela Barmash.

2   There have also been efforts to make more efficient use of scarce resources, as in the support of multiple patients connected to a single ventilator. See J Herrmann, et al., "Shared Ventilation in the Era of COVID-19: A Theoretical Consideration of the Dangers and Potential Solutions." *Respiratory Care*, May 6, 2020. Israeli rabbi Asher Weiss wrote a responsum permitting the connection of a second patient to the respirator in the expectation of saving two people, even if there is some risk to the first. See אשר מנחת הנשמנה במכונת חולים שני שיתוף 'ר ,הקורונה בתקופת. Thanks to Jason Rogoff for this source.

3   Lisa Rosenbaum, "Facing COVID-19 in Italy — Ethics, Logistics, and Therapeutics on the Epidemic's Front Line," *New England Journal of Medicine*, March 18, 2020. She shares a "a hypothetical scenario involving two patients with respiratory failure, one 65 and the other 85 with coexisting conditions. With only one ventilator, you intubate the 65-year-old."

4   Douglas White and Benjamin Lo, "A framework for rationing ventilators and critical care beds during the COVID-19 pandemic," *Journal of the American Medical Association*, March 26, 2020. As of late April 2020, 53% of American hospitals had not established triage policies. See Armand H. Matheny Antommaria, et al., "Ventilator Triage Policies During the COVID-19 Pandemic at U.S. Hospitals Associated with Members of the Association of Bioethics Program Directors," *Annals of Internal Medicine*, April 24, 2020.

5   Ezekiel J. Emanuel, et al., "Fair Allocation of Scarce Medical Resources in the Time of COVID-19," *New England Journal of Medicine*, March 28, 2020.

6   See also prior articles: "Public health: who should get influenza vaccine when not all can?" E.J. Emanuel, A. Wertheimer, *Science* 2006;312:854 5; "Standing by our principles: meaningful guidance, moral foundations, and multi-principle methodology in medical scarcity." G.C. Persad, A. Wertheimer, E.J. Emanuel, *American Journal of Bioethics*. 2010 Apr;10(4): pp. 46-8; "Principles for allocation of scarce medical interventions." G.C. Persad, A. Wertheimer, E.J. Emanuel, *Lancet*, 2009 Jan 31; 373 (9661): pp. 423-31.

7   This common claim is advanced by Ezekiel, et al., even if clinicians requiring artificial ventilation are unlikely to return to medical practice soon. If the pandemic is protracted, then surviving doctors and nurses may return to practice; knowledge of their protected status may bolster their resolve.

8   In their article at least the authors do not define the key terms "likely/unlikely" and "recover." Does "likely" mean a greater than 50 percent chance? Does "recover" mean full restoration to pre-infection function, or being stabilized to allow weaning from ventilation and discharge from the ICU and perhaps the hospital?

9   Although a medical worker who requires ventilation will not likely return to clinical work quickly, but they may return to the medical field eventually. Moreover, knowledge that medical workers will receive priority care in a crisis may encourage them

in their inherently risky work. There is no disagreement about priority allocation of personal protection equipment to health care workers. The argument here is more of a "reward" for workers if they fall sick that they will receive priority treatment.

10   As Michael Paasche-Orlow explained, this claim is not realistic. The pandemic was allocated resources unavailable to other types of patients, for example, catheterization for those experiencing heart attack, because the latter is not a contagious condition (personal communication).

11   Here they presumably mean that, by default, patients would be assigned do not resuscitate (DNR) orders, an idea that has been advocated by various researchers. See, "The Importance of Addressing Advance Care Planning and Decisions About Do-Not-Resuscitate Orders During Novel Coronavirus 2019 (COVID-19)." J. Randall Curtis, et al., *Journal of the American Medical Association*, March 27, 2020.

12   Jennifer Senior, "The Psychological Trauma that Awaits our Doctors and Nurses," *New York Times*, Mar. 29, 2020.

13   Ari Ne'eman, "I Will Not Apologize for My Needs," *New York Times*, March 23, 2020.

14   דברים פרק כח, נ. גּוֹי עַז פָּנִים אֲשֶׁר לֹא יִשָּׂא פָנִים לְזָקֵן וְנַעַר לֹא יָחֹן:

15   White and Lo write (7), "A central feature of this allocation framework is that it does not use categorical exclusion criteria to bar individuals from access to critical care services during a public health emergency. There are several ethical justifications for this. First, the use of rigid categorical exclusions would be a major departure from traditional medical ethics and raise fundamental questions of fairness. Second, such restrictive measures are not necessary to accomplish public health goals during a pandemic or disaster; it is equally feasible to assign all patients a priority score and allow the availability of resources to determine how many patients can receive the scarce resource. Third, categorical exclusion criteria may be interpreted by the public to mean that some groups are "not worth saving," leading to perceptions of unfairness and distrust. In a public health emergency, public trust will be essential to ensure cooperation with restrictive public health measures. Thus, an allocation system should make clear that all individuals are "worth saving" by keeping all patients who would receive critical care during routine clinical circumstances eligible, and by allowing the availability of beds and services to determine how many eligible patients receive them."

16   See Andrew Peterson and Jason Karlawish, "Ethics of Reallocating Ventilators in the COVID-19 Pandemic," *The BMJ* 2020;369:m1828, May 12, 2020.

17   Mishnah Horayot claims that a Torah scholar should be rescued before anyone else (including the high priest), but this Mishnah has been nullified in practice. For example, see Yisrael Meir Kagan (following Pri Megadim, OH 240, Eshel Avraham, who writes, וצ"ע בזמן הזה לית תלמיד חכם). Rabbi Kagan states, "there is no one today deserving of special treatment as a Torah scholar" (שער הציון סימן תקמז. מטעם דאין בזמננו דין תלמיד חכם). Rabbis Feinstein and Auerbach, among other 20th-century poskim, confirm this position. The Mishnah prioritizes saving men before women in some situations, and women before men in others, but later Jewish law has abandoned this approach. See discussion by Herschel Schachter, קדימה בהצלת נפשות, who notes that it is not possible to decide whose life is most valuable, and for this reason, the *poskim* do not base themselves on this Mishnah.

18   E. Dorff, esp. pp. 279-298. Other halakhic resources include Aryeh Dienstag, "Rationing During a Pandemic Flu," *Verapoh Yirape* (undated Yeshiva University journal, perhaps 2009, No. 2) and Avraham Steinberg, "Allocation of scarce resources," *Encyclopedia of Jewish Medical Ethics* (Feldheim, 2003).

19   Rabbi Dorff discusses *pikuaḥ nefesh* in his book, pp. 15-18 and p. 328, n.3, but does

not argue there for a quantitative aspect to this mitzvah.

20   See B. Pesaḥim 25b, Yoma 82b, and especially, Sanhedrin 72b-74a. The biblical source is 2 Samuel, chapter 20. There, King David's troops besiege the city where Sheva is sheltering. The rabbinic sources recast the scenario as one of gentile marauders who attack a Jewish caravan and demand one victim.

21   תוספתא מסכת תרומות (ליברמן) פרק ז. סיעה של בני אדם שאמרו להם גוים תנו לנו אחד מכם ונהרגהו ואם לאו הרי אנו הורגין את כולכם יהרגו כולן ואל ימסרו להן נפש אחת מישראל אבל אם ייחדוהו להם כגון שייחדו לשבע בן בכרי יתנו להן ואל יהרגו כולן אמ' ר' יהודה במי דברים אמו' בזמן שהוא מבפנים והן מבחוץ אבל בזמן שהוא מבפנים והן מבפנים הואיל והוא נהרג והן נהרגין יתנוהו להן ואל יהרגו כולן. תלמוד ירושלמי (וונציה) מסכת תרומות פרק ח דף מו טור ב /ה"ד. תני סיעות בני אדם שהיו מהלכין בדרך ופגעו להן גוים ואמרו תנו לנו אחד מכם ונהרוג אותו ואם לאו הרי אנו הורגין את כולכ' אפילו כולן נהרגין לא ימסרו נפש אחת מישראל ייחדו להן אחד כגון שבע בן בכרי ימסרו אותו ולא ייהרגו אמר רבי שמעון בן לקיש והוא שיהא שיהא מיתה חייב כשבע בן בכרי ורבי יוחנן אמר אף על פי שאינו חייב מיתה כשבע בן בכרי. בראשיתא רבה (תיאודור-אלבק) פרשת ויגש פרשה צד. תני סיעה של בני אדם שאמרו להם גוים, תנו לנו אחד מכם ונהרגנו, ואם לאו אנו הורגים אתכם, יהרגו כולם ואל ימסרו נפש אחת מישראל, ואם יחדוהו להן כשבע בן בכרי נותנין ואל יהרגו כולם, אמר רבי יהודה בד"א בזמן שהוא מבפנים והן מבחוץ, אבל הוא מבפנים והן מבפנים, הואיל והוא נהרג והן נהרגים, יתנו להם ואל יהרגו כולם, כגן שהוא אומר ותבוא האשה אל כל העם, [אמרה להם] הואיל והוא נהרג ואתם נהרגים תנוהו להם ואל תהרגו כולכם.

22   רמב"ם יסודי התורה פו'ק ה, הלכה ה. וכן אם אמרו להם עובדי כוכבים תנו לנו אחד מכם ונהרגנו ואם לאו נהרוג כולכם, יהרגו כולם ואל ימסרו להם נפש אחת מישראל, ואם יחדוהו להם ואמרו תנו לנו פלוני או נהרוג את כולכם, אם היה מחוייב מיתה כשבע בן בכרי יתנו אותו להם, ואין מורין להם כן לכתחלה, ואם אינו חייב מיתה יהרגו כולם ואל ימסרו להם נפש אחת מישראל.

23   שו"ת שרידי אש חלק ב סימן לח.

24   פרי מגדים אורח חיים משבצות זהב סימן שכח ס"ק א. מכל מקום אם יש אחד שוודאי מסוכן על פי הרופאים וכדומה, וזה ספק, ורפואה אחת אין מספקת לשניהן, הוודאי דוחה הספק.

25   שו"ת אגרות משה חושן משפט חלק ב סימן עה. אם יש לפנינו שני חולים ושניהם אפשר שיתרפאו בדרך הטבע ממחלות אחרות שאירע להם, אם להקדים החולה ששייך שיתרפא שיחיה יותר משנה שהוא לא אבד חזקת חיים שלו מחולה האחר מאחר שלפי דעת הרופאים לא יחיה יותר משנה שהוא בחשיבות טרפה להרופאים ועוד גרוע שלא יוכל לחיות יותר משנה וטרפה באדם הא שייך שיחיה אפילו הרבה שנים, אבל כשנידון הוא בשומת חיי שלהרופאים לא יהיה יותר משתי שנים אין נוגע שוב כלום להלכה דשניהם שוין לחשיבות דחזקת חיים, ואמירת הרופאים שלא יוכל לחיות לא מגרע כלום החזקת חיים שלו, וליכא בשביל זה דין קדימה וצריך הרופא לילך למי שנקרא תחלה ולמי שקרוב לביתו יותר וכשישווין בזה צריך להקדים לפי סדר מתני' דהורית (י"ג ע"א) ואם לא ידוע זה להרופא יהי' גורל, כן נראה לע"ד.

26   שו"ת מנחת שלמה תנינא (ב - ג) סימן פו. אולם להעביר מכשיר מחולה לאחר שהוא במצב יותר קשה או שיש לשני יותר סיבויים להצלה מסוופקני מאד, כי יתכן דחשיב כאילו הראשון כבר זכה במכשיר והחולה עצמו ודאי פטור מליתן מכשיר שלו לאחר אף אם השני יותר מסוכן, וכן אם כבר התחיל הרופא להתעסק עם חולה מסוכן דכמו שהעוסק במצוה פטור מן המצוה, כך הוא פטור - ואולי אסור - מלהניח את הראשון ולהתעסק עם השני כשעוסק בהצלתן בסכנה אף אם יש יותר סיכוי להציל את השני. אגיד לו נאמנה שאין אני קובע מסמרים בכל מה שכתבתי כי השאלות הן חמורות מאד, ואינני יודע ראיות ברורות.

27   שו"ת משנה הלכות חלק יז סימן קעה.

28   M. Sanhedrin 4:5; Avot DR"N A 31. We acknowledge the troubling fact that classical halakhic literature differentiates between saving Jewish and gentile lives. Both are ultimately to be saved, but the latter is "for the sake of peace" (מפני דרכי שלום). A redemptive (or wishful) reading of this expression sees it not as a form a Jewish diplomacy but of *imitatio Dei*, since God is known as Shalom/Peace, and has mercy over all God's creatures, as should we. In any event, we apply *pikuaḥ nefesh* to all human lives. And as noted above, the hierarchy found in M. Horayot is inoperative.

29   There is a middle example of laundry, and a debate about whether the upstream villagers may use up all the water for laundry since dirty clothes may cause physical

discomfort and perhaps disease. See comments of Ra"N.

30   This permission is not universally held, as shown by Rabbi Auerbach. However, it has support from Rabbi Klein, and accords with rabbinic sources going back to Tosefta that remove the shield of *pikuaḥ nefesh* from people who are deemed terminally ill and beyond rescue with or without this resource.

NOTES TO CHAPTER 7

EARLY CIRCUMCISION FROM MEDICAL NECESSITY

1   Rabbi Elliot Dorff composed a brief chairman's response for the CJLS that largely accords with my findings.

2   Healthy babies delivered at term are typically discharged about 48 hours after vaginal delivery and 96 hours after cesarean delivery. See "New Guidelines for Hospital Discharge of Newborns," *Contemporary Pediatrics,* May 21, 2015.

3   I thank pediatric urologist Zachary Liss, MD, for this information. I inquired with several additional physicians about diagnoses that could medically justify early circumcision. All offered these as hypotheticals, not as actual cases. Urologist Jeffrey Weingarten, MD, imagined a case of a heart defect requiring surgery on the infant; perhaps in such a case, there would be a rush to advance the circumcision. Family physician David Bar-Shain, MD offered that the newborn could be known to be incubating an infection, causing a rush to complete the procedure. These scenarios are unlikely today; it is impossible to know what medical concerns were considered by medieval physicians and rabbis.

4   Rabbi Yehoshua's position may reflect the importance of intention in the assignment of guilt for Shabbat violations. Since the *mohel* did not intend to circumcise the wrong child, he should not be liable for the violation.

5   Responsa of Rashba, Bar Ilan Responsa Project 28, "New responsa from manuscript" #141, Ms. K 499.

6   We ought not to ascribe authorial intent to this cross-reference, since such comments in the Shulḥan Arukh were likely added by a later anonymous editor. See Asher Siev [=Ziv], *Ha-Rema: Rabbi Moshe Isserles, His Life and Work* [Hebrew] (Yeshiva University Press, 1972).

7   Rav Hillel, son of Rav Naftali Zvi Hirtz, was born in Brisk, Lithuania in 5375 (1615). See his "Beit Hillel" comment to YD 262:1.

8   Rabbinic scholars have puzzled over why the medieval sages all followed the ruling here of Beit Shamai, not Beit Hillel, as is customary. It may be that this text has been corrupted, and that the debate was not truly over the requirement for HDB, but only whether it could be performed on Shabbat. See discussion by Isaac Klein, "Hatafat Dam," in *Responsa and Halakhic Studies* (Ktav, 1975), 94-104.

9   This view is explained later by Rabbi Aryeh Leib b. Shmuel Tzvi Hirtz (Poland, b.1630), *Shaagat Aryeh*, Dinei Milah #52; and Rabbi Yaakov Feraji Mahmah (Alexandria, b. ca. 1660), *Responsa Maharif* #47.

10   תלמוד בבלי מסכת ברכות דף ט: עמוד א. וכיון דעבר יומו בטל קרבנו.

11   Rabbinic tradition claims that several biblical heroes, including Adam, Seth, Job, Jacob, Joseph, Moses, Samuel, and Jeremiah, et al., were "born circumcised," and thus also exempt from the mitzvah of brit milah. See Avot D'Rabbi Natan A, chapter 2, appendix 2. This category is different from our case, when the child is born with a foreskin, and is thus obligated in brit milah.

12   Isaac Klein, "Hatafat Dam," in *Responsa*, p. 103. See responsa of Morris Shapiro, "Improperly Circumcised Children and Parents' Synagogue Membership," approved by CJLS, May 18, 1981, David Novak, "The Case of a Jew who was not Circumcised on the Eighth Day," p.64-65 [Hebrew] approved by CJLS on December 15, 1982, and Joel Roth, "*Hattafat Dam Brit*," CJLS minority opinion, March 10, 1983. I thank Micah Peltz and David Fine for the references.

13   The procedure is typically performed with a spring-loaded lancet of the sort used by diabetics for glucose monitoring. According to Dr. Alan J. Green, a certified obstetrician and *mohel*, the loose skin on the shaft just behind the head of the penis is lifted and pinched between two fingers, and the lancet is then applied to produce a drop of blood. A simple bandage will suffice to stop the bleeding. See also the illustrated guide of Dr. Sam Kunin. A colleague mentioned one contemporary rabbi's opinion that the changing of bandages following a medical circumcision is likely later to produce some drops of blood, suggesting that this itself could satisfy the obligation of *hatafat dam brit*. But if the circumcision is performed within 48 hours of birth, it seems highly unlikely that there would still be bleeding six days later when the mitzvah of brit milah becomes active, unless there is a medical complication. This suggestion therefore does not seem helpful to our case.

14   Or, as Rif prefers, וספקא דאורייתא לחומרא. See for example his comments to Ketubot 3b, and many others.

15   I thank Rabbi Avram Reisner for convincing me to reverse my initial position on this subject.

16   This distinction is associated with Rosh, but others are ambivalent, and prefer that the second blessing precede periah, the peeling back of the inner foreskin. See comments of Ta"Z to SA YD 265:1. He adds that if the father also serves as *mohel*, he says both the first and second blessings before cutting.

17   B. Shabbat 137b, s.v. *avi ha-ben omeir*, etc. See also Ta"Z cited above.

18   רא"ש מסכת שבת פרק יט סימן י. ואומר ר"ת ז"ל דברכה זו אינה דוקא על מילה זו שנעשית עכשיו קאי אלא מודה ומשבח להקב"ה שצוה לעשות מצוות זו כשתבוא עוד לידו ותקנו לה מקום זה לגלות ולהודיע דזאת המצוה נעשית לשם הקדוש ברוך הוא ולא לשם מורנא ולא לשם הר גריזים.

19   The former position would be supported by those who argue that the medical circumcision makes it impossible to fulfill the mitzvah of brit milah, and so HDB would not be indicated; David Novak's responsum cited above provides some support for this leniency. The latter position accords with the rabbinic consensus that such a child has not fulfilled the mitzvah of brit milah, that HDB is required, and that rabbis should not assist Jews in the neglect of this essential mitzvah. This position was argued by Rabbi David Lincoln, "Naming of an Improperly Circumcised Child," approved by CJLS, February 15, 1984.

NOTES TO CHAPTER 8

CONTEMPORARY CRITERIA FOR THE DECLARATION OF DEATH

1   I am grateful for special assistance given to me on this project by my father and teacher, Michael A. Nevins, M.D., my friend David Bar-Shain, M.D., and by my physician congregants at Adat Shalom Synagogue, specifically Bruce Silverman, Alex Steinbock, Richard Trosch, who are neurologists, as well as pulmonologists Leonard Rosenthal and Ronald Sherman. The bioethics subcommittee of the CJLS helped me research and sharpen this paper. I thank its chairman, Aaron Mackler, as well as Kassel Abelson, Elliot Dorff, Avram Reisner, Joel Roth, and Elie Kaplan Spitz for their guidance.

2   Sherwin B. Nuland, M.D. *How We Die: Reflections on Life's Final Chapter* (Alfred A. Knopf, 1994), p. 3.

3   For an extended study of this concept, see Michael Fishbane, Ph.D. *The Kiss of God: Spiritual and Mystical Death in Judaism* (University of Washington Press, 1994).

4   See Yechiel Michal Toktzinski, *Gesher Ha-Ḥaim* II:27 (Jerusalem, 1960).

5   Norman Fost, M.D., M.P.H. "The Unimportance of Death," in *The Definition of Death: Contemporary Controversies,* edited by Stuart J. Younger, Robert M. Arnold, and Renie Schapiro (Johns Hopkins University Press, 1999), pp. 161-178.

6   Baruch A. Brody, Ph.D. "How Much of the Brain Must be Dead?" in *The Definition of Death*, pp. 71-82. Derick T. Wade has suggested further expanding the continuum to include patients in a "minimally conscious state." See "The dis-integration of death," in *The Lancet*, Vol. 360 (Aug. 10, 2002), pp. 425-6.

7   See note 90 below.

8   I thank my father, Michael A. Nevins, M.D., for this description.

9   Margaret Lock, Ph.D., *Twice Dead: Organ Transplants and the Reinvention of Death* (University of California Press, 2002), p. 40.

10   See Martin S. Pernick, Ph.D., "Brain Death in a Cultural Context: The Reconstruction of Death, 1967-1981," in *The Definition of Death*, pp. 3-33, and the chapters, "Locating the Moment of Death," and "Making the New Death Uniform," in *Twice Dead* by Margaret Lock, pp. 78-126.

11   American Medical Association and American Bar Association, 1983.

12   For a harsh critique, see "As Good as Dead: Is there really such a thing as brain death?" Gary Greenberg in *The New Yorker* (August 13, 2001), pp. 36-41.

13   For example, see Ronald Cranford, M.D., "Even the Dead are not Terminally Ill Anymore" in *Neurology* 1998: 51:1515-16; D. Alan Shewmon, M.D., "Chronic 'Brain Death,'" in *Neurology* 1998:51:1538-1545; The Hastings Center Report of July-August 2001, and James Bernat, "Refinements in the Definition and Criteria for Death," in *The Definition of Death*. See also, "Brain Death: Still-unresolved issues worldwide," editorial in Neurology 2002:58:9-10 by Michael Swash, M.D. and Richard Beresford, M.D.

14   See Eelco F.M. Wijdicks, M.D., "The Diagnosis of Brain Death" in *The New England Journal of Medicine* 344:16 (April 19, 2001), pp. 1215-1221, and Dr. Fred Plum's protocol.

15   Based on personal conversations with emergency, pulmonology, and neurology specialists. Transplant teams follow separate protocols for determining death before harvesting vital organs.

16   Michael Y. Wang, M.D., Pamela Wallace, R.N., and J. Peter Gruen, M.D., "Brain Death Documentation: Analysis and Issues," in *Neurosurgery*, September 2002, pp.731-736. A similar claim is made by Sam D. Shemie, Christopher Doig and Philip Belitsky in "Advancing toward a modern death: the path from severe brain injury to neurological determination of death" in *Journal of the Canadian Medical Association* 168:8 (Apr. 15, 2003), pp.993-995.

17   Specifically, "the continued hypothalamic secretion of antidiuretic hormone (ADH) sufficient to prevent diabetes insipidus" in patients declared brain dead according to accepted protocol. James Bernat, M.D., in *The Definition of Death*, p. 86. However, Bernat argues that ADH secretion should not be classified as a "clinical function" of the brain, and therefore, is not an impediment to the diagnosis of brain death.

18   See *Twice Dead*; also, Masahiro Morioka, "Reconsidering Brain Death: A Lesson from Japan's Fifteen Years of Experience," in *The Hastings Center Report*, July-August 2001. Also see RD Truog, "Is it time to abandon brain death?" in *The Hastings Center Report* 1997; 27 (1):29-37.

19   See "Really, most SINCERELY dead: Policy and procedure in the diagnosis of death by neurologic criteria," *Views and Reviews, in Neurology* 62 (May 25, 2004), pp. 1683-1686.

20   See Fred Plum, M.D., "Clinical Standards and Technological Confirmatory Tests in Diagnosing Brain Death," in *The Definition of Death*, p. 53. Such a case was described in *The New York Times*, 10:8, 2002.

21   Plum, op cit., p. 39.

22   A more technically precise statement that addressed the issue of confounding factors was published in the *Journal of the American Medical Association* 246 (1981), pp. 2184-86.

23   New Jersey provides the exemption in the original statute; New York does so in a separate regulation.

24   Eelco F.M. Wijdicks, M.D., "Brain Death Worldwide: Accepted fact but no global consensus in diagnostic criteria" in *Neurology* 58 (January 1-2, 2002), pp. 20-25.

25   James L. Bernat, M.D., writes that EEG activity persists in some patients who are "unequivocally determined to be brain dead by accepted tests. This rudimentary EEG activity neither responds to sensory stimuli nor appears to represent coherent brain functioning. Rather, it represents isolated nests of neurons whose random and purposeless cellular electrical activity can be recorded technologically but whose functioning is utterly divorced from that of the organism as a whole." "Refinements in the Definition and Criteria for Death," in *The Definition of Death: Contemporary Controversies* (1999), p. 87. See Fred Plum, MD, in the same volume, pp. 42-43. False negatives are also possible with EEG. EEG is increasingly being supplanted by transcranial Doppler ultrasonography as a confirmatory test of brain death (see below, p. 13).

26   All translations are my own unless otherwise noted.

27   The Talmud Yerushalmi to Yoma 8:5 provides an interesting variant. In this version, the dispute concerns the best method of proving respiratory failure—at the nose or at the diaphragm. Cardiac criteria play no role at all. It is possible that even the Bavli's reference to checking "to his heart" refers to the rising and falling of the chest.

28 MT Hilkhot Shabbat 2:19.

29 SA OH 329:4.

30 Mishnah Berurah, 329:11.

31 In section V, we shall scrutinize Rabbi J. David Bleich's surprising argument that Rashi establishes the primacy of a cardiac standard.

32 MT Hilkhot Eivel, 4:5.

33 Beit Yosef, Yoreh De'ah 339:1. The Talmudic basis is found on Shabbat 151b.

34 Rema to OH 330:5. See Magen Avraham there, note 11.

35 See John M. Efron, *Medicine and the German Jews, A History* (Yale University Press, 2001), pp. 95-104. Margaret Lock also discusses the eighteenth-century panic over premature burial in *Twice Dead*, pp. 66-69. This uncertainty among Jews over proving a diagnosis of death was still a source of concern to Ḥatam Sofer (Y.D. 338). Some contemporary Jews even recalled a *beraita* from Tractate Semaḥhot (288) of a Jewish Rip Van Winkle, who was found alive twenty-five years after burial in a crypt--and who went on to marry and have children! Yet Rabbi Emden and then Ḥatam Sofer railed against viewing this story as a precedent.

36 In his commentary to the Rosh, *Ma'adanei Yom Tov*, Rabbi Lipman HaLevi Heller makes a fine distinction between the description of Eli as heavy, which he believes caused the fall, and elderly, which caused him to die even without his neck being gashed. p. 149a in the Vilna shas.

37 Yoreh De'ah, 370.

38 *Peirush Mishnayot*, Yosef Kapach translation, Mosad HaRav Kuk (5727), III:150.

39 רמב"ם הלכות טומאת מת פרק א. המת אינו מטמא עד שתצא נפשו אפילו מגוייד או גוסס, אפילו נשחטו בו שני הסימנים אינו מטמא עד שתצא נפשו שנאמר בנפש האדם אשר ימות, נשברה מפרקתו ורוב בשרה עמה, או שנקרע כדג מגבו או שהותז ראשו או שנחלק לשני חלקים בבטנו הרי זה מטמא אף על פי שעדיין הוא מרפרף באחד מאיבריו.

40 Because of the laws of *sheḥitah*, a Jew may eat the meat while it still quivers, but a non-Jew is forbidden the flesh based upon איבר מן החי. See Ḥullin 121b, and Tanḥuma (Buber) VaYeshev 6.

41 The Tur confirms this at Yoreh De'ah 22:1:

42 רש"י מסכת חולין דף כח עמוד ב. מאחר שלא הוזכרו ורידין - כלומר אין חיות תלויה בהן ואין צריך להזכירו אלא משום דם למה אתה מצריכו שחיטה.

43 See, for example, B. Shabbat 103a, and many similar sources. We may even discern in the future tense of "he will die" that decapitation leads to death rather than constitutes death.

44 *The Merck Manual of Medical Information, Second Home Edition* (Whitehouse Station, NJ: Merck & Co., 2003) p. 1437.

45 Rashi on B. Sanhedrin 72b s.v. *yatza rosho*. See Susan Grossman, "Partial Birth Abortion and the Question of When 'Life' Begins," p. 6. This responsum was approved by the CJLS, September 17, 2003. A different conclusion about the precise moment of birth was defined by Rabbi Avram Reisner in his responsum, *"Ein doḥin nefesh mipnei nefesh,"* approved by the CJLS on December 19, 2001.

46 For an excellent online resource, see www.braindeath.org/clinical.htm. See also the book, *Brain Death*, edited by Eelco F. M. Wijdicks (Lippincott Williams & Wilkins,

2001), esp. chapter 4.

47   *New England Journal of Medicine* 344:16 (April 19, 2001), pp. 1215-1221. See note 14 above, and his book, *Brain Death* (2001).

48   Andrew Newberg, MD, Abass Alavi, MD, Salina van Rhijn, MD, Adolfo Cotter, MD, and Patrick Reilly, MD, "Radiologic Diagnosis of Brain Death" in *Journal of the American Medical Association* 288:17 (Nov. 6, 2002), p. 2121. The six-hour wait is cited from the Quality Standards Subcommittee of the American Academy of Neurology, published in *Neurology* 45, 1995), pp. 1012-1014. In Michigan, the standard waiting period is 24 hours, according to a personal communication with Dr. Bruce Silverman.

49   See Stephen Ashwal, "Clinical Diagnosis and Confirmatory Testing of Brain Death in Children" in *Brain Death*, edited by Eelco F.M. Wijdicks (Lippincott, 2001), chapter 5. He writes, "the neurologic examination is more difficult to perform and interpret because of the smaller size of the patient, immaturity of certain development reflexes being tested, and pathopshysiologic differences due to the presence of open sutures and fontanels in the neonate and infant."

50   "Clinical Standards and Technological Confirmatory Standards in Diagnosing Brain Death," in Younger, *The Definition of Death*, p. 40.

51   Neurologist Bruce Silverman M.D., who regularly examines patients for brain death, has not ordered the radionuclide test once in the past 15 years (personal communication).

52   See note 47, "Radiologic Diagnosis of Brain Death."

53   V. Singh, JP McCartney, JC Hemphill 3rd, "Transcranial Doppler Ultrasonography in the Neurologic Intensive Care Unit," in *Neurology* (India), June 2001, Suppl. 1:S 81-9.

54   W. Mel Flowers, Jr., MD and Bharti R. Patel, MD, "Persistence of Cerebral Blood Flow After Brain Death," in *Southern Medical Journal*, (April 2000) Vol.93, No.4, 364-370, and in an earlier article, "Accuracy of Clinical Evaluation in the Determination of Brain Death" in *Southern Medical Journal* (Feb. 2000) Vol. 93, No. 2, pp. 203-206.

55   *Brain Death* (2001), p. 82.

56   Neurologist Richard Trosch, M.D. (personal communication).

57   B. Sanhedrin 72b.

58   Daniel C. Goldfarb, "The Definition of Death," and Seymour Siegel, "Updating the Criteria of Death," in *Conservative Judaism* (Winter 1976), pp. 10-39.

59   David M. Feldman, "Rabbinic Comment: Definition of Death and Dying," in *The Mount Sinai Journal of Medicine* Vol.51, No.1 (Jan.-Feb. 1984), pp. 73-76.

60   David Golinkin, "Responsum Regarding Organ Transplantation," in *Responsa of the Law Committee of the Rabbinical Assembly in Israel*, Vol. 5: 121-122 [Hebrew].

61   Avram I. Reisner, "Care for the Terminally Ill: Halakhic Concepts and Values" footnote #5, in *Life and Death Responsibilities in Jewish Biomedical Ethics*, edited by Rabbi Aaron L. Mackler (New York: Jewish Theological Seminary, 2000), pp. 278-281.

62   Elliot N. Dorff, "End-Stage Medical Care: Practical Applications," in *Life and Death Responsibilities*, p. 351.

63   Joseph H. Prouser, "Ḥesed or Ḥiyuv? The Obligation to Preserve Life and the Question of Postmortem Organ Donation," in *Life and Death Responsibilities*, pp. 455-456.

64   Aaron L. Mackler, "Respecting Bodies and Saving Lives: Jewish Perspectives on

Organ Donation and Transplantation," in *Cambridge Quarterly of Healthcare Ethics* (2001) 10, p. 424f.

65   Central Conference of American Rabbis, *Contemporary American Reform Responsa*, #78. Available online at: www.ccarnet.org.

66   Moshe Zemer, "Determining Death in Jewish Law," in *Death and Euthanasia in Jewish Law: Essays and Responsa*, edited by Walter Jacob and Moshe Zemer (Rodef Shalom Press, 1995), p. 108. I thank Rabbi Dorff for sharing this source with me.

67   J. David Bleich, *Time of Death in Jewish Law* (Berman, 1991). See also, "Neurological Criteria of Death and Time of Death Statutes," in *Jewish Bioethics*, edited by Fred Rosner and J. David Bleich (Ktav, 1979, 2000), reprinted from *Tradition* (Summer, 1977).

68   Fred Rosner and Moshe David Tendler, "Definition of Death in Judaism," in *The Journal of Halacha and Contemporary Society*, Vol.17 (Spring 1989), pp.14-31.

69   "Brain Death and Heart Transplants: The Israeli Chief Rabbinate's Directives," translated by Yoel Jakobovits in *Tradition* 24:4 (Summer 1989), pp. 1-14.

70   Yitzhok A. Breitowitz, "The Brain Death Controversy in Jewish Law." This article is available online at: www.jlaw.com/Articles/brain.html.

71   See Abraham S. Abraham, M.D., *Nishmat Avraham: Volume II Yoreh Deah, Medical Halacha for Doctors, Nurses, Health-Care Personnel and Patients* (Mesorah Publications, 2003), p. 310.

72   Fred Rosner, *Bioethics* (Ktav Publishing House, Inc., 2001). Chapter 22, "Definition of Death," p. 297.

73   *Time of Death*, pp. 131-135, esp. note 4.

74   op cit, p. 280.

75   *Time of Death*, pp. 148-154.

76   Moses Sofer, 1762-1839.

77   שו"ת חתם סופר חלק ב (יורה דעה) סימן שלח.

78   Shlomo Zalman Auerbach, *Minḥat Shlomo* II, 86:5 (1 Adar 5728: March 1, 1968). As we shall see, he eventually rejected the concept of brain death based on concerns about blood flow studies hastening death.

79   Tzvi Hirsh ben Jacob Ashkenazi, 1660-1718.

80   שו"ת חכם צבי סימן עז ד"ה אצבי"ה סבור.

81   שו"ת חכם צבי סימן עז. והרב האלקי כמוהר"ר יצחק לוריא זצוק"ל אשר רוח אלקים דבר בו הסכים למה שהוא מפורסם לכל אנשי העולם שהלב הוא משכן לנפש החיונית והוא המת באחרונה אחרי מיתת כל האברים הרחוקים והקרובים אליו ופירש בזה דברי נביאי בית אל.

82   Ahron Soloveichik, "Death according to the Halacha" in *The Journal of Halacha and Contemporary Society*, (Spring, 1989), pp. 41-48.

83   Section I:39.

84   "Neurological Criteria of Death," p. 333.

85   See *Nishmat Avraham*, p. 313f.

86   See their website, www.hods.org. They are neutral on the brain death controversy, presenting both sides of the debate.

87   Avraham Steinberg, "Moment of Death," in *The Encyclopedia of Jewish Medical Ethics*, translated by Fred Rosner, M.D. (Feldheim Publishers, 2003), V. II, p. 702. Emphasis in the original.

88   Auerbach rules that one may accept organs from a brain-dead donor in the diaspora, where it can be assumed that the donor is non-Jewish, and that doctors will remove organs regardless of the halakhah. In Israel, however, he forbids acceptance of such organs, for fear of encouraging the hastening of death in a goses.

89   If the proposed course of action is to remove futile treatments that are deemed an impediment to death, then a diagnosis of irreversible coma will suffice for a shift to palliative care. Dr. Hayim Brodie notes that the brain death diagnosis may also be used to justify withdrawal of life support for a patient who has no relative or guardian. Conservative Movement authors are divided about the withdrawal of artificial nutrition and hydration, but this controversy obtains in cases of coma, rather than brain death. See Rabbi Dorff and Rabbi Reisner in *Life and Death Responsibilities in Jewish Biomedical Ethics.*

90   A notable development in the field is the "Pittsburgh Protocol," which involves terminating artificial respiration, allowing the patient to go into cardiac arrest in the operating room and, after a few moments of official death, proceeding with the harvesting of vital organs. This procedure, which does not establish irreversibility, raises numerous ethical and halakhic difficulties, and is to be the subject of a separate study by Rabbi Dorff.

NOTES TO AFTERWORD / CHAPTER 9

AMONG THE MOURNERS OF ZION

1   This passage is cited in medieval sources such as Rosh to Moed Katan III:46, Sefer Eshkol Moed Katan 216:1, and Tur YD 393.

2   1365-1427, Laws of Bereavement, #14. I thank Alvan Kaunfer and his son, Elie Kaunfer, for directing me to this source and helping parse it. Alvan also shared a discussion of this subject in *Netiv Binah* by B.S. Jacobson, Section I, pp. 67-68.

3   This claim is odd, given other Midrashim (e.g. Mekhilta, Bo, Pischa 14, s.v. Miketz; Vayikra Rabba, 32:8), that assert that God's presence went into exile with the Jews. Moreover, in Avot 3:6 we learn that wherever Jews gather to study Torah, the Shekhinah is present. In Eikha Rabba (1:32-33) we read that the Shekhinah did not go into exile until the children (*tinokot*) were exiled.

4   Born 1423 in Hoechstadt, Bavaria. *Sefer Leket Yosher*, Yoreh Deah II: 85.

5   B. Brakhot 16b.

6   Prague, 1754-1826. *Teshuvot MeiAhavah*, I:172.

7   Semahot 4:13.

8   *Igrot Moshe*, OH 5:21.

9   *Tzitz Eliezer*, 17:7.

10   Personal communication.

11   I Chronicles, 29:11.

12   This is the comment of Tractate Sofrim 21: "One is not comforted over loss of the living, but the dead are eventually forgotten by the heart" (Psalms 31:13). But as Rabbi Shimon ben Eliezer teaches in Mishnah Avot (4:18), "do not comfort your friend when his dead lie before him."

13   *Encyclopedia Judaica*, (1st edition) v. 3, p. 946.

14   SA YD 388.

15   Moed Katan 27b.

16   Midrash Bereshit Rabbah 68:9, among other places.

INDEX

OF ENGLISH-LANGUAGE SOURCES AND NOTES

שו״ת ענה דניאל

תשובות בענייני טכנולוגיה והלכה

מאת

הרב דניאל יחזקאל נבינס

ספרי איזון

תשפ״ד